The Body of Property

The Body of Property

Antebellum American Fiction and the
Phenomenology of Possession

CHAD LUCK

Fordham University Press
NEW YORK   2014

Copyright © 2014 Fordham University Press

All rights reserved. No part of this publication may be reproduced, stored in a retrieval system, or transmitted in any form or by any means—electronic, mechanical, photocopy, recording, or any other—except for brief quotations in printed reviews, without the prior permission of the publisher.

Fordham University Press has no responsibility for the persistence or accuracy of URLs for external or third-party Internet websites referred to in this publication and does not guarantee that any content on such websites is, or will remain, accurate or appropriate.

Fordham University Press also publishes its books in a variety of electronic formats. Some content that appears in print may not be available in electronic books.

Library of Congress Cataloging-in-Publication Data

Luck, Chad.
 The body of property : antebellum American fiction and the phenomenology of possession / Chad Luck.
   pages cm
 Summary: "Explores the embodied aspects of ownership and private property as these emerge in a range of American literary texts across the late eighteenth and early nineteenth century"— Provided by publisher.
 Includes bibliographical references and index.
 ISBN 978-0-8232-6300-4 (hardback)
 1. American fiction—19th century—History and criticism. 2. Material culture in literature. 3. American fiction—18th century—History and criticism. 4. Property in literature. 5. Personal belongings in literature. 6. Law and literature—United States—History—19th century. 7. Law and literature—United States—History—18th century. I. Title.
 PS374.M39L83 2014
 813'.3093553—dc23

2014014677

Printed in the United States of America

17 16 15   5 4 3 2 1

First edition

A book in the American Literatures Initiative (ALI), a collaborative publishing project of NYU Press, Fordham University Press, Rutgers University Press, Temple University Press, and the University of Virginia Press. The Initiative is supported by The Andrew W. Mellon Foundation. For more information, please visit www.americanliteratures.org.

Contents

Acknowledgments   vii

Introduction: *Pierson v. Post* and the Literary Origins of American Property   1

1. Walking the Property: Ownership, Space, and the Body in Motion in *Edgar Huntly*   35
2. Eating Dwelling Gagging: Hawthorne, Stoddard, and the Phenomenology of Possession   83
3. Anxieties of Ownership: Debt, Entitlement, and the Plantation Romance   138
4. Feeling at a Loss: Theft and Affect in George Lippard   188

Epilogue. Wisconsin, 2004: Racial Violence and the Bodies of Property   236

Notes   241
Works Cited   271
Index   291

Acknowledgments

After thinking and writing for so long about the nature of ownership, I am acutely aware of how this book itself represents an especially rewarding and fortuitous form of shared property. Many brilliant and generous people have contributed crucial pieces to this project, and if the experience has produced any overriding phenomenology, it is that of profound gratitude.

The book began as a research project at Indiana University where I was fortunate enough to work with an absolutely stellar group of faculty. As director of the project from its earliest embryonic shudders, Jonathan Elmer offered up his remarkably agile intellect, his seemingly boundless creativity, and, most valuable of all, his warm friendship. Likewise, Jennifer Fleissner proved a tireless advocate of the project, contributing invaluable insights and suggestions to the scholarship and encouraging me to share the work as widely as possible. Paul Gutjahr provided crucial elements of historical context for the book, gently reminding me to tether my theoretical flights to carefully historicized readings. Nick Williams was the theoretical devil to Paul's historicist angel, challenging me with new readings, new philosophers, and new ways of imaginatively engaging the ontology of ownership. Together, this group constituted the single richest intellectual experience of my academic life, and to its members I am deeply grateful.

My work was also bolstered at Indiana by the close friendships and intellectual contributions I found in an incredibly talented and generous cohort. I benefited from conversations, reading groups, writing groups, and ample amounts of beer and wine with Melissa Adams-Campbell, Celia Barnes, Jon Blandford, Michael Taylor Brown, Tim Campbell, Lauren Curtright, Tobias Menely, Pete Molin, Sarah Murphy, Bryan Rasmussen, Brandi Stanton, Roger Stanton, and Rod Taylor. My scholarship, intellectual curiosity, and habits of mind were all immeasurably improved by these many friendships.

I have also been incredibly fortunate to find a robust and supportive scholarly community in the English Department at California State University, San Bernardino. My colleagues here have been remarkably encouraging, as I have worked to transform the early writing into a finished book. David Carlson, in particular, has been generous in reading draft after draft of the various chapters. And I have greatly profited from a range of enthusiastic interlocutors including Jenny Anderson, Juan Delgado, Sunny Hyon, Stephen Lehigh, David Marshall, Julie Paegle, and Jackie Rhodes. The department as a whole has proven to be a warm, welcoming, and vibrant academic home in which to finish the book.

Help and encouragement has come from a wider academic community as well, and I'd like to thank in particular Chris Looby for his early support of the book project and for his invaluable professional advice going forward. Peter Coviello and Duncan Faherty were both kind enough to shepherd early versions of my work through conference panel revisions. Betsy Philips and Becca Lewis have been valued readers and sounding boards for various aspects of the project. Jason Neal and Lisa Simon provided much-needed intellectual and emotional support as the book gestated in the Montana hinterlands. I also wish to thank Helen Tartar and Thomas Lay at Fordham University Press. Finally, I want to convey my gratitude to the editors of *Early American Literature* for their interest in selections from my first chapter.

In addition to the friendship and feedback I have received from all of these people, I was fortunate enough to garner a good deal of institutional support. At Indiana, my work benefited from research and writing time afforded by an Indiana University Chancellor's Fellowship, the Booth Tarkington Dissertation Fellowship in American Literature, and finally, by the university's Esther L. Kinsley Ph.D. Dissertation Award. At Cal State, San Bernardino, I have been grateful for the department's generous disbursement of release time and for a CSU Research Grant. All of this research support has been essential for my work, and I greatly appreciate it.

My deepest debt of gratitude, however, is reserved for family. My parents, John and Carlah Luck, have been enthusiastic supporters of my work even as the project expanded and the years rolled on. Not once did they ask me when I would finish the damn thing. Nicole, Jake, and Eli have helped recharge my intellectual batteries during our all-too-infrequent visits. And the Lewis family, too, has been a steadfast source of encouragement; though, for their part, they did ask when I'd finish the damn thing. To my wife, Jessica, of course, I owe my deepest thanks. Her keen intellect, scholarly insight, inexhaustible patience, and unshakable faith in the project carried me when nothing else would. Love itself is a kind of debt, and hers is one that I will never fully repay. As for Fletcher, little man, the next one is for you . . .

Introduction: *Pierson v. Post* and the Literary Origins of American Property

Of all that I had, I had nothing except through my body
Of all that I have or shall have, it is the same
That I am is of my body, and what I am is of my body
What identity I am, I owe to my body . . . . what soul I owe to my body,
What belongs to me . . . . that it does not yet spread in the spread of the
  universe, I owe to my body
Of all that I have had, I have had nothing except through my body
—WALT WHITMAN[1]

On December 10, 1802, along a deserted stretch of Long Island beach, two young men nearly came to blows over the carcass of a dead fox. The quarrel began as Jesse Pierson, a twenty-two-year-old schoolteacher from Southampton, New York, followed the shoreline home after a day of work in the town's one-room schoolhouse. Alone with his thoughts at first, Pierson gradually heard the clamor of shouts, galloping horses, and baying hounds drawing nearer. Abruptly, he spotted a terrified fox streaking down the beach, trailed at a distance by a band of mounted horsemen and their pursuing dogs. In a matter of moments, the fox had gone to ground in a nearby dry well and Pierson sprang into action. Picking up a broken fence rail, he moved to the mouth of the well, brained the fox, slung it over his shoulder, and set off once again toward home with his new prize.[2]

Before he had gone more than a few steps, however, he was confronted by Lodowick Post, leader of the now indignant hunters. Post demanded that Pierson return the fox, asserting that it was his (Post's) property by virtue of his hunter's rights: he had been in the process of hunting and killing the animal when Pierson had impertinently stepped in and stole it. Pierson, for his part, did not bat an eye, replying "It may be you was going to kill him, but you did not kill him. I was going to kill him and did kill him." This was followed by a series of escalating threats with neither man giving ground until at last Post vowed to haul Pierson into court. Three weeks later, the case was heard by John Fordham, justice of the peace in Southhampton, and the jury held for the original hunter, Post, awarding him seventy-five cents in damages.[3]

The award was paltry but entirely in keeping with the mundane contours of the disagreement. After all, an ownership dispute about a seventy-five-cent fox pelt retrieved on the far-flung reaches of an East Hampton beach hardly seems to warrant a court case, much less a substantive award. But the New York Supreme Court felt otherwise. After Pierson appealed the initial decision, the higher court agreed to hear his case and offered up their ruling on September 10, 1805. They found for Pierson—overturning the original ruling—and in doing so authored what has since become one of the most influential pieces of case law in American legal history. Over the past two hundred years, *Pierson v. Post* has gradually evolved from a bit of provincial hunting law into perhaps the best-known legal justification for the original acquisition of unowned property. The fox dispute has been given pride of place in law student casebooks since the late nineteenth century, often appearing on the first page. It has been cited in an "enormous range" of judicial decisions and law articles, and it has itself been the focus of intense legal scholarship over the last twenty years.[4] But how is it, we might ask, that an obscure early nineteenth-century case about a dead fox has come to occupy such a prominent position in our understanding of possession, ownership, and private property?

The New York Supreme Court of 1805 felt that the case raised a "novel and nice question" about the proper means of acquiring possession of a wild animal.[5] In particular, the issue was "whether Lodowick Post, by the pursuit with his hounds [. . .] acquired such a right to, or property in, the fox as will sustain an action against Pierson for killing him and taking him away?" (177). Pierson's attorney, Nathan Sanford, argued that "occupancy" of an animal is required to establish title: "There must be a taking," a physical, bodily capture; not even wounding an animal constitutes legal possession unless it is also physically seized (176). Counsel for the defense, Codwallader D. Colden, conceded that occupancy was indeed required to establish title, but he maintained that starting and pursuing a wild animal constitutes such because it functions as a declaration of intent to appropriate. For the justices, the case thus hinged on "the simple question of what acts amount to occupancy, applied to acquiring right to wild animals" (177). After pointedly rejecting the precedents of English common law—such cases could not apply because they generally took place on owned land—the court looked instead to classic natural law treatises, including those of Hugo Grotius and Samuel von Pufendorf, and held that occupancy required some form of "actual corporeal possession" of the animal (177). They remained circumspect, however, when describing the precise degree of physical control required to establish that possession. It might be "bodily touch or manucaption," but it might also include wounding, trapping, or killing the animal (182). Since the dispute between Pierson and Post did not involve any of these corporeal contacts, however, there was no need for the court to clarify the criteria. For them, it was enough to rule that property rights in wild animals could be established only through some sort of bodily occupancy.

Still, even after this emphasis on bodily control, it is not immediately clear why the court's careful articulation of property rights in a fugitive fox should go on to dramatically influence the course of American property law. The answer, I submit, lies precisely in the mechanism of "occupancy" so central to the case. By explaining how to take possession of, and establish title to, a wild animal, *Pierson v. Post*, albeit in roundabout fashion, addresses the thorny problem of original acquisition. That is, in the humble guise of a legal dispute about a seventy-five–cent fox pelt, the case posits a seminal justification for the appropriation of unclaimed properties more generally. In stating the facts of the case, for example, the Supreme Court decision is careful to note that the fox is hunted and killed "upon a certain wild and uninhabited, unpossessed and waste land" (175). (This is, in fact, the only direct citation maintained from the lower-court ruling.) Moreover, the legal category of wild animals, or *ferae naturae*, had long been recognized as a form of unowned property. Here, then, is a circumstance as close to a legally unencumbered "state of nature" as the justices might hope to encounter. In effect, *Pierson v. Post* represented a rare opportunity for them to engage the fraught topic of original acquisition, and their decision would help articulate both a conceptual legal framework and an ideology of property through which American citizens might more comfortably justify the appropriation of "waste" lands and all sorts of other "unowned" properties.[6]

Of course, the court's decision to invoke a "state of nature" and to employ the language of wilderness and waste also reveals an intellectual debt to classical economics and to John Locke in particular. Locke, Adam Smith, and a range of Scottish Enlightenment thinkers were all fond of positing an original state of nature, a primitive stage of society that existed before the advent of private property, up and out of which mankind gradually progressed. According to this theory, during the primitive phase, all property was held in common and everyone had an equal right to use it. As Locke explains in his *Two Treatises of Government* (1690), God "gave the World to *Adam* and his Posterity in common," and in this natural state, "no body ha[d] originally a private Dominion, exclusive of the rest of Mankind" (286). More pointedly, Locke directly equates this original state of nature with the "wild woods and uncultivated waste of America" (294). By describing a Long Island beach as a "wild and uninhabited, unpossessed and waste land," the New York Supreme Court thus effectively invokes the vacant, unclaimed spaces of Locke's America. In doing so, they underscore the ways in which *Pierson v. Post* is meant to speak not just to New York state hunting rights or to the ownership of fox pelts, but to the much larger question of how it is that Americans originally come to own anything at all.

American Literature and the Problem of Property

It is this question, along with a range of closely related concerns, that animates this book. What does it mean, exactly, to own something? How does a thing become mine? *Pierson v. Post*, I believe, is a crucial juncture in American legal history because it is one of the very few times that American jurisprudence directly addresses, more or less, the fundamental, ontological nature of property. This is a case in which the court attempts, however tentatively, to think through the very difficult problem of how an unclaimed object in the world is transformed into that peculiar phenomenon we call property. This is a case that peeks, for just a moment, behind the massive edifice of property law that simply assumes property as a legal given. Instead, *Pierson v. Post* tries to explain how ownership is established ex nihilo. It tries to provide a defensible foundation for original acquisition and thereby construct a base upon which appropriation of all sorts might stand. Indeed, the steadily increasing prominence of this case over the last two hundred years only underscores the theoretical importance of this move. Whenever American law becomes nervous about original acquisition, about that first link in the ownership chain, it looks to *Pierson v. Post*.

But this uneasiness about the ontological status of property is not unique to the American perspective. No less a figure than William Blackstone, godfather of the English common law, seems troubled by precisely these obscure foundations of ownership. In his seminal *Commentaries on the Laws of England*—easily the most influential legal text in America at the beginning of the nineteenth century—Blackstone famously begins by extolling the virtues of private property: "There is nothing which so generally strikes the imagination, and engages the affections of mankind, as the right of property; or that sole and despotic dominion which one man claims and exercises over the external things of the world, in total exclusion of the right of any other individual in the universe" (2: 2). In fact, a huge proportion of Blackstone's four-volume work goes on to detail the intricacies of how such exclusive rights can best be negotiated in the common law. But before he explains England's arcane property laws in excruciating detail, he pauses and observes that "there are very few, that will give themselves the trouble to consider the original and foundation of this right" (2). Indeed, he describes this reluctance in terms of uneasiness: "Pleased as we are with possession, we seem afraid to look back to the means by which it was acquired, as if fearful of some defect in our title" (2). Moreover, he thinks that these sorts of inquiries would be "useless and even troublesome in common life." It is better that men not "[scrutinize] too nicely" into the reasons behind the laws of property (2). Nevertheless, with that caveat in mind, Blackstone proceeds to offer a decidedly Lockean origin story to explain the genesis of property rights (complete with an analogy between the "beginning of the world" and pre-Columbian America) and finally concludes that "occupancy is the thing by which the title was in fact originally gained" (8). Like the *Pierson* ruling that would later cite him, Blackstone briefly confronts the ontological chasm yawning underneath the legal institution of property and then consoles himself with the mechanism of "occupancy."

Legal scholar Carol M. Rose calls this ontological uneasiness "Blackstone's Anxiety" and argues that its specter has haunted Anglo-American legal thought throughout the nineteenth and twentieth centuries. According to Rose, lawyers, judges, and legal thinkers have successfully avoided confronting nagging theoretical questions about the nature of property by adopting one of two coping strategies: either they offer up a quick utilitarian justification—property exists because it promotes efficient and productive resource management—or, they "[deflect] the entire issue by moving to a seemingly neutral, positive description of property's legal structures" (606).[7] But neither of these responses, neither the head-in-the-sand doctrinalism nor the utilitarian misdirection, effectively addresses the underlying issue, namely, how exactly does a thing become mine in the first place? Or, more broadly, what is this strange phenomenon of property that seemingly transforms the nature of things in the world?[8] Philosopher Alan Ryan underscores precisely this point when he observes that the English legal system—and Anglo-American political philosophy more generally—has "discouraged a question which Roman law encouraged, namely, 'What is it to be the *owner* of something?' or 'How does a thing become Mine?'" Ryan's conclusion is that this legal and philosophical complacency "seems to have diverted a certain psychological and metaphysical interest into other channels" (7).

One of the central aims of this book, *The Body of Property*, is to demonstrate that the imaginative literature of antebellum America constitutes just such an "other channel." I argue that whereas Anglo-American legal theory since John Locke has sidestepped anxiety-inducing questions about the nature and ontology of property, American writers in the eighteenth and nineteenth centuries eagerly took them up. Slave narratives, gothic romances, city-mystery novels, and a range of other literary forms all obsessively engaged the shifting terms of property discourse in what amounted to a culture-wide effort to understand the consequences and complexities of ownership. From Melville's meditation on maritime property rights in *Moby-Dick*'s "Fast-Fish and Loose-Fish," to Harriet Jacobs's anguished reflections on the hypocrisies of chattel slavery, antebellum writers relentlessly scrutinized the nature of, and justification for, an institution central to the political and economic edifice of the new nation. Free to move beyond the circumscribed discourse of contemporary jurisprudence, American writers set about plumbing the depths of property, exploring it as a set of contested theories and practices far richer and more malleable than had been acknowledged by legal and political philosophy alone.[9]

In taking up the difficult ontological issues that haunt the theory of ownership, antebellum writing also raises new, more pointed questions about the full spectrum of our property experience. That is, in seeking to better understand what it means to own something, antebellum writers also ask what it *feels like* to appropriate and retain properties, or, conversely, what it *feels like* to have them taken away. These writers, I will argue, reveal the extent to which individual embodied experience plays a fundamental role in taking possession of the world and—as we will see in Chapters 3 and 4—losing it. The sensate body, they suggest, is absolutely crucial to our understanding and enactment of property practices, and only by accounting for these corporeal and affective components will we begin to appreciate the experiential scope of ownership. Alan Ryan touches on this possibility when he identifies a "self-developmental" tradition of property at odds with the utilitarian instrumentalism of Blackstone and his Anglo-American progeny. Within this alternative tradition, typified by Hegel, Ryan notes that "the relationship between a man and what he *owns* is intrinsically significant; there is a substantial bond between a man and his property, a bond which repays philosophical analysis" (11). The writers of antebellum America are fascinated with precisely this bond between person and property, repeatedly returning to explore its contours. In doing so, they situate the sensate body at the heart of the property experience and dramatically reconfigure our understanding of the relationship between people and things.

One place to begin tracing this counter-history of property is in the pages of James Fenimore Cooper's 1823 novel, *The Pioneers*. Steeped in a variety of American origin myths and itself an origin point for many histories of the American novel, the book enjoys a certain seminal influence in the development of antebellum literary culture. This makes it all the more significant that the novel's opening pages focus on a property dispute suspiciously similar to the 1805 *Pierson v. Post* case. The narrative begins with Judge Temple and his daughter returning home on a sleigh through the mountains of central New York. They hear a pack of baying hounds approaching through the trees and are startled to see a "fine buck" bound across their path. The Judge fires both barrels of his fowling piece at the deer, apparently missing with both, but two quick additional shots ring out and the buck falls. The final shots, of course, come from Natty Bumppo and his young companion, Oliver Effingham, who emerge from the trees to claim their prize. But the Judge thinks it may have been his first two shots that actually brought down the deer and so an argument begins. "I would fain establish a right, Natty, to the honour of this death; and surely if the hit in the neck be mine, it is enough; for the shot in the heart was unnecessary—what we call an act of supererogation, Leather-stocking" (23). Natty responds with Pierson-like disdain: "You may call it by what larned name you please, Judge," but "It's far easier to call names, than to shoot a buck on the spring" (23). Natty, for his part, cedes his claim to Oliver whose bullet he believes actually killed the deer. And the young man bolsters his claim by pointing out where four of the Judge's five pieces of buckshot have buried themselves in a tree. The Judge laughs, "You are making out the case against yourself, my young advocate—where is the fifth?" With a dramatic flourish, Effingham throws off his overcoat and reveals a gunshot wound in his shoulder. "Here," he says simply.

Though perhaps a bit more melodramatic than the dispute between Pierson and Post, the argument over the deer raises similar questions about ownership rights in unclaimed property. Cooper may very well have read an account of *Pierson*—he was a close friend of James Kent, the presiding justice on the case—but either way the book's opening scene places issues of property and original acquisition at the center of the novel's thematic structure.[10] The interrupted hunt, like *Pierson v. Post*, asks readers to consider the finer points of how and why a person can establish title to a previously unowned wild animal. Oliver makes clear the stakes when he tells the Judge, "First let us determine the question of right to the satisfaction of both of us" (24). Indeed, this single statement might serve as an epigraph for the novel as a whole. This is because the deer debate figures as a microcosm of the larger property dispute that will unfold between Judge Temple and the Effingham family. Prior to the events of the novel, the Judge has taken possession of all the Effingham land holdings through some questionable business maneuvers at the end of the Revolutionary War. The murky ethical nature of these purchases, along with the contending land claims of local Indian tribes, renders the ownership of Temple's lands anything but clear. Thus, as many critics have noted, the central work of the novel's marriage plot is to resolve "the question of right" as to the ownership of Temple's property. When young Effingham—himself an adopted member of the Delaware tribe—marries Elizabeth Temple, all the contending property claims are conveniently reunited.[11] So, by opening the novel with a *Pierson*-esque squabble over the rights to a deer carcass, Cooper not only alerts us to the plot's larger investment in early national property disputes, he also signals a willingness to engage the thornier theoretical issues, those slippery "questions of right," that are central to *Pierson v. Post*.

But I'm also particularly interested in Oliver's bullet wound. When young Effingham throws back his coat to reveal "a hole in his under garment, through which large drops of blood were oozing," he initiates an odd corporeal subplot that will continue for the next seventy pages and that will effectively place Oliver's body at the center of the property dispute (24). Immediately upon learning of the wound, the Judge stops arguing over the deer and whisks a reluctant Oliver away to the Temple mansion where he can be attended to by the local doctor. Cooper then provides a detailed account of the surgery during which the bullet is removed from Oliver's shoulder, and the wound is bandaged. But as soon as the procedure is finished, the young hunter stands, pulls on his coat, and declares, "There remains but one thing more to be settled, and that is, our respective rights to the deer" (91). The Judge, surprised by the young man's tenacity, concedes the carcass, and the dispute is finally resolved in Oliver's favor. It is the curious prominence of Oliver's injury, however, that stands out here. Cooper carefully sandwiches the elaborate drama of Oliver's wound between the beginning and end of the property debate. Why this strange juxtaposition of wounds and property?

Cooper does this, I would suggest, in order to hint at the ways in which the corporeal body is integral to our experience and conception of property. The opening scenes of *The Pioneers* imply that the body is a crucial component of appropriation, that it is a site at which ownership is ultimately inscribed. Natty first looks to the bullet holes in the carcass of the deer when he is trying to determine ownership. But Oliver's body, too, becomes a site of appropriation when Judge Temple's bullet lodges in his shoulder. Standing in as a kind of extension of the deer (like Natty, after all, he wears a deer-skin overcoat), Oliver's wounded body foreshadows the Judge's eventual acquisition of Oliver and his land titles through marriage. This notion that wounds might be read as a kind of territorial marker is reinforced by another story of bodily injury that Natty tells upon seeing Oliver's wound. He reminisces about being shot by an Iroquois warrior: "I travelled seventy miles alone in the howling wilderness, with a rifle bullet in my thigh, and then cut it out with my own jack-knife" (27). Then, to revenge himself, he catches up to the Indian and opens fire: "I made a mark on the red-skin that I'll warrant he carried to his grave. I took him on his posterum [. . .] and rattled three buck shot into his naked hide" (27). Again, in the context of the deer dispute and of Oliver's analogous wound, Natty's language here of *marking* and *taking* links appropriation to embodiment. Cooper's text reveals how the experience of ownership gets routed through bodies and wounds. His narrative gestures at the corporeal underbelly of property, as it were, and alerts us to the crucial role of embodiment in antebellum accounts of ownership.

Whereas Cooper's novel begins to call our attention to these issues, antebellum literature considered more broadly works to flesh out a fuller account of property's corporeal underpinnings. Bedeviled by "Blackstone's Anxiety," American writers of this period map out a *phenomenology of possession*, a meaningful sense of how property comes to be, and they do so by repeatedly linking ownership to a richly realized experience of embodiment. This phenomenology identifies both affective and sensational components in the experience of property. That is, writers chart the complex emotional configurations that link persons to things—what does it feel like, for instance, to fear the imminent theft of the only property you own—but they also closely attend to the sensory experiences—the touches, tastes, smells, and sounds—that produce a feeling of ownership. In doing so, antebellum literature provides property with a body. No longer a legal abstraction, no longer simply a discursive construct, property is revealed in eighteenth- and nineteenth-century American texts to be a distinctly embodied phenomenon, one that troubles the too-easy separation of theory and practice and that yokes particular bodily experiences to specific historical circumstances.

Property in Antebellum Culture

The period between the Revolutionary and Civil Wars created an especially fertile context for thinking through issues of ownership because these decades were marked by an unprecedented upheaval in American property practices. As early as 1803, the Virginia judge and law professor St. George Tucker could describe the ongoing transformation as an "almost total change in the system of laws relative to property, both *real* and *personal*" (x).[12] The catalysts for change came in a variety of forms. Continuing westward expansion, for example, ensured that problems of "original" acquisition and Native American property rights would remain insistent issues for lawyers and prospective settlers. Moreover, this expanding national geography—and the associated desire for more efficient property transactions—caused American land law to shed itself of older, more cumbersome English restrictions on the distribution and exchange of real estate.[13] Inheritance law followed suit by divesting itself of many of the feudal legacies of the English system, including primogeniture.[14] Then as the nineteenth century wore on, the so-called Married Women's Property Acts further altered the gender politics of inheritance law. Rejecting the doctrine of coverture, whereby a woman forfeited her right to own and inherit property once she was married, the acts gradually enhanced women's legal standing vis-à-vis property both inside and outside marriage.[15] But perhaps the most insistent challenge to established property paradigms was the festering problem of chattel slavery. Pro- and antislavery discourse mobilized competing definitions of property and forced Americans to reexamine deeply held assumptions about the nature of ownership, market exchange, and commodification. All of these factors, then—race, gender, geography—contributed to a period of remarkable turmoil in both the theory and practice of property in America. As a result, American writers were awash in a flood of property discourse that gave them the incentive and opportunity to thoroughly rethink the nature of the institution. As Charles Brockden Brown opined in 1799, "No topic can engage the attention of man more momentous than this. Opinions, relative to property, are the immediate source of nearly all the happiness and misery that exist among mankind."[16]

Historians have generally made sense of this period of rapid change in property practices by pointing out that, in broader strokes, it reflects a gradual shift from an older idea of property as a "thing" to an emergent idea of property as a "bundle of rights." That is, historians chart a *trajectory of abstraction* in which legal definitions of property evolve from agrarian eighteenth-century models predicated on the civic republican idea of land as the exemplary form of (tangible) property, to commercial nineteenth-century models that understood property more as an abstract set of intangible rights often associated with entirely nonphysical assets (for example, shares of a corporation). Or, to put it another way, property was initially conceived in the seventeenth and eighteenth centuries as a relationship between people and things, but by the end of the nineteenth century it was widely viewed as a relationship of rights and duties obtaining only between people.[17] One clear measure of this change can be seen by comparing Blackstone's *Commentaries*, published from 1765–69, to James Kent's influential *Commentaries on American Law*, published from 1826–30. As Gregory Alexander points out, Blackstone titles his book on property law, "Of the Rights of Things," while Kent, sixty years later, replaces that terminology with simply the label "property," subdivided into "personal" and "real." This change, Alexander emphasizes, "both reflected and facilitated the commodification of property in legal consciousness by replacing a term—'things'—that seemingly limited the meaning of property to tangible objects with another term—'property'—whose measure was vastly more flexible" (138). According to this point of view, then, as the nineteenth century advanced, property was reconceived as an increasingly abstract legal form, as a bundle of rights that facilitated alienability and mobility while leaving behind the more physicalist notions of the eighteenth century.

Of course, this trajectory of abstraction in property law was part and parcel of a broader "Machiavellian Moment," a political and economic transition from a predominantly agrarian to an emerging market society with ever-more complex, and abstract, credit mechanisms.[18] Increasingly figurative conceptions of property, for example, proceeded apace with the wider adoption of paper money and with a growing reliance on public debt financing. More and more, economic life seemed to require the manipulation and exchange of "virtual" financial instruments. Literary critics as well as historians have used this trajectory of abstraction as a framework for exploring the complex interrelationship of literary and economic discourses during the eighteenth and nineteenth centuries.[19] In particular, the field of "new economic criticism," as practiced by scholars of both British and American literature, has relied on this abstraction narrative to make sense of the myriad cultural forms that emerge from a rapidly modernizing culture. Scholars of British literature, for instance, have examined the ways in which the new economy's abstract financial instruments instigated a broader crisis of representation that was refracted through eighteenth- and nineteenth-century imaginative works.[20] Similarly, Americanist critics have identified in early and antebellum American writings a range of cultural anxieties rising out of the rapid transition to paper currency and to a speculation-obsessed economy.[21] In short, recent economically inflected literary criticism has relied heavily on the abstraction narrative in order to better conceptualize the varieties of cultural work performed by eighteenth- and nineteenth century literature.

What I would like to suggest, however, is that this scholarly emphasis on abstraction and virtualization has effectively obscured the many ways in which a phenomenology of property, an embodied, corporeal experience of ownership, continued to influence American property discourse during (and after) the transition to a market economy. In particular, I aim to show that, while mindful of the economic abstraction unfolding around them, many antebellum novelists were eagerly delving in the opposite direction and exploring the bodily aspects of appropriation and expropriation. They were, in fact, actively *theorizing* the persistent role of the body in the acquisition and exchange of property. Without a doubt, the abstraction framework has facilitated a number of impressive works of literary and cultural scholarship focused on the changing contours of antebellum property. Stephen Best's recent study of the relationship between the cultural figure of the fugitive slave and the emergence of increasingly abstract forms of commodified personhood is one particularly incisive example of this.[22] But such work can overplay the virtualization of property. When Best, for example, describes the antebellum "ephemeralization and abstraction of property" as a "given," he diverts attention away from the insistently concrete and embodied accounts of ownership that pervade antebellum culture (14–15). Instead, I want to argue that only by attending closely to these literary phenomenologies of possession can we begin to appreciate how embodied experience informs diverse property relations in both antebellum America and our own historical moment.

More often than not, critics have characterized the literary response to increasing economic abstraction as one of deep-seated anxiety. The imaginative literature of the period is seen to reflect a growing uneasiness about the speculative, intangible, insubstantial nature of emerging market paradigms. Recent studies have diagnosed a litany of economically induced fears: the loss of a reliable money supply, the erosion of stable forms of personhood, the alarming reconfiguration of sexual and gender relations.[23] David Anthony goes so far as to suggest that by the mid-nineteenth century, America could best be described as "a kind of fiscal neurotic" (2). More specifically, in relation to property, critics have noted that the waning of civic republican models of "property as land" occasioned widespread anxiety about the potential breakdown of social structures predicated on that more "stable" economic foundation. Walter Benn Michaels, for example, finds in Nathaniel Hawthorne's work an insistent desire for some sort of stable property, some sort of "clear and unobstructed title" in a "world of fluctuation" (187, 193). In Charles Brockden Brown's oeuvre, Elizabeth Jane Wall Hinds discerns symptoms of a national "vertigo" caused by the shift from landed to portable property (11). And more recently, in his groundbreaking study of the relationship between antebellum literature and insurance underwriting, Eric Wertheimer identifies "the loss of property as a constant source of anxiety" for American writers (*xiv*). The trajectory of abstraction, it seems, does not sit well with antebellum writers accustomed to thinking of property in primarily materialist terms.

After diagnosing this abstraction anxiety, critics have gone on to uncover a range of creative coping mechanisms at work in antebellum literature. Perhaps the most prevalent of these is a pointed nostalgia for the older, more stable socioeconomic structures of civic republicanism and even mercantilism. Anthony, for instance, sees the sensationalist trope of buried treasure as an index of cultural desire for the more reliable gold-based currency of a mercantile paradigm, and Hinds discovers in Brockden Brown's work a pronounced longing for the "aristocratic, land-based economy of a more classical republican era" (22). Other critics focus on more paranoid defensive strategies, pointing out how antebellum literature often projects its economic anxiety onto the figure of a racialized or sexualized "other."[24] Still other critics detail sophisticated literary attempts to imagine some entirely new form of stable property insulated from the vicissitudes of market abstraction and circulation. Wertheimer, for example, describes the ways in which insurance underwriting is used to reinforce the ontological status of property, to shore up its "reality" and reliability, and Walter Benn Michaels sees the genre of the romance itself as a fantasy site for the protection of property, a place beyond the clutches of abstracting capitalism.[25]

These literary coping mechanisms, along with the economic anxieties that produce them, comprise an important discursive context for *The Body of Property*. The phenomenologies of ownership to which I attend unfold in direct relation to broader anxieties about economic change and the gradual "ephemeralization" of property. Indeed, the successive chapters of this book aim to chart an evolving correlation between abstraction and anxiety. As models of property become increasingly discursive and intangible, I argue, cultural anxieties about that property become correspondingly more expansive. The antebellum property fiction I engage here reflects these expanding anxieties by slowly increasing the spatial scale of its investigations. Beginning with an early focus on individual body-to-body appropriation, these texts slowly expand in scope to engage sprawling social networks and spatial circulation. My account of embodied ownership, then, is closely linked to the broader narratives of abstraction and anxiety that characterize antebellum property discourse. In fact, this phenomenology of possession can in some ways be understood as a further articulation of nineteenth-century America's literary coping mechanisms. After all, one reasonable way of coping with the increasing disembodiment of property would be for antebellum writers to underscore the ineluctably embodied aspects of ownership.

At the same time, however, the "anxiety and response" approach to the trajectory of abstraction perhaps overstates the resistant, or even reactionary, posture of antebellum writers. As Jennifer Baker has made clear in her recent analysis of debt and speculation in early America, there was also a vibrant "rhetoric of advocacy" in American letters that effectively complicates any merely anxiety-focused accounts. With that in mind, *The Body of Property* examines ownership as it unfolds in relation both to cultural anxieties about property and in relation to more optimistic or forward-looking possibilities. Thus, the book investigates working-class anxieties about losing property to greedy capitalists at the same time that it explores the powerful feelings of empowerment that accrue to some women and slaves in their evolving relationship to ownership. It is one of the principal claims of this book that phenomenologies of property function very differently in distinct historical—and spatial—circumstances. The affective and sensory configurations that link people to things are remarkably malleable; they shift with time and place and subject position. As a result, while acknowledging the cultural force of the anxiety paradigm, my analyses seek to remain open to property dynamics that unfold both inside and outside that framework. Challenging the larger historical trajectory of abstraction means not just highlighting the anxieties that resulted from it, but also attending to the ways in which antebellum writers thought through a remarkable variety of embodied alternatives.

Of course, one of the keenest observers of property's increasing abstraction across the nineteenth century is Karl Marx. Like his American counterparts, Marx is especially attuned to the anxieties and pathologies that spring from changing property paradigms and from the accelerating circulation of abstract commodities. As such, Marx would seem to offer a crucial contemporary perspective on antebellum property practices. And to some extent he does. In particular, Marx's theory of the worker's alienation from the products of his labor hints at the affective dimensions inherent in a person's relationship to things. Accordingly, his theory of alienation will figure prominently in our account of urban theft anxiety later in this book. Unfortunately, such contributions to a phenomenology of property are never central to Marx's project. Like a number of his nineteenth-century contemporaries, Marx maintains that property is primarily a social relation—in his terms, a particular "relation to the conditions of production" (*Grundrisse* 492)—and his aim is not to better understand the bodily components of ownership or the phenomenological nature of property, but to explode the entire social framework that enables it.

At times, especially in his earlier writings, Marx does occasionally gesture toward a more sophisticated phenomenological account of ownership, as when he speculates about the property relations that might come to supersede what he calls "capitalist private property." These new and multifarious forms of appropriation will apparently involve a range of sensational and affective experiences:

> Man appropriates his comprehensive essence in a comprehensive manner, that is to say, as a whole man. Each of his human relations to the world—seeing, hearing, smelling, tasting, feeling, thinking, observing, experiencing, wanting, acting, loving—in short, all the organs of his individual being, like those organs which are directly social in their form, are in their objective orientation, or in their orientation to the object, the appropriation of the object, the appropriation of human reality. Their orientation to the object is the manifestation of the human reality. (*Selected Writings* 100)

Here, Marx sounds almost metaphysical as he works to flesh out a fuller embodied conception of ownership beyond the reductive constraints of capitalist private property. But such passages are rare in Marx; he generally confines his analysis of property to a social relations model.

As a result, Marx's work spends little time exploring the central *ontological* questions that animate this book.[26] American writers, by contrast, were haunted by precisely these questions about the nature of ownership. Consequently, although Marx effectively voices nineteenth-century anxieties about capitalism's increasingly abstract economies, ultimately, he does not figure as prominently in my phenomenological analyses of property as he otherwise might. Instead, I look to a later group of thinkers and theorists.

A Phenomenology of Property

My investigation of embodied ownership in the eighteenth and nineteenth century will be greatly facilitated by some twentieth-century theory. The discourse of phenomenology, in particular, provides a rich conceptual framework with which to analyze the affective and sensational components of ownership. Phenomenology, of course, comprises a diverse body of thought, but one of the movement's shared goals has been an attempt to find a middle way between the opposed epistemologies of empiricism and idealism. From Husserl on, phenomenologists have sought to reconcile the empiricist claim that the world can only be known through direct, sensory experience with the idealist argument that knowledge of the world comes only through ideas and subjective experience. Rejecting both these extremes, phenomenology maintains that knowledge and consciousness are constituted through the intimate interrelationship of subject and object. Consciousness is always already consciousness *of* something and so subjectivity is inextricably bound to the objects of the world. This is the terrain of Maurice Merleau-Ponty's *entre-deux*, the "in-between" ground from which knowledge and consciousness spring.[27] Because of this in-between status, however, knowledge of the world is only ever given to the subject through experiential frames, structures of consciousness that apprehend and interpret the objective world. As a result, the central aim of phenomenology is to carefully describe these structures of consciousness, to investigate the "things themselves" as they appear to us by attending to the concrete, lived experience of the individual subject.[28]

It is, in particular, this sensitivity to the intimate relationship between subject and object that recommends phenomenology for an exploration of embodied ownership. If property is originally conceived within legal discourse as a relationship between people and things, then phenomenology's close attention to the links between subject and object promises a powerful interpretive framework for interrogating that bond. Indeed, as Merleau-Ponty makes clear, our perceptual grasp of the world, our connection to things and spaces beyond ourselves, unfolds as an appropriation, as a "relation of *having*" (202). In his view, phenomenology's "constant aim" should be to "elucidate the primary function whereby we bring into existence, for ourselves, or take a hold upon [. . .] the object [. . .] and to describe the body as the place this appropriation occurs" (178). Likewise, the proto-phenomenologist William James attends to the "instinctual impulse" of property: "It is clear that between what a man calls *me* and what he simply calls *mine* the line is difficult to draw. We feel and act about certain things that are ours very much as we feel and act about ourselves" (279).[29] In exploring these appropriative feelings and actions, phenomenology has developed a sophisticated language of sensation, spatial orientation, and affective attachment that will prove indispensable to any understanding of the diverse embodied experiences of property. Accordingly, this book builds on the ideas of influential phenomenological theorists such as Merleau-Ponty, Emmanuel Levinas,

Martin Heidegger, and Jacques Derrida, in order to construct a phenomenology of possession sensitive to the tastes, sounds, sights, and touches of embodied antebellum experience.

My use of phenomenology is self-consciously eclectic, even promiscuous, using bits and pieces of theory taken from divergent phenomenological traditions and employing them when and where they seem most potentially productive. In this way, I eschew any systematic "phenomenological criticism"—this is not Poulet's Geneva School approach, nor is it Iser and Ingarden's reader-response—in favor of what Brian Massumi calls the "exemplary method" of utilizing theory. Instead of flat *applications* of theory *to* a set of materials—an approach that tends to conform the material to the theory—Massumi advocates "extracting [theoretical concepts] from their usual connections to other concepts in their home system and confronting them with the example" (18). Doing so allows the target text, the specific example, more space to push back against the theory, to assert the creative, deforming force of its own particularities. Borrowing promiscuously from a range of phenomenologists, then, not only better matches specific phenomenological tools with specific instantiations of embodied property, it also helps catalyze productive new ways of thinking about the possessive relationship between people and things. If Anglo-American law has turned a systemic blind eye to questions about the nature and experience of property, then bringing vitalizing bits of phenomenology to bear on antebellum property narratives is one way to open up the system.

Narrative and the novel, in particular, are literary modes especially well-suited to capturing and recording this kind of rich sensory experience. As Paul Ricoeur has argued, narratives (both fictional and historical) effectively mediate between the author's phenomenological experience of the world and the reader's reconstitution of that experience in the act of reading. According to Ricoeur, a narrative text captures or "prefigures" elements of our shared being-in-the-world (that is, our shared bodily sense of how objects, sensations, and spaces can interact); the text then "configures" or recombines those elements into structured plots; and, finally, it offers them up to the reader to be "refigured" in a process of *embodied* interpretation. We are thus drawn to narrative because it leverages our shared phenomenological experience of the world and allows us to creatively imitate aspects of that experience while reading. Crucially, these elements of experience are neither isolated nor autonomous; rather, narrative texts present us with complex "configurations," intricate networks of feeling in which subjects and objects and spaces are bound together in affective and sensational circuits. Viewed in this fashion, antebellum narratives become a remarkably valuable account of the complex property relations that obtained between persons and things in the early years of the nation.[30]

Of course, one of the charges that has long bedeviled phenomenology is its perceived lack of historical sensibility. Husserl's famous method of phenomenological description, the much-remarked "transcendental reduction," functions as a "bracketing" or stripping away of social and historical contexts in order to more effectively focus on first-person experience and the structures of consciousness.[31] As a result, phenomenology sometimes seems to deemphasize historical situated-ness. But, as should be clear by now, *The Body of Property* is centrally concerned with understanding embodied ownership as a historical phenomenon that manifests itself in different ways at different times across the antebellum period. Because of this, my theoretical framework might be better described as a version of "neo-phenomenology," Rita Felski's term for an approach "that blends historical and phenomenological perspectives, that respects the intricacy and complexity of consciousness without shelving sociopolitical reflection" (18). In this way, my work extends the historicist sensibility of much recent nineteenth-century American studies scholarship on emotion and affect.[32] Building on this work, my book assumes that antebellum literary texts are rich repositories of phenomenological experience, "thick" descriptions of affective and emotional experiences that emerge within very specific historical circumstances. This is neo-phenomenology, then, scholarship that maintains a judicious balance between physiological influence and discursive context.

The nineteenth-century Americanist focus on emotion is part and parcel of a broader phenomenological conversation emerging in recent literary criticism, a "phenomenological turn" that seeks to revalue the sensate body as a productive site of analysis.[33] *The Body of Property* engages this broader conversation as well, exploring the ways in which embodied experience informs the antebellum dynamic of ownership and appropriation. But whereas much of this recent phenomenologically-inflected scholarship has focused on accounts of emotion and affect in particular, my approach expands the purview of embodiment to include a broader range of sensory experiences. "Feeling" is construed to mean not just affective states like sympathy, fear, or envy—though affect figures prominently in the phenomenology of possession—but also physical sensations like touch, taste, and vision. So, for example, while I include chapters on the pivotal affective experiences of debt anxiety and what I call "theft-distress," I also consider nineteenth-century diet reform and the crucial role that *eating* plays in the process of appropriation. My aim here is to expand our sense of the sensations to which phenomenological criticism gives access, for, as Mikel Dufrenne suggests in his *Phenomenology of Aesthetic Experience*, "what is irreplaceable, the very substance of the [aesthetic] work, is the sensuous or perceptible element [*le sensible*] which is communicated only in its presence" (11). Thus, while antebellum literary works certainly offer rich evocations of affect and emotion—evocations that have been analyzed to great effect by recent scholarship—these same texts also link that affect to complex constellations of sensory perception. The embodied experience of property unfolds along an intersecting network of "feelings" both affective and sensorial. Antebellum literature registers and reshapes this experience, limning its historical permutations and its particular spatial instantiations. And it is phenomenology, finally, that provides an interpretive frame capable of synthesizing these modes of consciousness.

Expanding the phenomenological field in this way serves a dual purpose. On the one hand, it provides a richer theoretical account of the full range of human sensation and emotion. On the other, it effectively locates antebellum property practices in relation to the much broader cultural shift from eighteenth-century rationalism to nineteenth-century emotion. That is to say, phenomenology's attention to both sensation *and* affect—its middle way between empiricism and idealism—make it an ideal lens through which to consider how the crucial transition from Lockean empiricism (the sensationalists) to Romantic idealism (the emotionalists) might impinge on changing notions of embodied possession. This cultural shift is an important context for evolving phenomenologies of possession because it informs the ways in which narratives of embodied ownership are revised and remade in response to changing philosophical priorities. A neo-phenomenological framework makes room for precisely this sort of historico-theoretical analysis, effectively tracking the cultural prominence of sensation and affect across the nineteenth century.

Given the theoretical and historical importance of this transition—of what Philip Gura calls "the great philosophical shift from eighteenth-century rationalism to nineteenth-century subjectivity" (47)—it behooves us to say a few further words by way of explanation. By the beginning of the nineteenth century, the broad-based influence of the European Enlightenment was on the wane in America. Lockean empiricism—as well as the alarming skepticism of Berkeley and Hume that seemed to follow from it—was being challenged by an emerging emphasis on emotion and personal intuition. The Second Great Awakening was particularly significant here, convulsing American culture in the 1790s and opening the gates for the exuberant emotions and religious revivalism of what Henry May terms the "Methodist Age." This revaluing of passion and sentiment then helped set the stage for an influx of Romantic writings—English, German, and French—that began in the late 1820s. Rejecting what Emerson would later call "paltry empiricism," Romantics like Samuel Taylor Coleridge championed "love and holy passion" as the necessary correctives to the arid and mechanistic approach of empirical science. The head needed to be balanced out by the heart. This confluence of religious, philosophical, and literary emotionalism helped push American culture out of its Enlightened phase and into the turbulent currents of midcentury Romanticism. In doing so, the focus on Lockean sensation gradually made room for a focus on emotion and affect.[34]

Of course, American Transcendentalism played a key role in this transition from empiricist sensation to Romantic affect. Channeling Coleridge, Madame de Staël, Thomas Carlyle, and others, the Transcendentalists likewise rejected Locke and his overreliance on sensory experience. The particular target of their wrath was the Scottish Common Sense school, long the reigning philosophical paradigm in American colleges and Unitarian churches. Common Sense philosophy had managed the difficult task of extending Lockean empiricism even into the moral realm, arguing that God had placed an innate "moral sense" in all human beings and that this provided moral impressions analogous to our sensory impressions. By reconciling empirical science with religious morality in this way, the Scottish school remained an attractive option for moderate defenders of the Enlightenment status quo.[35] For the Transcendentalists, however, it was a stubborn bastion of Enlightenment rationalism, and they set about dismantling it with the tools of Romantic idealism. In *Nature* (1836), for instance, Emerson denounces empiricism and its attendant "despotism of the senses" (*Prose and Poetry* 44), arguing instead for an idealism that "satisf[ies] the demands of the spirit" (49). "Idealism sayeth," he tells us, "matter is a phenomenon, not a substance [...] the world is a divine dream" (49). This is the crucial Transcendentalist move: we are better served by turning inward, focusing on the mind itself, and looking for traces of the divine within us rather than without. "Locke, Paley, Mackintosh, and Stewart," they merely speak "*from without*," according to Emerson, but "Spinoza, Kant, and Coleridge" speak "*from within*, or from experience, as parties and possessors of the fact" (*Prose and Poetry* 170). The "facts" for the Transcendentalists are thus not the sense impressions of Locke and the Scots, rather they are the emotions and intuitions that emerge from within the self, glittering markers of the divine.

Transcendentalism, then, plays a key role in the broad cultural shift from sensation to affect, from eighteenth-century rationalism to nineteenth-century emotion. As such, it constitutes an important cultural backdrop for changing phenomenologies of possession in antebellum America. Indeed, Transcendentalism's inward turn, its focus on self-culture and its close attention to the structures of individual consciousness, give it a proto-phenomenological outlook. Emerson and Thoreau, for instance, both generate rich evocations of phenomenological experience in their writing. Think of Emerson's luminous description of the "evanescence and lubricity of all objects" in "Experience" (*Prose and Poetry* 200), or of Thoreau's "delicious evenings" on the pond, "when the whole body is one sense, and imbibes delight through every pore" (*Walden* 107). In this vein, Transcendentalist writing occasionally elucidates the phenomenologies of property that I pursue in this book, particularly Emerson's treatment of debt and Thoreau's interest in diet reform. But Transcendentalism's idealist commitments also distance it from phenomenology's middle path between empiricism and idealism. Transcendentalist philosophy tends to reinforce an idealist binary of self and world, subject and object; Emerson's "lubricity of objects," after all, describes the way in which the world slips away from the self and "souls never touch their objects" (199). This idealist binarism is ultimately at odds with phenomenology's focus on the overlapping interrelation of subject and object, on the in-between spaces of persons and things. As a result, Transcendentalist writing is less pertinent to a phenomenological investigation of ownership than we might at first imagine. Perhaps more to the point, Transcendentalist accounts of private property tend to be of the disapproving, critical sort. Like Marx, many Transcendentalists—Orestes Brownson, George Ripley, Bronson Alcott—saw private property and the "cash nexus" mainly as an obstacle to be overcome, and they did not concern themselves with any sustained investigation of its ontology or phenomenology.[36] Thus, while Transcendentalism plays a central role in the broader cultural transition from sensation to affect, it plays a smaller role in this book's exploration of specific phenomenologies of property.

Still, the shift from sensation to affect is crucial to antebellum property narratives and to their evolving phenomenologies of possession. As nineteenth-century culture increasingly revalues subjective emotional experience, so too do American writers attend more closely to the affective components of ownership. In order to acknowledge this expanding phenomenological focus, *The Body of Property* is broadly structured around a similar progression from sensation to affect. The first half of the book explores the phenomenology of property as it emerges from a range of sensory experiences, most significantly touch and taste. Leveraging the eighteenth-century legacy of Lockean empiricism and sensational psychology, my first two chapters reveal antebellum writers wrestling with the sensuous particulars of ownership, with tactile, somatic, and gustatory experiences that are intimately bound up with the process of taking possession. Chapter 1 details Charles Brockden Brown's sophisticated engagement with Locke, Hume, and Condillac as he works out a theory of tactile boundaries on the Pennsylvania frontier. Chapter 2 follows Nathaniel Hawthorne and Elizabeth Stoddard as they investigate the ways in which eating and tasting enable a foundational form of alimentary possession. Both chapters underscore the ways in which Enlightenment rationalism and its focus on the formative powers of bodily sensation continue to influence theories of property and ownership well into the nineteenth century.

The second half of the book, by contrast, shifts its focus to the increasingly prominent role of affect and emotion in the nineteenth century. In particular, the third and fourth chapters concentrate on readerly affect, on the phenomenology of property as it manifests itself in the reader's embodied experience. Chapter 3 thus diagnoses the debt-related anxieties evoked among readers of the plantation romance, while Chapter 4 investigates fears of expropriation among working-class readers of the city-mystery novel. Here, antebellum writers are increasingly attuned not just to the affective elements so central to property experience but also to the political ends to which that affect might be yoked.

In this way, the two halves of this book trace a developing conception of embodied ownership across the first half of the nineteenth century. Writers who are unsettled by the period's more and more abstract notions of property begin to dig in the opposite direction, unearthing what they see as the crucially embodied aspects of ownership. One vein of this phenomenological excavation—growing out of the tradition of Enlightenment empiricism—emphasizes the ways in which bodily sensation inform our experience of property. The other vein—emerging from the Romantic celebration of emotion—emphasizes our affective ties to property and explores the political potential inherent in that link. Of course, the sensational and affective experiences of property are never entirely distinct from one another; emotional aspects of possession and dispossession are inextricably bound to the bodily sensations of the same. As a result, the historical shift from sensation to affect never proceeds in an entirely smooth and linear fashion: interest in the sensory elements of ownership still appears even as other writers turn to affect.

Hawthorne's work on eating and gustation, for instance, is published a few years later than Lippard's work on debt anxiety. Despite the sometimes fitful nature of this historical progression, however, my book aims to underscore its significance by adopting the successive two-part structure of sensation and affect.

The Space of Property

The Body of Property unfolds, then, in relation to two broad historical arcs: first, the increasingly abstract conception of property that develops across the eighteenth and nineteenth centuries (along with the increasing anxieties that follow from it), and, second, the gradual shift in focus from theories of sensation to theories of affect. As the book moves from its opening chapter on Charles Brockden Brown's 1799 novel, *Edgar Huntly*, through to its closing chapter on George Lippard's "city-mysteries" of the 1840s and 1850s, these two broad historical narratives will provide a useful framework for indexing the evolving phenomenologies of possession. However, one of the remarkable consequences of marrying history and phenomenology in this way is the emergence of space itself as a crucial third term in antebellum treatments of private property. American writers are persistently fascinated with the role that property plays in organizing and appropriating social spaces of all sorts. From frontier boundary disputes, to spatio-economic stratification in the city, to the permeable recesses of the private home, antebellum novels map out the spatial contours of possessive bodies in motion. The historical evolution of embodied property, they demonstrate, is intimately intertwined with spatial practice, so much so that it is virtually impossible to describe the experience of property without recourse to a spatial context.

For this reason, I have chosen to organize the book less around an overarching historical narrative, but according to a spatial topography of antebellum culture. Each chapter examines the phenomenology of possession (or dispossession) as it unfolds within one of four representative antebellum social spaces: the Native American frontier; the gendered space of the middle-class home; the Southern plantation; and the emerging urban metropole. This structure allows for a close-grained analysis of specific historical and cultural circumstances at the same time that it accords pride of place to the spatial frameworks in which experiences of property must unfold. This organizational scheme has the added advantage of providing slightly more discrete and coherent accounts of embodied property than a strictly historical structure would allow. As I mentioned earlier, the historical development of embodied property practices proceeds in a somewhat fitful fashion, not always following a smooth chronological progression. For some writers, explorations of affect may slightly precede a focus on sensation; for others, abstraction anxieties may emerge at an earlier rather than a later date. In broad strokes, the historical narratives provide a crucial piece of context, but in considering the particularities of individual authors, places, and properties—particularities sometimes separated by a decade or less—linear historical models can do more to obscure than to clarify. A spatial framework, by contrast, allows us to reveal phenomenologies of possession at work within the discrete networks, circuits, and architectures of antebellum life.

"Space," of course, is a notoriously capacious concept, and it is important to emphasize here that I mean by it something more complex than simply the empty container in which objects are located. I assume, rather, that space—like bodies and properties themselves—is in part a socially-constructed phenomenon. Our experience of space, our lived relation to it, is crucially conditioned by the economic and cultural circumstances in which we exist. The US interstate highway system, for example, is a historically specific mode of spatial organization produced by a certain set of economic and ideological imperatives. Lived spatial experience in twenty-first-century America is dramatically influenced by this spatial paradigm, in the same way that spatial experience in antebellum America was lived in relation to a system of river-based commerce and an expanding railroad. Human experience must always unfold within such a social space, within a structured context saturated with diverse and competing semantic networks.

Henri Lefebvre's pioneering work on social space is helpful here because he offers a model of space as a social product, as the constantly changing result of a "process of production" in which human beings "secrete" the very spaces in which they live (36, 38).[37] Lefebvre presents a powerful three-part "conceptual triad" to explain how it is that lived space gets dialectically produced (33). The triad includes three continuously interrelated aspects of spatial experience: the mental, the physical, and the social. The first of these—what Lefebvre terms "representations of space"—involves a culture's dominant conceptual theories of space. These are the abstract mental maps that impose a design or order on space. Lefebvre points, for example, to medieval conceptions of space that posit "the Earth, the underground 'world', and the luminous Cosmos" as spatial coordinates (45). Lefebvre describes the second aspect of his triad as "spatial practice," the physical and perceptual experience of space as it is generated and used by people in their everyday behavior. It is constituted of things like the habitual paths that we create in carrying out our daily movements (for example, from house to mailbox). Finally, Lefebvre calls attention to "representational space," or social space as it is "directly *lived* through its associated images and symbols" (39). This is distinct from mental space in that it focuses not on top-down ideological configurations of space, but rather on the role of local imagination and tradition and art and literature as it impinges upon spatial experience. Lefebvre has in mind here spaces like village churches and graveyards, local fields and landmarks, spaces inscribed with the social imagination of people who live in them.

Lefebvre's model of spatial experience is especially useful for our purposes because it makes room for the mutual interinfluence of conceptual apparatus, social exchange, and phenomenological experience. It sheds light on the ways in which embodied property practices are part of a complex dialectical interaction with the spaces that they produce and that produce them. In particular, his work helps us understand how phenomenologies of ownership emerge simultaneously with lived spatial experiences.[38] It follows from this that when literary texts capture and *configure* events and actions in the world, à la Ricoeur, they bring with them traces of the spatial relations that are inextricably part of those events and actions. That is, when Ricoeur describes narrative emplotment as a "synthesis of the heterogeneous" (66), he means for that heterogeneity to include the diverse experiences of space that help constitute being-in-the-world.[39] Again, it is the rich phenomenological repository of the antebellum text that will enable us to parse out the complex interweaving of bodies, properties, and spaces. The synthetic, configurational power of narrative allows it to capture the subtle and shifting dialectics that link spaces and embodied ownership in a powerful antebellum structure of feeling.

Accordingly, this book proceeds from the assumption that antebellum literary texts operate in at least two directions with regard to spatial experience. On the one hand, the texts effectively *reflect* the social spaces out of which they emerge. Following Ricoeur's lead, we can understand them to be capturing antebellum social spaces and then configuring those same spaces in complex relation to a network of circulating bodies and properties. On the other hand, these texts also work to *recondition* the reader's own experience of space. As Lefebvre makes clear, art and literature play a crucial role in defining a person's "representational space." Without question, we all inhabit a lived space that is overlaid with a matrix of symbolic and affective meaning. Lefebvre's triad alerts us to the ways in which that meaning is deeply influenced by the art and literature that takes up and represents those spaces. As a result, this book will consider not just the centripetal movement of social space *into* the body of the text, it will also attend to the centrifugal movement of textual spaces *out to* the body of the reader. It will examine, for instance, how the claustrophobic urban spaces of George Lippard's "city-mystery" novels aim to cultivate a feeling of spatial vulnerability in antebellum readers. In this way, the book persistently highlights the complex interplay of phenomenology, ownership, and spatial experience that characterizes antebellum culture.

Even a brief glance back at Cooper's *Pioneers* demonstrates the advantages of this spatially oriented approach as it pertains to issues of ownership and embodiment. Cooper's novel effectively places the (wounded) body at the center of a complex and long-standing property dispute involving Native American rights, British and American land claims, and the arcane mechanisms of interfamily inheritance. But, as a raft of critics have noted, Cooper's novel is also crucially concerned with geographical description and the organization of space. The book's subtitle, after all, is "A Descriptive Tale," and Cooper spends page after page detailing the natural landscape of upstate New York as well as the layout and architecture of the fictional town of Templeton. What quickly becomes clear, however, is that these two discourses—one of property and one of space—are intimately intertwined. Cooper's novel, I would suggest, directly links notions of embodied ownership to the evolving spatial practices of the early nineteenth-century New York frontier. More specifically, *The Pioneers* carefully locates its property questions in relation to two competing spatial paradigms: an older, communal model of shared land and resources, and a swiftly emerging model of capitalist enclosure and accumulation. The tension between these two overlapping paradigms constitutes the crucial spatial context in which the novel's exploration of property unfolds. The origins of ownership, Cooper implies, cannot be separated from the spaces of ownership.

Cooper's interest in the close connection between property and space is foreshadowed in *Pierson v. Post* itself. The opening of the 1805 ruling carefully situates the events of the case "upon a certain wild and uninhabited, unpossessed and waste land." This seemingly incidental bit of spatial context is necessary, of course, in order to emphasize the ex nihilo characteristics of this ruling. That is, the justices require a blank geographical slate so they can explain how it is that property comes to being out of a state of nature, out of a vacuum, as it were. But these initial spatial coordinates—no matter how brief—should alert us to the fact that spatial criteria play an important role in the experience and justification of property more broadly. More to the point, *Pierson v. Post* is a ruling on New York state hunting law and, as such, it calls attention to the ways in which hunting and game laws engage questions of boundary, trespass, right of way, and other mechanisms of spatial organization. Game law, to put it bluntly, determines who can hunt where according to which property rights. Such laws, then, are one place we might look to see how Cooper—and early American culture more widely—thinks through the imbrications of property and space.

Hunting practices in early America were distinguished by a fiercely democratic sense of how space and spatial boundaries ought to be determined and policed. Whereas English game laws were notoriously elitist—hunting rights in England were generally reserved for the landed nobility—American jurisprudence took pride in its more egalitarian treatment of forests and farm land. As early as William Penn's 1683 *Frame of Government of Pennsylvania*, state constitutions made a point of enshrining hunters' rights to open space, granting all inhabitants "Liberty to Fowle and Hunt upon the Lands they hold, and all other Lands therein not Inclosed" (*Statutes* 1: 344). This spatial precedent was reaffirmed by a host of legal cases well into the nineteenth century. In the 1818 case of *M'Conico v. Singleton*, for example, a South Carolina landowner sued a hunter for trespassing on his property. The court summarily rejected the landowner's claim, noting that "the right to hunt on unenclosed and uncultivated lands has never been disputed." The ruling went on to emphasize that "the forest was regarded as a common" and that wild animals were "common property" (qtd. in Freyfogle and Goble 44). As the nineteenth century wore on, however, these common spaces began to give ground (literally) to more restrictive property practices, practices that reinforced the right of landowners to exclude hunters from even unenclosed private land. Such changes helped facilitate the increasing commodification of land-as-property, and by implementing them, the American legal system gradually forsook its long-standing protection of the hunting commons.[40]

Nineteenth-century game laws thus highlight an evolving tension between the open spatial paradigm of the forest commons and an increasingly insistent model of private, enclosed space intimately associated with capitalist exchange and accumulation. Cooper's narrative, for its part, carefully leverages this same tension by juxtaposing the older space of the commons—closely linked to Natty and his hunting practices—with the emerging space of capitalist enclosure—represented by Judge Temple and his plans for economic development. When Natty first contests the Judge's claim to the fallen deer, for instance, he does so by asserting the older legal tradition of the forest commons: "There's them living who say, that Nathaniel Bumppo's right to shoot on these hills, is of older date than Marmaduke Temple's right to forbid him [...] who ever heard of a law, that a man shouldn't kill deer where he pleased!" (25). Later, during the village's wasteful slaughter of the pigeons, Natty again invokes the notion of communal forest space and chides the Judge's efforts to cultivate them. "Put an ind, Judge, to your clearings," he cries. "Wasn't the woods made for beasts and birds to harbor in? and when man wanted their flesh, their skins, or their feathers, there's the place to seek them" (248).[41]

The Judge and his minions, by contrast, are consistently linked to the mechanisms of private property and to what Dana Nelson calls the "guardian logic of privatization" (169).[42] When the Judge first visits the region, after all, he brings with him a team of surveyors to begin marking out property lines (8). We gradually learn that his plans for development involve digging a network of canals, sinking mines, and laying out the gridlines of his eponymous village, "in a manner that aped the streets of a city" (41). This rage for spatial enclosure and control is represented as the flipside to Natty's unrestricted space of the commons. "What right," Sheriff Jones asks the Judge, "has the Leather-stocking, to shoot in your woods, without your permission?" He continues, "If I were in [the Judge's] place, I would stick up advertisements, to-morrow morning, forbidding all persons to shoot, or trespass, in any manner" (93). In this way, game laws in the novel are used to juxtapose two alternative models of social space in early nineteenth-century America, two models, moreover, that cannot be separated from antebellum property practice.

The most important articulation of this tension occurs in the fraught figure of Natty's wilderness hut. The mysteriously opaque space of Natty's dwelling, I would suggest, sits at the intersection of these two competing spatial paradigms. That is, the hut exhibits characteristics of both unrestricted communal space *and* the circumscribed space of capitalist enclosure. On the one hand, the hut figures as an emblem of shared possession, of common property, and of liminal spatial boundaries. Natty, Chingachgook, and Oliver Effingham all jointly share the secret of the hut, for example. All have access to its interior, and all possess a stake in maintaining the safety of its contents. As a result, the hut signifies not just individual possession but shared property, communal property. Moreover, the curious liminality of the hut—its marginal location and ambiguous architecture—helps trouble any system of firm boundaries and strict enclosures. Situated "on the margin of the lake, under a rock, that was crowned by pines and hemlocks," and covered with "fragments of small trees, and branches of oak and chestnut," Natty's hut blends seamlessly into the landscape itself (144, 207). It straddles the margins of lake and forest, town and wilderness, nature and culture, and, in so doing, unsettles the distinctions and demarcations crucial to Judge Temple's logic of individual accumulation.

At the same time, however, the hut figures as its own opposite, as a site of profound privacy and stubborn enclosure. Natty and his companions, for example, zealously guard the contents of the hut from prying eyes, and they regularly check the integrity of "certain complicated and ingenious fastenings" that secure the entrance (207). Not even the narrator is allowed inside this most private of private spaces. More to the point, the hut conceals Major Effingham, the rightful heir to the Judge's massive landholdings, and a "solution" of sorts to the novel's insistent questions of ownership. The Major's presence in the hut clearly links the space to this larger exploration of property rights and to abiding anxieties about justified ownership.[43] In this way, then, the hut sits at the epicenter of the novel's complex network of possessive and spatial tensions. It represents a paradoxical conflation of openness and closure, communality and privacy. Most importantly for our purposes, it closely ties the novel's property disputes to the fate of the book's two competing spatial paradigms.

It should come as no surprise, then, that the novel's final treatment of the hut reveals a good deal about the close imbrication of space and property in both Cooper's text and in antebellum culture more broadly. In particular, the fate of Natty's hut seems to parallel the fate of the commons as it plays out in relation to the historical ascent of capitalist enclosure. That is, if the hut figures as the site of struggle between an older paradigm of communal space and a developing paradigm of individual ownership, then the novel ultimately chooses a clear winner: the enclosed, privatized, and clearly demarcated spaces of capitalist development and accumulation.

Cooper's text signals this transition through a carefully choreographed destruction of Natty's hut and then through the subsequent circumscription and enclosure of the empty hut-space itself. Toward the end of the novel, Natty faces arrest at the hands of a posse comitatus because he has killed a deer out of season and violated Judge Temple's game laws. His hut is thought to conceal evidence of the kill, so the posse, led by Sheriff Jones, maneuvers through the woods in order to surprise Natty and capture him at home.[44] Cooper's description of the posse's approach, however, is notable for its emphasis on the language of encirclement and spatial constraint. After reminding his troops that Natty is both an "out-law" and "suspected of other misdemeanours and offences against private rights," Jones instructs his men to "form [them]selves in a complete circle around his hut" (355). Having done so, the circle slowly constricts, growing tighter and tighter, only to discover at last that nothing remains of the dwelling except a still smoldering pile of ashes. Then, as the posse stands speechless, "a tall form stalk[s] from the gloom into the circle," and Natty confronts his captors (356). "You've driven God's creaters from the wilderness," he cries, "and you've brought in the troubles and divilties of the law, where no man was ever known to disturb another" (356). He continues with a speech that is simultaneously a blistering indictment of the "wasty ways" that come with capitalist enclosure and a lament for the lost space of the forest commons. He makes this clear when he compares the posse's pursuit to "hungry hounds on the track of a worn-out and dying deer" (357). As in the opening scene of the novel, where wounded man and wounded deer are conflated, Natty figures himself here as the common property of the forest, as an emblem of the communal space that is disappearing. A few pages later, he directly targets the Judge's practice of enclosure and development:

> Your betterments and clearings have druv the knowing things out of the country; and instead of beaver-dams, which is the nater of the animal, and according to Providence, you turn back the waters over the low grounds with your mill-dams, as if 'twas in man to stay the drops from going where He wills them to go. (387–88)

It is a stark narrative of spatial transformation and one that is acted out in miniature via the enclosure and destruction of Natty's liminal hut. As an ambivalent space of shared ownership, the hut stands as a challenge to Judge Temple's paradigm of individual ownership and, as such it must be destroyed.[45]

Yet even destroying the hut does not seem to fully contain and constrain the threat of transgressed boundaries and communal property. For that, the novel appends yet another act of circumscription and enclosure. At the very end of the book, Natty prepares to leave the settlement behind and to head out into the untrammeled forests of the West. Before he does so, however, he makes one last visit to the site upon which his hut previously stood. There, he finds the space "entirely cleared of rubbish, and beautifully laid down in turf" (449). Moreover, "this little place was surrounded by a circle of mason-work" and could be entered only by a "small gate" (450). The space of the hut has been transformed into a cemetery containing the graves of Chingachgook and Major Effingham. More to the point, however, the gated, fenced enclosure signals the passing of the space of the commons. In the struggle between the spatial practices of an older forest commons and an emerging space of private accumulation, Cooper lets us know that the capitalist paradigm has won. The ambiguous, shared space of Natty's hut has ceded at last to the regime of fences, clearings, and "betterments." The novel thus narrates the vanishing of communal space in the same way that it narrates the vanishing of Indian bodies. And, in so doing, it illuminates the ways in which spaces, properties, and possessive bodies are all intimately intertwined in antebellum efforts to understand ownership.

It is this complex interrelationship between spatial dynamics and antebellum phenomenologies of possession that dictate the spatial organization of this book. The four main chapters represent a cross-section of crucial antebellum social spaces, each of which sheds light on a particular aspect of embodied ownership. But the book's spatial progression is also designed to trace a gradually increasing radius of bodily experience, one that begins with individual tactile orientation in the Pennsylvania woods, then expands through the intimate circuits of domestic space, through the farm-scale labor patterns of the plantation, and finally into the anxious sprawl of urban life. Each chapter aims to expand the scale of embodied ownership, exploring the ways in which our sensational and affective experience of property links us to greater and greater circuits of influence and action. A phenomenology of possession, we learn, is not limited merely to what we can physically feel and grasp; instead, it extends outward along the expanding radius of our sensory and affective engagements.

One advantage of this telescopic approach is the discovery of bodies and properties interacting with one another in places and at scales that are otherwise invisible. Foregrounding the spatial praxis of the plantation, for example, brings into focus conflicts of geographic appropriation between slave and slave owner that might otherwise remain hidden. In a broader sense, however, the book's expanding social spaces also effectively index the increasing abstraction and anxiety that gradually come to characterize antebellum property. That is, as private property is increasingly viewed as an abstract, discursive construct—one designed to circulate freely through the furthest reaches of the market—the spatial scale of cultural anxiety also increases. No longer are anxieties limited to the relations between persons and things, between an individual and his immediate possessions. Instead, unease about the nature of property begins to infect wider and wider circuits of exchange: the space of the home, of the plantation, of the city. In this way, the progressively larger spaces of this book roughly map out the historical trajectory of property abstraction and the increasing cultural anxiety that attends it.

Intriguingly, the figure of the hut—so central to Cooper's *Pioneers*—proves to be a curiously persistent index of these spatial anxieties as they develop across our collection of antebellum property narratives. From *Edgar Huntly*'s contested frontier hut, to Matthew Maule's doomed shack in *House of the Seven Gables*, to the rudimentary slave cabins of the plantation, to the humble "mechanic's huts" of George Lippard's working-class city, the image of the hut appears again and again as a fraught symbol for narratives of ownership and spatial appropriation. In particular, as the scale of cultural anxiety expands to encompass homes, plantations, and cities, the hut becomes a site of sympathy, a perhaps nostalgic emblem of a time when ownership was imagined to be simpler, more straightforward, and less subject to the circulations of "virtual" property. Thus, Lippard's working-class huts can signify the rightful claims of disenfranchised labor and Maule's destroyed shack can attest to his family's hereditary rights. Even the slave cabins become a source of affective identification: antislavery texts employ the huts as a symbol of the slave's exploitation, proslavery texts use them as markers for the paternal largesse of the master. In this way, the recurring trope of the hut tracks many of the larger historical arcs in this book: it underscores growing anxieties about the abstract definition of property; it marks the changing spatial paradigms that define property practices; and it reflects the nineteenth-century inclination to issues of affect and emotion.[46]

These larger historical arcs, then, provide a framework for my book's exploration of antebellum phenomenologies of possession. But the precise sequence of chapters follows an expanding spatial scale related to, but distinct from, broader historical trajectories. Accordingly, each chapter develops its own historical particularities in relation to these larger arcs, but does so with an eye on the exigencies of a given social space. More specifically, my first chapter links *Edgar Huntly*'s complex treatment of eighteenth-century sense psychology not just to issues of ownership but to questions about the nature of space itself. I contend that in the novel's famous cave sequence, Brown ingeniously narrativizes Condillac's dictum that "touch teaches vision" and in so doing enacts a subterranean model of spatial orientation that directly evokes the "plenum versus vacuum" debates of Locke and Hume. The novel then yokes this spatio-sensory exploration to an array of eighteenth-century property laws that focus on the creation of boundary lines. In particular, I argue that Brown's fictional account of settler-Indian violence on the Pennsylvania frontier is designed to imaginatively re-walk the infamous "Walking Purchase" treaty of 1737 in which the Delaware tribe was defrauded of 750,000 acres. Chapter 2 then slightly expands the spatial scale to argue that Hawthorne and Stoddard each rework the discourse of antebellum diet reform into a nuanced theory of property and domestic space. In *House of the Seven Gables* and *The Morgesons*, respectively, the two authors identify the phenomenological experience of eating as a fundamental aspect of appropriation, a primordial form of "alimentary possession." At the same time, I contend, both authors capitalize on the medico-physiological language of the diet reformers in order to analogize the alimentary body and the space of the home. Doing so reveals the ways in which eating helps condition the inside/outside structure of domestic space.

Chapters 3 and 4 not only mark the shift from eighteenth-century sensation to nineteenth-century affect, they also continue to expand the scale of social spaces through which property anxieties emerge. In particular, these two chapters shift the focus from appropriation to the more troubling experience of expropriation. As social spaces expand, these chapters suggest, the threat of dispossession and loss become evermore insistent. Thus, Chapters 3 and 4 explore the experiences of debt and theft as they emerge on the plantation and in the city. Chapter 3, in particular, examines the exploitative property relationship of master and slave as it is depicted in the proslavery novels of William Gilmore Simms and in the popular slave narratives of Frederick Douglass, Harriet Jacobs, and Charles Ball. By contrasting these two genres, I reveal a dialectical phenomenology of debt and entitlement underlying the master-slave relation. Slaveholders, I argue, are plagued by a persistent anxiety of ownership, an unconscious fear that they owe rather than own their slaves. What is more, I show that this tension between feelings of debt and feelings of entitlement also structures the space of the plantation itself. I end the chapter with a reading of John Pendleton Kennedy's *Swallow Barn* in which I demonstrate how the owner's spatial mastery of the plantation is challenged by the slaves' bodily appropriation of various counter-spaces. My fourth chapter then argues that the sensationalist "city-mystery" novels of George Lippard yoke the affective power of gothic sensationalism to a radical critique of possessive market society. I show that Lippard's urban exposés work to induce in his readers a phenomenology of theft, a feeling of what it is like to have property stolen. Adapting Silvan Tomkins's groundbreaking taxonomy of affect, I maintain that Lippard cultivates a form of "theft-distress," or kleptophobia, specifically through his representation of urban space. His novels invert the standard gothic architecture of enclosure and entrapment in favor of a frightening, and market-generated, permeability and perforation. This affective strategy was particularly compelling for Lippard's working-class readers, I suggest, because it creatively appropriates the "capitalist-as-thief" imagery so popular with the 1840s labor press and with socialist thinkers like Thomas Skidmore and Pierre Proudhon.

In short, by organizing the book around a series of gradually expanding social spaces—something like a set of Russian nesting dolls—I highlight the myriad ways in which antebellum property narratives actively resist a straightforward narrative of abstraction and "virtualization." Instead, these texts reveal the complex and continuing dialectical interaction between individual embodied experience and larger sociohistorical structures. The counter-history of antebellum property, we discover, is buried precisely in these diverse spaces of embodied possession and dispossession.

1 / Walking the Property: Ownership, Space, and the Body in Motion in *Edgar Huntly*

In April 1799, four months before the first volume of *Edgar Huntly* was published in Philadelphia, a short preview of the novel appeared in the New York periodical, *The Monthly Magazine and American Review*. This "Fragment," as it was called, consisted of about four chapters taken from the middle of the finished book. In order to introduce the fragment, the editor of the magazine saw fit to include a brief two-paragraph letter, ostensibly written by Edgar Huntly himself:

> Mr. Editor,
> The following narrative is extracted from the memoirs of a young man who resided some years since on the upper branches of the Delaware. These memoirs will shortly be published; but, meanwhile, the incidents here related are of such a kind as may interest and amuse some of your readers. Similar events have frequently happened on the Indian borders; but, perhaps, they never were before described with equal minuteness.
> As to the truth of these incidents, men acquainted with the perils of an Indian war must be allowed to judge. Those who have ranged along the foot of the *Blue-ridge*, from *Wind-gap* to the *Water-gap*, will see the exactness of the *local* descriptions. It may also be mentioned that "*Old Deb*" is a portrait faithfully drawn from nature.[1]

The letter is signed "E. H.," but of course it is the handiwork of Charles Brockden Brown, himself the author of the novel and editor of the magazine. As such, the piece initially seems to function as little more than a fairly standard bit of self-promotion. Upon closer scrutiny, however, the letter reveals a conspicuous preoccupation with geography, both physical and political. The narrative, we learn, will take place "on the upper branches of the Delaware," more specifically, in the area between the Wind-Gap and the Water-Gap on the eastern side of the Blue Mountains. The events of the narrative will be those "frequently" associated with "Indian borders." And the "perils of an Indian war," it seems, will be closely linked to boundary issues and to local topography. Nor will these topics be engaged in abstract terms. Brown is careful to emphasize the "minuteness" and "exactness" of his descriptions. In doing so, he implies that the novel will be best understood by placing it in a very particular geographical and historical context. It is not simply "the frontier" that interests Brown, but the zone of contact between whites and Indians in eastern Pennsylvania, between the Delaware river and the Blue Mountains.[2]

This region is particularly significant to a novel about "Indian borders" because it comprises the heart of the infamous Walking Purchase of 1737. One of the most flagrant abuses of Indian land claims in American history, the Purchase involved the defrauding and dispossession of the Delaware tribe at the hands of John and Thomas Penn (sons of William). Having produced an old Indian land deed of decidedly dubious authenticity, the two brothers demanded to take possession of their "ancient" claim. The Delaware were railroaded into ratifying the deed, which asserted that the amount of property in question would be determined by the distance a man could walk in a day and a half from a particular starting place. When it came time to actually walk the walk, the Indians were outraged to find that the Penn brothers had pre-marked the trail and that they had hired three trained athletes to do the walking. Nevertheless, the walk took place (sixty-four miles were covered), a very liberal interpretation of the boundaries was made, and the Delaware were summarily dispossessed of 750,000 acres. Crucially, the path that the walkers followed crossed the Blue Mountains precisely in the area laid out by Brown's two-paragraph preface.[3]

As a number of critics have argued, the connection between *Edgar Huntly* and the history of the Walking Purchase is vitally important because it helps illuminate Brown's racial and political sensibilities while at the same time fleshing out early national accounts of the Indian.[4] What I would like to suggest, however, is that the Walking Purchase also appealed to Brown because it raised questions, specifically philosophical questions, about the nature of private property, about the process of boundary formation, and about the organization of lived space. What does it mean to own something? How do we distinguish our spaces from those of other people? How does space itself come into being? These questions, I believe, constitute a central concern of the novel in their own right, and they also directly influence our understanding of Brown's politics. The philosophical register of *Edgar Huntly* makes clear the ways in which Brown was engaging Enlightenment luminaries like Locke and Hume in order to wrestle with the questions posed by the Walking Purchase. In effect, the novel yokes more abstract investigations of boundary, property, and space to the particular circumstances of late eighteenth-century Pennsylvania.

Brown himself spoke to the possibilities of a philosophically self-aware literature in an essay he wrote for *The Monthly Magazine*. In August 1799, the same month that the first volume of *Edgar Huntly* appeared, Brown published "Walstein's School of History," an odd, ruminative piece in which he describes the philosophical and aesthetic tenets of a fictitious professor of history at a school in southern Germany. The essay seems to be an opportunity for Brown, via the figure of the professor and his students, to reflect on some of his own philosophical and aesthetic concerns. He argues that good history writing needs to display many of the same techniques as good fiction writing: a "minute explication of motives," a "well-woven tissue of causes and effects," the "power of engrossing the attention" (*Rhapsodist* 145). More importantly, this type of writing should contribute to a certain kind of moral enrichment. "By exhibiting a virtuous being in opposite conditions," Walstein explains, he is "displaying a model of right conduct, and furnishing incitements to imitate that conduct" (148).

This kind of moral instruction is effective, however, only to the extent that it is able to translate abstruse philosophical ideas into more accessible historical narratives. "Abstract systems, and theoretical reasonings," Brown writes, "were not without their use, but they claimed more attention than many were willing to bestow [...]. A mode by which truth could be conveyed to a great number, was much to be preferred" (150). That mode, he goes on to explain, is one in which the writer pays close attention to concrete historical circumstance. "Truth flows from the union and relation of many parts," he asserts, and chief among these, is "the detail of actions." Such details "exchange the fleeting, misty, and dubious form of inference, for a sensible and present existence" (151). In short, by bringing sophisticated philosophical ideas down to earth in the form of a psychologically and historically concrete narrative, an author can maximize his moral efficacy.[5] Accordingly, we might expect Brown's own fiction to provide an imaginative framework in which high-minded philosophical discourse can be tested against the constraints of history and lived experience.[6]

Bearing in mind Brown's desire to marry the philosophical and the historical, the abstract and the concrete, this chapter explores the ways in which *Edgar Huntly* seeks to ground two prominent strands of Enlightenment philosophy in the particular time and space of eastern Pennsylvania at the end of the eighteenth century. I aim to show that Brown specifically invokes the philosophical discourses of sensational psychology and Enlightenment property theory in order to place them into meaningful conversation with one another and with the history of Indian-settler conflicts in the region. More particularly, I argue that Brown draws on the sense psychology of Locke, Hume, and the French *philosophe*, Condillac, in order to posit a sophisticated phenomenological model of body-space relationships. This model allows Brown to more closely consider both the embodied and the social processes through which spatial boundaries get produced. Frontiers and frontier space, the novel suggests, cannot be understood apart from individual, embodied acts of spatial delimitation; that is, spatial boundaries get produced via a continuous process of small-scale phenomenological encounters between individual and Other. At the same time, for Brown, the production of boundaries also implies an initial appropriation, a taking possession, of the newly delineated space. Brown, I maintain, directly relates his treatment of body-space relationships to the property theories of Locke and Hume. By actively linking embodiment and appropriation, *Edgar Huntly* is able to chart a distinctive third path between materialist and contractual models of private property.

According to Brown's theory of fiction, however, these theoretical investigations need to be grounded in a particular time and place in order to achieve their desired moral effect. *Edgar Huntly* accomplishes this by evoking the historical context of Indian-settler violence in Pennsylvania. In particular, the novel wrestles with the problematic history of the Walking Purchase and the subsequent dispossession of the Delaware tribe. What I would like to suggest is that Brown's philosophical emphasis on embodiment has the additional, and radical, effect of restoring the vanishing body of the Indian to the history of border disputes and treaty violations. This is where the moral work of the novel begins. Brown's philosophical arguments self-consciously call attention to bodies that have been erased, both literally and discursively, from the narrative of Pennsylvania history. Restoring those bodies to the narrative unsettles the moral framework of white colonial property claims. So just as

Walstein recommends, in *Edgar Huntly* abstract philosophical reasoning gets tied to concrete history in the service of moral instruction.

By framing the novel's sophisticated philosophical arguments within the context of Indian-settler property disputes, this chapter works to shift critical conversations about Brown away from the now familiar question of his political identification.[7] Instead, the chapter helps open up the relatively underexamined issue of Brown's status as a writer of philosophical fiction. W. M. Verhoeven has recently argued that Brown criticism is overdue for just this sort of correction. Verhoeven calls for more analysis of Brown's "negotiations with eighteenth-century philosophical and historical thought" and of his "place in the tradition of what has been called 'philosophical history.'"[8] Significantly, some earlier work on Brown did indeed consider his use of sensational psychology, albeit in a fairly generalized fashion.[9] This chapter is an effort to add to those earlier forays and to suggest some of the remarkable ways in which Brown linked sensational psychology to other philosophical concerns, particularly property theory.

At the same time, however, the chapter follows Brown's own suggestion and considers the connection between his "theoretical reasonings" and the historical exigencies of the Pennsylvania frontier. This has the benefit of actively linking the "philosophical" criticism to some of the same historical and political issues that have preoccupied more recent Brown scholarship. The general trope of the frontier has of course long been important to readings of *Edgar Huntly*,[10] but in considering the Walking Purchase in particular, Sidney Krause and John Carlos Rowe have recently disagreed about the political implications of Brown's treatment. By factoring in the role of the body and of property theory, my argument forces a reassessment of Brown's historical project here.[11]

At the same time, the novel's complex phenomenology of possession also forges a link between domains of eighteenth-century thought that are often considered in isolation. Intellectuals from Brown's time to the present, have, for example, frequently approached the scientific and political writings of philosophers like Locke as largely independent works.[12] Brown's novel suggests that this formulation may be an unnecessary dichotomy and that the two domains can be productively linked. And in terms of more contemporary theoretical debates, Brown's model of spatial production and appropriation seems to weave together phenomenological and social constructionist understandings of space. Whereas phenomenology views space as the product of an individual body moving and sensing its way through the environment, social constructionism sees it instead as a kind of social morphology, the result of social behaviors and economic forces. Brown's narrative suggests that these explanations need not be mutually exclusive; in fact, the production of space is best understood as a combination of both.

In order to effectively address these questions and to map out the complicated relationships that Brown constructs, this chapter is divided into three sections. The first of these describes Brown's intervention into the debates of the sensational psychologists. Rejecting the predominantly visual bias of much Enlightenment thought (including that of Locke and Berkeley), Brown's novel turns instead toward the ideas of the French *philosophe*, Condillac, a writer who emphasizes the crucial role of touch. This, in turn, helps Brown establish the importance of a fully embodied, multisensory relationship between individual and environment. The second section extends this discussion into a consideration of space and spatial boundaries. Theories of sense perception were (and are) intimately bound up with theories of space. *Edgar Huntly* makes it clear, following David Hume, that the production of space is fundamentally a phenomenological process. Finally, the third section links this embodied production of space to an act of appropriation. To produce a spatial frontier, the novel suggests, is also at some level to stake a claim to the spaces created. Exactly how this appropriation might occur, and how it might reframe a history of Indian-settler violence is the central concern of this chapter.

Condillac's Statue and the Primacy of Touch

By the time he published *Edgar Huntly* in 1799, Brown had read deeply and widely across a range of Enlightenment thinkers and his fascination with sensational psychology was well-established. He was guided in these studies by his membership in Elihu Smith's "Friendly Club," a regular gathering of thinkers and literati in New York that was designed to foster lively discussion and intellectual community. The group read extensively in works of philosophy, art, politics, and history.[13] Crucially for Brown, their reading list included not just British empiricists like Locke, Berkeley, and Hume, but also a varied selection of more radical French thought.[14] As a result, Brown was able to track the debates about sensory perception as they developed over time and across national boundaries. Evidence of this deep-seated interest in sensation can be found in all four of his major novels, but the theme is especially prominent in *Edgar Huntly*.[15] The novel repeatedly considers the role and function of the senses in conditioning an individual's relationship to the environment, and it does so by turning to specific texts—even specific passages—involved in the sensational psychology debates.

Brown wastes no time in *Edgar Huntly* before signaling his interest in issues of sensation and embodiment. The opening paragraphs of the novel fixate on the ungovernable nature of the narrator's sense impressions as they threaten to overwhelm his ability to construct a coherent narrative. Epistolary in form, the novel is constructed as a collection of letters sent from Edgar to his fiancée, Mary Waldegrave. Edgar begins the first of these letters disconcerted and upset. The "series of events" through which he has lately passed, he warns Mary, has utterly "absorbed his faculties" and "hurried away [his] attention." Up to this point, it has been impossible "to disengage [his] senses from the scene that was passing or approaching." He wonders if the incidents can even be "recalled and arranged without indistinctness and confusion" (643). One of the initial tensions in the novel is thus between the immediacy of bodily sense experience and the pause, or "repose," needed for reflection, composure, and ultimately, composition. Such a tension broadly parallels the insistent psychological question of how the mind is able to form higher-order thoughts and "judgments" out of raw sense data. (The French *philosophe*, Condillac, in fact, specifically proposes the mechanism of "attention.") But for the moment, it is enough to note that Brown's first two paragraphs establish an investment in sensation that will reverberate throughout the book.

The fear of narrative incoherence that Edgar voices in these initial paragraphs also nicely prefigures the crazed, convoluted plot that will unfold over the course of the entire novel. Edgar's tale begins with his discovery of a mysterious Irish immigrant, Clithero Edny, whom he witnesses sleepwalking under a giant elm tree on the edge of the settled territories. This arouses Edgar's suspicions because his own dear friend Waldegrave (Mary's brother) has recently been murdered by unknown assailants under the very same tree. Edgar begins following Clithero, tracking him as he somnambulates through the frontier wilderness. Eventually, he learns the mournful story behind the Irishman's exile to America. Convinced of Clithero's innocence in relation to Waldegrave's murder, Edgar dispenses with any ideas of revenge and dedicates himself instead to the benevolent support of the exile. At this point, however, Edgar is beset with some difficulties of his own when he learns that the liberal inheritance of his fiancée (the seed money for their future together) actually belongs to someone else. The night after receiving this news, Edgar goes to bed upset, only to awaken disoriented in a subterranean pit in the middle of the wilderness. The second half of the novel follows Edgar through a series of violent confrontations with Indians as he makes his way back across the frontier and into the familiar territory of white settlement.

Edgar's dogged pursuit of Clithero through the Pennsylvania woods is crucial not just for the peculiar relationship of "benevolence" that it establishes between the two men but also because it effectively sets up a contrast between vision and touch that is central to debates among the sensational psychologists. As Edgar tracks Clithero through "Norwalk," that is, the rugged, hilly region between the Wind-gap and the Water-gap, he repeatedly oscillates between moments of panoramic vision and moments of near blindness in which he must often rely on the sense of touch. The two men move from precipitous views that are "in the highest degree, rugged, picturesque and wild," into "dreary vale[s]" where "the faintness of star-light was all that preserved my senses from being useless to my own guidance" (656). They hike from "deepest thickets" and "darkest cavities" to "the most difficult heights," approaching "the slippery and tremulous verge of the dizziest precipices" (659). At one point, Edgar follows Clithero's trail into a cave of "intense dark." Having (strangely) forgotten to bring a lamp or torch, he is compelled "to resort to hands as well as feet": "I proceeded with the utmost caution, always ascertaining, by out-stretched arms, the height and breadth of the cavity before me" (726). Eventually, his hands lead him through the cave and out onto a "projecture of rock" high up on a cliff face. Here, he pauses to take in the view: "A large part of this chaos of rocks and precipices was subjected, at one view, to the eye. The fertile lawns and vales which lay beyond this, the winding course of the river, and the slopes which rose on its farther side, were parts of this extensive scene. These objects were at any time fitted to inspire rapture" (728). From expansive vision to groping darkness and back again, Edgar's movements persistently juxtapose the visual and the tactile.[16]

Nowhere is this contrast more clear than in the moment at which Clithero disappears into the mouth of a mountainside cave. Edgar draws up short, unwilling to pursue the Irishman into "the windings of the grotto" (656). Instead, he stations himself directly in front of the entrance and waits for Clithero to reappear. Recognizing that his sight will be of little avail in the gloom—it is nighttime and the entrance is "hemmed in on all sides by lofty and precipitous cliffs"—Edgar resolves to depend on his hearing and his sense of touch: "I stretched my hands before it, determined that he should not emerge from his den without my notice. His steps would, necessarily, communicate the tidings of his approach. They could not move without a noise which would be echoed to, on all sides, by the abruptnesses by which this valley was surrounded" (656). It is, in its way, a remarkable image: a blind man standing before the darkened mouth of a cave with arms outstretched and ears cocked, waiting. Edgar is a kind of raw sensorium here, a body finely attuned to its environment. But significantly, this is a nonvisual mode of attention. Sight is curtailed and the other senses—most importantly, touch—assert themselves.

Brown's shadowy circumscription of European landscape conventions begins here to reveal his antivisualist inclinations. Edgar's up-and-down, light-and-dark pursuit of Clithero underscores the ways in which vision can abstract and distance an individual from the environment. The hyper-visuality of landscape discourse positions the viewer as an outsider, a disembodied eye, as it were, who can only survey the scene from above, literally out of touch with the world below.[17] Once the viewer descends into the landscape, into the enclosed and intimate spaces of darkness represented by the elm tree and the cave, vision loses its constitutive power and the sense of touch begins to assert its importance. A crucial effect of this shift from visual to tactile is an emphasis on the contact that occurs between individual and the world, between subject and object. Whereas vision, particularly landscape vision, maintains a distance between the viewer and the scene, touch effectively draws the two together. Tactile sensation makes room for, in fact requires, intimate contact with an Other in a way that vision does not.

Brown's shift in emphasis from vision to touch parallels the arguments of sensational psychologists as they develop over the course of the eighteenth century. In his *Essay Concerning Human Understanding* (1690), John Locke had famously argued that vision is the predominant sense. He held that a person learned to habitually associate particular visual impressions (that is, "the ideas of light and colours") with different kinds of information from the other senses (for example, "the far different ideas of space, figure, and motion"). Vision is linked to touch, say, through gradual experience, "by a settled habit." But for him, sight takes precedence; it is "the most comprehensive of all our senses" because it synthesizes heterogeneous sense data and because, ultimately, it is the sense that "convey[s] to our minds" the information we will use to make "judgements" (*Essay* 145).[18]

Later philosophers, however, quickly disagreed and began to gradually elevate the status of touch in the human experience of the world. In his *Essay Towards A New Theory of Vision* (1709), Bishop Berkeley argued that Locke made the mistake of thinking that human beings have an inherent ability to identify *shapes*. That is, Locke assumed that a person would, from the beginning, be able to visually distinguish squares, circles, and so forth, and to then mentally associate those visual shapes with tangible, tactile sense data. Berkeley rejected this reasoning and strenuously maintained that "the extension, figures, and motions perceived by sight are specifically distinct from the ideas of touch called by the same names, nor is there any such thing as one idea [. . .] common to both senses" (24). Instead, Berkeley maintained that sight was learned from the ground up, as it were. The mind possesses absolutely no underlying ideas that might link sight and touch, and seeing must be learned entirely through experience. What is more, touch plays the fundamental role here: "Having of a long time experienced certain ideas, perceivable by touch as distance, tangible figure, and solidity, to have been connected with certain ideas of sight, I do upon perceiving these ideas of sight forthwith conclude what tangible ideas are by the wonted ordinary course of nature like to follow" (7). The privileged status of vision has begun to erode.[19]

The most radical assertion of the primacy of touch, however, occurs in the work of Etienne Bonnot, abbé de Condillac. A friend of both Rousseau and Diderot, Condillac was the French *philosophe* most responsible for introducing Lockean empiricism to France; his *Essay on the Origins of Human Knowledge* (1756) was subtitled "A supplement to Mr. Locke's essay." But like Berkeley, Condillac was frustrated by what he perceived as Locke's failure to explain the precise mechanism through which knowledge is derived from the senses. He felt that Locke's assertion that "all ideas come from sensation or reflection" unnecessarily distinguished external sense-data and internal mental operations. At the beginning of his *Treatise on the Sensations* (1754), Condillac explains that his main purpose is to correct this unnecessary distinction and to "show how all our knowledge and all our faculties come from the senses or, to be more precise, from sensation" (155). In this way, Condillac's empiricism is more radical than either Berkeley or Locke in that it maintains *absolutely all* human knowledge ultimately derives from sense-data. There is no innate judge or reflector separate from and above the initial sensory experience. To manage this conflation, Condillac proposes that specific sensory impressions result from a kind of "attention" that our mind bestows on particular aspects of sensory experience, for example, by focusing on the background sound of a ticking clock (which would normally go unnoticed). Once the "sensation becomes attention" it makes a lasting impression on the mind; it becomes memory. The existence of memory along with new sensations allows for a "twofold attention" that results in "comparison." This, in turn, leads to the faculty of judgment (160). Thus, for Condillac, all higher mental faculties grow out of the fundamental sensory experience of the environment.[20]

Touch, however, is the one sense that undergirds the experience of all the others. Condillac expands on Berkeley's claim that "seeing" is a learned behavior by asserting that, in fact, it is touch that "teaches the other senses to judge external objects" (266). Significantly, he entitles Part Two of the *Treatise*, "On Touch, Or The Only Sense That Judges External Objects On Its Own" (223). The visualism of Locke's theory has been rejected here in favor of a tactile prejudice, a deep-seated conviction that all other sensory information is filtered through an experiential framework provided by touch. To make his case, Condillac employs the rhetorical device of an imaginary statue who is endowed with each of the five senses, one at a time and in combination. In his words, "We imagined a statue internally organized like ourselves, and animated by a mind deprived of every kind of idea [. . .] and we reserved for ourselves the freedom to open [its senses] at will" (170). This hypothetical construct allows Condillac to consider individually the role of each of the senses in the process of cognition and the development of self-knowledge. Thus, chapter titles in the *Treatise* include descriptions like "Of a Man Limited to the Sense of Sight," "Of the First Knowledge of a Man Limited to the Sense of Smell," and "On Sight with Smell, Hearing and Taste." He concludes, among other things, that without touch (and the associated ability to move), the perceiving subject would have no knowledge of the space in which it exists or of external objects. Space, for him, is not primarily a visual construct, but a tactile one, growing out of the mobile body.

Already in Edgar's midnight pursuit of Clithero, we have seen Brown set up an opposition between the visual and tactile modes of experience. But it is in chapter 16 during the pivotal cave sequence that Brown draws closest to the works of Condillac. At this point in the narrative, Edgar abruptly regains consciousness in a pitch-black space having no knowledge whatsoever as to where he is or how he has arrived there. Like the statue, he is bereft of all sensory input: "When enabled at length to attend to the information which my senses afforded, I was conscious, for a time of nothing but existence." His thoughts are "wildering and mazy," and although consciousness is present, it is "disconnected with the loco-motive or voluntary power" (779). Compare this with the account rendered by Condillac's statue in a chapter entitled "Of a Man Who Remembers Having Received the Use of His Senses One After the Other": "At the first moment of my existence I did not know at all what was taking place in me; I distinguished nothing as yet; I had no consciousness of myself" (332). Edgar's status as a blind man is emphasized: "My eyes [. . .] were opened; but the darkness that environed me was as intense as before." "I turned my head to different quarters, I stretched my eye-lids, and exerted every visual energy, but in vain. I was wrapt in the murkiest and most impenetrable gloom." The only explanation that initially suggests itself to him is "the belief that I was blind" (779). Then, however, as with the statue, sense-data begins to trickle in one sense at a time. "Since my sight availed nothing to the knowledge of my condition, I betook myself to other instruments" (780). What follows for Edgar is a gradual rediscovery of the body and the self as he slowly accumulates bits and pieces of sensory information.

His first impressions are of sensations *within* his own body, the proprioceptive feeling of physical pain. Opening his eyes causes him "a pang more acute than any which I ever experienced." His "limbs [are] cold" and he is "sensible of pain in [his] shoulders and back" (779). This mirrors the initial experience of the statue whose first sensations impress him "in proportion to the extent of the pains or pleasures that accompany them." Indeed, by directing his attention, it is pleasure and pain that subsequently "develop all [the statue's] faculties" (333). Edgar, after registering his own physical pain, immediately turns his attention to the sensory information available to his touch. "The spot where I lay," he recalls, "was rugged and hard." So he staggers to his feet and begins a tentative investigation: "I stretched out my hands on all sides but met only with vacuity. I advanced forward. At the third step my foot moved something which lay upon the ground" (780). This turns out to be his own tomahawk, but it offers him no clues so he continues groping. "My hands at length touched a wall. This, like the flooring, was of stone, and was rugged and impenetrable. I followed this wall" (780). The tactile exploration continues for awhile, but it is sufficient here to point out that Condillac's statue embarks on the same quest as it awakens to its environment. "I place my hands on myself, I place them on what is around me. In that moment a new sensation seems to give substance to all my states. Everything takes on solidity at my fingertips" (333).

As the chapter continues, Edgar repeats the same crucial sensory experiences described by Condillac. Spurred on by a steadily increasing hunger, Edgar turns to his sense of hearing: "I once more tasked my understanding and my senses, to discover the nature of my present situation and the means of escape. I listened to catch some sound" (782). He hears an indistinct rush of wind, "sometimes near and sometimes distant," but this only confuses him because, as he puts it, "If my hands were true I was immured between walls through which there was no avenue" (782). So he tries his own voice instead and is rewarded with a cacophony of echoes. This turns out to be a serendipitous development, however, because "part of that uncertainty in which I was involved, was instantly dispelled by it." He recalls his earlier pursuit of Clithero into the darkened cave and concludes that "the effect produced by my voice on this occasion resembled, with remarkable exactness, the effect which was then produced" (782). In short, he has figured out where he is. Such echo-location dovetails nicely with Condillac's assessment of the role of hearing for his statue: "The statue will perceive distance and location of an object by ear, whenever they are the same as under the conditions in which it has made many experiments" (272). The parallels continue with the sense of taste. After encountering and killing a panther in the pit, Edgar's ravenous hunger drives him to the unthinkable: feasting on the raw flesh of the cat. "My hunger had arrived at that pitch where all fastidiousness and scruples are at an end. I crept to the spot. [...] " Despite the fastidiousness of that ellipsis, however, in the next paragraph Edgar details the *taste* of the carcass, shivering as he remembers "the yet warm blood and reeking fibres of a brute" (786). Condillac describes a similar connection between hunger, taste, and touch: "*Hunger makes it seize indifferently whatever is offered* [...]. Then the statue tries to bite everything at hand [...] and its first choice is to nourish itself on those things that are most readily available" (302).

Edgar's sensory reawakening continues throughout the chapter, ending only when he finally climbs out of the pit and gropes his way to the gleams of a campfire kindled by marauding Indians. But the parallels with Condillac are already clear. While it is difficult to say definitively whether Brown is working directly from Condillac's text, he is plainly fascinated with the same unique idea of a man gradually accumulating sensory powers. This idea, and the darkness of the cave, allows him to emphasize the significance of the nonvisual senses, to explore those forms of perception we often overlook, or take for granted. Against the visualist bias of much Enlightenment thought, Brown opts instead to follow the trail blazed by Condillac. The *philosophe* famously argued that "touch teaches vision," and Brown leverages this maxim throughout *Edgar Huntly*. For him, it is touch that undergirds all the other senses. It is touch that situates the body within, and not above, the landscape. Most importantly, it is touch that draws the individual and the world together into intimate contact. Boundaries, borders, and the space of the frontier are produced not simply by political will, but also through precisely this sort of contact between bodies in motion.

Touching on the Other: Bodily Frontiers and the Production of Space

Brown's fascination with Condillac's statue leads, almost inevitably, to a related investigation into the nature of space itself. Locke, Berkeley, Hume, and the French *philosophes* all attempted to explain the ontology of space on the basis of our initial sensory experience. Locke and Hume aligned themselves on opposite sides of a long-standing debate about whether space could best be understood as a *vacuum* or a *plenum*. Berkeley, himself a plenist, rejected the Newtonian concept of "absolute space" (that is, space as an empty container in which bodies move) and argued instead that the idea of space simply could not be conceived apart from a body.[21] Condillac, not surprisingly, is distinguished by the emphasis he places on the role of touch in the experience of space. Eschewing the visualist tendencies of Berkeley and Locke, he calls attention to the multisensory, fully embodied nature of our relationship to the environment, and to tactile relationships in particular. In a chapter helpfully entitled "On the Manner in Which a Man Limited to a Sense of Touch Begins to Discover Space," Condillac explains the statue's spatial awakening: "It seems to it that the space must be drawn from its own being, that objects are extended beneath its hands at only the expense of its own body; and the more it compares itself with the space that surrounds it, the more it feels its outer limits constrict" (239). A few pages later, he continues, "Wherever the statue finds no resistance whatever, it judges that there is none and it forms the idea of empty space" (249).

Condillac's conception of space here is notable for two characteristics: its tactile foundations and its self-generated nature. For Condillac, our idea of space grows out of a primordial sensory experience in which we learn, through touch, to distinguish our own body from the space surrounding it. The higher intellectual functions (for example, "judgment" and "ideas") then rely upon that initial tactile encounter and comparison. But there can be, in effect, no notion of space without specifically tactile sensations and bodily movement. More radically, however, Condillac posits a model of space that is *produced* from the body itself. Space is "drawn from [the body's] own being" and extended around itself at its own "expense." This is a far cry from the Newtonian idea of space as a preexisting expanse in which bodies eventually orient themselves. Instead, Condillac suggests that space has meaning only to the extent that it emanates from our own phenomenological body. We are not located a priori inside a space-as-container; rather, the space in which we live is actively produced by our mobile bodies.[22]

In this way, Condillac's work continues to provide a theoretical context in which Brown can explore relevant philosophical issues, in this case, the nature of space. Brown again follows Condillac's lead here by dramatically emphasizing the key role of the sensate body in the production of space. But the novel then takes a further step, adding to Condillac's thinking: Brown goes on to consider not just the phenomenological but also the social aspects of spatial production. *Edgar Huntly*, I would suggest, articulates a sophisticated model of spatial production in which the orientational powers of the phenomenological body are carefully linked to larger, socially-produced forms of space. The mobile body, Brown implies, establishes both the individual spatial framework in which we exist, as bodies, and the patterns of movement, contact, and exchange that delineate our larger properties, territories, and networks. The spaces we inhabit and through which we move are created in the overlap between phenomenological experience and social interaction.

For Brown, the essential point of contact between sensory space and social space occurs with the body of the Indian. In the moment of contact, particularly tactile contact, between white subject and Native American Other, a boundary is created that is simultaneously phenomenological and social. The limits of the body and the limits of a spatial territory are enacted, and reenacted, through repeated contact. In this way, the novel argues that the larger sociocultural formation of the geographical frontier (which Edgar travels back and forth across) cannot be separated from small-scale phenomenological encounters between the individual sensate body and an Other. Those small-scale encounters reaffirm an individual bodily "frontier" at the same time that they enact and maintain the larger and more abstract geographic boundary. The frontier wilderness setting of the novel calls attention to precisely this process of encounter and delimitation. By simplifying the tactile encounter with the Indian to its most schematic, unencumbered form (that is, outside the complex overlapping social spaces of the town or city), the novel carefully turns our attention to those foundational moments of spatial production, to one body touching another.[23]

Brown's own philosophical path to this blending of embodiment and social interaction lies through Locke and Hume. But in order to follow him, it will be helpful to return briefly to Henri Lefebvre's theory of social space. As I discussed in my introductory chapter, Lefebvre understands lived space to emerge from the dialectical interaction of our conceptual, phenomenological, and social experiences of space. But it is Lefebvre's detailed account of that phenomenological element that is especially helpful for understanding Edgar's experience in the cave. Echoing Condillac, Lefebvre argues that the abstract concept of space has no meaning unless there is an "axes and an origin [. . .] a right and a left" (169). Like Berkeley and Hume, he underscores the necessity of beginning with "a body—not bodies in general, nor corporeality, but a specific body, a body capable of indicating direction by a gesture, of defining rotation by turning round, of demarcating and orienting space" (170). In this way, we can say that a body *produces* space. In Lefebvre's formulation, "each living body *is* space and *has* its space: it produces itself in space and it also produces that space" (170). Gestures, in particular, play a key role because they are the primary means by which the fundamental axes of orientation are established. "Gesture" should here be understood not in the limited sense of hand motion, but rather movements of the entire body: "It seems that it is not so much *gestures* which do the qualifying as the body as a whole" (174). Movements such as sitting up and lying down, or turning the body around, effectively establish directional signifiers like left/right, up/down, and front/back.[24]

Immediately, this sort of gestural orientation recalls Edgar's behavior upon regaining consciousness in the pit. He remarks that his initial return to consciousness is "disconnected with the loco-motive or voluntary power." At first, his disorientation is marked by a complete detachment from the orienting mechanisms of the body; he cannot move and thus cannot set up any sort of spatial framework in which he might begin to place himself. "From this state a transition was speedily effected," he tells us. "I perceived that my posture was supine, and that I lay upon my back." But after a painful struggle to regain control of his limbs, he attains "a sitting posture" (779) and thus puts into place at least one component of his body's own space. He rides out his panic for awhile and then performs two more crucial gestures in quick succession: "After various efforts I stood upon my feet. At first I tottered and staggered [. . .]. I advanced forward" (780). Standing erect reinforces the up/down axis put into place by his sitting up and then he sets his body in forward motion. This is a critical step in the creation of a spatial framework because it produces a number of ancillary demarcations. Notions of forward and backward are clearly established, but so are the ideas of left and right, and front and back. When Edgar reaches out his hands and encounters the wall of the pit, the general concepts of near and far come into play although they remain hobbled by the "utter darkness" of the pit, which disables him from "comparing directions and distances" (781). In this way, as Edgar begins a series of embodied, gestural movements within the cave, he begins to *produce* a space of the body, a space springing from his own physio-sensory experience.²⁵

The intimate interrelationship of Edgar's body and the gradually expanding space around it is also indicated through Brown's careful evocation of specific bodily rhythms. Lefebvre asserts that internal physiological states externalize themselves by exerting an influence on the organization and meaning of the space "occupied" by the body. "Through the mediation of rhythms [...] an animated space comes into being which is an extension of the space of bodies." In particular, Lefebvre points to the most obvious rhythms, the ones most closely associated with the individual body: "breathing, the heartbeat, thirst, hunger, and the need for sleep" (207). As these bodily rhythms impinge on the consciousness of the individual, they motivate movement and action within the surrounding space. Responding to and fulfilling these internal requirements thus become important factors in the production and arrangement of space around the body. In Edgar's case, the most insistent physiological rhythm is that of hunger, and when the "cravings" first make themselves felt, they immediately spur a renewed investigation of the pit. That investigation flags, however, as Edgar's hunger drives him to eat the shreds of his linen shirt. But the shirt does little to assuage him and the "inroads of hunger" quickly reassert themselves. Finally, he tomahawks the panther and gorges himself on the carcass. But, again, his respite is brief as he is "now assailed by the torments of thirst" (787). What is more, his bouts of hunger and thirst are repeatedly interrupted by exhausted collapses into fitful sleep. Again and again, the interaction of Edgar's body with the space around it is structured by the insistence of physiological rhythms.

What Lefebvre and Condillac make clear is that Brown is deeply committed to exploring a phenomenological space of the body at odds with the prevailing philosophical conception of space as an empty container. I say "prevailing" because although at the end of the eighteenth century there were several competing theories of space, the Newtonian tradition of "absolute space" was clearly in ascendance. During the period of the early republic, the tradition had its most prominent articulation in Locke's *Essay*. In a chapter on "The Simple Modes of Space," Locke declares in no uncertain terms that "*space is not body*, because it includes not the idea of solidity in it; *space and solidity* being *as distinct ideas*" (166). A few pages earlier, Locke explains that such solidity is "the idea most intimately connected with, and essential to body" (125).²⁶ He leaves no doubt as to the separate and distinct natures of space and body; there is no possibility of a mutually constitutive, or *productive*, relationship here. Furthermore, like Newton, Locke's space is a vast emptiness in which various material bodies move around: "All beyond it [the universe] is one uniform space or expansion, wherein the mind finds no variety, no marks" (165). Such an assertion places Locke firmly on the side of the *vacuum* in the long-standing philosophical debate about whether space itself can best be understood as a vacuum (an absence of matter) or as a *plenum* (a continuous distribution of matter).[27] In fact, he answers one of the plenist objections to the theory of the vacuum by maintaining that God must certainly have the ability to "annihilate" any body in existence, including even "this book, or the body of him who reads it." As a result, "it is evident, that the space, that was filled by the parts of the annihilated body, will still remain, and be a space without a body" (170). Locke's space, then, is a version of Newton's empty container. It is, as Locke scholar John Yolton explains, a "space devoid of body, the absolute space, the infinite abysses of space" (82). It is also diametrically opposed to the embodied space Brown is bent on exploring.

It is not only Condillac, however, who opposes Locke's model of empty space. The most pointed rejoinder to the Lockean spatial paradigm was written by that most skeptical of all empiricists, David Hume. Unlike Locke, Hume denies that the idea of space can exist apart from the idea of bodies. Addressing the issue in *A Treatise of Human Nature* (1739–40), Hume asserts that "however we may express ourselves, we must always confess, that we have no idea of any real extension without filling it with sensible objects, and conceiving its parts as visible or tangible" (47). For Hume, the only way we can have any idea or understanding of space is through the *relational association* of objects that we can see or feel. Since there is no direct sense-data to attest to the existence of space (that is, we can't touch or taste or hear or see space itself), it is only through extrapolation that we come to have an idea of it: "We have therefore no idea of space or extension, but when we regard it as an object either of our sight or feeling" (31).[28]

This emphasis on the embodied, sensory foundation of our spatial experience prompts Marina Frasca-Spada to describe Hume's approach as "a phenomenology of the initial stages of perceptual acquaintance with the world" (182). But more to the point, she calls attention to a crucial passage in Hume's argument. In trying to explain exactly how it is that human beings arrive at a notion of space based solely on their sense perceptions, Hume offers the following example: "Suppose, that amidst an entire darkness, there are luminous bodies presented to us, whose light discovers only these bodies themselves, without giving any impression of the surrounding objects" (42). The relationship of these "two luminous bodies" (42) gives shape to the darkness and allows us to conceive of a distance or space between them. But Hume is adamant that it is never the darkness that generates this idea of space; it is rather "the objects themselves, and [...] the manner [in which] they affect our senses" (42). Frasca-Spada helpfully elucidates: "Vacuum is absence and cannot be represented. But perceiving two-bodies-separated-by-an-invisible-and-intangible-distance is perceiving a configuration, a whole including the two bodies' mutual position and distance as well as the bodies themselves [...]. Here Hume states that the idea of space derives from the whole configuration, with the invisible and intangible distance being part of its 'manner of appearance'" (179–80). All of which underscores the distinction between Hume's plenist inclinations and Locke's belief in the vacuum.[29] Whereas Locke argues that space exists independently from the realm of material objects, Hume insists that the only experience of space we can ever have is one that grows out of our embodied relationship to the sensual environment around us.

Brown was familiar with Hume's writing via his participation in the Philadelphia Friendly Club. There is tantalizing evidence, however, of an even more direct connection in *Edgar Huntly*.[30] The centerpiece of Hume's anti-Lockean model of space is the example he offers of "two luminous bodies" that appear "amidst an entire darkness." Significantly, Edgar himself encounters two strikingly similar objects as he gropes his way around the gloomy cave. Having clambered out of the pit and onto a ledge, he comes face to face with the two glowing eyes of the panther. "The darkness," he tells us, "was no less intense than in the pit below, and yet two objects were distinctly seen": "They resembled a fixed and obscure flame. They were motionless. Though lustrous themselves they created no illumination around them. This circumstance, added to others, which reminded me of similar objects, noted on former occasions, immediately explained the nature of what I beheld. These were the eyes of a panther" (785). These are also, it seems to me, Brown's version of Hume's "two luminous bodies." The most telling aspect of his description here is the fact that the eyes, "though lustrous themselves [...] creat[e] no illumination around them." This is a language and phrasing that almost directly echoes Hume's two bodies, "whose light discovers only these bodies themselves, without giving any impression of the surrounding objects." Then, to underscore the spatial register, Brown has Edgar aim the tomahawk at "the middle space between these glowing orbs" (786). The "middle space" between two luminescent objects is precisely where Hume locates the origin of our extrapolated ideas of embodied space. But as he repeatedly emphasizes, this is not as simple an intellectual process as seeing or feeling such an "empty space" and then concluding that space exists. In fact, "'tis impossible that the dark and undistinguishable distance between two bodies can ever produce that idea" (42). Instead, it is the presence of the two bodies themselves that explain "why we falsely imagine we can form such an idea. For there is a close relation betwixt that motion and darkness, and a real extension, or composition of visible and tangible objects" (43). In other words, we have at some time in the past seen or felt a "real extension" between objects. (We might remember, for example, the visible "extension" of a panther's head between its eyes. We should also note here that Edgar explicitly compares the configuration of the panther's eyes to "similar objects, noted on former occasions.") Then, by the process of false analogy, we assume that this new *invisible* or *intangible* space between objects actually exists, even though we have no direct sensory impressions to confirm that. Why exactly are we prone to make this perceptual error? According to Hume, it is because "we may establish it as a general maxim in this science of human nature, that wherever there is a close relation betwixt two ideas, the mind is very apt to mistake them, and in all its discourses and reasonings to use the one for the other" (44).

Edgar's tomahawk throw into the "middle space" between the panther's eyes thus serves as a particularly apt literary device for Brown. At the same time that it calls attention to the Humean concept of relationally defined space, it also symbolically destroys the false Lockean notion of an empty space that can exist apart from, and independent of, material objects and direct sensory impressions. In a way, Edgar's tomahawk delivers a fatal blow to the notion of space as a vacuum, at least within the narrative confines of the novel. What is more, the lethal tomahawk nicely underscores Brown's pursuit of a sensual, embodied alternative to such a space by dramatically revealing an actual *body* in the "middle space." Initially the space between the glowing eyes appears to be an empty vacuum, but the edge of the tomahawk uncovers a "warm" and "reeking" body that Edgar cannot only touch and smell, but also taste and consume. And while this violent deconstruction of Lockean space may be hard to swallow at first, doing so is ultimately necessary for Edgar's survival.

It is worth noting as well that the tomahawk invokes a political register here that begins to move our discussion beyond empiricist debates about space. Because it is a tomahawk, in particular, that reveals the presence of a body in what seemed to be an empty vacuum, the scene hints also at the potential presence of Native American bodies in the supposedly "empty" spaces of America. As I discussed in the Introduction, Locke's political philosophy (in *Two Treatises*) frequently refers to the "vacant places" (293) and "uncultivated waste of *America*" (294). This rhetoric was frequently used as a legal justification for dispossessing Native American from their lands. So Edgar's overdetermined tomahawk sets up an intriguing parallel here between Locke's political and empirical philosophies: just as Locke's theory of space-as-vacuum erases the constitutive role of material bodies, so too does his theory of property effectively erase the Native American bodies who were actually filling the "vacant" spaces of America before white settlers arrived. In effect, the tomahawk figures as a kind of double retaliation against Locke: it rejects the Lockean model of body-less space, and it simultaneously suggests an unacknowledged Native American presence within Locke's narrative of uncontested appropriation.

More broadly speaking, then, the fateful tomahawk returns us to the issue of boundary-formation and to the body of the Indian. Where, we might ask, does the space produced by one's own body come to an end? If Edgar's ordeal in the cave stages a primordial production of bodily space, where do we locate the limits of that space? Or more provocatively, what happens when one lived space encounters another space-producing subjectivity? Although ignored in Condillac and Hume, such questions are particularly resonant in a novel of the frontier that concerns itself with intercultural boundary disputes. Building on the models of the empiricists, Brown's novel suggests that the production of space proceeds hand in hand with the production of spatial boundaries. The same relationship between self and Other that calls space into being is also the delineation of a spatial limit. In this case, the Other in question is the Delaware Indian and the spatial boundaries being created are the frontiers dividing white and Indian spaces.

Michel de Certeau, in a particularly helpful account of how space is represented in narrative, explains this process of spatial delimitation through contact with the Other. He argues that "the determination of space is dual and operational," an "interlocutory" process that unfolds between "acting subjects" (126). Emphasizing the importance of intersubjective relationality, Certeau believes that space comes into being through an active, "operational" negotiation between two subjects. But then he specifically addresses the issue of boundaries: "[Spaces] result from the operations of distinctions resulting from encounters. Thus, in the obscurity of their unlimitedness, bodies can be distinguished only where the 'contacts' ('*touches*') of amorous or hostile struggles are inscribed on them" (127) Here, Certeau implies that the expanding phenomenological space of sensate bodies, that is, the "obscurity of their unlimitedness," is curtailed and circumscribed only at points of amorous or hostile contact. Simply put, the limits of phenomenological space are established through the process of intimate contact with an Other. He goes on to note that this is "the paradox of the frontier: created by contacts, the points of differentiation between two bodies are also their common points. Conjunction and disjunction are inseparable in them. Of two bodies in contact, which one possesses the frontier that distinguishes them?" (127). We will return to the crucial issue of possession a bit further on, but for now it is enough to consider how the production of spatial frontiers rely on small-scale points of contact.[31]

Edgar's ordeal in the cave is itself a painful process of establishing spatial boundaries, albeit with nonhuman actants. (Certeau acknowledges the importance of subject interactions with "things, animals, human beings" [126].) First, his hands trace out the rocky confines of the pit itself, then he kills and feeds on the panther, an act which effectively appropriates the space of the cave for himself. But the novel is most interested in the negotiation of spatial boundaries as it occurs between competing social spaces. Time and time again, the narrative describes Edgar's hostile encounters with a string of Native American marauders. It is here, at the level of individual bodily contact, the novel suggests, that the contours of the white-Indian frontier are most clearly demarcated. A liminal, shifting space of back-and-forth negotiation, the frontier is constantly produced and reproduced through a process of violent, embodied encounter between two competing spatial paradigms.

Upon emerging from his exile in the pit, Edgar's first sight is of a small band of Indians sleeping around a campfire in a cavern on the mountainside. They have a white captive with them, a young farmer's daughter. Immediately, their presence throws him into a state of spatial and geographical disorientation. He wonders if "some mysterious power" has cast him into "the heart of the wilderness." "Was I still in the vicinity of my paternal habitation, or was I thousands of miles distant?" (790). Space and spatial boundaries have been destabilized for Edgar, and much of the remaining narrative will center on his efforts to reestablish some semblance of a clear dividing line. He quickly recounts for himself the regional geography, noting that the area of Norwalk has long functioned as a kind of de facto frontier space separating "Indian country" and the "English settlements" (791). In fact, Norwalk has historically been the "rude surface" across which Indians have made their "destructive inroads" into the colonial properties, a fact that explains the earlier violent fate of Edgar's own parents (791). As an acknowledged frontier and as a space previously marked by violent encounters, Norwalk and the

Indians' cavern represents precisely the sort of contested liminal space in which boundary definition would be called for.³²

And Edgar does not disappoint. He immediately initiates what will become a lengthy series of gruesome Indian killings through which he can reassert the spatial boundaries of the frontier. Creeping past the four sleeping Indians, he exits the cavern only to discover a fifth warrior standing guard outside, perched on the edge of a cliff. Hesitating only for a moment, Edgar hurls his tomahawk into the Indian's chest, killing him instantly and sending him plunging over the precipice. Edgar's first contact with an Indian thus results in a violent assertion of territorial authority and appropriation. A frontier is actualized in its most tangible form through bodily contact, through a violent negotiation of sorts. But it remains for subsequent encounters to underscore the specifically tactile nature of this interchange. Brown's penchant for gore will reinforce the emphasis on touch he has already established via Condillac.

Having rescued the young female captive from amidst the four remaining Indians, Edgar flees the mountains and takes refuge in a rude, abandoned hut on the outermost edges of the colonial settlements. Unfortunately for him, three of the cavern Indians are in hot pursuit and they soon track him to the hut. A gunfight ensues in which Edgar slays all of them and is himself grazed by a bullet across the cheek. As soon as the smoke has cleared, a group of white settlers arrive to provide support, but weakened from lack of food and loss of blood, Edgar loses consciousness. When he awakens, the settlers have gone, taking the girl but leaving him, apparently mistaking him for dead. His return to consciousness is a gruesome one, however. He managed to faint directly on top of the body of his final Indian victim, the two of them forming a bloody pile at some distance from the hut. "My head had reposed upon the breast of him whom I had shot in this part of his body. The blood had ceased to ooze from the wound, but my dishevelled locks were matted and steeped in that gore which had overflowed and choked up the orifice" (812). Here, Certeau's "amorous" and "hostile" contacts seem to have been conflated into an image of horrific tactile intimacy. Effectively sleeping with his head on the breast of the Indian, Edgar's tableau obliquely implies a version of romantic proximity. At the same time, however, the Indian's wound marks the violence of the encounter. In either case, Edgar's contact with the Indian is intimate and tactile, again instantiating bodily and spatial boundaries.

The last of the five Indians catches up with Edgar as he pauses to drink at a nearby spring. Once again, Edgar benefits from the advantage of surprise and drops the Indian with a single shot. This time, however, the bullet is not fatal and the Indian is simply wounded, albeit grievously. "He rolled upon the ground, uttering doleful shrieks, and throwing his limbs into those contorsions which bespeak the keenest agonies to which ill-fated man is subject" (816). The "dictate of compassion and of duty" compels Edgar to end the man's suffering, so he once more levels his musket at the Indian's head. But instead of finishing the grisly deed, his "faltering hand render[s] this second bullet ineffectual" (816). Twice wounded by gunfire, the Indian is still alive. So Edgar, horrified, affixes a bayonet to his musket and drives it into the Indian's heart. The sequence is notable for the fact that the increasingly gruesome violence parallels an increasing bodily intimacy. First, a bullet at a distance, then a bullet at point blank range, and finally a bayonet twist in which Edgar kills with the force of his own hands. The encounter between white and Indian is here reduced to a razor-sharp point of contact. But Edgar has one final act left to commit before leaving the Indian behind: "Prompted by some freak of fancy, I stuck his musquet in the ground, and left it standing in the middle of the road" (817). It is a fraught image. The violent point of contact between individual and other is here actively transformed into a spatial demarcation. If the frontier is to be found anywhere, Edgar suggests, it is under the sign of the bloody encounter between white and Indian bodies.

The entire novel is in fact structured around a series of such small-scale, body-to-body contacts between white settlers and Native Americans: Waldegrave's murder at the hands of a rogue Delaware; the early destruction of Edgar's own parents by an Indian raiding party; the death of Edgar's uncle during hand-to-hand combat with an Indian warrior, and so on. While Edgar's gruesome destruction of the five marauders provides perhaps the most minute account of this brutal contact, the repetition of similar encounters throughout the narrative underscores the ways in which Edgar's spatial delimitation occurs in the broader context of a history of violence. Brown's focus on sensational psychology effectively draws attention to the role of Indian bodies in the production of frontier space, but, in these instances, it is a violent role. The Indian body is touched, but only with a tomahawk or a bayonet.

Certeau, however, also raises the possibility of *amorous* contact as a way to establish bodily and spatial boundaries. The intimate tactile encounter of two bodies, he suggests, need not always be violent. Such a suggestion holds intriguing possibilities for *Edgar Huntly*. While our previous discussion seems to make it clear that violence is the only mode of encounter between whites and Indians in the novel, this explanation is complicated by the peculiar case of Clithero Edny. As any number of

Brown critics have noted, Clithero is himself repeatedly equated with Indians in the book.[33] He haunts the wilderness, dressed in a "scanty and coarse garb [. . .] his arms, bosom, and cheeks [. . .] overgrown and half-concealed by hair" (730); he moves into a frontier hut that was previously occupied by Old Deb and her Delaware compatriots; he is persistently associated with the panther, an animal that Edgar insists on describing as a "savage." And perhaps most convincingly, as Jared Gardner has shown, in the context of late eighteenth-century America, the "beastly" Irish were persistently imagined in terms synonymous with the "savage" Indians. Perceived as a social threat both "uncivilized" and politically radical, Irish immigrants were often stigmatized with the very same language used to describe the perceived Native American threat. This discursive context, along with the weight of textual evidence, makes a compelling case for Clithero's implicit representation as Indian avatar.[34]

But Edgar's relationship with Clithero differs markedly from his relationship with the more conventional Indians. Instead of resorting to lethal violence, Edgar develops an obsessive, and perhaps even erotic, sympathy for the Irishman. It is this manic species of benevolence that propels Edgar on his lengthy pursuit of Clithero and that inspires his ill-fated attempt to redeem the madman at the end of the novel. But the shape of Edgar's feelings for Clithero are revealed almost immediately in the book. When he spies Clithero's "tall and robust" figure, "half naked" in the gloom under the elm tree, it manages to "rouse up [his] whole soul" (647). And once he sees the sleepwalker begin to weep, his heart is won over: "Every sentiment, at length, yielded to my sympathy [. . .]. Tears found their way spontaneously to my eyes" (648). Later, after Clithero has exiled himself to the wilderness, Edgar finds him sleeping in a mountain cave. "I longed with vehemence for the return of day. I believed that every moment added to his sufferings, intellectual and physical, and confided in the efficacy of my presence to alleviate or suspend them" (760). Edgar's ardent sympathy here, sympathy for a man also coded as Native American, opens up the possibility of a nonviolent counter-narrative to the brutal encounters between Edgar and the Delaware.

The unexpected depth and energy of Edgar's feeling for Clithero has been the focus of several recent critics. Stephen Shapiro highlights the erotic dynamic between the two men, provocatively arguing that the novel expresses "a nascent ideal of male-male sexuality," and that, in fact, "*Edgar Huntly*'s theme is the potential for and fate of homoerotics."[35] Elizabeth Dillon, for her part, suggests that the pronounced "bodily interest" that pertains between Edgar and Clithero is not so much homoerotic as it is political in nature (167). Dillon maintains that Edgar's desire is a desire "to produce a body of his own—that is, to produce himself as embodied." Through a kind of "mimetic or identic contact" with Clithero, Edgar hopes to match Clithero's "somatic being." Edgar's goal is to produce a radical (in the sense of the French Revolution) republican identity through "fraternity and a literal identity or sameness with other male bodies" (177). In short, Edgar "seeks a *republican embodiment* or a bodily equality with other men around him, in which what matters is less any visible marker of his identity than establishing the sheer physical being that he holds in common with fellow men" (177).[36]

Dillon and Shapiro effectively call attention to the importance of the "bodily interest" that draws Edgar and Clithero into closer and closer proximity. But both critics also focus almost exclusively on the cohesive, or aggregating, effects of this erotic sympathy. That is, both see the bodily attraction of the two men as a strategy for the creation of a new group identity. For Dillon, it is a radical republican brotherhood; for Shapiro, it is a homoerotic collectivity. But as Certeau reminds us, there is a paradox to contact: the common points are also points of differentiation, of boundary demarcation. For this reason, while I agree that there is an identificatory impulse linking Edgar and Clithero, I would also emphasize the way in which their bodily contacts paradoxically function as separations, or "operations of distinctions," as Certeau calls them. Just as the violent contact between Edgar and the Indians serves to demarcate spatial boundaries, so too does Edgar's "amorous" contact with Clithero trace the outlines of a nonviolent spatial frontier.

Before specifically considering the boundary-defining qualities of these amorous contacts, however, it is worth reminding ourselves of the explicitly tactile register in which Brown couches them. We have already seen a hint of this tactile fixation in the image of Edgar waiting for Clithero with his hands outstretched in front of the cave entrance. But it is implied as well in the opening scene under the elm in which Edgar's sympathy for Clithero arouses a desire "to advance nearer and hold his hand" (648). Much later in the book, after Clithero has been attacked by the marauding Delaware and been brought, wounded, to the same house as Edgar, Edgar cradles him in his arms: "I was sensible of nothing but compassion. I acted without design, when seating myself on the floor I raised his head and placed it on my knees" (876). Even in their final encounter inside Deb's hut, just before Clithero runs off to attempt Mrs. Lorimer's murder for the second time, Edgar cannot resist touching Clithero. "I took his hand, and affectionately pressing it, said, do you not know me?" (892). The almost compulsive manner here in which Edgar is drawn to Clithero's body reveals a desire not just for "mimetic or identic contact," but specifically a desire for tactile contact, for bodies touching bodies.

This particular kind of contact is essential because it invokes the paradox of the frontier: it separates at the same time that it brings together. One way that Brown emphasizes this boundary-defining quality is to locate the Edgar-Clithero encounters in precisely the same spots that white-Indian violence has occurred, for example, the elm tree, Old Deb's hut, wilderness caves in Norwalk. In this way, Brown links the amorous Clithero contacts directly to the Indian contacts and their violent spatial demarcation. But even the nature of the Edgar-Clithero encounters themselves manifest a peculiar, and paradoxical, tendency toward separation. The two men are continually having their interviews interrupted, either by outside intrusions or by Clithero's abrupt departures. After hearing Edgar's request for an explanation of his bizarre behavior, Clithero mumbles his assent and then abruptly runs off to his room. He doesn't appear again for days. Similarly, the moment he finishes telling Edgar his story, "he started from the spot where he stood, and, without affording me any opportunity of replying or commenting, disappeared amidst the thickest of the wood" (718). Or again, at the end of the novel, when Edgar divulges the address of Mrs. Lorimer, Clithero vows to kill her and, "so saying, he darted through the door and was gone in a moment, beyond my sight and beyond my reach" (894). The tactile proximity of Edgar's "reach" (remember he had just taken Clithero's hand) seems to immediately trigger a centrifugal separation. Clithero is touched only to disappear.

This paradoxical conflation of proximity and separation is artfully captured in the scene in which Edgar discovers Clithero's wilderness hideaway. Having groped his way through the dark cave into which he saw Clithero disappear, Edgar emerges to the sublime prospect of Norwalk's rocky waterfalls and precipitous cliffs. Directly in front of him, he discovers a huge chasm that separates him from the far slope. Brown musters all of his landscape talents to describe the "dizzy" height, the "perpetual mist," and the "desolate and solitary grandeur" that envelops the scene (729). "Since the birth of this continent," he tells us, "I was probably the first who had deviated thus remotely from the customary paths of men" (730). No sooner has he said this, however, than he spies Clithero standing on the far slope. Where isolation and separation were thought to reign, he paradoxically finds social connection. The sight of Clithero arouses Edgar's manic sympathy, of course, and he immediately begins envisioning some sort of tactile contact between the two: "to set by him in silence, to moisten his hand with tears, to sigh in unison" (732).

But the desire for tactile union is held in tantalizing abeyance: "Though so near, the gulf by which we were separated was impassable" (731). It is a resonant image because it encapsulates the productive tension between contact and differentiation that characterizes all of Edgar and Clithero's relations. As with the violent Indian encounters, Edgar's benevolent brushes with the Irish "savage" are both unions and demarcations.

Through Clithero, the Indian-by-proxy, the novel makes room for an "amorous" alternative to the violent boundary creations enacted through Edgar's killing of the Delaware. Whether this turns out to be a historically viable alternative remains to be seen, but regardless, it underscores Brown's fascination with boundary formation and the production of space. Phenomenological space, that is, space springing from a mobile sensate body, Brown suggests, requires a circumscription, a limit against which it can define itself. Such a limit, the book argues, can best be understood in terms of an intimate, embodied negotiation between self and other, a negotiation that is both phenomenological and social. Although that negotiation need not always be violent, the novel implies that within the context of the eighteenth-century Pennsylvanian "frontier," it often is. Individual bodies touching one another may allow space to come into being, but such contact is also a struggle for control, a struggle for possession. Who owns that frontier and the spaces created on either side of it? These are questions with which Brown's novel is obsessed. In considering them, we can begin to see the crucial connections that link the novel's interest in sensation and space with its other primary concern: the discourse of private property.

Walking the Property: Mobility and the Appropriation of Space

The issue of boundaries, of course, has long been a key concern of property law and theories of ownership. At least as far back as ancient Rome, legal philosophy has paid close attention to the nature and contours of the boundary line. Roman jurists argued that occupation of a *res nullius*, a thing without an owner, in fact required the existence of spatial boundaries.[37] Only objects or areas of land with recognizable limits were capable of being possessed. Hugo Grotius, the prominent seventeenth-century legal theorist and author of *The Laws of War and Peace* (1625), explains:

> Occupation takes place only in the case of a thing which has definite limits. For this reason Thucydides calls unoccupied land "devoid of boundaries," and Isocrates characterized the land taken

over by the Athenians as "having boundaries fixed by us." Liquids, on the contrary, have no limits in themselves. "Water," says Aristotle, "is not bounded by a boundary of its own substance." Liquids therefore cannot be taken possession of unless they are contained in something else; as being thus contained, lakes and ponds have been taken possession of.[38]

Grotius is using Aristotle to bolster his own argument that the sea can never be privately possessed (and is thus open for Dutch shipping interests), but he also effectively underscores the role of boundaries in the act of possession. According to most legal theory, private property, in the form of either objects or land, can occur only within the constraints of recognizable spatial limits.

Whether Brown was familiar with Grotius's specific argument, he was certainly familiar with the legal philosophical tradition of which Grotius was a part. Brown studied law for six years in the offices of Alexander Wilcocks, a distinguished Philadelphia lawyer. He was at this time also a member of the "Legal Society," a law club that considered hypothetical cases in order to analyze, and rule on, particular legal issues. This education, in addition to Brown's later participation in the philosophy-heavy Friendly Club, suggests that by 1799, he would have had a thoroughgoing knowledge of not only Blackstone's *Commentaries* and Coke's *Institutes*, but also the political philosophy with which the legal writers engaged. This philosophy, which included the likes of Grotius, Pufendorf, Hobbes, Locke and Hume, was intimately concerned with the nature and function of private property. Interest in boundaries and ownership followed from these philosophers just as readily as it followed from Brown's more pragmatic professional engagement with land deeds, quitclaims, and ground rents.[39]

Certainly, possession and property rights are insistent themes in *Edgar Huntly*, repeatedly manifesting themselves in a variety of convoluted subplots that wind their way through the novel. Edgar's own dispossession and displacement, for example, is a source of constant anxiety for him. Having lost his parents to an Indian raid while still a child, he and his two surviving sisters have lived under the protection of an uncle. But the death of his uncle, also at the hands of marauding Indians, exposes both him and his sisters to the malevolence of the uncle's son. As he tells his fiancee Mary, "The ground which furnished me with bread was now become the property of one, who, if he could have done it with security, would gladly have mingled poison with my food" (845). Edgar thus loses both a patrimony and a "ground" he can call his own. His plight mirrors that of Old

Deb, the Native American matriarch who haunts the margins of the white settlement. She represents the last of the Delaware tribe who previously inhabited the region around the Huntly farm. (In fact, Edgar explains in passing that the Delaware village was "built upon ground which now constitutes my uncle's barn yard and orchard" [820].) Like Edgar, she has been dispossessed of her inheritance, pushed to abandon her "ancient seat" by the "perpetual encroachments of the English colonists" (820).

Recent scholarship on *Edgar Huntly* has begun to explore the novel's complex engagement with these property issues.[40] Sydney Krause, in particular, has drawn attention to the historical significance of the "perpetual encroachments" suffered by Old Deb's Delaware tribe. Krause maintains that by subtly calling attention to the shameful history of treaty violations, Brown's novel "awakens dark thoughts about the whites' past treatment of Native Americans" (473). For Krause, Edgar's giant elm tree functions as a symbolic reminder of the original property agreements made under William Penn's "Treaty Elm," agreements that were subsequently violated by the colonists. The most notorious of the white "encroachments," of course, was the Walking Purchase itself, and Krause suggests that by setting his novel where he does (in the heart of the Purchase), Brown establishes an "ironic parallel" between such pseudo-treaties and his own fiction (469).[41]

Krause's work is invaluable for its placement of *Edgar Huntly* in the crucial context of Indian-white relations on the frontier. But I want to push the implications of this context a bit further. The Walking Purchase, I believe, was of particular interest to Brown not just because it emblematized the problematic history of Indian-white property disputes, but also because it specifically engaged the philosophical issues of bounded space and mobile embodiment. A remarkable conflation of spaces, bodies, and properties, the story of the Walking Purchase represented a kind of philosophical "perfect storm" for a man of Brown's demonstrated interests. In it, questions of boundary creation were directly linked to the figure of the mobile body and to justifications of ownership. I would suggest that *Edgar Huntly* presents Brown with an opportunity to explore and experiment with the nexus of philosophical issues raised by the Walking Purchase. In the novel, as in the Purchase, the phenomenology of spatial boundaries is closely tied to the discourse of private property. To limit and to bound through contact with the other, the narrative implies, is also to take possession. In this way, the novel reveals a critical phenomenological component to the experience of acquiring property.

But Brown's invocation of the Walking Purchase is not simply an exercise in philosophical argument. Instead, Brown makes good on his oft-stated commitment to ground philosophical abstraction in specific historical circumstances. In this case, he orchestrates a fictional reconsideration of the Purchase itself. That is, *Edgar Huntly* effectively re-walks the Walking Purchase in light of Brown's philosophical investigations. The new model of embodied appropriation that he explores encourages a reexamination of Indian-white property relations on the frontier. In particular, his model asks the reader to pay attention to the body of the Indian and its essential role in the production and appropriation of space. Abstract philosophy is here put in the service of Brown's moral historiography.

Brown's efforts begin with the philosophy, however, and once again Locke and Hume will loom large. At the end of the eighteenth century, Locke casts as long a shadow over theories of private property as he does over sensational psychology and theories of space. The ontology of property he provides in his *Two Treatises of Government* remains the dominant paradigm throughout the eighteenth and nineteenth centuries. (Indeed, as I noted in the Introduction, it remains an important influence in contemporary property law.) In the *Two Treatises*, of course, Locke is faced with the task of rejecting the philosophical justifications (à la Robert Filmer) of absolutist, monarchical government. To do so, he rejects the appeals to history, tradition, and common law made by Whig apologists and invokes instead the precedent of natural law. Because it depends directly on the rule of God, such natural law trumps the hierarchical authority of the sovereign and establishes the basic equality of all men. According to Locke, all men are born free, equal, and with the power of rational thought. This freedom and rationality means that men have a natural—literally God-given—right to govern one another according to the dictates of reason. A radical claim at the time, Locke's argument implies that the foundation of just government rests on the shoulders of the individual, not in the traditional authority of the sovereign.

Property plays a key role here for Locke because it is property that ultimately provides the motive for men to organize themselves into a society. While God has granted mankind in general the fruits of the earth (as attested to in Scripture), this provides only for a kind of common property, an original communism. Individual property, by contrast, enjoys insufficient protection in this pre-civil state of nature. Held in common, one's property is subject to the claims and exigencies of others. As a result, men decided early on to organize themselves into lawful societies with the central goal of securing individual property rights. Private property thus becomes both the driving force behind initial social organization and the primary institution that this organization must protect.[42]

For our purposes, however, it is Locke's innovative and influential theory of just *how* objects and land become property that is most significant. Locke famously proposes that an individual comes to possess something by "mixing" his labor with it. He understands natural law to mean that "every Man has a *Property* in his own *Person*" and that "The *Labour* of his Body, and the *Work* of his Hands, we may say, are properly his." It follows from this that "whatsoever then he removes out of the State that Nature hath provided, and left it in, he hath mixed his *Labour* with, and joyned to it something that is his own, and thereby makes it his property" (288). This sort of mixing, he makes clear, extends to the appropriation of land through cultivation: "*As much Land* as a Man Tills, Plants, Improves, Cultivates, and can use the Product of, so much is his *Property*" (290). Working the land "mixes" the labor of the individual into the ground, transferring that mysterious "something" from person to object and transforming raw nature into private property.

This argument for ownership through cultivation was increasingly used in eighteenth- and nineteenth-century America as a rationale for dispossessing native peoples. According to Locke scholar Barbara Arneil, "Preachers, legal theorists, and politicians all used Locke's theory of property to define the cultivation of land by American citizens as the only the legitimate means to claim property." Such an argument represented a radical change: "Occupancy for thousands of years was suddenly and dramatically superseded by Locke's distinctly English form of labour as the basis of holding land" (170).[43] In *Edgar Huntly*, the displacement of Old Deb's tribe in order to make way for English farming settlements suggests just this sort of Lockean rationale. In fact, Old Deb herself articulates a version of the traditional "first occupancy" counter-argument to Locke. "She conceived," Edgar tells us, "that by remaining behind her countrymen she succeeded to the government, and retained possession of all this region. The English were aliens and sojourners, who occupied the land merely by her connivance and permission" (822). One of the central conflicts in the novel thus revolves around the tension between a widely accepted (among colonials) Lockean justification of land rights and a tenacious older argument based on first occupancy rights.

What I would like to suggest, however, is that while Brown is familiar with both of these discourses, his novel moves instead toward a third option: property as a social convention. Rejecting Locke in particular, the novel again looks to David Hume as a viable alternative. Hume strenuously argues in *A Treatise of Human Nature* that property is nothing other than "a convention enter'd into by all the members of the society to bestow stability on the possession of those external goods, and leave every one in the peaceable enjoyment of what he may acquire by his fortune and industry" (314). Or more succinctly, "Our property is nothing but those goods, whose constant possession is establish'd by the laws of society; that is, by the laws of justice" (315). An early contributor to the virtualization of property, Hume represents an explicit rebuke of Locke's labor-mixture approach, which Hume characterizes as a needless mystification.[44] For Brown, however, Hume's approach is attractive not simply because it rejects Locke, but also because it offers a *relational* model of ownership analogous to Hume's relational model of space.

Humean property theory reveals itself most clearly in the pivotal scene with the mysterious visitor, Weymouth. Appearing out of the blue and disappearing just as quickly, Weymouth's presence at the center of the novel initially suggests nothing more than an awkward bit of narrative stitching on Brown's part. But given that Weymouth's arrival bears directly on the issue of property rights and given that Edgar immediately follows this interview by sleepwalking into the pit, the scene merits some closer scrutiny. A complete stranger, Weymouth shows up at Edgar's door and stakes a claim to the eight thousand dollars that Mary (and by extension, her fiancee, Edgar) has inherited from the murdered Waldegrave. According to Weymouth, this was money he had given to Waldegrave to safeguard for him while he was traveling overseas. Weymouth had previously made a fortune speculating in mercantile commodities, but in a final bid to achieve financial independence, he had invested everything in a cargo of "wine from Madeira" (765). The ship was lost and with it Weymouth's entire fortune, except for the relatively tiny remainder he had deposited with Waldegrave. Learning of Waldegrave's death, he has come to Edgar to ask for the money.

Initially, Weymouth's request is far from convincing. He has no evidence to corroborate his story: there is no will, as Edgar makes clear to him, "nor was any paper discovered, by which we could guess at [Waldegrave's] intentions" (763). Weymouth himself has nothing in the way of a receipt and admits as much: "I have only my assertion to produce in support of my claim" (771). In effect, the loan was entirely unknown to anyone but Waldegrave and Weymouth. Weymouth is able, however, to provide a fairly accurate timeline of the financial transactions between himself and Waldegrave; these estimates match the date on a bank-receipt in Waldegrave's records. Ultimately, this is enough for the benevolent Edgar: "You will perceive how much this coincidence, which could scarcely have taken place by chance, is favourable to your claim" (772). Convinced of Weymouth's honesty, Edgar pledges to "exert all [his] influence" to get Mary to restore the money (772).

The significance of the scene, however, lies not merely in Edgar's impressive magnanimity, but also in its close connection to Hume's discussion of private property. For Hume, the institution of property is inseparable from the concept of *justice*: "A man's property is some object related to him. This relation is not natural, but moral, and founded on justice" (315). The existence of property, he believes, is predicated on people's willingness to abstain from using the possessions of others. Such abstinence depends upon the realization that taking another person's property would constitute an injustice. More simply perhaps, one has to have a sense of right and wrong in order to understand why one should respect others' property rights. Hume hammers on this relationship between justice and property. "The origin of justice explains that of property. The same artifice gives rise to both" (315). And by "artifice," Hume means a social convention, a relation between individuals that has been established outside of the purely natural world. In essence, he is arguing that property and justice are mutually constitutive and that both of them are social constructions.

His treatment of property becomes particularly relevant to *Edgar Huntly*, however, in terms of the specific hypothetical examples he provides. "I suppose a person to have lent me a sum of money, on condition that it be restor'd in a few days; and also suppose, that after the expiration of the term agreed on, he demands the sum: I ask, *What reason or motive have I to restore the money?*" (308). The answer of course is a person's socially-constructed sense of justice. But more to the point, this moral conundrum bears a striking resemblance to the situation Edgar faces with Weymouth. Moreover, in the course of his reasoning, Hume addresses several possible counter-explanations that resonate with the novel. Does it change anything, Hume wonders, "if we suppose, that the loan was secret"? (309). Waldegrave's mysterious eight-thousand-dollar deposit is similarly distinguished by its inscrutability. There are no records and no outside witnesses of the loan. Then Hume considers whether a person's desperate need to help their family might not be a better explanation for the origin of justice. "What if I be in necessity, and have urgent motives to acquire something for my family?" (310). Again, this eventuality is echoed in Brown's narrative. Edgar is stricken by the knowledge that returning the money to Weymouth will "blast that scheme of happiness" on which he and Mary have "so fondly meditated" (774): "Our flattering prospects are now shut in. You must return to your original poverty" (776). As in Hume's hypothetical question, Edgar makes the decision to respect property rights even in the face of "urgent motives" pushing him to help his fiancee.

In this way, Brown constructs a version of Hume's philosophical test case. Doing so allows him to emphasize the relationship between justice and property and, by extension, to invoke the social, relational qualities of Hume's model. Weymouth's concluding comments drive the connection home. "I know that my claim has no legal support: that, if this money be resigned to me, it will be the impulse of spontaneous justice, and not the coercion of law to which I am indebted for it" (773). Similarly, Edgar assures him that "neither Mary Waldegrave nor I are capable of disguising the truth or committing an injustice" (771). The novel's echo of Humean terms here suggests that Brown is keenly aware of the social, contractual aspects of ownership and appropriation. As he works out his own understanding of property, it seems clear that metaphysical Lockean "mixing" will give way to a formulation in which property is understood as a social relation between moral actors.

At this point, however, a crucial distinction needs to be made between Hume's socio-discursive model and the novel's own investigation of property. In rejecting Locke, Hume emphasizes the "artificial" or socially-constructed nature of property; it is "a convention or agreement betwixt us" (315). Such a formulation presages the nineteenth-century virtualization of property and, in contrast to Locke, leaves the material *bodies* of the actors behind. "Convention" and "agreement" imply that property rights are entirely discursive, that they arise through social communication and are ratified through legal discourse. Brown's novel, however, sets itself against precisely this sort of disembodiment. On the contrary, it repeatedly highlights the embodied characteristics of our experience in the world, particularly our tactile experience. This was the import of invoking Condillac's statue in the cave and of revealing the body-filled *plenum* between the panther's eyes; this was why so much attention was paid to Edgar's contact with the Indian and with Clithero. So how are we to reconcile the novel's focus on embodiment with Humean property's seeming disregard of the body? Is property simply a discursive practice entirely detached from phenomenological experience?[45]

In fact, I would argue that one of the central functions of the novel is to reconcile this tension between body and discourse by enacting a kind of embodied relationality, through mobility, that blends phenomenological experience with discursive interaction. The mobile body, Brown's narrative suggests, conjoins distinct spaces in such a way as to enable a dialogic relationship between them. That is, Edgar's ceaseless mobility, his obsessive movement back and forth across the Pennsylvania frontier, structures space itself as a discourse. Distinct spaces are not only produced by the mobile body, but they are also placed into particular relationships with one another; they are articulated as a spatial syntax. At the same time, this relationship is dialogic; as Certeau earlier suggested, it requires the presence of an interlocutory body. Thus, in *Edgar Huntly*, as mobile bodies come into contact, they are continually reaffirming their presence to one another, negotiating spatial boundaries and staking claims. It is in this way that mobility organizes spaces and bodies. It functions, in short, as a rhetoric of space.

Certeau's work on spatial practices is again helpful here. In a chapter entitled, "Walking in the City," Certeau famously argues that walking is a "space of enunciation" (98); it is an improvisational appropriation of the larger spatial system in which the walker is moving. In this way, it is directly analogous to the speech act (following Saussure, Austin, Searle, and so on), in which an individual speaker operationalizes a larger linguistic system for his or her own particular speech performance. Certeau emphasizes that the act of walking has "a triple 'enunciative' function," two of which are particularly helpful in regards to *Edgar Huntly*: first, "[walking] is a process of *appropriation* of the topographical system;" and second, "it implies *relations* among differentiated positions, that is, among pragmatic 'contracts' in the form of movements" (98). The first of these functions speaks directly to the appropriative effects of the mobile body. Certeau is explicit about this, noting that walking constitutes a "style of tactile apprehension and kinesthetic appropriation" (97). Here, we see that movement of the body, specifically the phenomenological body, enables an initial taking possession of the environment through which it moves. The second function is equally important, however, in that it posits "differentiated positions," that is, other interlocutors. "The walker constitutes, in relation to his position, both a near and a far, a *here* and a *there*." This, in turn, "has the function of introducing an other in relation to this 'I' and of thus establishing a conjunctive and disjunctive articulation of places" (99). In the same way that the speech act implies an interlocutor with whom the exchange can occur, so too does the mobile body call forth "here" and "there," other spaces distinct from, but in direct communication with, the space of the individual body. Movement thus produces a spatial syntax that organizes the spaces of self and other into meaningful but constantly shifting configurations.

Walking, of course, figures prominently throughout *Edgar Huntly*. There is Edgar's indefatigable pursuit of Clithero through the wilds of Norwalk. There is Clithero's account of his own perambulations through the nighttime streets of Dublin. There is the constant circulation of Old Deb and her marauding Delaware tribesmen, hiking the narrow trails that link wilderness and settlement space. Most dramatically perhaps, there is Edgar's prolonged flight across the countryside after he awakes in the cave.[46] One of the effects of all of this movement is a series of intimate tactile encounters, both sympathetic and hostile, between whites and Indians. The encounters paradoxically acknowledge the presence of other bodies at the same time that they differentiate them. Through an interlocutory process of movement and contact, Edgar highlights the proximity of other bodies at the same time that he produces a set of spatial boundaries characteristic of the frontier.

Significantly, however, Brown's narrative goes on to imply that these acts of spatial demarcation are also acts of appropriation. Edgar's bizarre thrusting of the Indian musket into the middle of the road is perhaps the most dramatic example of this. The musket marks the violent frontier established by Edgar's encounter with the pursuing Delaware, but it also signals his possessory rights over the territory it delineates. In a pantomime of geographic appropriation that evokes the planting of the sovereign's flag in earlier voyages of discovery, Edgar claims the contested space whose boundaries he has helped create.[47] Similarly, Waldegrave's murder under the giant elm functions as both a liminal point of contact between settler and native and a violent assertion of property rights. Edgar describes "the situation of the Elm" as located (like the musket) "in the midst of a private road" and "on the verge of Norwalk" (646). Here, on the frontier between cultivated and uncultivated space, white and Indian again come into bodily contact, again reinforce a spatial boundary, and again make a territorial claim. (Waldegrave's murder, of course, is an act of retribution on the part of dispossessed Delawares who have been pushed off their ancestral grounds.)

In a more figurative register, we might also note the conspicuous placement of both the musket and the elm tree precisely in the middle of a road. This curious detail effectively underscores the significance of movement and mobility in Brown's model of appropriation. Not only do the musket and the tree mark the edges of white and Indian space, they also point toward vectors of motion, toward that transitory space of the road in which people move from one place to another, eventually coming into contact. Indeed, given the perpetual motion of characters in the novel, it makes perfect sense that crucial moments of contact and appropriation would be framed not by stillness or stasis, but by a space of mobile transition. In this way, the musket and the elm function as remarkably evocative images for Brown: they draw together bodies, spaces, properties and the trope of movement that winds throughout the novel.

The richest evocation of all these issues, however, can be found in Old Deb's hut, an early literary precursor of Natty Bumppo's own fraught frontier shelter. As a crucial boundary marker between white settler space and the territory of the displaced Delaware tribe, Deb's hut is a point of repeated, and violent, contact between whites and Indians. Ownership of the hut changes several times during the course of the novel, oscillating back and forth between native and colonial. Originally, we learn, the hut was built by an enterprising Scottish emigrant who "cleared a field in the unappropriated wilderness" twenty miles to the west of the existing colonial borders (823). This bid for spatial appropriation is apparently an affront to the Delawares because the Scotsman quickly disappears, purportedly murdered by Deb's visiting tribesmen. This initial violent contact, however, has the effect of establishing the hut as a provisional spatial limit with significant ramifications for property rights in the region. Controlling the hut, it seems, implies control over the spaces it delimits. Immediately after the Scotsman's disappearance, Deb takes possession and, in so doing, reconfigures the spatial routines of both Indians and whites. Edgar tells us that after her move, her cantankerous character remains the same, "but her circuits were new" (823). What is more, the new location prevents him "from ever extending [his own] pedestrian excursions to her present abode" (823). In effect, the transfer of ownership dictates a new set of spatial boundaries in which whites and Indians can circulate.

But as the references to Edgar's "pedestrian excursions" and Deb's "periodical rambles" (823) make clear, the boundary claims represented by the hut are also continually enacted by walking bodies. On one side are the forest footpaths and village networks of the displaced Delaware. On the other are the frontier farms and squatter's huts of the white settlers. Social space is produced and appropriated on either side by the furious motion of circulating bodies. Any notion of a clear boundary separating these two spaces, however, is belied by the oscillating ownership of the hut itself. From the Scotsman, to Deb, to Edgar, to Clithero, the repossessed hut signals the ambiguous, contested nature of spatial demarcation and appropriation. It also signals the fact that any such demarcation is a continuous process, a series of repeated encounters between mobile bodies. Possession, Brown suggests, results not from a mysterious Lockean transfer of "something" between self and object (that would be the model of the unfortunate Scottish emigrant), nor from a purely discursive agreement between contracting agents. Rather, it grows out of bodies in motion, bodies contacting one another in an interlocutory process of spatial delineation.

Such a model of spatial appropriation dovetails nicely with Certeau's concept of "kinesthetic appropriation." Whites and Indian crisscross the landscape on foot, taking possession through the medium of the sensate body. But it also begins to get at Certeau's notion of spatial syntax, that is, his observation that walking produces a rhetoric of space, "a conjunctive and disjunctive articulation of places." The musket, the elm, Deb's hut, all of these points of contact use mobile bodies to juxtapose distinct spaces. But ultimately it is not walking, per se, that best reveals the rhetorical characteristics of spatial appropriation. Rather, it is sleepwalking. The trope of somnambulism allows Brown to highlight the ways in which spaces get woven together in conjunctive, or disjunctive, syntactic structures. When Edgar awakes in the cave, for example, the immediate effect is a jarring juxtaposition, both for Edgar and for the reader, of two spaces that would normally remain topographically separate: "One image runs into another," as Edgar has it (778). The comforting candlelight of his bedroom gives way directly to the cold stone and inky abyss of the pit. In this way, somnambulism effectively adjoins bedroom and cave, thereby calling attention to the paratactic qualities of walking.

Normally, walking sutures together distinct spaces into a meaningful syntax; that is, moving from one space to the next, the walker chooses a trajectory and enunciates a kind of spatial sentence. In doing this, however, the walker is generally oblivious to the syntactic function of movement itself. He or she disregards the linking movements that connect spaces. Certeau describes this disregard in terms of the rhetorical figure of asyndeton, that is, "the suppression of linking words such as conjunctions and adverbs, either within a sentence or between sentences." Thus, walking also "skips over links and whole parts that it omits [...] every walk constantly leaps, or skips like a child, hopping on one foot. It practices the ellipsis of conjunctive *loci*" (101). Edgar's sleepwalking, however, actually underscores the importance of these spatial ellipses. Without some experience of the movement that must link bedroom and cave, the meaning of the two spaces becomes incomprehensible. Simply put, neither Edgar nor the reader can make any sense of these spaces without the interstitial tissue of the walk to connect them. Paradoxically perhaps, by fully erasing the syntactic function of the walk, the novel emphasizes its significance. At the same time, the spatial ellipsis dramatized by sleepwalking is directly mirrored in the narrative ellipsis between these two chapters. The reader ends chapter 15 in Edgar's bedroom and begins chapter 16 in the cave with no clear idea of how the two scenes might be connected. The effect is to further tighten the analogy between spatial and narrative syntax. Walking, the novel suggests, is simply another form of narration.

Somnambulism thus provides Brown with a tool for investigating the relational, interlocutory aspects of spatial production and appropriation.

It calls attention to the way that appropriated space gets discursively articulated, or "enunciated," at the same time that it is produced by material bodies. Locke and Hume represent these two poles of property theory within the text, that of embodied materiality and that of social discourse, respectively. According to Brown's novel, however, these are not the only two options. *Edgar Huntly* charts a third option, that of locomotion, which combines aspects of both. But the trope of sleepwalking does more than simply reinforce the combinative possibilities inherent to movement; it also directly challenges the assumptions of Locke and Hume themselves. Neither Locke's embodied essentializing nor Hume's discursive negotiating can, it suggests, provide a fully viable model of ownership and property rights.

Locke's theory in particular is undercut by the phenomenon of somnambulism. This is because sleepwalking itself is a kind of "possession" in which an individual loses control of his own body. Clithero, for example, describes his somnambulistic trances in terms of a demonic seizure: "It was the daemon that possessed me. My limbs were guided to the bloody office by a power foreign and superior to mine" (711). Somnambulism is thus a dramatic example of a situation in which an individual's body has become alienated from his consciousness; it has become an object, a piece of property subject to outside appropriation. This presents serious problems for Locke's labor-mixing theory because ownership of one's own body is the foundation upon which his entire theory rests. In the crucial third paragraph of the "Of Property" chapter, Locke makes this clear: "Though the Earth, and all inferior Creatures be common to all Men, yet every man has *Property* in his own *Person*. This no Body has any Right to but himself" (287). According to his natural-law perspective, preserving our own life and liberty are worshipful duties to God meant to demonstrate our good stewardship of the body he has given us. Because of their divine origin, neither life nor liberty can ever, under any circumstances, be alienated and considered the property of someone else.[48] But the novel's focus on sleepwalking calls this claim into question. Both Edgar and Clithero demonstrate that the body is indeed alienable, that the "empire of my muscles," as Clithero calls it, can be readily appropriated by an outside force.

By contrast, somnambulism also tempers the Humean disavowal of the body. In arguing for property as an entirely discursive construction, Hume wants to oppose rational mind and irrational body, conscious mental restraint and ungovernable physical appetites. Left to his own devices, an individual is subject to his natural "passions," and "this avidity alone, of acquiring goods and possessions [. . .] is insatiable, perpetual, universal, and directly destructive of society." What is more, "there is scarce any one, who is not actuated by it; and there is no one, who has not reason to fear from it, when it acts without any restraint, and gives way to its first and most natural movements" (316). The restraint comes, of course, only from a "general sense of common interest," which "all the members of society express to one another" (315). This is Hume's notion of property as social convention; mindful social agreement reins in the errant bodily passions. Sleepwalking, however, suggests that the "natural movements" of the body can never be entirely constrained by discourse.[49] The natural passions, the desire to acquire goods and possessions, will always reassert themselves, even if only unconsciously. Because of this, the body will always exceed complete discursive control.

So sleepwalking serves as a particularly serendipitous trope for Brown. It challenges the assumptions of Lockean and Humean property theory at the very same time that it elucidates the role of the body in spatial appropriation. But, significantly, there is also a certain ambivalence in the figure of the sleepwalker as it relates to issues of property and ownership. As Clithero's "possession" should make clear, sleepwalking might be better understood as a dramatic form of dis-possession in that it represents a loss of sovereignty over one's own body. Brown himself is certainly interested in the prospect of dispossession since it seems to be the defining experience of almost all the characters in the novel: Clithero's dispossession is echoed by Edgar's loss of inheritance; Weymouth is dispossessed of his fortune; Sarsefield loses his shot at Mrs. Lorimer's wealth and is forced to wander the Indian subcontinent for twenty years; most egregiously, Old Deb and the Delaware are dispossessed of their land and exiled to the west. Time and again throughout the book, characters are stripped of their property and pushed into motion, pushed into a sometimes conscious, sometimes unconscious attempt to repossess what they've lost. In this context, the figure of the sleepwalker seems ideally suited to represent Brown's frontier narrative: a man dispossessed of his own body and displaced by forces seemingly beyond his control.

This still leaves us with the question of why it is that Brown focuses on the theme of dispossession at the same time that he is articulating a complex model of possession. I think the answer lies in Brown's stated desire to ground his philosophical ideas in a specific historical context. The history of eastern Pennsylvania is not a simple triumphalist narrative of westward migration. Rather, it is a violent chronicle of betrayal and fraud. Given this background, it stands to reason that Brown would closely attend to the dark side of appropriation, to the ways in which ownership can be subverted or rearranged. If anything, the narratives of

Edgar, Clithero, and Old Deb call attention to the instability of appropriation, to the way in which possession of any sort can be quickly and violently transformed into dispossession. When faced with the unseemly history of spatial appropriation in early Pennsylvania, Brown's remarkable philosophical model is forced to recalibrate itself to unpleasant realities.

This tension between high-minded theory and low-down practice is exactly the opportunity Brown is seeking. By applying the salutary power of philosophical inquiry to the shameful history of land claims and boundary disputes in Pennsylvania, Brown's novel can offer a moral corrective to a narrative of deceit. Sleepwalking comprises only one aspect of a complex theoretical effort on Brown's part to reassert the importance of the body in our conceptions of space and property. Restoring the body in this way serves the purpose of moral instruction by calling attention to the significance of other bodies in the process of appropriation and disappropriation. Brown's model of possession is not just interlocutory; it is interlocutory *and* embodied. This means that it requires the presence of an Other's body with which to come into contact. In the context of the Pennsylvania frontier, that other body gets figured as the Indian. This is a morally charged move for Brown to make because it runs counter to a larger cultural tendency to erase the body of the Indian. Instead, *Edgar Huntly*'s phenomenology of possession makes it clear that the spaces, boundaries, and properties of early Pennsylvania were produced in continuous contact with Native Americans.

Of course, it is the Walking Purchase that figures most prominently here, both because it conflates all of the novel's key philosophical issues (boundaries, spaces, possession, and mobility) and because it represents the most infamous perversion of native property rights in Pennsylvania history. *Edgar Huntly*, I maintain, invokes the narrative of the Purchase (in a more careful and comprehensive fashion than has yet been acknowledged) in order to reconsider the philosophical and political issues it raises. The novel effectively re-walks the Walk, recalling our attention to the presence of Indian bodies and thereby destabilizing white narratives of appropriation. This is the moral work of Brown's philosophical fiction.

Other critics have identified the Walking Purchase as one important aspect of the general context of Indian conflict that informs *Edgar Huntly*.[50] But as Brown's preface in the *Monthly Magazine* suggests, this bit of history proves to be considerably more significant to the narrative than it might first appear. The preface's careful attention to geographic detail ("the foot of the *Blue-ridge*, from *Wind-gap* to the *Water-gap*") immediately situates the events of the novel in the heart of the Purchase, a locale Brown's contemporary readers would have immediately recognized. Furthermore, the novel traces a path nearly identical to that taken by the walkers. The three trained runners hired by the Penn brothers began from a boundary-marking chestnut tree in Wrightstown (very close to Edgar's "natal township" of Solebury) and then walked in a northwesterly direction for some sixty-four miles. They moved through the area known as "the Forks of the Delaware" (where Weymouth informs us that Edgar lives) and then crossed the Blue Mountains at Lehigh Gap.[51] This spot is about fifteen miles west of the Wind-gap. From there, the lone remaining walker, one Edward Marshall, continued across a rugged valley to the slopes of Pocono Mountain. This valley seems to be precisely the terrain that Edgar must navigate after crossing (underneath) those same Blue Mountains. He finds himself "in the midst of a vale, included between ridges that gradually approached each other [to the eastward]. This vale gradually widened as it tended to the westward, and was, in this place ten or twelve miles in breadth" (824). Then, as he tries to make his way back home, he finds himself at "the foot of the southern barrier," blocked, that is, by the Blue Mountains that separate him from his uncle's farm. Brown has his protagonist literally following in the footsteps of the original walkers.

Edward Marshall himself bears more than a passing resemblance to the fictional Edgar. A "famous walker," Marshall was said to have worn "very thin and flexible moccasins" while on the walk and to have "carried a hatchet."[52] What is more, he seems to have been known for his distinctive rifle, "a flint-lock" with "the name of the German maker, or the place where made, stamped on the barrel." The gun recalls Edgar's own rifle, a gift "of extraordinary workmanship" from Sarsefield who received it from "an English officer, who died in Bengal" (804). Like Marshall's weapon, Edgar's is identifiable by the unique "cyphers" that mark it (802). There is also the fact that Marshall's gun was purportedly used to kill "unnumbered Indians." But perhaps the strongest link between Edward and Edgar is the history of Indian retribution that characterizes Marshall's life after he participates in the Walking Purchase. Singled out for Delaware vengeance, Marshall's family was attacked on their farm in 1756 and his daughter and pregnant wife were killed. But Marshall himself was away from home, so the Delawares returned a few months later, killing his son Peter. Again, Marshall, like Edgar, was away during the attack and escaped harm. Whether Brown intended Edgar to be a fictional version of the original walker, the parallels between the two men underscore the close connection between the narrative of the Walking Purchase and the novel's plot.

It is also worth taking Brown at his word when he informs us in the magazine preface that Old Deb is "a portrait faithfully drawn from nature." There is good reason to believe that Brown's cantankerous Delaware matriarch was inspired by the figure of Hannah Freeman, or "old Indian Hannah," as she was known during Brown's time. Christened "the last of the Lenape" by local historians, Hannah lived just a few miles to the west of Philadelphia on the Brandywine River in Chester County, where she died in 1803. Like Old Deb, Hannah was left behind when the bulk of the Delaware tribes moved west to escape European encroachment. Hannah's kin retired to Shamokin, while in Old Deb's case "they abandoned their ancient seats and retired to the banks of the Wabash and Muskingum" (820). More telling perhaps is the fact that Hannah "used to travel much about [. . .] followed by her dogs and pigs—all stopping where she did" (Watson 161). This dovetails nicely with Deb's dogs: "They were her servants and protectors, and attended her person or guarded her threshold, agreeably to her direction [. . .] when she entered a farmhouse, [they] waited her return at a distance" (821). Hannah was said to have displayed "a proud and lofty spirit [and] she often spoke emphatically of the wrongs and misfortunes of her race, upon whom her affections still dwelt" (Watson 161). Such indignation, of course, is echoed in Old Deb's long-simmering resentment: "Her imagination brooded for a long time, over nothing but schemes of revenge" (886).[53]

I am less interested, however, in establishing exact correlations between Brown's characters and actual historical figures than I am in demonstrating how thoroughly the events, actors and issues of the Purchase inform the narrative of *Edgar Huntly*. Old Deb's Hannah-esque resentment links her directly to the history of dispossession inaugurated by the Purchase. Likewise, Edgar's close resemblance to Marshall suggests that Brown is in some way reexamining issues of guilt and vengeance associated with the Walk. Add to this the geographical specificity that Brown takes pains to establish in the magazine preface, and it becomes clear that the novel is creatively reworking the narrative of the Walking Purchase. But the framework for this reevaluation is distinctly philosophical in nature. Brown is especially interested in reconsidering the theoretical issues raised by the Walking Purchase and determining to what extent a new philosophical perspective might alter our understanding. Brown is fascinated by the body's role, particularly the Indian body's role, in the production and appropriation of space. It is essential, then, to briefly consider the treatment of the Indian body in the history of the Purchase itself.

Like most land transactions involving settlers and Indians, the Walking Purchase was meant to secure absolute, or fee simple, ownership of the land for the settlers: in effect, the buyer had total control over the land purchased and could do with it as he saw fit. This was in stark contrast to the more complex communal and usufruct property systems of the Native Americans. Overlapping possession, shared usage, and seasonal variation all gave way to the more abstract, idealized principle of absolute, individual ownership.[54] What this meant, both literally and discursively, was that the bodies of Indians were removed to make way for the legally unencumbered spaces of white ownership and development. Not only were tribes like the Delaware being gradually moved further and further west, but also their absence was being legally codified and enforced via property law.[55]

The Walking Purchase provides a particularly dramatic example of this material and discursive erasure. The text of the deed itself emphasizes the expulsion of Indians and Indian claims almost to the point of panic:

> We, [the Delaware representatives], Do, for ourselves and all other the Delaware Indians, fully, clearly, and Absolutely Remise, Release, and forever Quit claim unto [the Penn brothers], All our Right Title, Interest, and pretentions whatsoever of, in, or to the said Tract or Tracts of Land, and every Part and Parcel thereof, So that neither We, or any of us, or our Children, shall or may at any time hereafter, have Challenge, Claim, or Demand any Right, Title or Interest, or any Pretentions whatsoever of, in, or to the said Tract or Tracts of Land, or any Part thereof, but of and from the same shall be excluded, and forever Debarred.[56]

The extinction of Delaware claims is repeated compulsively here, demanding for the Penn brothers not just ownership of the land but legal assurances that absolutely no vestige of Indian presence or right could possibly remain. The language is replete with intensifiers that attest to the desire for total removal: "Absolutely," "forever," "We, or any of us, or our Children," "at any time," "any Pretentions whatsoever." According to the deed of the Purchase at least, erasure of the Indians must be complete.[57]

Given this desire for removal, it should come as no surprise that the actual walk itself also effectively enacted the disappearance of Indian bodies. When the walkers started off from Wrightstown, they were initially accompanied by three Indian representatives whose job it was to validate the terms and execution of the walk.[58] But when it became clear to the Indians that the hired walkers were moving at speeds closer to a run than a walk, that they were following a marked path, and that they were accompanied by horses with supplies, the Indians first protested loudly, and then abandoned the walk in disgust.[59] (They subsequently referred to it as the "hurry walk.") In this way, what began as an example of possession through embodied relationality, of spatial boundaries defined through movement and interlocution, quickly collapsed into a possessive soliloquy. The interlocutory bodies of the Indians fell away from the Walk and disappeared from the narrative of possession.

Of course, the broader erasure of the body from theories of American property was already in progress in 1799. But *Edgar Huntly*'s rethinking of Locke and Hume has the effect of restoring that body, both theoretically and historically. The novel's philosophical work calls attention to the role of mobile bodies in the production and appropriation of space. This work, when juxtaposed with the novel's invocation of the Walking Purchase, encourages a reconsideration of how bodies get figured, or not figured, in that historical narrative. The repeated contacts between whites and Indians in the novel, violent or otherwise, constitute a rebuke of the myth of the vanished Indian body. Again and again, Edgar demonstrates that spatial boundaries are delineated through intimate, tactile encounters; his mobile body repeatedly collides with that of the Indian and, in so doing, corporealizes it. That is, Edgar's encounters affirm the corporeal presence of Indians in a way that historical narratives like the Walking Purchase emphatically do not.

The encounters are violent because in bringing back the corporeal history of the Purchase, Brown's novel brings with it the history of violence inscribed on those bodies. It is here that *Edgar Huntly* performs its moral work. By calling attention not only to the stubborn fact of Indian presence on (and ownership of) the land, but also to the region's narrative of violence and fraud, the novel unsettles the moral framework of white property claims. Spatial appropriation may be achieved through the interlocutory encounters of white and Indian bodies, but if those encounters are generally violent in nature, the legitimacy of ownership is called into question. Property stories like the Walking Purchase often ignored the context of violence in which appropriation took place because to do otherwise would be to undercut the moral foundation of the property claims. But in Brown's retelling, violence between whites and Indians takes center stage and the novel dramatizes precisely this ignored aspect of appropriation.

This is the function of literature that Brown foresaw for his own work. The historical and geographical particularity of *Edgar Huntly* lends a moral weight to the narrative that abstract philosophies of ownership do not possess. Whereas Locke and Hume remain remote from the moral and historical complexities of specific people coming into contact and vying for particular possessions, Brown's novel puts its theoretical feet on the ground. It explores the phenomenon of spatial production and appropriation as it has looked in the recent history of Pennsylvania, and as it might look in the future of the frontier. In this way, literature, that is, philosophical fiction, is able to attend to specific historical consequences that philosophy alone often overlooks. But as Brown's novel particularizes the abstract in this way, it also demonstrates the morally ambiguous nature of possession. There is no guarantee that property acquired by way of Brown's model is somehow morally sanctified. On the contrary, *Edgar Huntly* makes it clear that violence is always a looming threat when people come together and vie for ownership of space, and that when such violence does erupt, claims become murky and morally suspect. Edgar, Old Deb, and the Delaware end up dispossessed and displaced in the novel not because they fail to enact Brown's model of possession, but because they do so in a violent fashion. When possession is acquired through violence, the novel suggests, it may swiftly give way to dispossession.

Anxieties of this sort—anxieties about the ambiguous purview of ownership and about the ephemeral nature of property itself—only grow more insistent as the nineteenth century gets under way. The rising influence of market culture (foreshadowed by Weymouth's disastrous mercantile speculations) increasingly treats property not as an embodied phenomenon, not as a phenomenological relationship between persons and things, but as an abstract commodity, as a legal construct designed to facilitate easy movement and exchange. Such "virtualization" is unsettling: What is property, exactly, if not tangible objects, and what is to prevent it from being transformed or taken away? After *Edgar Huntly*, antebellum culture becomes progressively more worried about this potential for loss and dispossession.

What is more, the scale of such anxieties begins to expand as new property concerns emerge in spaces and discourses previously thought to be insulated from the market. No longer are questions about the nature of ownership and appropriation limited to the proximate spaces of the body and to what a person can touch. For their part, antebellum writers respond to this growing anxiety by continuing to engage the phenomenology of possession, continuing to explore the embodied underpinnings of ownership, but doing so in larger and larger and spatial contexts. Literary treatments of domestic space, in particular, mark the next iteration of embodied possession in nineteenth-century American property narratives. Midcentury accounts of domestic space extend the proximate scale of Edgar Huntly's walking body into the expanded "body" of the home. Appropriation gets refigured not as body-to-body contacts but rather as alimentary exchanges between inside spaces and outside spaces. Owning property is investigated on a larger spatial scale, as a phenomenon of dwelling, a kind of corporealized "householding" intimately connected to the circulation of possessions through the home.

2 / Eating Dwelling Gagging: Hawthorne, Stoddard, and the Phenomenology of Possession

> *Of all corporeal operations, digestion is the one which has the closest connection with the moral condition of man.*
> —JEAN ANTHELME BRILLAT-SAVARIN, *THE PHYSIOLOGY OF TASTE, OR TRANSCENDENTAL GASTRONOMY* (1825)

Midway through *Totality and Infinity*, his seminal work on the phenomenology of the other, Emmanuel Levinas makes the surprising claim that property and possession absolutely require the existence of the home. "The primordial function of the home," he tells us, "does not consist in orienting being by the architecture of the building and in discovering a site"; rather, "it makes labor and property possible" (156). It does so by providing a space in which material objects, or what Levinas calls "the element," can be collected and held in reserve: "The uncertain future of the element is suspended. The element is fixed between the four walls of the home, is calmed in possession" (158). Levinas's argument is startling here not only because it directly links the genesis of property to the space of the home, but also because it reverses our intuitive sense of possessive causality. That is, we generally think of our home as the end result of a series of incremental acquisitions: land, building, furniture. It represents not the beginning, but the culmination of our possessive power. But for Levinas, "The home that founds possession is not a possession in the same sense as the movable goods it can collect and keep" (157). Instead, it is a precondition for property of any kind. "The very project of acquisition presupposes the recollection of the dwelling" (162).[1]

Such a claim is an innovative contribution to theories of possession and ownership. Levinas suggests here that property cannot be understood simply as a metaphysical relation between people and things (Locke), or as a contractual relation between acting subjects (following Hume). Instead, he argues that a particular kind of spatial experience, that of dwelling and the home, must mediate between intending subjects and the external world they seek to appropriate. Implicit in his argument are two key questions, both of which bear directly on our larger investigation into the embodied nature of property and its specific nineteenth-century instantiations. First, Levinas asks what it means to own a thing. How is it, he wonders, that we can ever come to possess things outside of ourselves? What exactly happens during the process of acquisition or appropriation? This question leads to a second: What is the nature of domestic space, and how is it related to the "project of acquisition"? In attempting to answer these questions, Levinas produces a set of ideas that are remarkably useful for thinking about property and its peculiar relationship to the contours of domestic space.

Levinas is not alone in fruitfully juxtaposing issues of property and domestic space. Nineteenth-century domestic fiction in America betrays a similar obsession with these twin themes. Novels as varied as Harriet Beecher Stowe's *Uncle Tom's Cabin*, Susan Warner's *The Wide, Wide World*, and even Herman Melville's *Pierre*, all reveal a deep-seated fascination with the intricacies of property exchange and the interior spaces of the home. But among such writers, Nathaniel Hawthorne and Elizabeth Stoddard stand out for the sophistication and self-consciousness with which they scrutinize the links between ownership and domesticity. Like Levinas, both Hawthorne and Stoddard seem to sense that domestic space and private property are in some way deeply dependent upon one another. In *The House of the Seven Gables* and *The Morgesons*, the two authors respectively take up the questions of how ownership is established, how possession might be distinguished from property, and how the "project of acquisition" is profoundly intertwined with the experience of domestic space. In short, the fictional houses of Pyncheon and Morgeson provide productive settings in which the writers can construct their own theories of ownership and domestic space. By peering in their windows, as it were, we can gain a better sense not just of how possession and the space of the home might be linked, but exactly how this connection was worked out in antebellum culture.

By the middle of the nineteenth century, of course, property practices were evolving from the early national context of Brockden Brown's *Edgar Huntly*. Most significantly, perhaps, the accelerating rise of market capitalism continued to encourage an increasingly abstract, or "virtual," conception of private property. In legal and financial circles, at least, the older notion of property as a substantive, embodied relation between person and thing was swiftly dropping away in favor of the more mobile, more flexible, more market-friendly formulation of property as a "bundle of rights." This growing abstraction brought with it growing anxieties about the ephemeral nature of property. Cold commodities, unscrupulous financiers, byzantine credit devices, all of the trappings of market culture unsettled the antebellum relationship to private property. This anxiety—manifest across a broad swath of American literature at the time—would prove to be an especially crucial catalyst for Hawthorne and Stoddard's own specific investigations of ownership.

One particularly virulent strain of property anxiety emerged in relation to the rapidly changing gender politics in the first half of the nineteenth century. Following close on the heels of the new market economy, the ideology of "domesticity" and "separate spheres" installed itself at the center of antebellum culture. A complex set of social practices—both discursive and material—domestic ideology imagined the home as a restorative "private sphere" in which women served as nurturers and moral guides. This feminine space was understood to act as a necessary counterbalance to the masculine "public sphere," an extradomestic marketplace of bruising commerce and competition.[2] Property, however, posed a special problem for this gender schema because its circulation tended to complicate the notion of rigid distinctions between the spheres. Not only did property literally move across the divide between private and public, inside and outside, but women were quickly gaining property rights unheard of at the beginning of the nineteenth century.[3] Changing property practices thus destabilized the supposedly sacrosanct bounds of the feminine sphere and added to anxieties about the cultural role of ownership.

Antebellum writers were particularly sensitive to this upheaval, generating a cascade of domestic literature that carefully reconsidered the concepts of *dwelling* and *home* in relation to existing property paradigms.[4] Indeed, the increasingly fraught space of the home emerged as a kind of proving ground for new phenomenologies of possession. But this relationship between dwelling and possession in American literature does not begin with the midcentury middle-class home, of course. Literary accounts of ownership have long been associated with that most unassuming of dwelling places, the humble hut. As a result, one way to gauge the evolving notions of property and home as they appear in Hawthorne and Stoddard is to glance quickly, once again, at the tenacious literary trope of the hut. In gradually giving ground to the middle-class home, I would suggest, representations of the hut index a subtle "domestication" of property, a growing antebellum desire for control over the unruly circuits and spaces of ownership.

Old Deb's hut, if we recall, is characterized by a certain fluidity of title, a certain malleability of ownership reflected in the succession of owners who take serial possession of the dwelling: the unfortunate Scotsman who built it, Old Deb, Edgar himself, and then Clithero. Owners are interchangeable here, circulating in and out over time, each one assuming the territorial rights associated with the hut. Twenty years later, however, when Cooper has Natty Bumppo build a hut at the edge of Lake Otsego, this more transitory, circulating model of property is slowly giving way to a more circumscribed sense of ownership: Natty's doors are closed, his locks fastened. And even though Natty and his dwelling are closely connected to older forms of communal property, the eventual destruction of his hut—and the enclosure of his hut-space—signals the emerging stature of private space and individual control. This suggests that as broader antebellum anxieties about abstraction and unchecked circulation increase, property narratives respond with fantasies of increased privacy and increased control. The hut no longer signifies simply as a marker of territorial appropriation; it signals instead a growing desire for possessive stability.

This trend continues with the publication of *The House of the Seven Gables* at midcentury. As in earlier texts, Hawthorne's hut—the squatter's cabin of the wronged Matthew Maule—represents the desire for uncontested title: Maule's original occupation of the land gives him a clearer claim to the property than Colonel Pyncheon. In this case, however, Hawthorne pushes the antebellum fantasy of stable property to the point of pathology: the hut is swallowed up by the Pyncheon mansion, subsumed into the larger house that gets built over its ruins; the mansion, in turn, shuts its doors on the outside world, turning inward, hoarding its possessions, and hinting at the dangers of too much privacy, too much control. In effect, Hawthorne's novel "domesticates" property, locking up the hut within the supposedly secure confines of the home.

On the one hand, then, literary treatments of the hut in the early decades of the nineteenth century reveal an increasing desire for possessive control. On the other hand, however, they also suggest that the spatial scale of ownership anxiety is increasing. Our series of literary huts marks a shift from the proximate tactile spaces of the body to the wider circuits of domestic space. The tight spaces and tactile encounters of *Edgar Huntly* encourage a phenomenology of possession predicated on intimate contact between individual possessive bodies. By 1823 and *The Pioneers*, Natty's hut has concealed those bodily contacts behind the log walls of his dwelling. Now, the secret of property relations unfolds inside the expanded space of the hut. Natty's rude home figures here as a kind of transitional structure, an embryonic form of dwelling and owning somewhere in scale between individual body and middle-class home.

Finally, when Hawthorne and Stoddard are writing at midcentury, the figure of the hut is literally incorporated, swallowed up by the larger domestic space of the Pyncheon mansion. It is a telling image of property's changing spatial implications: as anxieties about the reach of the market increase, so too do the spaces of antebellum property narrative.

In this way, then, attending to the literary fate of the hut prepares us to better understand the peculiar phenomenologies of possession that emerge in Hawthorne and Stoddard's midcentury domestic spaces. Their explorations of property unfold in the midst of this cultural revaluation of the home. Given this fact, it perhaps comes as no surprise that when Hawthorne and Stoddard chart their own phenomenologies of property they look to the decidedly domestic realm of eating and food preparation. It is not tactile sensation that is crucial to understanding embodied possession for these two authors; rather, it is gustatory experience. Both authors, I would like to suggest, are especially interested in the domestic discourse of eating and diet reform that emerged in the late 1830s.

At this point in time, an energetic phalanx of health reformers including Sylvester Graham, William Alcott, and Mary Gove Nichols, took it upon themselves to educate Americans about the alimentary dangers of intemperance, overindulgence, and overstimulation. "Excessive alimentation," Graham pronounced, "is one of the greatest sources of evil to the human family in civic life" (qtd. in Nissenbaum 127). The reformers advocated various versions of an ascetic diet: vegetarian, without alcohol or spices, and in the case of Graham, centered on the staple of home-baked whole-wheat bread. "There is," he opined, "a far more intimate relation between the quality of the bread and the moral character of a family, than is generally supposed" (*Bread* 124). Hawthorne and Stoddard, I contend, appropriate elements of this discourse and rework them into a theory of property and domestic space. Diet reformers effectively called attention to the material and social significance of the phenomenological, alimentary body. Hawthorne and Stoddard capitalize on this attention by revealing the ways in which this same alimentary body helps structure the linked experiences of ownership and domestic space.[5]

By turning our attention to the alimentary underpinnings of property and the home, Hawthorne and Stoddard help elaborate the discursive links that connect diet reform and the ideology of domesticity. Social historians generally understand diet reform to be a response to the growing influence of market economies in the middle of the nineteenth century. As the old-style, self-reliant, household economies gave way to an increasing consumerism, so the thinking goes, diet reformers appeared with a compelling call to arms: repudiate the temptations of sensual indulgence that the consumer economy brings with it and return to the wholesome dietary restraint of times past. Such a regimen was appealing because it implicitly promised to stave off the anxiety and change associated with the rise of the unfamiliar market.[6] At the same time, this was a conservative message, one that sought to resist socioeconomic change and evolving gender roles. By extolling the virtues of a nurturing mother dutifully preparing homemade food in the kitchen, the discourse of diet reform worked to reinforce the notion of the separate spheres. Stephen Nissenbaum points out, for example, that "when Sylvester Graham romanticized the life of the traditional household, he unknowingly helped prepare women to find a new role as the guardians of domestic virtue, just as he helped prepare men—himself included—to adjust to the demands of the capitalist marketplace" (18).[7] In this way, diet reform occupied a conflicted position in relation to changing cultural politics. On the one hand, it represented what we might think of as a progressive critique of bourgeois capitalism. On the other, it played a significant role in the enforcement of a restrictive domestic ideology.

When Hawthorne and Stoddard invoke the discourse of diet reform in their novels, they do so in a similarly complex and conflicted fashion. For both of them, eating and digestive physiology constitute an absolutely essential aspect of the linked experiences of possession and of domestic space. Beyond this similarity, however, the two authors diverge in their treatment of food and diet. Hawthorne, in the spirit of the Grahamite philosophy he engages, contents himself with diagnosing the pathologies of market capitalism. With a species of defensive nostalgia that would have been familiar to Graham himself, Hawthorne chronicles the dangers of an alimentary economy run amok, one that hews too closely to the consuming appetites of the marketplace. Stoddard, for her part, goes on to locate an alternative, potentially radical, model of property exchange within the confines of maternal, domestic space. Instead of a "haven from a heartless world," she imagines home as a space in which the dueling alimentary economies of commodity and gift vie for the upper hand. In the possibility of the gift, specifically food given as a gift, she finds the basis for an alternative domestic space, one that confounds the separate spheres model and that reconceives the roles of eating and possession.

Domestic ideology and the discourse of the separate spheres are, of course, ongoing concerns among scholars of antebellum American fiction. In the twenty years since Jane Tompkins first challenged Ann Douglas's unflattering assessment of America's "feminized" antebellum writers, literary critics have been busy building a progressively more sophisticated account of domesticity and its cultural influence. In 1998, Cathy Davidson issued an influential call to arms in *American Literature* entitled "No More Separate Spheres!" In it, she suggests that the stubborn persistence of the separate spheres binary, both in historiography and literary criticism, hinders more subtle, more textured investigations of antebellum culture. She points to the work of Amy Kaplan and Lora Romero as examples of how scholars might productively set aside the paradigm of the separate spheres and begin to examine domesticity as a more fluid cultural phenomenon, one that spans private and public contexts and that performs different kinds of cultural work depending on its specific location.[8]

It is within this context of what we might call a "post-separate spheres awareness" that I would like to approach Hawthorne's and Stoddard's texts. Diet reform offers a productive framework in which to reexamine not just the phenomenology of possession and space, but also the protean forms of nineteenth-century domesticity itself. Gillian Brown has persuasively argued that domestic ideology in general, and *The House of the Seven Gables* in particular, enacts a "thematics of disembodiment" whereby women's bodies are dissociated from their household labor and from their very sense of self-identity (65). Brown has in mind here the "spiritualizing" tendencies of domesticity, the desire to see women in terms of a "transcendent femininity" rather than as a material, corporeal presence (64). These "thematics of disembodiment," according to Brown, are part of a larger cultural strategy to construct a "private domain of individuality apart from the marketplace" (3). In short, the private sphere, de-corporealized and removed from the material circulations of capital, becomes the foundation for a new kind of modern selfhood.[9] Compelling as it is, this account of domesticity seems to me to overlook the myriad and subtle ways in which domestic discourse specifically calls attention to the corporeal aspects of the "feminine" sphere and women's work. Certainly, Hawthorne and Stoddard are aware of the spiritualizing, disembodying tendencies of domesticity, but they are also attuned to its materializing energies, to the ways it effectively inserts both male and female bodies into material economies, that is, into circuits of property exchange. No longer relegated to the abstract domain of moral suasion, women in these novels are imagined in terms of their material, corporeal influence. Here, the path of "feminine" power circulates not simply from "heart to heart," but more provocatively, from stomach to stomach.

Eating and digestion sit at a crucial intersection of theoretical and historical concerns in nineteenth-century domestic fiction. Hawthorne and Stoddard are fascinated with precisely this overlap, this overdetermined knot of private spaces, private properties, and alimentary bodies that characterizes nineteenth-century America. Indeed, their interest in eating and digestion extends so far as to flavor their own sense of aesthetic purpose as writers. In his "Preface" to *The House of the Seven Gables*, Hawthorne remarks that while the judicious writer of "Romance" has "a certain latitude," he should not stray too far from the dictates of realism. "He will be wise," Hawthorne says, "to mingle the Marvellous rather as a slight, delicate, and evanescent flavor, than as any portion of the actual substance of the dish offered to the Public" (3). Hawthorne imagines his own fiction here as a kind of confection, a delicate meal served up for the public's discerning palate.[10] In a similar vein, Stoddard's novel repeatedly conflates the act of reading with the act of eating. In the opening pages, the precocious ten-year-old protagonist reveals a fondness for any and all food-related narratives. She likes the "Shepherd of Salisbury Plain," for example, "because it makes [her] hungry to read about the roasted potatoes the shepherd had for breakfast and supper" (6); later, as a teenager, she describes herself as a "devourer of books which I could not digest" (56). Like Hawthorne, Stoddard seems to understand her own aesthetic project in terms of a culinary economy: books are prepared by writers and then devoured by hungry readers. Within this alimentary circuit, however, the artful writer has an opportunity to mix and mingle various ingredients to different effect.

The goals of this chapter are thus twofold, one philosophical and one historical. First, in a more philosophical vein, it aims to uncover and interpret these respective models of possession. How, it asks, can Hawthorne and Stoddard help us understand what it means to own something? What it means to take possession? In order to achieve this goal, the chapter is divided into three sections, each of which focuses on a particular component of possession or property. Section one investigates the "beginnings of property," the initial phenomenological experience of appropriation, of consuming an object by taking it inside oneself. Section two focuses on the more familiar notion of possession as an object that we hold within our power, within our space of control. This section, following Levinas, pays close attention to the crucial role of domestic space in enabling "possession proper." Finally, section three considers what happens when individual possessions begin to move in circuits of social exchange. I will argue here that the move to sociality is precisely what distinguishes phenomenological possession from private property. In addition to the philosophical argument of the chapter, however, there is also a second, intertwined historical claim. In drawing on the discourse of antebellum diet reform, Hawthorne and Stoddard do not simply produce a new model of possession. They also force us to reconsider the kinds of cultural work to which this discourse was put. Stoddard, in particular, reveals subversive potential hidden in the seemingly conservative ideology of diet reform. Her efforts, along with Hawthorne's, encourage us to rethink the political and economic ramifications of both diet reform and domesticity.

Possession Without Acquisition: Eating, Enjoyment, and the "Beginning of Property"

Like every animal, [men] begin by eating, drinking, etc. that is, not by 'finding themselves' in a relationship, but by behaving actively, gaining possession of certain things in the external world by their actions, thus satisfying their needs.
—KARL MARX, "COMMENTS ON ADOLPH WAGNER"

The opening sentence of John Locke's famous disquisition on private property contains a telling reference to eating and digestion. Chapter V of the *Second Treatise* begins by asserting that "Men, being once born, have a right to their Preservation, and consequently to Meat and Drink, and such other things, as Nature affords for their Subsistence" (285). The need for nourishment, apparently, will figure prominently in Locke's political theory of appropriation. Initially, however, it's not entirely clear what role alimentation will play. As we saw in the last chapter, Locke's theory revolves around the notion of labor mixing. In his words, "Whatsoever [a person] removes out of the State that Nature hath provided [. . .] he hath mixed his *Labour* with, and joyned to it something that is his own, and thereby makes it his *Property*" (288). This is the rationale whereby a farmer who tills an unclaimed plot of land effectively appropriates that plot by mixing his bodily labor with it. But it is not at all apparent why eating should factor into this formulation in any significant way. How exactly, we might ask, does alimentation illuminate Lockean property theory?

One answer lies in the opening sentence. When Locke declares that people have a "right to their Preservation," he makes it clear that eating and the need for nourishment constitute a justification of appropriation. That is, we must eat to survive, and therefore we have a natural right to remove things from a common state of nature and consume them for our own personal nourishment. Locke clarifies this point with another alimentary example. "He that is nourished by the Acorns he pickt up under an Oak, or the Apples he gathered from the Trees in the Wood, has certainly appropriated them to himself. No Body can deny but the nourishment is his" (288). Again, the need for nourishment warrants the appropriation. As the chapter continues, however, it becomes clear that this physical need also indexes a psychological drive, a desire that underlies the moral rationale. Men not only *need* to take possession of the natural world, they *desire* to take possession because it provides them pleasure. Locke emphasizes that God gave men the world "for their benefit, and the greatest Conveniences of Life they were capable to draw from it" (291). The natural world is not meant to provide simply "Subsistence"; rather, it is also a source of benefit and convenience, in short, pleasure. Eating is crucial for Locke because it enacts this desire at the same time that it justifies it. In this way, alimentation is the point of origin for all appropriation. The needs and desires it represents are what Locke calls the "*beginning of Property*" (289).

The pleasures of appropriation, however, also lead to a difficulty for Locke. "If gathering the Acorns, or other Fruits of the Earth, &c. makes a right to them, then any one may *ingross* as much as he will" (290). In other words, if mixing one's labor with an object is all that is required in order to take possession, what is to stop a particularly greedy person from appropriating more than his fair share? Locke's answer again has recourse to the act of eating. "The same Law of Nature, that does by this means give us Property, does also *bound* that *Property* too." More specifically, it is bounded by the biblical injunction of 1st Timothy: "*God has given us all things richly to enjoy.*" Locke focuses here on the phrase "to enjoy," interpreting it to mean "As much as any one can make use of to any advantage of life before it spoils" (290). This passage sees Locke more directly acknowledging the role that pleasure, or enjoyment, plays in the process of appropriation. But more importantly, the language of "spoilage" identifies eating as the limit to what can be appropriated. We can only take possession of those things we can ourselves consume before they spoil. "Whatever is beyond this," Locke warns, "is more than his share, and belongs to others" (290). Of course, this formulation is complicated by the appearance of durable goods and money, but in the primordial context Locke is addressing here, eating establishes not just the beginning of property, but its limits as well.[11]

Like Brockden Brown, Hawthorne and Stoddard are still writing in the long shadow cast by Locke's work on property. The two novelists are keenly interested in the same issues of appropriation and alimentation that Locke engages, and his efforts provide a broad theoretical precedent for their own investigations.[12] Before considering their work, however, it is necessary to address one more crucial question raised by Locke's theory. In short, what about the body itself? That is, how does a person come to have a property in his own body and thus in himself? Locke declares in no uncertain terms that "every Man has a *Property* in his own *Person*. This no Body has any right to but himself" (287). This corporeal ownership is the reason that a person owns his own labor and the work of his own hands. It is also, therefore, the foundation of Lockean possessive individualism. Because a person owns his own body, he owns himself. He is the "proprietor of his own person or capacities." But how exactly does this self-ownership come about? Locke himself is silent on the subject. Self-possession is simply assumed. Emmanuel Levinas, writing two hundred and fifty years after Locke, hints at a possible answer to this very same question. Self-possession, he suggests, just like the appropriative powers that follow from it, may begin with the primordial act of eating.[13]

Like Locke, Levinas turns his attention to the origins of possession and property, and like Locke, he identifies eating as the embodied experience that first enacts a primordial appropriation. Using language that echoes Locke's much earlier work, Levinas characterizes eating as "enjoyment," that is, as the act of feeding on the elements of the world in order to sustain oneself. "Nourishment, as a means of invigoration," he writes, "is the transmutation of the other into the same, which is the essence of enjoyment: an energy that is other [. . .] becomes, in enjoyment, my own energy, my strength, me. All enjoyment is in this sense alimentation" (111). Already with the use of the possessive pronoun, Levinas identifies eating as a form of elemental appropriation; what is other becomes mine. But he goes on to make the connection more explicit. Enjoyment, he explains, is "possession without acquisition"; it is possession "which 'possesses' without taking" (158). This is a puzzling claim, but also, I believe, absolutely crucial for understanding the nature of possession. Levinas is suggesting that eating constitutes a mode of possession distinct from, but related to, the more familiar type of appropriation. Enjoyment signifies an "immediate relation" with the material world. It is an enjoyment experienced by "the sensibility steeped in the element" (158). In other words, enjoyment is a sensory experience, a phenomenological experience of tasting, consuming, possessing the world. Possession *proper*, as we might call it, requires a suspension, a holding in reserve, an abeyance. It is food not consumed but stored away. This is the sense in which we can be said to have, and hold, a possession. Eating and enjoyment, on the other hand, enact an immediate, primordial appropriation, an appropriation of and through the senses. It is precisely these two modes of possession, I would suggest, that Locke is negotiating in his account of the "beginnings of property." As it does for Levinas, eating for Locke represents a primordial form of appropriation, one that foregrounds the agency of the sensate body.

But what is it exactly, we might ask, that gets possessed in this "possession without acquisition"? Isn't Levinasian "enjoyment" simply another word for "consumption"? The answer to these questions, I would submit, also gets at the answer to the Lockean question of self-ownership, that is, how do we come to possess our own bodies and selves? To put it concisely, Levinas implies that what we come to possess through this mysterious process of "possession without acquisition" is in fact the embodied self. "In enjoyment throbs egoist being," he writes, hinting at the self-creating potential of alimentation (147). Or again, "Enjoyment is not a psychological state among others, [as empiricist psychology has it], but the very pulsation of the I" (113). He takes pains to emphasize the essential role of eating here: "This sinking of one's teeth into the things which the act of eating involves [. . .] is the way the I, the absolute commencement, is suspended on the non-I" (129). The "sensibility" of eating, the pleasurable sensation of consuming food for nourishment, cultivates an awareness of the embodied self distinct from the world around it. This alimentary experience is thus the very foundation of "egoist being." "In enjoyment," Levinas elaborates, "I am absolutely for myself. Egoist without reference to the Other, I am alone without solitude [. . .] outside of all communication and all refusal to communicate—without ears, like a hungry stomach" (134). Eating enacts an awareness of the sensate body that is simultaneously an awareness of the individual self. This is the answer to Locke's implicit question about self-ownership: this is how a person comes to "possess" his own body and his own self. Such self-possession, however, is not quite synonymous with the more familiar mode of possession that follows from it. Rather, eating is the phenomenological foundation upon which possession proper rests. It is, in short, possession without acquisition.

What Locke circles around, and what Levinas only hints at, Hawthorne and Stoddard take up as a central feature in their domestic novels. Both *The House of the Seven Gables* and *The Morgesons* explore the nature of what we might call *alimentary possession*, that is, this bodily process through which individuals appropriate elements of the external world and in so doing come to a sense of themselves as selves. Operating in a discursive space opened up by the exhortations of the diet reformers, Hawthorne and Stoddard carefully map the physical and ideological significance of the "hungry stomach." More specifically, they concern themselves with the appropriative powers of alimentation, with the ways in which eating structures both possession and self-possession. However, their shared focus on alimentary possession leads to very different conclusions. Whereas Hawthorne will ultimately find reason to fear the voracious potential of self-possessive appetites, Stoddard will find reason to hope. From her perspective as a middle-class white woman, alimentary self-possession represents an important step toward greater social and economic influence. For Stoddard, the path to agency leads through the appropriating stomach.

In Hawthorne's case, the links between eating and appropriation begin early in *The House of the Seven Gables*. The "preface" to the novel invokes a culinary metaphor to describe Hawthorne's own aesthetic: he describes his writing as a "dish offered to the public." Having done so, he immediately goes on to assure the reader that eating such a "dish" "infringes upon nobody's private rights" (5). That is, reading his delectable novel will not, despite what any potential plaintiffs might think, constitute a property crime. Instead, reading it is analogous to "appropriating a lot of land which had no visible owner" and which nobody else can claim (5). Eating and property rights are conflated here in a manner that forecasts the theoretical stakes of the coming narrative. To drive home the point, Hawthorne returns to his culinary metaphor. "The personages of the Tale," he explains, "are really of the author's own making, or, at all events, of his own mixing" (5). The qualifying phrase "of his own mixing" evokes both the culinary image of a chef mixing up his own dish, and the Lockean implication of labor mixing. Products of his labor, the characters in the book are Hawthorne's own private property, but they are also available for consumption by the reader. Digesting the book is the way to take possession of them.[14]

Hawthorne's gustatory preface serves as an ideal appetizer to the larger narrative because in its own way *The House of the Seven Gables* is a story obsessed with eating. Alongside the drama of hereditary guilt and family decay, there is a persistent interest in the practice and experience of alimentation. After he helps condemn the obstructionist homesteader Matthew Maule to a gruesome death on the gallows, Colonel Pyncheon marks his victory by inviting the village to a sumptuous feast. Plying them with "ale, cider, wine, and brandy, in copious effusion," as well as an ox, a massive venison "pasty," and "a cod-fish of sixty pounds," the Colonel invites the whole population to "a ceremony of consecration" for his new house (11). Later in the book, the momentous arrivals of Phoebe and Clifford Pyncheon are both marked by elaborately prepared breakfasts that serve to cement their position in the household. Phoebe herself is continually feeding spice-cake to the heirloom chickens who strut about the garden, tasting the brackish well-water like little "wine-bibbers round a probationary cask" (130). Later still, as Judge Pyncheon's corpse sits stonily in the parlor of the house, Hawthorne details the delicacies of a dinner he is missing: "Real turtle [...] and salmon, tautog, canvasbacks, pig, English mutton, good roast-beef" (234). The description spans several pages.

It is not simply eating, in general, that concerns Hawthorne, however, but more specifically the phenomenon of alimentary possession. When old Colonel Pyncheon throws his feast, "the mere smell" of which is "at once an invitation and an appetite," it is meant to demonstrate his unobstructed title to Matthew Maule's land and to the newly built Pyncheon house that sits on top of it (11). Eating marks the process of taking possession. Hawthorne makes this clear by referring to the feast as a "ceremony of consecration," a phrase that connotes not only the setting aside of a sacred property, but also the transubstantiation of bread and wine into the body and blood of Christ. Colonel Pyncheon's communion meal effectively appropriates Matthew Maule's possessory rights, just as the seven-gabled house itself swallows Maule's hut. Similarly, when encroaching poverty forces the reclusive and decrepit Hepzibah Pyncheon to open a street-level "cent-shop" in one of the seven gables, her first customer is Ned Higgins, a small boy with a "grand appetite." He is a "little cannibal" who happily devours the gingerbread figures on display in the shop window (52). As with the Colonel's appropriation of Maule's property, Ned's emblematic purchase is described as a "cannibal feast" and marked by the "crumbs and discoloration" that are "exceedingly visible about his mouth" (46). Taking possession is understood to mean taking a bite.

Describing Ned's snack as a "cannibal feast," however, seems to cast an unflattering light on this sort of alimentary possession. Ned's voracity and his "exceedingly visible" mouth hint at a potential for violence in this sort of property exchange. Indeed a number of critics have read Ned's "cannibal feast" as the incursion of destructive market forces into the protected sphere of domestic privacy. This is, so the thinking goes, the critical moment at which Hepzibah is forced into direct contact with the exploitative and devouring capacities of consumer capitalism.[15] While acknowledging the risks associated with this moment of contact, I would like to suggest that Ned's appetite might be better understood as a more ambivalent feature in the text. His "grand appetite" is, first and foremost, a model of healthy incorporation to be contrasted with Hepzibah's own anemic presence and near-starvation diet. She has been feeding, we are told, mostly on the "shadowy food of aristocratic reminiscences" (34) and has "incurred her present meagerness by often choosing to go without her dinner rather than be attendant on the rotation of the spit, or ebullition of the pot" (87). She is, in short, a ghost: almost all spirit and no body. Ned's appetite represents a possible strategy for reappropriating and renovating her own flesh. Hawthorne tells us as much when he describes the transformation wrought by Hepzibah's exchange with Ned. "The healthiest glow, that Hepzibah had known for years, had come now"; and the touch of Ned's copper coin has a "galvanic" influence on her, inspiring her with "energy to get some breakfast, at which [...] she allowed herself an extra spoonful in her infusion of black tea" (47). Ned's appetite is ultimately not something for Hepzibah to fear, but a suggestion as to how she might repossess herself.[16]

Hepzibah is not the only member of the Pyncheon family who suffers from mental and physical disintegration. Her invalid brother Clifford, wrongfully imprisoned for thirty years, has himself deteriorated to a shadowy, incorporeal presence. When he finally returns to the House of the Seven Gables, he seems on the brink of disappearing altogether. "Continually," Hawthorne tells us, "he faded away out of his place [...] leaving his wasted, gray, and melancholy figure—a substantial emptiness, a material ghost—to occupy his seat at the table" (92). He "stare[s] vaguely about," and moves slowly "with as indefinite an aim as a child's first journey across a floor" (90). But again, as with Hepzibah, the solution to his dissolution lies in the restorative power of eating. Recalling Clifford's epicurean tastes, Hepzibah exerts herself to prepare a succulent breakfast of "the finest mackerel," the "sweetest" Indian cakes, and "real Mocha [...] worth its weight in gold" (86–88). Her brother is galvanized by the sight of the sumptuous fare. "He ate food with what might almost be termed voracity, and seemed to forget himself [...] and everything else around him, in the sensual enjoyment which the bountifully spread table afforded" (93). When he tastes the coffee, it acts upon him "like a charmed draught," causing him to cry out, "More, more! [...] This is what I need! Give me more!" The effects of the meal are dramatic: "He sat more erect, and looked out from his eyes with a glance that took note of what it rested on [...] a certain fine temper of being was now brought out in full relief" (94). Hawthorne's description is particularly telling in that Clifford first "forgets himself" in his sensual reverie before eventually gathering his thoughts and composing himself. In a manner that prefigures the "egoist being" of Levinasian enjoyment, Clifford enacts a striking alimentary repossession of the self.

Yet, alimentary possession of this sort is not without its risks. Little Ned's characterization as a "cannibal" hints at the danger of an uncontrolled appetite turning on its own kind. As Locke realized, if this appetite is allowed to "ingross as much as [it] will," it may exceed the bounds of simple self-possession and eat away at the social fabric. The same intense self-regard that gives the alimentary appetite its restorative power also threatens to collapse it into a dangerous, all-consuming self-absorption. Clifford's hunger borders on precisely this sort of destructive self-indulgence, a fact that Hawthorne gestures toward with his description of Hepzibah's painstaking breakfast preparations. Determined that Clifford's breakfast mackerel will be perfect, Hepzibah watches the fish "with as much tender care and minuteness of attention as if—we know not how to express it otherwise—as if her own heart were on the gridiron" (87). In effect, when Hepzibah feeds Clifford the mackerel, she is offering up a part of herself for consumption. Alimentary possession is imagined here as a disturbing sort of sibling cannibalism; Clifford's appetite enables a metaphorical self-sacrifice on the part of Hepzibah. The fact that the two are siblings also raises the grim specter of self-cannibalism. Clifford's reembodiment proceeds only at the expense of his sister's body, and so, in a kind of aristocratic *ouroboros*, the family eats itself to sustain itself. A bit later in the book, Hepzibah prepares another breakfast for Clifford, this time feeding him the lone egg produced by the family's heirloom chickens. Hawthorne has made it clear that we are to read the chickens as an analogue for the Pyncheons themselves, telling us that they are "a symbol of the life of the old house" (132). As with the mackerel, then, Hepzibah's egg serves as another entree for Clifford's cannibal gourmandise. Here is the dark underbelly of alimentary possession. While tasting, swallowing, and digesting constitute a crucial form of embodied appropriation and self-definition, they also enable a destructive and narcissistic turn to the self. In a kind of possessive individualism run amok, the self-cannibal appropriates not just the outside world, but also his own internal substance.[17]

Nevertheless, while Hawthorne's novel weighs the potential benefits of alimentary possession alongside its potential risks, ultimately, the book adopts a cautionary stance toward the power of eating. Like the diet reformers with whom it is engaging, the novel is more concerned with the likely pathologies of eating than it is with the possibility of healthy alimentary exchange. Indeed, Sylvester Graham's warning that "excessive alimentation is one of the greatest sources of evil to the human family" might have served as an apt epigraph for the Pyncheon family saga: this is a narrative more about indigestion than digestion. Or, to be more precise, it is a story of dysphagia. For all the attention given to stomachs, mouths, and particularly throats, more often than not, the narrative describes a failed attempt to swallow and incorporate. Self-cannibalism represents only one possible perversion of proper alimentation. Even more significant are the novel's repeated instances of choking and failed ingestion. These moments of failed consumption serve two purposes: on the one hand, they again link the process of alimentation to the process of taking possession. So, when Judge Pyncheon is repeatedly thwarted in his efforts to reacquire the Pyncheon legacy, he is also repeatedly unable to take alimentary possession of the objects (and the people) around him. On the other hand, like Ned's cannibalistic appetite, the moments of dysphagia also foreground the dangers of unbridled acquisition. Too much intemperate eating, the novel warns, leads to an inability to consume anything at all.

Judge Pyncheon is the key figure of failed ingestion in the book. Ironically, Hawthorne contrasts the Judge's inability to effectively consume things during the narrative with his renowned appetite and overwhelming corporeality. When the Judge makes his first visit to the cent-shop, Hawthorne notes "the massive accumulation of animal substance about the lower region of his face" and characterizes his look as one of "fleshly effulgence" (101). His massive body, we learn, is an inheritance passed down from the Colonel, an ancestor who was himself distinguished by "all his English beef" (231). To sustain this "full-fed physiognomy" (103), the Judge is subject to an "ogre-like appetite" that transforms him into a "great beast" at dinner. "Persons of his large sensual endowments," Hawthorne tells us, "must claim indulgence, at their feeding-time" (236). Nor are the Judge's appetites confined to the dinner table. He is as "greedy of wealth" (106) as the old Colonel and desperately desires to reacquire both Clifford and the Pyncheon house, the two of which, he believes, will lead him to an old Indian property deed. Hawthorne also hints, ever so delicately, that the Judge's voracity extends to the women in his life. Like his ancestor who had "worn out three wives" because of "certain transgressions to which men of his great animal development [...] must continue liable," the Judge has sent one wife to her grave, "merely by the remorseless weight and hardness of his character in the conjugal relation" (107). His hunger, it seems, knows no bounds.

Yet one of the novel's central concerns is precisely those moments at which the Judge's hunger is frustrated. Before he can return to his own home and enjoy the elaborate dinner of "salmon" and "tautog" mentioned above, the Judge abruptly chokes to death in the parlor of the Pyncheon mansion. His lifeless corpse sits ashen-faced in the Colonel's old chair while the narrator mockingly offers it some wine, exclaiming, "It would all but revive a dead man! Would you like to sip it now, Judge Pyncheon?" He cannot, of course, but this is precisely Hawthorne's point. With a kind of self-righteous glee, the narrator continues, "Make haste, then! [. . .] Be present at this dinner!—drink a glass or two of that noble wine!" But, no, "for once the Judge is entirely too late for dinner!" (235–36). Intended to initiate his candidacy for governor of Massachusetts, the dinner would have marked his greatest acquisition of power. Instead he is denied the food and denied his political reward.

While still alive, he suffers a similar setback when he attempts to become "better acquainted" (102) with the nubile young Phoebe. She is working behind the counter in the cent-shop when the Judge enters and introduces himself. Once he realizes that the "young rosebud" is a distant cousin, he takes advantage of their kinship in order to steal a kiss. But, "just at the critical moment," Phoebe recoils so that the Judge "with his body bent over the counter, and his lips protruded, was betrayed into the rather absurd predicament of kissing the empty air." She does so, we are told, because "the man, the sex, somehow or other, was entirely too prominent in the Judge's demonstrations" (103). As naive as she may be, Phoebe instinctively recognizes the voracious threat of the Judge's protruding lips. To be sure, there is a sexual component to his advances, but this is only a particular form assumed by his larger appetite. The Judge moves to consume and appropriate Phoebe just as he consumes everything else in his life. Yet here again, he is frustrated in his attempt.

As the scene continues, the Judge's frustration manifests itself in the novel's most persistent symbol of failed ingestion: the hereditary Pyncheon gurgle. Embarrassed by Phoebe's evasion, the Judge makes a peculiar noise in his throat, "a queer and awkward ingurgitation" that is "not altogether voluntary, [. . .] a slight bronchial complaint" (108). The noise startles Phoebe not so much on its own account, but because it recalls a celebrated legend of the Pyncheon family in which the austere Colonel was cursed by doomed Matthew Maule. According to "fireside tradition," as Maule stood on the gallows preparing to die, he pointed at the Colonel, and intoned, "God will give him blood to drink!" (9). The subsequent scene of the Colonel's death confirms the curse. His body is found in an oaken chair, with "blood on his ruff" and saturating his beard. Some versions of the legend even describe the "print of a bloody hand" on the ruff, or a skeleton claw at his throat (15–16).

For our purposes, the gurgle is significant because it marks a crucial obstruction of alimentation. The Colonel, and later the Judge, are both unable to properly consume elements of the outside world, a fact that mirrors their inability to obtain unobstructed title to the house. Possession and alimentation go hand in hand. At the same time, the fate of choking on their own blood should be read as a cautionary tale about the dangers of excessive appetite. The Colonel and his descendant have fallen prey to what Hepzibah calls "this hard and grasping spirit in our blood" (204); they have overindulged their appetites to the point that they can no longer consume. Gluttons for power and property, they are literally choking on their own greed. Again echoing the abstemious diet reformers, Hawthorne underscores the pathological potential inherent in ingestion and alimentary possession.

But then Hawthorne makes an unexpected move. He reverses the direction of alimentation and suggests that the gurgle functions not only as an obstacle to ingestion but to expulsion as well. The Colonel and Judge, it seems, can neither swallow any more of the world nor regurgitate anything of their own. They are frozen by an "awkard ingurgitation." This expulsive paralysis is most clearly expressed when Holgrave, the radical daguerreotypist who will eventually marry Phoebe, reads to her a short story he has written about the Pyncheon curse. In it, he describes a dream that Alice Pyncheon has while she is mesmerized by the grandson of Matthew Maule. The dream features three figures: Colonel Pyncheon, the original Matthew Maule, and Matthew Maule's son, the builder of the Pyncheon house. The ghostly Colonel Pyncheon, complete with bloodstain on his ruff, struggles to divulge the secret of the missing Indian deed. But when he tries to speak, the two Maules "pressed their hands over his mouth; and forthwith—whether that he were choked by it, or that the secret itself was of a crimson hue—there was a fresh flow of blood upon his band" (179). Ambiguously suspended between ingestion and expulsion, the gurgle effectively blocks the exchange between inside and outside in either direction. Healthy alimentation and healthy expression are both trapped in the passageway of the throat.

The image of the obstructed Pyncheon throat is a striking one and, I believe, essential to an understanding of the phenomenology of possession in Hawthorne's novel. The mouth and throat constitute a key point of exchange between internal body and external world. Jacques Derrida helpfully calls our attention to precisely this fact in his essay "Economimesis." Rejecting Kant's claim that "pure" art exists outside the crass claims of economic exchange and animal bodies, Derrida maintains that in fact the two are intimately connected. More specifically, they are linked in the space of the mouth. He points out that the mouth is the site at which both ingestion and linguistic expression take place; it is where taste decides what will come in and what will be emitted. "The split between all the values that at one moment or another are opposed will pass through the mouth: what it finds good or what it finds bad, according to what is sensible or ideal" (16). In other words, the mouth itself spans the gap, *is* the gap, between word and flesh. "Is the *os* [mouth] of the system, the place of tasting or of consumption but also the emitting production of the *logos*, still a term in an analogy? [. . .] Is it not itself the analogy, towards which everything returns as towards the logos itself?" (16). As both inlet and outlet, as embouchure, the mouth reveals the embodied connection between Kant's separate economies. Art and nature are linked in a continuous circuit of exchange.

Ultimately, such a formulation does not satisfy Derrida, however, because in some ways it is even more totalizing than Kant's. Nothing escapes this new value-economy. Negative pleasures as well as positive ones are all assigned a place in the hierarchy. Yet, as a good deconstructionist, Derrida maintains there must be an outside to this system, a third term to disrupt the binary. "What is the border or the absolute overboard of this problematic? [. . .] What is it that does not enter into this theory thus framed, hierarchised, regulated? What is excluded from it and what, proceeding from this exclusion, gives it form, limit, and contour?" (20–21). Derrida's answer returns us to the predicament of the Pyncheon gurgle. "What it excludes," he tells us, "is what does not allow itself to be digested, or represented, or stated." In short, "Vomit lends its form to this whole system" (20). Vomit is precisely that which cannot be assimilated to the system of exchange initiated by the mouth. It is the "non-transcendentalisable, the non-idealisable" (22); it can neither be taken in ("digested") nor emitted ("stated"). It represents the complete breakdown of a system of exchange between interior and exterior, as well as between embodiment and idealization. "If one could name it or represent it, it would begin to enter into the auto-affective circle of mastery or reappropriation. An economy would be possible" (22). In fact, even utilizing the term "vomit" begins to reify the experience into something appropriate-able. So Derrida ends the essay by explaining that "What is absolutely foreclosed is not vomit, but the possibility of a vicariousness of vomit, of its replacement by anything else" (25).

The Pyncheon gurgle represents just this sort of vomitive foreclosure. The dream figure of Colonel Pyncheon tries to speak, tries to divulge the secret he possesses, but it remains lodged in his throat, a gurgling obstruction. Gervayse Pyncheon, having lost possession of his daughter Alice to Maule's mesmerist grandson, also desperately tries to speak, but can "make only a gurgling murmur in his throat" (179). The gurgle is the unsayable, the unrepresentable, but it is also the indigestible, that which cannot be eaten or appropriated. It marks the absolute limit and breakdown of the possessive, alimentary economy in which the Pyncheons have been located. The Judge can neither ingest nor express, but remains trapped in a moment outside the "circle of mastery or reappropriation." Nor is it a coincidence that the Judge is a judge. As Derrida makes clear, the circulation of both sensible and discursive forms moves through the mouth, the organ of taste and judgment. "The taste decides," as Brillat-Savarin puts it in *The Physiology of Taste* (1825), and the magnitude of the Judge's dilemma can be measured by the fact that he can no longer judge at all. Denied his ability to decide what comes in and what goes out, he dangles in the gap between inside and outside, between body and discourse, between possession and dispossession. Ultimately, this liminal state is untenable, and the Judge and Colonel fall victim to their suspension. Literally stuck in their craw, they expire.

Hawthorne is not alone in attending to the hazards of eating and alimentary possession. Stoddard's novel, too, faces up to the risks associated with possessive incorporation. In the case of *The Morgesons*, however, the most pressing dangers associated with eating and possession lie not in a gluttonous, Pyncheon-esque overindulgence; rather, they lie in the practice of ignoring bodily appetites altogether. Stoddard is specifically concerned with the ways in which domestic ideology seeks to deny bodily appetites to women. As Gillian Brown has alerted us, domestic discourse often employs a "thematics of disembodiment" in which women's actual, material bodies are deemphasized in favor of their perceived moral and "spiritual" characteristics. Such discourse effectively imagines the middle-class white woman as an "angel in the house," a submissive, bodiless agent who attends to her family's every need without unnecessarily asserting her own corporeality. But Stoddard is having no part of this "spiritualizing" myth. She carefully punctuates her novel with images of hungry women, women both suffering and satiating their bodily appetites. In doing so, she helps counter the elisions of domesticity and helps rematerialize the female body.

Alimentary possession is the key strategy for accomplishing this. By turning attention to the ways in which eating enables not just possession, but more particularly, self-possession, Stoddard adapts the model of alimentary possession to her own ends. Building on the Lockean and Levinasian claims that eating and enjoyment enable the possession of one's own body, and thus one's self, Stoddard emphasizes alimentation as both the means and the mark of female self-possession.[18] Women, she suggests, need to have done with the sort of self-sacrifice and self-negation epitomized by Hepzibah's assiduous attention to Clifford. Instead, they need to take possession of their own bodily appetites. This celebratory stance vis-à-vis alimentation differentiates Stoddard's novel both from Hawthorne's work and from the anxious invective of the diet reformers.

While mindful of the potential pathologies of alimentary consumption, *The Morgesons* turns the ideology of diet reform on its head.

Female appetite is represented most prominently in the figure of Cassandra Morgeson. The bildungsroman narrative follows Cassandra from her earliest days as a willful child, through her love-struck teenage years, and finally into the concessions and compromises of sober adulthood. Throughout, Cassandra is distinguished by her uncommonly strong sense of self-empowerment. "That child," Aunt Merce declares in the first sentence of the novel, "is possessed." But we quickly learn that this "devilish" possession is better understood as a form of vigorous *self-possession*: Cassandra defies the wishes of her complacent mother, teases her Puritanical grandfather Warren by pinching his cat, and mocks the local evangelical minister. In short, she flouts the conventions of proper feminine behavior. In the estimation of the flabbergasted villagers, "Locke Morgeson's daughter can do anything" (60).

Significantly, Stoddard makes a point of carefully and repeatedly linking Cassandra's "devilish" self-actualization to her prodigious appetite. As her sense of individual agency grows, so too does her bodily hunger. "What an appetite I had," she recalls, remembering the silent meals she shared with her grandfather during her year-long visit. Even the taciturn old man had remarked on her ravenous hunger, worrying that "the creature will eat us out of house and home" (47). Later, when Cassandra goes to Rosville to live with the family of her older cousin Charles and his wife Alice, she is enamored with their exquisitely prepared food. In a Clifford-esque rapture, she describes the meals: "The lamb chops were fragile; the bread was delicious, but cut in transparent slices"; the sponge cake "felt like muslin in the fingers; I could have squeezed the whole of it into my mouth" (69). But her enjoyment of the food is inhibited by the fact that her cousin's family doesn't eat enough of it to suit her tastes. The ham is "most savory, but cut in such thin slices that it curled [...]. The boiled eggs were smaller than any I had seen." "I am afraid I am an animal," she confesses to her mother; "Did you notice how little the Morgesons [her cousins] ate?" (71). Within the constraints of conventional domestic culture, Cassandra's alimentary self-possession is an aberration. Indulging her appetite is seen as a concession to the very body she should be trying to ignore. Late in the book, Cassandra guiltily confesses that she has long been subject to selfish "contrary desires." Her sister Veronica responds with a telling question: "What do they find to feed on?" (219). For Stoddard, eating and appetite represent the path to self-possession. A woman comes into her own, literally, by acknowledging and acting on her bodily hunger.

As we have hinted, however, Cassandra's refreshing corporeality always exists in tension with the body- and appetite-denying tenets of domesticity. Stoddard registers the force of these tenets most dramatically in the peculiar figure of Veronica. In contrast to Cassandra's vigorous embodiment, Veronica, like Hepzibah, is characterized by her frail physicality and lack of appetite. She repeatedly refuses to eat while her robust older sister indulges herself: "I was faint from the want of food, and when Temperance prepared us something I ate heartily. Veronica drank a little milk, but would taste nothing" (207). At one point, in fact, Veronica decides "to live entirely on toast" (51). The result of Veronica's abstemiousness is a persistent physical debilitation: she is "diminutive and pale," and she suffers from "long and mysterious illnesses, which made her helpless for weeks" (13). What is more, Veronica spends much of her time "confined to her room," both because of her ill health and because she has little interest in the world outside her domestic sphere (59). "Do you never tire of this limited, monotonous view?" Cassandra asks her while the two of them stand in Veronica's room looking out the window. Veronica's reply reveals a contentment with her domestic constraint: "If the landscape were wider, I could never learn it [...]. Why, morning and night are wonderful from these windows. But I must say the charm vanishes if I go from them" (135). Veronica's distance from Cassandra's self-possessed embodiment marks her as a casualty of domestic ideology; she is a woman denied the vivifying effects of alimentary possession.[19]

Cassandra's adult experience provides perhaps the most remarkable demonstration of the link that Stoddard makes between eating and possession. After her mother's unexpected death, Cassandra makes a fateful decision to forego her own life, that is, her own self-possessed, self-directed existence, in order to take care of the family and the family home. "You may depend on me," she dejectedly tells her old Aunt Merce, "I will reign, and serve also." It is a succinct description of the woman's role as imagined by domestic ideology. She will rule within her domestic sphere, but to do so successfully, she must become a servant. "I [...] never mean to have anything to myself—entirely, you know" (215). Her self-possession and her ability to possess, to "have anything," are both being relinquished. This sacrifice, however, is imaged in specifically alimentary terms. In a bizarre, postfuneral dinner scene, Cassandra surveys all the food that has been laid out for visitors. Then, without warning, she grabs the tablecloth, yanks it, and sends the whole meal crashing to the floor. She abruptly sits down and begins "picking out the remains" (215). "I scarcely tasted what I ate. A wall had risen up suddenly before me, which divided me from my dreams; I was inside it, on a prosaic domain I must henceforth be confined to" (216). It is a stark image of domestic imprisonment viewed through an alimentary lens. Cassandra recognizes, despairingly, that social custom and family ties require her to abandon her own life plans. And significantly, that loss is marked by the loss of her formerly prodigious appetite. In effect, she can no longer taste her freedom or her food. When a frightened servant warns Cassandra, "You'll choke yourself with that dry bread," it becomes clear that the alimentary economy has broken down (216). Like the gurgling Judge Pyncheon, Cassandra is here unable to eat, unable to take part in the process of alimentary possession.

Unlike Judge Pyncheon, however, Cassandra's plight is not meant as a warning about the dangers of sensual indulgence and intemperate consumption. On the contrary, it is intended to index the mental and physical damage that results from ignoring women's bodily appetites. At several points throughout the novel, Cassandra remarks on her Aunt Merce's unseemly habit of "chewing on cloves, flagroot, or grains of rice. If these articles were not at hand, she chewed a small chip" (5). When placed alongside the other images of famished women in the text, Aunt Merce's incessant nibbling serves as an apt illustration of the privation suffered by many middle-class women under the constraints of domesticity. Denied not just the means of satisfying their desires, but much acknowledgment of the desires at all, women were pushed toward a kind of sensory starvation.[20] In this way, Stoddard's treatment of eating and alimentation constitutes a thinly veiled rebuke of the asceticism prescribed by the diet reformers. Appetite and sensation are not a problem here, they are a solution, and Cassandra's bid for alimentary self-possession effectively revalues both.

Stoddard's celebration of appetite distinguishes her from Hawthorne's more anxious account, but, that difference notwithstanding, the two clearly share an interest in the alimentary underpinnings of possession and self-possession. The eating-inflected relationship between possession and self-possession is a central theme for both authors. Their two novels suggest, in fact, that eating functions as a phenomenological foundation for both the construction of the self and the acts of appropriation that follow from it. The intense sensory experience of eating and enjoyment calls self-reflective attention to the individual body, separating it from the world around it. At the same time, eating enacts a "possession without acquisition," an appropriation of objects in the external world that does not hold them in reserve, but simply consumes them. This is the "beginning of property" to which Locke alluded, and it is the starting point for the investigation of domestic space that Hawthorne and Stoddard set into motion.

Home Bodies: Domestic Space and Possession Proper

Is it not plain that not in senates, or courts, or chambers of commerce, but in the dwelling-house must the true character and hope of the time be consulted?
—RALPH WALDO EMERSON, "DOMESTIC LIFE"

In the "Higher Laws" chapter of *Walden*, Thoreau offers up his own transcendentally flavored recipe for radical dietary reform. Uncomfortable with the carnivorous, animalistic appetites he knows himself to possess, Thoreau strives instead to maintain an ascetic vegetarian diet of fruits and grains, "eaten temperately." "Like many of my contemporaries," he writes, "I had rarely for many years used animal food, or tea, or coffee, etc.; not so much because of any ill effect which I had traced to them, as because they were not agreeable to my imagination. The repugnance to animal food is not the effect of experience, but is an instinct" (179). He goes on to say that, in principle at least, he holds the diet reformer in high esteem: "He will be regarded as a benefactor of his race who shall teach man to confine himself to a more innocent and wholesome diet" (180). Then, in a characteristically transcendental move, Thoreau links embodied particularities to a more abstract metaphorical register: he equates individual bodies with individual houses. "Every man is the builder of a temple, called his body, to the god he worships, after a style purely his own, nor can he get off by hammering marble instead. We are all sculptors and painters, and our material is our own flesh and blood and bones" (184). By imaging the body as house in this way, Thoreau emphasizes its constructed, and therefore malleable, nature. As a structure always in the process of being built, the body is open to change, open to a radical renovation predicated on the strictures of a wholesome diet. Eating properly promises a new body that is simultaneously a new home.[21]

Thoreau was neither the first dietary writer, nor the last, to recognize the usefulness of this architectural metaphor. In fact, the trope of the "body as a house" was in widespread use among antebellum reformers. Like Thoreau, health and diet advocates were drawn to the image of the corporeal domicile, a body-home that could be snugly built, tidily organized, and swept clean. In 1834, for example, William Alcott, cousin of the Transcendentalist reformer Bronson Alcott, published an anatomical treatise for young adults entitled *The House I Live In*. Alcott is specific and exhaustive in his equation of bodies and homes. The book's chapters are organized around an architectural blueprint that links particular anatomical features with various structural elements of a house. Thus, one chapter explores the "pillars" of the house as they are represented by the foot, ankle, and thigh-bones. Another describes the hips as the "sills of the house" and the cranium as the "cupola." "I have called the mouth, and ears, and nostrils, doors," he tells us, "the eyes may, with propriety, be regarded as windows" (56). By the time he describes the epiglottis as a "trap-door" and the stomach as a "spacious saloon," the discerning reader may question the metaphor's elasticity, but the conflation of house and body is firmly established. Interspersed among these anatomical chapters are instructions pertaining to bodily hygiene, correct styles of dress, and, most importantly, diet. If the house I live in is to remain well-cared for, I will need to be temperate in my eating habits.[22]

Given their interest in both the contours of domesticity and the strictures of diet reform, the ubiquitous "body as house" metaphor would prove irresistible to Hawthorne and Stoddard. With it, the protected interior spaces of the home could be provocatively mapped onto the consuming appetites of individual bodies and stomachs. Rather than simply invoking the same old metaphor, however, the two authors take it upon themselves to energetically rework the trope, inverting it so as to suggest the ways in which we might also understand the house as a body, not just the body as a house. More specifically, I would argue, their two novels call attention to the crucial role that eating plays in structuring our experience of domestic space. Our sense of home and dwelling, they suggest, emerges from a process of alimentation that is both phenomenological and social. For them, the physical structure of the house is intimately tied to the alimentary experiences of individual bodies and to the relations that occur between those bodies. What is more, these links between eating and domestic space have significant ramifications for the phenomenology of possession. The novels suggest, in fact, that it is domestic space that enables full possession. That is, in order to move from Levinas's ephemeral "possession without acquisition" to a more durable and familiar form of appropriation, we require the "collecting" space of the home. Eating, it seems, enables not just self-possession, but possession proper.

Hawthorne wastes no time in equating domestic architecture with the human form. On the first page of the book, the narrator tells us that the sight of the Pyncheon mansion has always affected him "like a human countenance" (6); this initial analogy touches off a series of metaphors that proliferate throughout the novel. Holgrave's mesmerizing short story about Alice Pyncheon describes the House of Seven Gables as a "jolly-looking mansion" whose "great chimney in the centre, should symbolize the old fellow's hospitable heart" (165). Phoebe senses the same pulsating life as she prepares to leave the house and return to her own home in the country. The "heavy-hearted old mansion" has grown on her, she realizes: "Look where she would, lay her hand on what she might, the object responded to her consciousness, as if a moist human heart were in it" (189). More interestingly, for our purposes, the narrator repeatedly notes the propensity of the house to choke on its own effluvia. At one point, a violent windstorm drives the smoke from the chimney back in again, "choking the chimney's sooty throat with its own breath" (193). Then again, after the Judge's gurgling death, a blustery wind rattles the house, making "a vociferous but somewhat unintelligible bellowing in its sooty throat" (238). The parallels here between Pyncheon mansion and Pyncheon body are so pronounced as to be almost gratuitous, but Hawthorne makes his point: just as human bodies can be productively imagined as houses, so too can houses be seen as bodies. In some way or another, he suggests, domestic space reflects and responds to individual bodily experience.[23]

But how exactly? What is the nature of this relationship between house and body? To answer these questions, we need to turn again to the curious trope of the Pyncheon gurgle. Hawthorne uses the gurgle to establish a structural analogy between the Pyncheon house and the obstructed throat of the Judge. But aren't we simply talking about an analogy here, a metaphorical correspondence between the inside of the body and the inside of the home? In *Metaphors We Live By*, Lakoff and Johnson famously argue that human conceptual systems grow out of our embodied experience of the world. The metaphors we use to organize our thoughts, to structure our experience of the world, and to communicate with others, "arise from the fact that we have bodies of the sort we have and that they function as they do in our physical environment" (14). For instance, the experience of orienting our bodies in space—like Huntly in the cave (up-down, back-front, left-right, and so on)—provides us with conceptual categories that we can use to make meaning: "for example, HAPPY IS UP. The fact that the concept HAPPY is oriented UP leads to English expressions like 'I'm feeling *up* today.'" "Such metaphorical orientations are not arbitrary," Lakoff and Johnson insist, "they have a basis in our physical and cultural experience" (14).

One of the most fundamental, and therefore influential, examples of such "metaphorical orientation" is the category of what Lakoff and Johnson call the "container metaphor":

> We are physical beings, bounded and set off from the rest of the world by the surface of our skins, and we experience the rest of the world as outside us. Each of us is a container, with a bounding surface and an in-out orientation. We project our own in-out orientation onto other physical objects that are bounded by surfaces. Thus we also view them as containers with an inside and an outside. Rooms and houses are obvious containers. (29)

Our own sense of ourselves as a container, a vessel with an inside and an outside, allows us to "project" an inside-outside structure onto other objects. This is how we come to understand and experience other objects as containers. Such is the mechanism, I would suggest, that Hawthorne gestures toward with his fictional equation of houses and bodies. To his way of thinking, domestic space is not merely an arbitrary echo of the body's interiority, it is in fact a direct metaphorical (and therefore embodied) extension of it. The home, we might say, is a metaphor we live in.

The role of eating is crucial here, I believe, because it is the phenomenological process that most effectively establishes the initial sense of inside and outside, the notion of our body as a container. The visceral, or more properly, interoceptive sensations of chewing, swallowing, and digesting all contribute to the perception of an interior space within the body. We posit an inside and an outside because through alimentation we can literally feel the space inside of us, separated from the space outside by the container-boundary of our body. Maggie Kilgour elucidates this process in her analysis of eating and incorporation: "The model for the antithesis [of inside and outside] is based in bodily experience and the sense that what is 'inside' one's own body is a coherent structure that can be defined against what lies 'outside' of it" (4). Kilgour is following Freud who highlights the significance of the primary oral phase in distinguishing internal and external space: "Expressed in the language of the oldest, that is, of the oral, instinctual impulses, the alternative runs thus: 'I should like to eat that, or I should like to spit it out'; or, carried a stage further: 'I should like to take this into me and keep that out of me.' That is to say: it is to be either *inside* me or *outside* me."[24] The embodied experience of eating thus produces the experiential metaphor of the container. This metaphor, in turn, conditions our experience of domestic space: through it, we come to know the house as a "body" with its own internal space.[25]

Already we have seen that Hawthorne constructs the House of the Seven Gables in such a way as to emphasize its anatomical, anthropomorphic characteristics and, more specifically, to hint at its alimentary inclinations. But the novel's connection between eating and domestic space becomes most evident in its treatment of the architectural feature of the *threshold*. Again and again in the book, characters remark upon and are confronted by the thresholds of houses and of rooms, by that point of transition between inner and outer space. We might briefly recall, for example, the fraught moment at which Hepzibah finally opens her little cent-shop, an act which removes "the only barrier betwixt herself and the world" and which sends her weeping into the inner parlor of the house (37). That same door is marked by "the tinkling alarum" of a doorbell, an "ugly and spiteful little din" that sets "every nerve of [Hepzibah's] body in responsive and tumultuous vibration" (38). Earlier, when the town gathers to celebrate the original construction of Colonel Pyncheon's house, they are stopped at the ominous closed door of the Colonel's study (behind which his dead body awaits). There is too the fateful moment of Phoebe's arrival at the House of Seven Gables, in which she confronts Hepzibah at the "antique portal" of the front door. Hepzibah peers through the side-windows and discovers a "face to which almost any door would have opened of its own accord" (61). The image of the doorway is in fact so ubiquitous in the novel that it might almost be said that Hawthorne's domestic space is nothing but thresholds.

Indeed, such a claim begins to make more sense once we acknowledge the vital analogy linking thresholds with mouths. As with the mouth and the process of eating, the threshold is the structure that brings into being the possibility of an inner space. Martin Heidegger highlights this structuring power. "The threshold," he writes, " [. . .] sustains the middle in which the two, the outside and the inside, penetrate each other. The threshold bears the between. What goes out and goes in, in the between is joined in the between's dependability."[26] But the threshold not only joins inside and outside, it also establishes the very possibility of those two spaces. Like the tasting mouth, it separates what goes in from what stays out, delineating inner and outer space. Phenomenologist Richard Lang makes the connection between mouth and threshold explicit: "[The doorway] is the portal, resembling a mouth, through which outside and inside communicate." He goes on to elucidate the connection between the consuming body and the surrounding house: "Through incorporation, I have the very distinct experience of my home enveloping me as a kind of extended tissue of my own body. The home has been transformed into a region through which courses my life as it courses through my body" (204). For Lang, the processes of bodily incorporation and what we might call domestic incorporation constitute parallel economies. The home effectively "extends" the individual phenomenological experience of eating, and therefore of alimentary space, to the larger container-body of the house.

Hawthorne drives home the threshold-mouth analogy by persistently imaging food as the means of moving into and out of the space of the house. To the extent that Hepzibah opens up the mansion at all, she does so almost exclusively to facilitate the circulation of food. Ned Higgins and the foodstuffs available in the cent-shop are one example, but there are many others. In order to prepare Clifford's sumptuous breakfast, Hepzibah is forced to invite the fishmonger into the house. "With energetic raps at the shop-window, Hepzibah summoned the man in, and made purchase of what he warranted as the finest mackerel in his cart" (86). Late in the novel, when Hepzibah and Clifford have fled the horror of the Judge's death and the mansion is locked up tight, the townspeople who try to gain entrance are all interested in giving or taking away food. A frustrated housewife pounds on the doors trying to purchase some pork for her husband's breakfast. A well-meaning butcher does the same in the hopes of giving Hepzibah a choice "sweetbread of lamb" (250). The baker comes by, as does a "man of root beer." The cumulative effect of this gustatory circulation is to underscore the function of the house itself as a second, digestive body. Like the individual bodies to which it is linked, the home ingests objects and people. As such, it requires liminal spaces, "mouths" or "throats" like the cent-shop, in which inside and outside can be exchanged.

The relatively simple terms of this alimentary analogy, however, conceal a more complex set of implications. On one level, Hawthorne's equation of thresholds and mouths highlights the way in which our eating-inspired concept of space conditions our experience of the home: simply put, we understand and experience the home as an extended container-body because that is the organizing phenomenological concept provided to us by alimentation. What is perhaps less obvious, however, is that eating also enacts the *dissolution* of spatial boundaries. As both Kilgour and Freud point out, eating establishes the boundary between inside and outside by deciding what will come into the body and what will stay out, but it also demonstrates the porousness of that boundary. Eating is the process through which the external passes into the internal; in Levinasian terms, "nourishment [...] is the transmutation of the other into the same" (111).[27] In this way, eating simultaneously constructs and deconstructs the boundary between self and world.

The further implication, as Hepzibah's reluctant intercourse with the townsfolk makes clear, is that the house is an ineluctably social entity. According to Hawthorne, the space of the home cannot be understood in exclusively phenomenological terms. As was the case with Brockden Brown and tactile space, Hawthorne's domestic space emerges at the intersection of the phenomenological and the social. Like the body to which it is linked, the space of the home relies on the movement of objects and people into and out of its walls. These are the exchanges that both maintain and, paradoxically, dissolve the boundaries of the domestic sphere. Alimentation, whether of the body or of the home, thus includes both a self-possessive, individuating aspect as well as a relational, dialectical aspect; it is both phenomenological and social. Without such social exchange, domestic space loses any "sense" of interiority. That is, without any alimentary movement to distinguish the inside from the outside, the home can no longer be experienced as a self-contained space at all. Domestic space flattens out and collapses in on itself.

This, of course, is precisely what has been happening within the moribund walls of the House of the Seven Gables. Distinguished by its "long lapse of mortal life," the house serves mainly as a drafty tomb for the vanishing Pyncheon line (6). Clifford and Hepzibah remain trapped in the house for most of the novel, unable to initiate a healthy alimentary exchange with the outside world. The mansion's stubborn thresholds present an insurmountable obstacle to movement and circulation. "We are ghosts!" Clifford laments when the two of them attempt to leave the house and attend church one Sunday morning. "They pulled open the front-door, and stept across the threshold," but could not then take "one step further." Clifford correctly identifies their dilemma, linking the fate of their vanishing bodies to the social isolation of the house. "We have no right among human beings—no right anywhere, but in this old house, which has a curse on it, and which, therefore, we are doomed to haunt!" (146). The social and phenomenological exchange enacted through eating has reached a fateful impasse here. Since crossing the threshold sustains the internal-external distinction, sustains, in effect, domestic space, their own interior space is collapsing in on itself. Shrinking back into the entryway, "they found the whole interior of the house tenfold more dismal, and the air closer and heavier" (146). Denied the generative power of alimentary exchange, their bodies and their home are moving toward dissolution.

It is the curious dilemma of Judge Pyncheon, however, that best illustrates the pathological consequences, both phenomenological and social, of unsuccessful alimentary exchange. The Judge's frustrated movements in relation to the mansion's interior effectively enact the choked alimentation signaled by his hereditary gurgle. Blocked throats and blocked thresholds overlap as he is repeatedly denied entrance to the house. The

Judge wants inside, of course, so that he can interrogate Clifford about the location of a missing property deed, a document that the Judge believes will restore a vast tract of land to the Pyncheon family. But despite multiple attempts, the Judge is persistently arrested at, or in, the threshold itself. The very first time the Judge appears in the novel, for example, he is standing in the shadow of the Pyncheon elm, eyeing the house and preparing to enter the cent-shop. "But, as it chanced, his purpose was anticipated by Hepzibah's first customer, the little cannibal of Jim Crow" (52). Blocked by Little Ned, the Judge abandons his purpose and hurries off down the street.

This failure of access is repeated several times, most comically during his clumsy encounter with Phoebe. In this instance, he gains entrance to the cent-shop, but encounters a series of obstacles which again prevent his movement into the interior of the house. After grilling Phoebe for information, the Judge attempts to move forward. "But is Clifford in the parlor?" he asks, "I will just step in and see" (109). Phoebe counters by offering to call Hepzibah and then places herself between the Judge and "the private regions of the house" (110). Still moving toward the inside door, the Judge shoves her aside, exclaiming "I am at home here, Phoebe, you must recollect, and you are the stranger. I will just step in" (110). But before he can do so, he is once again obstructed, this time by a roused Hepzibah. "She now issued forth [. . .] to defend the entrance." "She made a repelling gesture with her hand, and stood a perfect picture of prohibition, at full length, in the dark frame of the door-way" (110). After a few more attempts to cross the threshold, all of which are stopped by either Hepzibah's body or Clifford's plaintive voice, the Judge retires in a rage.

Stopped precisely at the entrance to interior space, the Judge is unable to enact any sort of alimentary exchange. He can neither ingest anything himself (Phoebe or Clifford), nor can he be "ingested" into the domestic space of the house. As with the gurgle, alimentary exchange has been arrested here; only in this case, it is an entryway to the house, rather than the Judge's throat, that has become blocked. Hawthorne seems eager to emphasize the notion that the cent-shop is a liminal space, a dependable "between" in Heidegger's terms, that acts as a conduit between inside and outside. It is the last semipublic space before penetration into the actual "private regions of the house." It is also located in a "gray medium" between the fully lit outside world and dark spaces of the mansion. In short, the cent-shop functions as one of the house's "throats," and the Judge's stoppage here recapitulates a larger version of his own dysphagia. As goes the individual body, so goes the space of the home.

The analogy of mouth and threshold enacted by the Judge underscores the importance of eating and alimentation to Hawthorne's conception of domestic space. The house is experienced as an extended body, a phenomenological metaphor that echoes the alimentary space of the individual stomach. What is more, the novel hints at the ways in which this domestic interiority itself requires a kind of alimentation, a circulation of people and things into and out of the house. This gets at the nascent sociality of Hawthorne's model: without social exchange, without the threshold-crossing movement of insiders and outsiders, of self and other, there can be no distinction between internal and external, private and public.

In this way, Hawthorne's model of domestic space blends the phenomenological and the social in a fashion analogous to Brockden Brown's frontier space, where mobile bodies linked tactile experience to social circulation. But Hawthorne's account is ultimately pessimistic. Sensitive to the increasing antebellum anxiety engendered by such market circulation and social exchange, he focuses on a pathological version of domestic space, presenting a model of the alimentary home as it is choking and dying. Perhaps because of this, the social aspects of domestic space give ground to the more explicitly phenomenological concerns of embodied metaphor. His concern is more with dysphagia than with what a healthy exchange might look like. In order to better understand the social aspects of eating and domestic space, then, we will need to turn to *The Morgesons* and to Stoddard's more sanguine model of social alimentation.

Initially, it seems as if *The Morgesons* might forego the physiological analogy of house and body in favor of a more figurative parallel between house and psyche. Clearly, for Stoddard, domestic space serves as an index of female independence and self-autonomy. Houses and rooms reflect the degree to which female characters have achieved some measure of self-actualization and control over their own destiny. When, as a young woman, Cassandra decorates her own room, she does so in an elaborate fashion, opting for "blue chintz" upholstery, amber-painted walls, "shelves covered with blue damask," and a "wooden mantel shelf, originally painted in imitation of black marble." Here, the space of the home joins consumer appetites to a sense of self-possession: "It already seemed to me that I was like the room" (143). By appropriating goods made available by a new consumer economy (an economy with which her mercantilist father is deeply involved), Cassandra effectively outfits a room of her own.[28] She echoes these sentiments later in the novel when her newly married sister Veronica moves out of the family home. "The day they moved was a happy one for me. I was at last left alone in my own house, and I regained an absolute self-possession, and a sense of occupation I had long been a stranger to" (248). Owning a home and owning oneself are virtually synonymous experiences for Cassandra because, for her, domestic space is an extension of the self.

But the analogy of home and psychological self is only one aspect of Stoddard's treatment of domestic space. Like Hawthorne, she too is interested in linking the space of the home to the more overtly physiological characteristics of the alimentary body. In her case, however, she chooses to draw attention to the physical movements, the social flow, of people into and out of the dwelling. In *The Morgesons*, eating structures the space of the home by drawing people together within a tight sociospatial framework; in so doing, it produces an interior space distinct from the outside world. The need for food and the need for social interaction are conflated here as Stoddard reminds us that eating is not simply an isolated, individual phenomenological experience. It is also, necessarily, a process of relation and exchange with other bodies. The crucial connection between home and body still obtains in Stoddard's novel, but in this case the emphasis is on the home-body's continuous commerce with the other bodies circulating into and out of it.

More specifically, for Stoddard, the centripetal pull of domestic space is centered on the kitchen and dining rooms. The Morgeson dining room, we learn, is "large and central [. . .] a caravansary where people dropped in and out on their way to somewhere else" (24). The room draws not just family, but "infirm old ladies," sea-captains' wives, ministers, and "chance visitors," all who come for "dinner and supper" (22). During the preparations for her mother's funeral, Cassandra notes that the "the kitchen was the focus of interest [. . .] for meals were prepared at all hours for comers and goers" (209). And when young Cassy spends a year at her grandfather Warren's home, she notices a similar attractive force surrounding the well-room. "The well was so near the church that the house was used as an inn for the accommodation of the church-goers who lived at any distance [. . .]. A regular set took dinner with us." The well also functioned as "a watering-place for the Sunday-school scholars, who filed in troops before the pail in the well-room, and drank from the cocoanut dipper" (33). The alimentary centers of the house, those locations specifically associated with eating or drinking, direct the flow of people into and out of the domestic space.

In fact, such space seems to be produced by this very movement of consuming bodies. Stoddard's description recalls Henri Lefebvre's assertion that "space is social morphology: it is to lived experience what form itself is to the living organism" (94). According to Stoddard, when it comes to domestic space in particular, the most important aspect of lived experience is alimentation. Bodily needs map out a social morphology of the home. For the Morgeson family, home is characterized by the constant inflow and outflow of visitors, a circulation that mirrors the alimentary economy of the body. As with Hawthorne, there is a doubling here between individual experience and the house. Individual alimentary needs structure the larger domestic space in such a way as to mirror the economy of the individual stomach. The phenomenology of alimentation extends outward into space and then folds back into itself.

The relational, social quality of Stoddard's model distinguishes itself by virtue of its emphasis on visitation. The constant coming and going that is centered on the kitchen and dining room results in a more open and welcoming space than that of the hermetically sealed Pyncheon mansion. "When the want of society was felt," Cassandra tells us, "we sought the dining-room, sure of meeting others with the same want" (24). This openness leads her to observe that in the Morgeson house, "our most public moments were during meal-time" (24). Paradoxically, eating renders what should be the family's most private, inward-turning moment into a version of public exchange. In this way, we find a peculiar openness, a hospitality, at the center of the Morgeson's domestic interiority. Stoddard is gesturing to the ineluctably social characteristics of domestic space and she is doing so by demonstrating that eating enacts the same sort of paradoxical relation with the outside world. That is, the experience of one's own body and one's own house as interiorized spaces distinct from an exterior world, absolutely requires an openness to, and exchange with, that externality.[29]

Both Hawthorne and Stoddard, then, capitalize on the productive metaphorical overlap between houses and bodies that was so familiar to nineteenth-century diet reformers. The two authors use this analogy to explore the ways in which the phenomenology of eating structures our experience of domestic space. The home, they suggest, extends the interiority of the alimentary body by continually enacting a process of ingestion and expulsion, a process that effectively instantiates a boundary, albeit a permeable one, between inside and outside. But what, we might ask, does this alimentary production of domestic space have to do with our larger investigation of ownership and property? How does it relate to the earlier discussion of alimentary possession? Hawthorne and Stoddard understand eating to be a form of "enjoyment," a primordial "possession without acquisition" that sets the stage for more familiar forms of appropriation. For them, as for Locke, eating represents the "beginning of property." But how, then, does our alimentary account of domestic space contribute to this property discussion?

Again, it is Levinas who suggests an answer. If eating is "possession without acquisition," Levinas argues, possession itself, that is, possession *with* acquisition, is something that can only occur through the medium of the dwelling. The home establishes a relation with "a world to be possessed, to be acquired, to be rendered *interior*" (157). The sensual enjoyment of "the element," the possession without acquisition that occurs when we eat, is suspended and delayed by the space of the home. The "I" is able to step back and "recollect" itself, separate itself from the world. "The movement by which a being builds its home, opens and ensures interiority to itself, is constituted in a movement by which the separated being recollects itself" (157). At the same time that the home provides a space for this self-conscious recollection, however, it also provides a space for collection: the home allows an individual to hold and possess, rather than immediately enjoy, the element. Within the dwelling, "The uncertain future of the element is suspended. The element is fixed between the four walls of the home, is calmed in possession. It appears there as a thing, which can, perhaps, be defined by tranquillity—as in a "still life" (158). This tranquillity is the central quality that distinguishes possession proper from mere enjoyment. "Possession removes being from change," Levinas explains. "Possession masters, suspends, postpones the unforeseeable future of the element" (160, 158). In a manner that evokes the Heideggerian emphasis on "preserving," Levinas maintains that the space of the home functions as a gathering place, a place of re-collection, both for the individual subject and for the newly "suspended" possessions that have been removed from the element.[30]

In a particularly apropos image, Levinas describes possession proper as an act in which the hand "gathers the fruit but holds it far from the lips, keeps it, puts it in reserve, possesses it in a home" (161). The act of eating and enjoyment, of alimentary possession, is postponed in order to bring about a durable good, an object that persists over time and that rests in the space of the home.[31] Hawthorne and Stoddard, I submit, are intrigued by something very like this Levinasian postponement. Their interest in the origins of domestic space calls attention to its arresting, or "tranquilizing," characteristics. In both novels, possession is linked to the accumulative capabilities inherent in a suspended domestic "still-life." Alimentation and enjoyment is essential, they suggest, to the organization and experience of domestic space, but once established, that same domestic space then enables possession. It allows us to have and to hold objects that we would otherwise simply consume and enjoy.

We have already seen Stoddard equate ownership of a room and of a house with an increased sense of *self*-possession. But there is also a way in which her domestic spaces highlight the accumulative, "collecting" potential central to the notion of possession proper. Cassandra's elaborately furnished room is packed with "too many things": cabinets, stuffed chairs, a table, a lush carpet, curtains, "a long mirror," the decorative mantel (143, 136). This plenitude is matched in her sister Veronica's bedroom, a boudoir "like no other place." "A table stood near the window, methodically covered with labelled blank-books, a morocco portfolio, and a Wedgewood inkstand and vase" (134). Her bed is flanked by hanging shelves covered with books and her closet contains "drawers and boxes for everything which pertained to a wardrobe" (135). Nor is the Morgeson family alone in its domestic accumulation. Later in the novel, Cassandra makes an extended visit to the home of her old school friend Ben Somers. The Somers clan pride themselves on their aristocratic lineage and on their preeminent standing among the Puritan blue bloods of Belem, Massachusetts. That wealth is reflected in a bewildering clutter of goods: "The room, vast and dark, was a complete litter of tables and sofas. The tables were loaded with lamps, books, and knick-knacks of every description; the sofas were strewn with English and French magazines, novels, and papers" (162). For Stoddard, the space of the home is a space for gathering, a place in which possessions are collected and held over time.

Of course, one can and should read this profusion of material goods as a reflection of the burgeoning consumer culture of mid-nineteenth-century America. But there is also a way in which Stoddard is specifically underscoring a static accumulation here, a suspended collection of goods that comes to rest in the home. There is a sense of "too many things," a sense that the home gathers and gathers without ever really consuming or using the objects. Significantly, Stoddard's emphasis seems to activate the less familiar etymological connotations implicit in the terms "housekeeping" and "household." Domestic space, she suggests, is inextricably bound to the notion of appropriation, to the keeping and holding of objects that might otherwise be lost to enjoyment.[32]

Hawthorne, for his part, takes this same notion of domestic suspension and amplifies it, ultimately making it a central theme of his novel. The Pyncheon mansion is distinguished by its suspended internal existence: time has ground to a halt within its walls and the detritus of family history fills its rooms. Hepzibah's life for the past thirty years has been frozen among the "ghosts and ghostly reminiscences" that people the house (64). Clifford, returned from his exile in prison, exists in a kind of "suspended animation" (139). The furniture, the interior decor, the mundane objects of domestic existence, all of these things remain collected within the walls of the mansion, material emblems of time at a standstill. Hawthorne's house, it seems, embodies not just a spatial dysphagia but a temporal one as well.

Hawthorne's fascination with this sort of Levinasian postponement manifests itself via a persistent narrative emphasis on the figure of the heirloom. Heirlooms, of course, are objects that remain within a given house (whether that house be genealogical or architectural) over long periods of time. In this way, they objectify the static, suspended qualities that characterize Levinasian domestic space. The heirloom marks the capacity of a house to hold or keep things over time, to make goods "durable," that is, finally, to make possession possible. *The House of the Seven Gables* is replete with heirloom objects, from the ancient "Cookery Book," with which Hepzibah prepares Clifford's breakfast, to the old "china tea-set" passed down from Phoebe's "great-great-great-great-grandmother," to Alice Pyncheon's haunted harpsichord (86, 68). Indeed, even the house chickens exemplify the heirloom link between domestic space and duration through time. "An immemorial heirloom in the Pyncheon family," the birds are kept in the mansion's central garden, "hindered from escape by buildings, on three sides, and the difficult peaks of a wooden fence on the other" (130). Here, in the enclosed domestic space of the garden, the "immemorial" breed has come to rest, enjoying a kind of suspended existence in which past and present collapse into each other. And although the chickens themselves are potentially food for the family, instead of being consumed, they remain in stasis, held "far from the lips," put in reserve, and possessed in the home.

Perhaps the most significant heirloom in the book is the glowering portrait of old Colonel Pyncheon that hangs on the wall of the gloomy parlor. A symbol both of the family's history and its hereditary guilt, the portrait signals the unchanging nature of domestic space and time. The same issues and concerns that confronted the Colonel continue to exert an influence on the lives of Hepzibah and Clifford. Like the painting itself, the past endures; it waits, suspended. But, as we learn at the end of the book, the painting also conceals an old Indian property deed that bestows a vast tract of land in Maine to the Pyncheon family. In other words, Hawthorne carefully links the defining Pyncheon heirloom to an act of possession. Read figuratively, the image seems to suggest that the secret to possession resides at the center of the home. There, literally suspended, is the heirloom, an object that testifies to the arresting, gathering capabilities of domestic space. If eating's transitory "possession without acquisition" is to transform into possession proper, Hawthorne implies, it must do so by putting things in domestic reserve.

Both novelists, then, hint at the crucial role played by domestic space in our experience of possession. The "four walls of the home," they suggest, constitute a space of postponement and delay, a space in which "the element," to use Levinas's term, is no longer immediately enjoyed, but rather put into reserve. At the same time, they reveal how such space is organized and understood through a phenomenology of eating, through, that is, a process of differentiating inside from outside. And so, just as tactile sensation delineated an intimate space of possession for Brockden Brown, here gustatory sensation expands the radius of possessive space to encompass the "possession proper" of the home. Of course, Hawthorne and Stoddard are not alone in their focus on eating: they are actively reworking the alimentary discourses of nineteenth-century diet reformers, energetic activists who are themselves attuned to the social and political potential for change residing in the stomach. This context of diet reform will prove especially important to the novelists as they go on to consider the difference between the individual experience of possession and the social exchange that is private property.

Mother's Milk: Private Property and the Feminine Economy of the Gift

The only gift is a portion of thyself. Thou must bleed for me.
—RALPH WALDO EMERSON, "GIFTS"

Up to this point, we have been conceiving of possession largely as a relationship between persons and things, that is, as an individual phenomenology of appropriation in which a single subject experiences the process of coming to own a thing. Through the mechanism of alimentation, the novels suggest, an individual gradually separates himself from sensual absorption in the world; he gradually develops a sense of himself distinct from "the element" and then takes possession of that self. At the same time, alimentation bequeaths a sense of inside and outside, and the intimate space of the home then comes into being as an extension of this interiority. Finally, this intimate space of "recollection" enables the individual to set things aside, to put them in reserve, in short, to own them.

Once an individual has begun to gather possessions in this way, however, those objects then become available for exchange. Suddenly, what was initially a relationship between persons and things now has the potential to become a relationship between people. This moment, then, is a crucial point of contact between an individual phenomenology of possession and a larger, social and discursive instantiation of ownership. This is the point at which "making something mine" places me in a position of potential conflict vis-à-vis other members of society: they may contest what I claim as my own. What I would like to suggest, following Levinas, is that this move to social relations and exchange is precisely the move from possession to property. In effect, possessions become property the moment they begin to circulate. Levinas explains:

> Property alone institutes permanence in the pure quality of enjoyment, but this permanence disappears forthwith in the phenomenality reflected in money. As property, merchandise, bought and sold, a thing is revealed in the market as susceptible of belonging, being exchanged, and accordingly as convertible into money, susceptible of dispersing in the anonymity of money. But possession itself refers to more profound metaphysical relations. A thing does not resist acquisition; the other possessors—those whom one cannot possess—contest and therefore can sanction possession itself. Thus the possession of things issues in a discourse. (162)

When things are removed from "the pure quality of enjoyment," they become possessions within the home. But immediately, "forthwith," they are revealed to be "susceptible of belonging, being exchanged, and [...] convertible into money." That is, they are in danger of becoming mobile "property" or "merchandise, bought and sold." Possessions, by contrast, "refer to more profound metaphysical relations," in short, to the phenomenological relationship between person and thing. At the same time, however, the notion of possession requires the presence of "other possessors," those who can contest, enable, and "sanction" possession itself. Making something mine would be a meaningless act without other possessors who could potentially own that same something. In this way, although possession is distinct from the socio-discursive phenomenon of private property, it necessarily includes within it the potential for social exchange. In Levinas's formulation, possession "issues in a discourse."[33]

Hawthorne and Stoddard, of course, are acutely aware of the social and discursive aspects of property. Such, after all, is the increasingly familiar model of abstract ownership that has been gaining ground among Anglo-American legal theorists since the eighteenth century. Moreover, as we have seen—and as many critics have pointed out—both novelists are closely attuned to the growing cultural anxiety associated with this abstraction: namely, the fear that market capitalism and its anonymous commodities threaten to unravel the social fabric.[34] Consider, for example, Hepzibah's agonized decision to abandon her aristocratic past and become a cent-shop merchant. "In this republican country," Hawthorne explains, "amid the fluctuating waves of our social life, somebody is always at the drowning point" (35). Or, in Stoddard's case, there is Cassandra's father, a speculator in mercantile trade whose "business fluctuates like quicksilver" and whose fortunes eventually collapse (220). But this anxiety about mobile commodities and market capitalism does not supersede the novelists' interest in the alimentary underpinnings of possession. On the contrary, Hawthorne and Stoddard are intent upon demonstrating the ways in which alimentary possession undergirds, and indeed, influences, more familiar notions of property as social exchange. To their way of thinking, the social practice of private property, just like the individual experiences of self-possession and possession, depends upon the phenomenological substratum of alimentation. Simply put, the experience of eating continues to condition the circulations of property exchange.

Eating functions for these authors as more than a simple metaphor for a consumer economy. The act of alimentation is also itself a literal means of exchange between self and other, between interior and exterior spaces. Indeed, we might say that eating constitutes the primordial exchange, the inaugural relation between child-self and mother-Other. As such, the act of alimentation looms large in any attempt to understand more complicated systems of human commerce. Hawthorne and Stoddard, I believe, are particularly sensitive to this deep-seated connection between eating and property exchange. Their texts reveal the extent to which the mechanisms of bodily alimentation can be read into the circulations of property. What is more, the texts foreground the pivotal role that domestic space plays in mediating this relationship between eating and mobile property. Their two novels, I want to argue, suggest that the home is a privileged site for the construction and maintenance of two alternative versions of property exchange: the commodity and the gift. Domestic space is the matrix in which these two contrasting economies vie for the upper hand. Put another way, the acts of alimentation that occur within the home work to reinforce a particular form of property exchange. Significantly, both authors suggest that these two economies, commodity and gift, are closely tied to masculine and feminine gender roles: while Hawthorne laments the pathologies of the "masculine" market, Stoddard does him one better and uncovers the radical potential of a "feminine" gift-economy. In both cases, however, it is alimentary exchange that provides the key.

Perhaps not surprisingly, the cultural context of diet reform once again provides an essential touchstone here for the two authors. Sylvester Graham, in particular, serves as a crucial backdrop because he so clearly distinguished what he saw as the nurturing, maternal space of the home from the corrosive, corrupting influence of the market. In order to do so, he called popular attention to an unlikely cause célèbre: whole-wheat bread. In a spirited, almost fanatical, defense of traditional bread making that would help cement his reputation as the "prophet of bran bread and pumpkins," Graham extolled the virtues of homemade bread, particularly, bread made by caring mothers in the kitchen. There are, he makes clear, few issues of greater moment: "There are probably few people in civilized life, who [. . .] would not say, that they consider bread one of the most, if not the most important article of diet which enters into the food of man" (*Bread* v). Indeed, for Graham, the baking and eating of good bread has consequences that reverberate not just within the body, but within the family, and then within the nation. Wives and mothers need to understand the importance of good bread "in relation to all the bodily and intellectual and moral interests of their husbands and children, and in relation to the domestic and social and civil welfare of mankind, and to their religious prosperity, both for time and eternity" (106).

But it is Graham's insistence on the distinctly domestic and maternal components of good bread that most merits our attention. Public bakers, he warns us, regularly adulterate the bread with unwholesome "chemical agents" calculated to make it whiter, or lighter, or sweeter to the taste. Using "alum, sulphate of zinc, sub-carbonate of magnesia, sub-carbonate of ammonia, sulphate of copper," and "even chalk, pipe clay and plaster of Paris," unscrupulous bakers routinely deceive their customers, all in order "to increase the lucrativeness of their business" (43–44).[35] The depredations of these market capitalists, however, are for Graham in stark contrast to the selfless, nurturing care provided by America's baking mothers.

> It is the wife, the mother only—she who loves her husband and her children as woman ought to love, and who rightly perceives the relations between the dietetic habits and physical and moral condition of her loved ones, and justly appreciates the importance of good bread to their physical and moral welfare—she alone it is, who will be ever inspired by that cordial and unremitting affection and solicitude which will excite the vigilance, secure the attention, and prompt the action requisite to success, and essential to the attainment of that maturity of judgment and skilfulness of operation, which are the indispensable attributes of a perfect bread-maker. (105–6)

It is maternal love, then, a love "as woman ought to love," that is crucial to the physical and moral welfare of the family and the nation. Of course, Graham also emphasizes the importance of using hand-ground flour or Indian meal, and of producing the bread "within the precincts of our own domestic thresholds" (49). But it is the near-mystical quality of maternal care that he obsessively repeats. "The best bread-makers I have ever known," he effuses, "watch over their bread troughs while their dough is rising, and over their ovens while it is baking, with about as much care and attention as a mother watches over the cradle of her sick child" (97). In fact, anything less bespeaks a certain "sluttishness" in the preparation (101).[36]

Initially, Graham's exhortations seem to reflect an especially pronounced version of the separate spheres ideology. He imagines a clear divide here between the greedy, self-interested actions of commercial bakers and the self-sacrificing, family-saving labors of solicitous mothers and wives. Men, it seems, make their way in the bruising, depraved world of the market, and women preserve a nurturing haven at home. But, upon closer consideration, the social and political significance of Graham's work seems more ambivalent. On the one hand, he presents a pointed critique of market capitalism: without the humanizing moral influence of the domestic sphere, he suggests, the atomizing, alienating market will poison personal, familial, and finally civic relationships. It is this aspect of Graham's work that has led some historians to characterize his ideas as "a declaration of physical independence from the capitalist marketplace" (Nissenbaum 127). By detaching consumption from the excesses of the market, Graham looks to return economic and moral power to families and individuals. His efforts, the thinking goes, are part of a larger reform movement that attempts to constrain bourgeois consumerism: "'Temperance, vegetarianism, and purity become rallying cries for groups attempting to control the disturbing appetites of the middle class" (Burbick 57).

On the other hand, Graham's critique reaffirms the problematic gender distinctions endemic to the ideology of the separate spheres. The principal role for women, he makes clear, is as cooks and caregivers, nurturing mothers whose primary sphere of influence is in the kitchen. Indeed, Graham's treatise on bread making is explicitly nostalgic, wistfully hearkening back to an imagined past in which women dutifully fulfilled their culinary obligations. "Who that can look back thirty or forty years to those blessed days of New England's prosperity and happiness, when our good mothers used to make the family bread, but can well remember how long and how patiently those excellent matrons stood over their bread troughs, kneading and moulding their dough?" (92–93). Ultimately, historians tend to emphasize these conservative retro-politics over Graham's more subversive critiques of capitalism. Nissenbaum, for example, concedes that what was born "in an effort to resist and deny the reality of marketplace capitalism [. . .] ended by reinforcing that reality" (137). And Burbick goes so far as to suggest that Graham's fanatical ideas about bread making "implicitly [attack] the traditional caretakers of the body, that is, women" (85).

The ambivalent significations of Graham's work provide a rich context for Hawthorne and Stoddard to engage and adapt. It seems clear, for instance, that both authors subscribe to some version of Graham's anti-market sensibility. Hepzibah's plight, that is, her precarious economic position "at the drowning point," seems to reflect a deep distrust on Hawthorne's part of the mercurial forces of the market. Judge Pyncheon serves as a frightening illustration of the dangers of intemperance and greedy overconsumption: he epitomizes the "hard and grasping spirit" in the Pyncheon blood and, as a result, stands in for a nineteenth-century consumerist zeitgeist. At the same time, we should note Phoebe's peculiar penchant for domestic ministry. She renovates the moribund Pyncheon mansion with "a kind of natural magic," an ability to "give a look of comfort and habitableness to any place" (64). And she displays a conspicuously Grahamite flair for kitchen work. When Hepzibah is preparing Clifford's welcome-home breakfast, she enlists Phoebe's aid. "The country girl [. . .] proposed to make an Indian cake, after her mother's peculiar method, of easy manufacture, and which she could vouch for as possessing a richness, and, if rightly prepared, a delicacy, unequalled by any other mode of breakfast-cake" (86). The recipe sounds as if it has been directly lifted from Graham's treatise, and with it Hawthorne underscores the distinction between Phoebe's selfless domestic efforts and the Judge's avaricious consumerism.

Stoddard's distrust of the market emerges in her description of Locke Morgeson's mercantile fortunes. After enjoying an early prosperity, his business ventures wobble and then fall, leaving him and his family deeply in debt. "My business fluctuates like quicksilver," he tells Cassandra, "and it is enormously extended" (220); she later learns that he "had been insolvent for five years" (231). The financial collapse throws the family into disarray: servants are let go, consumption is curtailed in favor of an "old-fashioned asceticism," and Cassandra is forced to take over a number of household duties (224). As in Hawthorne, market instability and overconsumption threaten to ruin domestic tranquility. Against the dangers of the market, Stoddard proposes a generous, supportive economy of maternal provision and care. Temperance, the family's cook and surrogate mother, hints at the Grahamite roots of this maternal economy while they are all traveling in Boston. In the parlor of their boarding house, they encounter three "cadaverous" missionary children hungrily devouring some bread. Temperance is aghast at their deprived state. "Good Lord!" she exclaims, "what bread those children are eating! It is made of sawdust" (65). For Stoddard, as for Graham, maternal neglect is typified by the image of unwholesome bread.

Initially, then, it may seem that Hawthorne and Stoddard respond to increasing market anxieties in the same way: that is, they both look to the Graham-esque tableau of the woman in the home as a bulwark against economic uncertainty and moral dissolution. In so doing, they seem to reinforce, or at least accept, the problematic gender divide implicit in Graham and the separate spheres ideology. Women, they imply, belong in the kitchen; it is from this space that they can best maintain a safe haven from the excesses of the market. But this reading of Hawthorne and Stoddard, I believe, ignores crucial distinctions in their respective reactions to the perceived problem of market encroachment. In fact, it is precisely their *divergent* responses that best reveal each author's view of eating-inflected property exchange. Hawthorne, for his part, does indeed look to domestic ideology, and more specifically, to the sustenance-providing female, as a means of countering the market. But his approach is not as simple as opposing the haven of the home to the depredations of the market. Instead, he imagines (albeit problematically) a reconciliation of market and home in which Phoebe extends her salutary influence even to the public circulations of market exchange. Stoddard, by contrast, explores a more radical challenge to the economic status quo. Rather than using the woman in the home as a means of reinforcing or enabling commodity capitalism, she locates in her the potential for an alternative, gift-based economy. Property exchange, she suggests, need not be limited to the quid pro quo commerce of consumer capitalism. There is, in the figure of the nurturing mother, the potential for a very different sort of "feminine" economy.

In *The House of the Seven Gables*, the most obvious threat of market incursion into the home occurs in the form of Hepzibah's cent-shop. The tiny store marks the interpenetration of private and public, domestic and commercial. Hepzibah, of course, is appalled at these circumstances, appalled that in her poverty she must be "transformed" from "the patrician lady [...] into the plebeian woman" (35). Nor does it seems that she will be able to manage this transformation very successfully. Her business and customer service skills are atrocious: she fails to stock any of the thread, tobacco, root beer, or yeast that customers desire. A frustrated housewife takes Hepzibah to task for this last omission. "A cent-shop, and no yeast!" she explodes. "That will never do! Who ever heard of such a thing? Your loaf will never rise, no more than mine will today. You had better shut up shop at once!" (48). Significantly, Hepzibah and her shop fail to facilitate the quintessential domestic duty of bread making. As of yet, there is no successful reconciliation of market and home.

That all changes, of course, when Phoebe arrives on the domestic scene. The epitome of the domestic ideal, Phoebe is endowed with quasi-supernatural powers of homemaking; it doesn't take Hepzibah long to figure out that Phoebe is better suited to running the shop than she will ever be. "What a nice little housewife you are!" Hepzibah exclaims. "Do you do other things as well?" (68). She does. In particular, she applies her impressive domestic skills to harmonizing home and market. She enables the circulations of market exchange to peacefully coexist within the domestic sphere. "I have done all the shopping for the family at our village store," Phoebe assures Hepzibah. "And have had a table at a fancy fair, and made better sales than anybody." Then, crucially, she makes it clear that these commercial skills grow out of a properly gendered domestic upbringing. "These things are not to be learnt; they depend upon a knack that comes, I suppose [. . .] with one's mother's blood. You shall see I am as nice a little saleswoman as I am a housewife" (69). And indeed, this proves to be the case. Phoebe's effervescent personality is perfectly suited to customer service; she accurately advises Hepzibah on "various methods whereby the influx of trade might be increased, and rendered profitable, without a hazardous outlay of capital," and, most importantly, she knows how to "manufacture yeast," how to "brew a certain kind of beer, nectareous to the palate, and of rare stomachic virtues," and how to "bake and exhibit for sale some little spice-cakes, which whosoever tasted would longingly desire to taste again" (70). In short, Phoebe adapts the qualities of the ideal homemaker, the sustenance-providing mother, to the exigencies of market capitalism.

Graham, however, would not be pleased. Although Hawthorne clearly evokes the cherished image of the bread-making mother infusing her "little spice-cakes" with maternal love, he also capitulates to the selfish interests of the market. According to Graham, good bread, wholesome bread, should stay within the home because it is only a mother's love and care that can invest it with the necessary nutrients. Once bread begins to be bought and sold, it loses that "natural sweetness and richness" (93). Indeed, Phoebe's role as a commercial whiz might be understood as a particular perversion of Graham's vision. Instead of providing the selfless maternal nutriment expected of mothers, Phoebe actually takes to selling gingerbread to little Ned Higgins. What should be a benevolent exchange, the archetypal gift of food between a woman and a child, here becomes yet another profit-making transaction. Hawthorne, it seems, has literally sold out motherhood, replacing the sacrosanct mother in the kitchen with a smiling simulacrum in the cent-shop.

The effect of this substitution is to undercut Hawthorne's critique of the market. Having pathologized the vicissitudes of capitalism and exposed the excesses of consumerism, Hawthorne here suggests that, in fact, the market can be reconciled with the nurturing space of the home. By applying the characteristics of domestic care to the sphere of commerce, Hawthorne implies, we can mitigate the corrosive influence of capitalism. In effect, Hawthorne seems to advocate a species of accommodationism: given the proper kind of commerce, capitalist consumption and moral health can coexist. (It is perhaps telling that the end of the novel removes Phoebe from her commercial career and places her back at the center of a traditional family home with Holgrave as her husband. By so doing, Hawthorne backs away from his accommodationism, restoring the more comfortable division between private and public, domestic and commercial.)

Stoddard, by contrast, is much less interested in accommodation. Her response to the rising influence of the market is not to imagine ways in which its values might be amicably reconciled with the values of the domestic, "feminine" sphere. Nor does she adopt the conventional separate spheres opposition of protected home and corrosive market.[37] Instead, she turns to the home itself, to the figure of the mother and to the practice of feeding, in order to uncover the outlines of an alternative economy, an alternative form of property exchange at odds with commodity capitalism.

Before we attend to the subversive potential of Stoddard's maternal economy, it is important to note that many of the mothers in her novel are far from nurturing and supportive. On the contrary, they are often portrayed as pathological figures who not only fail to feed their children properly, but who threaten outright violence. Over the course of the book, Cassandra makes three extended visits away from home, each of which involves an encounter with a surrogate mother-figure. The first visit is to her grandfather Warren's silent house, where there is no living grandmother, only the hapless figure of Aunt Merce. The second visit is as a teenager to the house of Charles and Alice Morgeson. Here, Cassandra and Charles fall in love, but before they can consummate their affair, they are involved in a carriage accident which kills Charles and injures Cassandra. Wife Alice performs the role of the dutiful mother and cares for Cassandra as she recuperates. Significantly, however, her maternal attention takes on a decidedly sadistic tone. In a bizarre scene of nutritional deprivation, Alice refuses to feed her bedridden patient the chicken broth she requires. Alice forces her to wait an hour before bringing in the soup at all and when she finally does, it is a "thin, impoverished liquid." "There is no chicken in it," Cassandra complains, to which Alice responds, "I took it out." Cassandra bursts into tears and Alice ultimately relents, bringing her a bit of meat, but to Cassandra's eyes, it is "an infinitesimal portion" (124). Whether Alice's actions are a kind of sublimated revenge for the affair, this odd exchange reads as a symbolic inversion of maternal self-sacrifice: instead of the nurturing plenitude of mother's milk, Alice offers the child only a thin gruel.[38]

Cassandra's third visit is to the Somers home in Belem. In Mrs. Somers, she encounters a mother fiercely protective of her family wealth; the woman immediately suspects Cassandra to be a gold digger in pursuit of her sons. Cassandra does eventually fall for Desmond, and he for her, but during the course of her stay in the Somers house, Cassandra is gradually made aware of Mrs. Somers's diabolical character. Desmond himself describes the family as "a devil's household," explaining to Cassandra that they are all afraid of his imperious mother (191). And her devilry, Stoddard implies, is linked to the mistreatment of children. The first night that Cassandra spends in the Somers house, for instance, she is kept awake by the "wail of a young child," a "continued crying, which [she] could not locate" (169). When she finally does encounter the baby, "puny and anxious-looking," it is set out on the dining table during a dinner party, where "its energies were absorbed in swallowing its fists and fretfully crying" (169). Stoddard's language and imagery suggest a disturbing maternal apathy: the crying child has been reduced to chewing on its own fists in a futile attempt to receive the sustenance its mother has not provided it. In a moment of candor, Ben offers a potential explanation for his mother's cruelty: "the part of us which is Pickersgill hates its like" (172). A few months later, the baby is dead.[39]

Stoddard's depiction of maternal pathology is carefully linked to financial greed or to participation in the market itself. After Charles's death, Alice immediately decides that she will take over management of his cotton mills. "I am changed," she tells Cassandra. "When perhaps I should feel that I have done with life, I am eager to begin it" (125). But this is the very same conversation during which Alice tortures Cassandra by withholding food. Maternal self-sacrifice, it seems, falls victim to the self-absorption associated with market capitalism. Likewise, Mrs. Somers is the acknowledged steward of her family's wealth. She brought it with her into the family, and she is intent upon parsimoniously managing its disbursement. Her emasculated, bedridden husband is "endowed only with the privilege of settling her taxes" (169). Unlike Hawthorne, when Stoddard brings domestic "femininity" into contact with the market, the result is not a productive reconciliation of the two spheres. Rather, it is an erosion of maternal care, a wearing away of the alimentary bonds that link mother and child. While market involvement may make a certain model of selfhood more readily available to property-holding women, that selfhood comes at a cost. Women are drawn, or better yet interpellated, into a more conventionally masculine model of the self: aggressive, self-absorbed, and capable of violence.

Against this corrosive influence, against these seeming perversions of maternal feeding, Stoddard entertains the possibility of a subtle, but significant, revaluation of the maternal economy itself. That is, she turns away from the circulations of market exchange and looks instead toward the circulations of property within the home. In the primordial exchange of food between mother and child, Stoddard locates an alternative relationship, a gift-based economy predicated on a different set of values than those of market capitalism. Stoddard shifts the focus away from self-absorbed possessive individualism and toward an ethic of generosity. She does so by contrasting the destructive alimentary relationships enacted by Alice and Mrs. Somers with a network of female caregivers, solicitous feeders who surround and nurture both Cassandra and her siblings.[40]

The primary figures in this alimentary network are the two family cooks, Temperance Tinkham and Hepsey Curtis. Temperance is the envy of the town, a prized chef who lavishes "fresh waffles," "apple-fritters," and "buttered shortcake" on Mrs. Morgeson's tea circle (19). But her central role is as personal diet coach for the anorexic Veronica. She continually encourages Veronica to eat more than the meager bread and toast on which she prefers to snack. "Do eat your supper" becomes a kind of mantra characterizing the relationship between the two (13). Likewise, when the infant Arthur falls asleep at the table, "she drum[s] on his plate with a spoon" to make sure he eats (51). Temperance stands in here for the distant mothers in the book who fail to provide their children with the necessary sustenance. Hepsey, for her part, is perpetually kneading dough, preparing preserves, sugaring doughnuts and, above all, making sure that Cassandra has all she can eat. When Cassy returns from the year-long stay at her grandfather's house, for example, Hepsey's first response is to prepare a massive dinner: "I have made an Indian bannock for you, and we are going to have broiled sword-fish, besides, for supper. Is it best to cook more, Mrs. Morgeson, now that Cassandra has come?" (50). Indeed, it is Hepsey's generosity that Cassandra fondly recalls while staying with Charles and Alice: "Hepsey is a good woman, mother; do give my love to her [. . .] she was always making up some nice dish; tell her I remember it, will you?" (71).

In contrast to the parsimony of Alice and Mrs. Somers, then, Hepsey and Temperance enact a nurturing alimentary economy of generosity and giving. Whereas the biological mothers in the novel provide only the barest minimum of emotional support—always absent, distant, or otherwise occupied—and only the paltriest physical sustenance for their daughters, the two cooks are images of maternal plenitude, crying over, caring for, and constantly feeding Cassy and Veronica.[41] This is a Graham-esque economy of self-sacrifice: indeed, at one point, Temperance is actually "mixing dough" and crying with happiness over Cassandra's return (128). The image is telling in that it conflates emotional investment with food production. These two kinds of maternal support are closely linked in the book and offered up as a kind of gift economy. Hepsey and Temperance, that is, foster an exchange of goods that foregoes the capitalist inclinations of Alice and Mrs. Somers, and that echoes instead the primordial gift of mother's milk to the child. (Temperance, we learn, regularly provides Veronica with glasses "full of milk" to go with her diet of toast [239].)

Of course, Hepsey and Temperance are both paid employees of the Morgesons, a fact that initially seems to undercut their status as selfless caregivers: If they are paid for their services, to what extent can this relationship constitute a gift economy? But Stoddard seems to anticipate this very question, going to great lengths to represent the two women's commitment to the family in emotional rather than financial terms. They fulfill the conventional role of the mother, caring for the sisters when they fall ill, piercing ears, worrying over hair, and crying over absences. During one of Veronica's illnesses, for example, Cassandra finds Temperance "tucking the clothes about her, kissing her, and calling her 'deary and her best child'" (147). Later, Temperance marries, comes into her own modest fortune, and leaves the Morgesons for a while, only to return for good and without pay. "I know that I am needed," Temperance explains, "but you mustn't say a word about pay—I can't stand it" (236). For Stoddard, at any rate, Hepsey and Temperance transcend the selfish circuits of a market economy and offer themselves as maternal surrogates, emblems of a generous gift exchange.[42]

Hélène Cixous highlights the subversive potential of such a gift economy, calling particular attention to its gendered aspects. In *The Newly*

Born Woman, Cixous argues that capitalist economies are motivated by a particularly masculine "fear of expropriation, of separation, of losing the attribute" (80). Participants valorize the self and all its attributes and obsessively seek to retain them. The flip side of this fear is a desire for appropriation, a desire to master and possess those things that elude the self. This desire undergirds all economies of the "*propre*," that is, all economies based on the possession and exchange of private property (79). As a result, the masculine inclination is only to *give* property in the knowledge that you will get something in return. This is gift-as-commodity. But there is another version of the gift, one that traces out a distinctively feminine economy. "All the difference lies in the why and how of the gift, in the values that the gesture of giving affirms, causes to circulate; in the type of profit the giver draws from the gift and the use to which he or she puts it" (87). For the man, "loss and expense are stuck in the commercial deal that always turns the gift into a gift-that-takes. The gift brings in a return." But the woman, "with open hands, gives herself [. . .]. She doesn't try to 'recover her expenses.' She is able not to return to herself" (87). This is the "economy of femininity," "the relationship to the other in which the gift doesn't calculate its influence" (92).

The foundational relationship for Cixous's feminine economy is the gift-relation between mother and child, particularly, the connection established through the gift of mother's milk. Philosopher Alan Schrift explains her argument: "Mother and child do not stand in a relationship of self vs. other, opposing parties within competing interests, and the gift to the child of a mother's love or a mother's breast is not comprehensible in terms of quantifiable exchange values or the law of return that governs an economy based on the exchange of commodities" (12). As with Locke and Levinas, Cixous returns to a primordial scene of alimentation in order to understand the nature of property exchange, but in her case, the focus on mother-child feeding allows her to discern an economy untethered from the anxious expropriations of capitalism. In place of the revenues and profits sought within a masculine economy, Cixous highlights the social relationships, the *rapport*, established through the exchange of gifts. Rather than corroding or destroying the bonds that link people together, as was the case with Alice and Mrs. Somers, Cixous's "mother's milk" economy creates them.[43]

These gift-enabled social relations help explain the open domestic space of the Morgeson household. The interior spaces of Cassandra's various homes, I suggested earlier, are structured by the alimentary movement of people into and out of them. Family members and visitors alike are drawn to the feeding centers, to the kitchen and the dining room, in order to share a semipublic meal. This circulation both heightens the home-body analogy (that is, the home ingests people in the same way the body ingests food) and maps out a social morphology of inside and outside space. But Cixous reveals the extent to which this social welcome is also crucially an act of generosity. The gift of food maintains social and familial ties here, binding people together in a productive exchange of inside and outside.

Indeed, it is precisely this openness, this giving of gifts, that Levinas identifies as the kernel from which dwelling springs. In order to withdraw from the world and "recollect" oneself, we require "a new event": "I must have been in relation with something I do not live from. This event is the relation with the Other who welcomes me in the Home, the discreet presence of the Feminine" (170). More specifically, Levinas sees this relation with the feminine as a gift exchange. "I must know how *to give* what I possess," he writes. "Only thus could I situate myself absolutely above my engagement in the non-I" (171). What Stoddard's account of maternal care suggests is that this "discreet" relationship with the feminine, a relationship that Levinas situates "on another plane than language" (155), is precisely the bond of the feeding mother and the eating child. The first social relationship is a gift relationship, and in *The Morgesons*, that maternal economy structures the contours of an open domestic space.

It is clear that Stoddard intends this alternative form of property exchange to exist in tension with the more self-interested transactions of the market economy. While staying with the Somers family and enduring the suspicions of Mrs. Somers, Cassandra visits the wealthy widow, Mrs. Hepburn. Mrs. Hepburn is taken with Cassandra and bestows upon her a valuable pair of earrings and "a brooch of aqua-marina stones." Cassandra is stunned: "Is it possible that I am to have them? Why do you give them to me?" (177). In answer, Mrs. Hepburn quotes a few lines from Milton's *Comus*, effectively equating Cassandra with the river nymph Sabrina. The comparison is particularly apt because in *Comus*, the innocent Sabrina is forced to flee the persecutions of a jealous stepmother. Mrs. Hepburn's allusion is a covert acknowledgment of both Cassandra's predicament and her innocence. In effect, Mrs. Hepburn's gift establishes an intimate social bond between the two women, a bond that mitigates the social isolation Cassandra is experiencing at the hands of Mrs. Morgeson.

The gift of jewelry is not all that Mrs. Hepburn has to offer Cassandra, however. As she prepares to leave the widow, the old woman insists that she stay long enough to have a cup of "hot caudle." When Cassandra raises the "small silver tumbler" to her lips, she notices that there is an engraving on the side: "The Bequest of a Friend." The moment is significant for two reasons: first, it is another example of Stoddard calling attention to the socially cohesive power of the gift. With the caudle, Mrs. Hepburn highlights and reinforces the gift-connection she first established with the jewelry. Second, this is a gift of food (or drink). Mrs. Hepburn functions as yet another of Cassandra's surrogate mothers, a woman metaphorically providing the gift of sustenance for her child. Even more significantly, hot caudle was traditionally a drink (sweetened wine or ale with spices added) given to women during childbirth. In short, then, Mrs. Hepburn's gift underscores not just social cohesion but specifically an alimentary economy that ties together both women and their children in a circuit of generosity. Cixous's feminine economy achieves a certain symbolic resonance here.

Stoddard's efforts in *The Morgesons* highlight the subversive potential of this alternative gift economy. In contrast to the exploitative and expropriative values of a "masculine" market, Stoddard explores the possibilities of the gift. By turning inward, as it were, to the economy of the home and family, Stoddard attempts to revalue Graham's nostalgic kitchen politics. She attempts to uncover a more substantive, more fundamental alternative to market values than Hawthorne's essentially accommodationist account. In the primordial alimentary relationship of mother and child, she discovers the blueprint for another way, another means of social exchange that eschews the stark self-interest of possessive individualism. Together, Hawthorne and Stoddard reveal the home to be an alimentary and ideological battleground upon which the circulations of property are infused with particular meanings and constrained to particular paths. Once a possession begins to move, begins to be exchanged between individuals, it is transformed into private property; it has "issued in a discourse." But as these authors suggest, there is more than one discourse. There is both commodity and gift.

* * *

In a remarkably productive fashion, Hawthorne and Stoddard make the most of the antebellum fascination with diet reform. They use the discourse as an intellectual springboard, a thematic catalyst for exploring the ways in which eating conditions the related experiences of possession and domestic space. Like Charles Brockden Brown, the two move beyond a superficial engagement with their cultural moment in order to become cotheorizers of property, possession, and the home. Like Brown,

Hawthorne and Stoddard map out a taxonomy of possession in which the phenomenological aspects of appropriation are linked to the social. Not only does eating structure the experiences of alimentary possession and the contours of domestic space, it also conditions the circulation of property outside the home. Property and possession, these novels make clear, cannot be fully understood without taking the stomach into account.

The further implication of Hawthorne and Stoddard's philosophical work is that neither can we fully understand the historical function of domesticity without closely attending to the role of the alimentary body. Our phenomenological approach reveals the ineluctably embodied nature of domestic ideology. While other critics of domesticity have emphasized its "thematics of disembodiment," that is, its tendency to erase both the bodies and the physical labor of women in the home, our phenomenological reevaluation of Hawthorne and Stoddard suggests precisely the opposite. It suggests that domestic ideology—whether in the form of novels or of reform tracts—maintains a crucial investment in the sociopolitical dynamics of embodiment. Hawthorne and Stoddard, viewed through a phenomenological lens, challenge the notion that domestic novels must embrace a Stowe-esque disavowal of the body. For although Little Eva may enact a Protestant vilification of the flesh, Cassandra and Hepzibah make it clear that appetite, alimentation, and the body are all crucial components of domestic discourse. Female bodies are not necessarily erased or exiled to insignificance in the domestic sphere. Instead, diet reform discourse—as Hawthorne and Stoddard demonstrate—offers an avenue for reinserting the female body into property economies both inside and outside the home.

First in Brockden Brown and then in Hawthorne and Stoddard, we can discern a countercurrent to the trajectory of abstraction that characterizes antebellum property practices more broadly. All three authors respond to the "virtualization" of property, to the nation's increasingly disembodied conception of ownership, by reasserting the importance of sensate bodies—be they Native American or female—in the process of appropriation. For Hawthorne and Stoddard, the increasing anxiety about property is linked especially closely to the concerns of domestic life. As a result, their work highlights a "domestication" of property, a shift in focus from tactile negotiations on the frontier to alimentary exchanges in the middle-class home. This expansion in the spatial radius of property anxiety and property practice will continue over the course of the next two chapters as we examine the contested spaces of the plantation and the city. Just as growing anxieties about abstract, unpredictable market culture fed into the domestic models of Hawthorne and Stoddard, so will those same anxieties influence the phenomenology of possession as it unfolds in the plantation romance and the city-mystery.

At the same time, Chapters 3 and 4 open up a new area of emphasis by turning our attention more specifically to the *affective* elements of embodied ownership. Whereas Chapters 1 and 2 have focused on sensory experience—touch and taste—the second half of this book will expand the purview of our phenomenological approach to account for some of the complex *emotional* dynamics associated with owning—and losing—property. The *feeling* of property encompasses not just physical sensations but complex relationships of affective attachment.

This shift from sensation to affect reflects a broader cultural shift from eighteenth-century rationalism to nineteenth-century emotion. The legacy of Enlightenment empiricism—prominent in Brockden Brown and still visible in Hawthorne and Stoddard—gives way to the nineteenth-century fascination with Romantic subjectivity. One way to mark this change is to note the shift in emphasis away from Locke and toward Hegel. Hegel's German Idealism will prove to be an increasingly useful framework for exploring the affective phenomenology of ownership as it develops across the nineteenth century. Even Hegel's apostate disciple, Marx, will help call attention to the affective potential inherent in property fiction. By following their lead, and by moving from the confines of domestic space to the contested geography of the plantation, we will continue fleshing out antebellum America's phenomenology of possession.

3 / Anxieties of Ownership: Debt, Entitlement, and the Plantation Romance

> DEBT, *n. An ingenious substitute for the chain and whip of the slave-driver.*
>
> —AMBROSE BIERCE, *THE DEVIL'S DICTIONARY*

Over the course of the 1850s, as the sectional crisis between free and slaveholding states grew increasingly antagonistic, Southern planter and ideologue George Fitzhugh published a series of influential proslavery tracts. Beginning in 1850 with the pamphlet *Slavery Justified* and culminating in 1857 with the incendiary treatise *Cannibals All!, or Slaves Without Masters*, Fitzhugh mounted an audacious defense of white supremacy and black subjugation. His strategy in all of these works, broadly speaking, was twofold: first, he aimed to expose what he saw as the social and economic hypocrisy of a Northern market society that criticized Southern slavery while it ignored the abject plight of its own lower-class "wage slaves"; second, he sought to establish the moral superiority of the slaveholding South. In particular, Fitzhugh aimed to justify "slavery in the abstract," to produce a comprehensive, philosophically defensible account of slave society.[1] His arguments, of course, are just as repellent now as they were to many of his contemporaries, both Northern and Southern. But at the same time, as Eugene Genovese has pointed out, his racist social theories also effectively lay bare the "essence" of the slaveholders' worldview.[2] In effect, Fitzhugh offers a chilling distillation of slavery's most fundamental ideological tenets.

Fitzhugh is especially interested in the affective dynamics of the master-slave relationship. In his 1854 book, *Sociology for the South*, he devotes a chapter to what he calls "Domestic Affection." Here, he articulates a familiar refrain of many proslavery apologists: slaves, he asserts, are best understood as cherished members of the master's extended "family."

They live and prosper under "the broad panoply of domestic affection," a place of refuge where "the winds of heaven may not visit them too roughly" and where, like "the ox, the horse, the sheep, the faithful dog," they can "cluster around their protecting master" (105–6). True, he concedes, this paternal relationship is despotic, "But the family government, from its nature, has ever been despotic" (105). Indeed, Fitzhugh goes on to argue in *Cannibals All!* that the master's potential despotism is handcuffed by his deep sympathy for the weak and the helpless. "Our hearts bleed at the robbing of a bird's nest; and the little birds, because they are weak, subdue our strength and command our care." In fine Orwellian fashion, Fitzhugh terms this despotic sympathy "The Strength of Weakness." Because of it, "the humble and obedient slave exercises more or less control over the most brutal and hard-hearted master" (205).

On one level, of course, Fitzhugh's writings are a key instance of proslavery myth making. He is working to repackage the fundamentally economic, and coercive, relationship of chattel slavery into an ideology of benign paternalism. That is, he is looking to transform a property relation into a relation of the heart, to transmute iron shackles into "bonds of affection."[3] In so doing, Fitzhugh deftly adapts antebellum anxieties about the rise of market society into a defense of the agrarian economics of slavery: the "familial" relation existing between master and slave, he argues, is far more humane, more nurturing, than the cold calculations of Northern capitalism. Thus, in the same way that Northern writers like Hawthorne and Stoddard were becoming increasingly uneasy with the incursions of abstract capital, so too were Southern writers like Fitzhugh balking, albeit to very different social and political ends.[4]

On another level, however, Fitzhugh's polemics also underscore the shift from eighteenth-century rationalism to nineteenth-century emotion that characterized antebellum culture more broadly. When Fitzhugh invokes domestic affections, heart-felt sympathy, and patriarchal love, he is using the language and rhetoric of Romantic emotion. In the South, as in the North, Enlightenment epistemologies were giving ground to the emotionalism and individualism of the Romantic revolution. Awash in a powerful mixture of evangelical revivalism and Romantic philosophy, Southern writers looked to the register of emotion and affect to articulate their views, including, crucially, their views on slavery.[5] Fitzhugh reminds us, then, that as antebellum writers continued to explore the phenomenological aspects of ownership, they were increasingly attentive to a different order of *feeling*, namely, that of emotion and affect. More specifically, Fitzhugh's sentimental rhetoric underscores the importance of affect in any assessment of the master-slave dynamic. Such relationships, he implies, are inextricably bound up with the representation and experience of emotion.

The most famous attempt, of course, to analyze the affective dynamic of master and slave occurs in G. W. F. Hegel's 1807 masterwork, *The Phenomenology of Spirit*. In a section entitled "Self-Consciousness," Hegel lays out a theory of subjectivity and social identity that relies on the interaction of dominant and subordinate actors. Hegel argues that self-awareness begins when an individual is able to resist and control his physical appetites. In mastering the sensual body, a person is able to accomplish "the movement of absolute abstraction, of rooting-out all immediate being, and of being merely the purely negative being of self-identical consciousness" (113). But absolute abstraction requires the rooting-out of *all* desires, including crucially, the desire for life itself. Ultimately, then, the only way to demonstrate total freedom is to risk one's life in a mortal struggle, to show others that you can relinquish, if need be, your own life. "It is only through staking one's life that freedom is won [. . .] the individual who has not risked his life may well be recognized as a *person*, but he has not attained to the truth of this recognition as an independent self-consciousness" (114). Self-awareness will emerge when two opposing selves engage in a life-or-death battle for recognition, each trying to demonstrate his freedom from sensual desire. But this agonistic approach does not work if either of the two individuals is killed. If that happens, the loser is dead and the winner has no one to attest to his freedom; thus, neither individual achieves self-consciousness. So, instead of one person destroying the other, a relationship of dominance is established. The winner of the struggle grants the loser his life in exchange for the loser's continuous recognition of the winner's freedom and mastery. The defeated individual becomes a "dependent consciousness whose essential nature is simply to live or to be for another." This constitutes the master-slave relationship. In Hegel's words: "The former is lord, the other is bondsman" (115).

There is another difficulty, however. Because the slave has chosen to live rather than to die, he has become something less than a full person; he is a "dependent consciousness." This means that the quality of his recognition is less than what the master requires for his own full, independent self-consciousness. Alexander Kojève terms this paradox the "existential impasse": in subjugating the slave, the master reduces the value of the slave's recognition and, in so doing, destroys any chance for his own recognition by another fully independent consciousness (19). Moreover, since the slave performs all of the master's labor, the master becomes dependent on the slave, inverting the initial hierarchy of independence and dependence. This is the surprising conclusion of Hegel's model: the master's independence turns out to be a degraded form of the freedom eventually experienced by the slave. How does the slave experience freedom? "Through his service he rids himself of his attachment to natural existence in every single detail; and gets rid of it by working on it" (117). Instead of simply consuming the natural world, as his new master does, the slave works on the world and offers it up to the master; he does not consume it. Thus, "Work [. . .] is desire held in check, fleetingness staved off; in other words, work forms and shapes the thing" (118). Through the enduring nature of these works, the slave comes to understand and experience his own permanence, his own freedom from desire.[6]

Hegel's account of the master-slave dialectic has been enthusiastically taken up by scholars of American slavery and the antebellum South. In his seminal work, *The Problem of Slavery in the Age of Revolution*, for example, David Brion Davis lauds Hegel's phenomenological model as "the most profound analysis of slavery ever written" (558). Davis himself goes on to apply the model to a creative rereading of the relationship between Toussaint L'Ouverture and Napoleon Bonaparte. More recently, in *Slavery and Social Death*, Orlando Patterson has revised Hegel's dialectic into an influential model of master-slave relations he terms "human parasitism." In his formulation, the master "feeds" on the slave in order "to gain the very direct satisfactions of power over another, honor enhancement, and authority" (337). At the same time, however, the parasitic master is also dependent on the host/slave who feeds him, thus preserving the dialectical dynamic.[7] Patterson also incisively observes that the master class generally enacts some sort of ideological smokescreen, à la Fitzhugh, in which they reverse the terms of the parasitical relationship and portray the slave as the dependent and the master as the benevolent provider (337–40).

Patterson's model is a powerful heuristic for exploring what he calls the "political psychology" of slavery (11). But Patterson also makes a point of distancing his own social-psychological approach from previous scholarship that has emphasized property as a key aspect of plantation social relations. "The notion of property certainly has an important place in any discussion of slavery," he concedes, "but it is in no way one of the constitutive elements" (17). Following Marx, Patterson maintains that a focus on property and "legalistic" definitions of slavery simply obscures the more important social "relations of dependence" that actually define the institution (19). Property, for him, is more an epiphenomenon than a crucial, causal factor.[8] Instead, Patterson wants to extend and refine the "political psychology" pioneered by Hegel.

It is here, at the intersection of Hegelian phenomenology and property discourse, that I would like to intervene. When Patterson deemphasizes issues of property and ownership, it seems to me that he is overlooking Hegel's own focus on precisely these phenomena. In his *Elements of the Philosophy of Right* (1821), Hegel elaborates on the process through which a slave comes to a sense of himself as a free person. He explains that for an individual to be free, he must create for himself "an external *sphere of freedom*," specifically through the medium of private property (73). That is, he must concretely embody his will in the objective world so that others can recognize and attest to his freedom. This is precisely the process of work and labor through which slaves come to experience freedom. "It is in this way [through work]," Hegel tells us, "that consciousness, *qua* worker, comes to see in the independent being [of the object] its *own* independence" (*Phenomenology* 118). Hegel makes the connection to property explicit: "The circumstance that I, as free will, am an object to myself in what I possess and only become an actual will by this means constitutes the genuine and rightful element in possession, the determination of *property*" (*Philosophy* 76–77).[9] In short, property relations, contra Patterson, are absolutely crucial to Hegel's phenomenology of master and slave.

What I would like to suggest is that the master-slave dialectic is best understood as a complex interrelationship of phenomenological experience and property relations. Indeed, as this book argues, property itself possesses a phenomenological component, and this becomes especially clear in the context of master-slave interactions. More specifically, I aim to show that the back-and-forth struggle of master and slave is conditioned by a dialectical phenomenology of debt and entitlement. That is, the affective experience of the master is haunted by a feeling of debt, by a lingering fear that he owes something to the slave from whom he has taken so much. Likewise, the phenomenology of the slave is informed by an outraged feeling of entitlement, a sense of what it is to be owed something for your sacrifice. In this way, *owing* and *being owed*, indebtedness and entitlement, constitute key components of what Eric Sundquist has called the "phenomenology of slavery," that "dialectic of opposing wills [. . .] subject to continual borrowings and absorptions of power, alterations of ascendancy, and recognitions that the ontological planes of bondage and mastery could from time to time [. . .] become inverted" (40). Rather than relegating property relations to the background of this dialectic, I want to demonstrate that they are absolutely central to it.[10]

In order to better trace these intersections of property and phenomenology, I would like to turn to the genre of the antebellum plantation romance. As a version of the literary pastoral, the plantation romance is obsessed with narratives of property, inheritance, real estate, and, in particular, debt.[11] This focus on property makes the genre a particularly productive site at which to explore the affective experience of ownership. At the same time, plantation fiction addresses, albeit in a problematic fashion, the complex dynamics of the master-slave relationship. Although often reduced to cartoonish racist stereotypes, African American characters nevertheless crowd the margins of these novels, persistently calling attention to the tensions and anxieties that bind master and slave. I aim to mine the genre, then, for its insights into the particularly property-inflected contours of this master-slave dynamic.

Of course, antebellum plantation novels are a problematic genre. Much of the critical work on plantation fiction that has emerged over the last thirty years has taken the genre to task for helping to create and perpetuate a disturbing proslavery ideology. "Every line and every scene in this literature," Susan Tracy asserts in a representative critique, "was written to assure the reader of the natural superiority of men to women, of whites to blacks and Native Americans, and of the planter class to all other classes" (5). In short, the novels espouse a reactionary worldview that celebrates not just aristocratic ideals and Southern honor, but white supremacy and retrograde paternalism.[12]

While I certainly agree with these critiques, I am also interested in moving past simple critical denunciation and toward a more probing interrogation of the texts, one that sees them as a valuable window on both the ideological debates and the phenomenological experiences that characterized plantation culture. In particular, I want to read the plantation romance in relation to the contemporary genre of the slave narrative, a literary tradition that presents a much different picture of the master-slave dynamic and of property relations in the South. By reading these two genres dialectically, I hope to present a richer, more nuanced view of how master and slave experiences informed one another and of how the phenomenology of property on the plantation emerged from a Hegelian contest of wills.

In so doing, my chapter participates in what Houston Baker Jr. and Dana Nelson have called the "new Southern studies," a recent scholarly movement that seeks to understand Southern texts in a more historically and discursively sophisticated fashion. Specifically, my analysis explores a distinctively Southern cultural tension that Paul Jones describes as a conversation "between conservative and progressive literatures, each offering a vision of the South as they saw it or as they wanted it to be" (8–9). While much of the "new Southern studies" has focused on the crucial work of expanding the "Southern" canon, my chapter returns to the scene of the crime, as it were, to the central genre of the plantation romance, in order to view it with new eyes.[13] My focus on the phenomenology of property reveals the genre to be a rich, if problematic, repository of affective experience. But read in tension with slave narratives, the romances offer a valuable perspective on ownership, space, and the phenomenology of slavery.

On one level, this dialectical approach to white and black experiences of ownership on the plantation yields a much clearer sense of how the master-slave dynamic is crucially influenced by property relations. The feelings of debt and entitlement emerge as key components in the affective economy linking master and slave. On a broader level, this dialectical phenomenology helps to shed light on the experience of ownership in general. That is, the paired experiences of debt and entitlement enacted in these texts also reflect an anxiety of ownership that characterizes the phenomenology of property more generally. As Hegel proposes, and as Levinas concurs, property itself is a dialectical or discursive experience in which ownership comes into being through the challenge of other claims. It only makes sense to say we "own" something if there are other potential owners who might claim it. This underlying anxiety of contest, of counterclaim and alternative ownership, is dramatized in the writings of the antebellum South. Revealing that contest of appropriation is one of the rewards of this chapter.

To accomplish these goals, the chapter is divided into four sections. The first examines the complex cultural signification of debt in the antebellum South. The second section analyzes William Gilmore Simms's popular romance, *Woodcraft*, in light of this Southern debt culture. *Woodcraft* is particularly valuable for the attention it devotes to the planter's affective experience of debt. The third section reverses the discursive field and examines the slave's "senses of entitlement" by closely attending to a range of slave narratives, including those of Douglass, Jacobs, and Charles Ball. Finally, the fourth section explores John Pendleton Kennedy's *Swallow Barn*, unearthing a dialectical phenomenology of debt and entitlement in the very space of the plantation. Here, we will chart a further expansion of the phenomenological radius of possessive space, extending the range of sensory and affective experience to the edges of the slave estate. At the same time, by shifting our focus away from the experience of appropriation and toward the dynamics of expropriation and loss, this chapter marks a turn in our larger investigation of property, a turn toward the darker aspects and anxieties of ownership that will continue for the remainder of the book.

Southern Discomfort: Debt in the Slaveholding South

It is a very onerous business, this of being served, and the debtor naturally wishes to give you a slap. —RALPH WALDO EMERSON, "GIFTS"

George Fitzhugh's celebration of "domestic affection" effectively foregrounds the emotional economy of master and slave. At the same time, however, his sentimental account hints at a more literal sort of economy underlying the plantation's supposedly tender exchanges. He writes:

> Domestic affection cannot be calculated in dollars and cents. It cannot be weighed, or measured, or seen, or felt—except in its effects. 'The wind bloweth where it listeth and no man knoweth whence it cometh or whither it goeth.' Its holy fountain is concealed in deeper recesses than the head of the Nile, and in its course it dispenses blessings from the rich overflowings of the heart, ten thousand times more precious than that sacred river ever gave to the land of Egypt. Political economists, politicians and materialists ignore its existence, because it is too refined for their comprehension. The material world engrosses their attention, and they heed little those moral agencies that Providence has established to control the material world. (106)

Initially, the passage seems to reinforce Fitzhugh's overall goals: it transforms financial concerns into affective ones, and it subordinates the material world to the dictates of higher "moral agencies." But, more subtly, it also suggests that the master-slave relation takes the form of a gift economy rather than a crass market exchange. For Fitzhugh, domestic affection is a "fountain," a bountiful, overflowing spring that "dispenses blessings" more precious than the Nile's gift of life. He conceives of this as a form of "true" benevolence, or what Derrida calls an "aneconomic" gift, a donation outside the circuits of exchange.[14] There is no quid pro quo reciprocity here, no return expected for what the fountain bestows. Fitzhugh imagines the master's paternalism as a one-way interaction, a flowing of rich gifts from the beneficent owner to the grateful slave.[15]

Significantly, this benevolence seems to proceed according to a logic of disembodiment. There is a gothic inflection here, a ghostliness that shimmers at the edges of Fitzhugh's imagery. His domestic affection is a wellspring "concealed in deeper recesses." It is "too refined" for crass materialists, and "cannot be weighed, or measured, or seen, or felt—except in its effects." Immaterial and invisible, this paternal sentiment moves about unfettered, like a ghostly wind. It has left behind the troublesome corporeality of real slave bodies interacting with violent and coercive masters. It operates now only in the rarefied domain of moral suasion.

What I would like to suggest is that the affective economy of the master-slave relation is indeed haunted, but not by ethereal gusts of domestic affection. Rather, it is plagued by the specter of the debt-relation, by a fear of white indebtedness brought about by the exploitation of black slaves. Buried underneath the obsessive fantasy of selfless sentimental love and aneconomic gift giving, there lies a persistent anxiety about market reciprocity, about the quid pro quo of market exchange. This is the great dilemma of the slave owner: to the extent that the slave is recognized as a human being, he also merits treatment as a possessive individual, as an independent actor in exchange relations. If this is the case, then the owner is greatly in arrears. The violent expropriation of the slave's labor and the brutal subjugation of the slave's person have tilted the balance sheets dramatically in favor of the slave. He is owed something and the master is in his debt. This anxiety of indebtedness, this phenomenology of debt, haunts the master's experience of the master-slave relation.

Debt and debtorship were subjects of great interest in antebellum Southern culture (as they were in the burgeoning market economy of the North). But in order to fully understand debt in the South, we first need to understand the social contours of gift giving. As the passage from Fitzhugh suggests, the notion of the gift was central to the self-conception of the master class. The ideal of paternal benevolence, of the planter as a wealthy gift-giver bestowing his largesse on everyone around him, helped promote the traditional republican vision of a virtuous, disinterested leader wisely ruling the populace from a vantage point above the base concerns of a capitalist economy.[16] As a result, the image of the munificent planter appears again and again in plantation literature. While visiting a New England village, for example, the planter protagonist of Caroline Hentz's novel, *The Planter's Northern Bride*, distinguishes himself by giving large sums of money to the needy. Appalled by the poor health and abject living conditions he finds among "the thousand toiling operatives of the Northern manufactories," Mr. Moreland hands out money like candy. "When Moreland reached the low, dark-walled cottage which Nancy pointed out as her home, he gave her back her bundle, and at the same time slipped a bill into her hand, of whose amount she could not be aware. But she knew by the soft, yielding paper the nature of the gift, and something whispered in her that it was no niggard boon. 'Oh, sir,' she cried, 'you are too good'" (28).

On the fictional plantations themselves, the master's largesse is just as pronounced. In Kennedy's *Swallow Barn*, Frank Meriwether takes it upon himself to visit his slaves in the quarter. Upon arrival, he is swarmed by a crowd of happy bondsmen who look to him for gifts. After giving one slave a handful of money to buy a new saddle, Meriwether cheerfully remarks, "I seldom come here without finding myself involved in some new demand, as a consequence of my donation. Now he wants a pair of spurs which, I suppose, I must give him" (452). Indeed, planter generosity is celebrated to such a degree that financial improvidence functions something like a badge of honor. In Simms's *Woodcraft*, Captain Porgy's financial difficulties are due in no small part to the fact that he has a habit of giving out money to the less fortunate around him. His more frugal sergeant, Millhouse, takes him to task: "Captain Porgy could never, so far as I see, git the right sense of charity and ginerosity. He was always a wasting himself on people who hadn't nothing [. . .]. Ef there was a poor camp woman that had lost her man in a skrimmage, the cappin was the first to empty his pockets into her lap. I've seed him do it a dozen times" (279). According to the cultural ideal of the gift-giving planter, a lack of concern for financial matters actually signals a superior moral virtue. This is a value system that, in theory, rejects the selfish calculus of a market economy and posits republican disinterest as the model of social behavior.

Of course, the practice of gift giving and the image of the selfless planter were not quite as disinterested as they might initially seem. As Fitzhugh's fountain implies and as historian Kenneth Greenberg observes, "Between master and slave, gifts could only flow in one direction." In fact, "One of the central characteristics of the condition of enslavement, as seen through the eyes of masters, involved the inability to give gifts" (65). Masters were the ones with the power to bestow and slaves were defined by their receptivity and subordination. Any deviation from that pattern of one-way exchange would grant the slaves some sort of mastery over the masters. Planter benevolence, then, functioned as a stable marker of racial hierarchy and unequal master-slave power relations.[17]

At the same time, gift giving between white male planters was a complex process of social negotiation. If the act of receiving a gift placed one in a subordinate or dependent position, then it threatened to reduce a planter to something approximating the position of a slave. Gift giving between planters could thus call into question all their cherished notions of independence and patriarchal power. As a result, intricate social rituals were developed for allowing planters to respond with counter-gifts that would preserve their social status as benevolent patriarchs.[18] Again, this jockeying for position in the white social hierarchy underscores the ways in which the cultural fantasy of the selfless, disinterested planter concealed a more self-interested social practice.

The myth of benevolent paternalism turned on the notion of the "true gift," on the belief that an entirely selfless bequest could be made without expecting anything in return.[19] The social realities of plantation culture, however, suggest that the practice of gift giving is better understood in terms of reciprocal obligation. Giving a gift, in short, incurs a *debt*. This is the anthropological definition of gift giving first proposed by Marcel Mauss in his groundbreaking study of the gift in Native American and Polynesian cultures. According to Mauss, there are no disinterested gifts, only exchanges that place the receiver in various forms of social debt to the giver. While these debts serve to bind people together in networks of social obligation, they also establish a hierarchy in which the giver holds power over the receiver.[20] The paradox of the gift, however, is that while it incurs a debt, while it expects some form of reciprocation, it must always *appear* to be disinterested, with no strings attached. This disparity between selfless appearance and selfish reality is what allows the myth of the benevolent planter to remain in place. While planter gifts to slaves actually yield a very pragmatic financial benefit—an exploitative power hierarchy and a docile pool of slave labor—such gifts can also be presented as evidence of the planter's virtue, affection, and financial disinterest.[21]

Certainly, Southern planters were aware of the fact that a gift could bring with it the burden of debt, of reciprocal obligation. After all, this notion of gift-as-debt was central to the network of social ties that constituted plantation society. As Greenberg explains, in the antebellum South, "To be immersed in a system of reciprocal gift giving was to be part of a community of free men. In fact, gift exchange was one of the defining features of that community" (70). Moreover, this communal gift exchange was inextricably bound up with the larger network of patronage and debt obligation that likewise characterized plantation culture. In his study of early American debt practices, for example, Bruce Mann argues that Southern planters, particularly those involved in the tobacco economies of the Virginia tidewater, were thoroughly entangled in debt relations. "One of the grand ironies of the period," Mann maintains, "is that it was the tobacco planters who proclaimed their independence most ardently yet who were most deeply enmeshed in debt" (131). These debts encompassed the more familiar financial relationships with banks and creditors, as well as interpersonal relationships that leveraged community reputation and family ties. Bertram Wyatt-Brown notes, "In fact, it could be said that the gentry ranks, even more than the yeomanry, were meshed together through intertwined promissory notes, indentures, and other forms of financial entanglements [. . .]. The tendency was to look upon debt as a permanent condition of life and therefore something that should be made to serve other ends than just financial transaction" (345). Gift relations, then, easily bled into the more explicitly demanding strictures of debt. Gift and debt were, for Southern planters, flip sides of a very familiar social coin.

But this same ambiguity, I would like to emphasize, was a source of anxiety for the Southern slaveholder. Underneath the façade of benevolent largesse and communal bonding, there persisted the disturbing possibility of dependence and subordination. To owe something, to be in someone's debt, was to come perilously close to the position of a slave. Of course, anxieties about debt and other economic difficulties were not limited to the slaveholding South. As the Northern economy continued its transition to market capitalism and to increasingly abstract financial devices, speculation and the dangers of debt became a growing concern.[22] But such debt anxiety, I want to argue, was particularly acute within a social structure that insisted upon an immutable master-slave hierarchy. Southern social dynamics would not tolerate any reversal of the master-slave power relation. To do so would be to endanger the very foundations of the social order.

The threat of slaveholder subordination and dependence constitutes the most explicit feature of Southern debt anxiety. If a planter's debt burden became too great, or if creditors demanded repayment all at once, the planter's independence could be forfeit, and he could be subject to social and legal punishment. Perhaps not surprisingly, the greatest threat was from banks and creditors outside the local network of communal debt. British investors, for example, had a bad habit of abruptly calling in debt during diccy economic periods. This could ruin highly leveraged planters.[23] Peyton Randolph, attorney general of the Virginia colony, complained in 1759 that British creditors were "a Kind of lording Tyrants over their unfortunate Debtors," and that they were constantly inventing unscrupulous new strategies "to keep the poor Dogs of Debtors deep in their Books, and render the Redemption of their Freedom impossible." Thomas Jefferson himself, after the revolution, maintained that British creditors were manipulating tobacco prices in order to render debts "hereditary from father to son, for so many generations, so that the planters were a species of property, annexed to mercantile houses in London."[24]

Jefferson's characterization of indebted planters as a "species of property" makes explicit the fear at work here: debt has the potential to reduce the planter to a condition resembling enslavement. Mann demonstrates that as the nineteenth century wore on and popular pressure to reduce the penalties for insolvency grew, the discourse equating debtors and slaves likewise increased.[25] In its most dramatic instantiation, this imagery served as the masthead for a newspaper published from inside a New York debtor's prison. The banner of *Forlorn Hope* features the image of a kneeling black man in a tattered loincloth chained together with a ragged-looking white man standing next to him. The banner underneath reads: "Liberty Suspended But Will Be Restored" (see Fig. 1 below). Clearly, the masthead (and the newspaper in general) is trading on early abolitionist sympathies: the slave as well as the wayward debtor, it appears, will have his liberty restored. But despite a politics diametrically opposed to that of Southern planters, the masthead does make clear the cultural prominence of the debtor-as-slave analogy. The possibility that an owner of slaves might himself become "enslaved" to heartless creditors was an especially disturbing prospect for Southern whites who defined themselves in opposition to subjugated blacks.[26]

But there is a second, subtler, aspect of slaveholder debt anxiety that I want to focus on here. At its core, the fear of debt slavery was an anxiety about the transformation of social debt into market debt. Planters existed in a culture that understood debt in terms of social obligation, communal reputation, and honor. Indeed, debt was so closely related to gift-giving practices that the two were often indistinguishable. The impertinent claims of foreign creditors, however, abruptly dispensed with this social understanding of debt and insisted upon the crass strictures of contract law and market claims. What had been understood as a version of gift relation or as a social obligation had now become a precise reciprocity, a market exchange between socioeconomic equals. The stratified social hierarchy of planter culture did not figure in the account books of outside creditors. Instead, market reciprocity ushered in an unsettling egalitarianism.

But if the illusion of one gift economy—that of social obligations circulating between white men of property—can give way to the strict reciprocity of market debt, might not that other "gift" economy—the one between master and slave—yield to a similar reciprocity? This is, for slaveholders, the more unsettling debt anxiety that haunts the master-slave relation. What if the supposedly affective interactions between owner and slave can more accurately be described as reciprocal, market-based property exchanges? Such a reconfiguration of the master-slave dynamic would be morally and economically devastating to the planters' self-image and worldview. The real burden of debt in this case would not

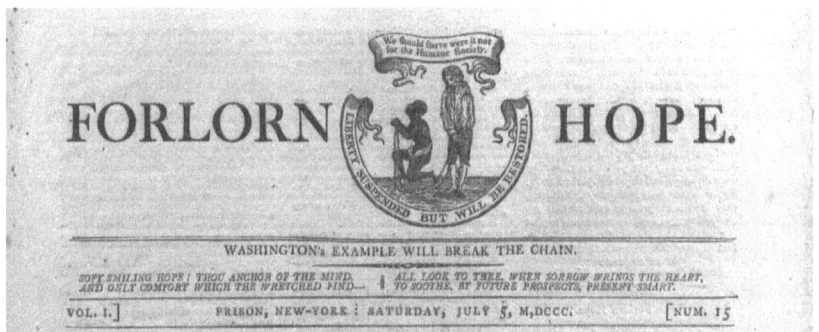

FIGURE 1. Masthead from *Forlorn Hope*, July 5, 1800; NEG #49720. Collection of The New-York Historical Society.

be on the slave, whatever paltry "gifts" he may have received from his owner. Rather, the burden would rest on the master, both for his exploitation of the slave and for his violent expropriation of slave labor.

Owning and Owing: *Woodcraft* and the Phenomenology of Debt

Have these genealogists of morals had even the remotest suspicion that, for example, the major moral concept Schuld [guilt] has its origin in the very material concept Schulden [debts]? —FRIEDRICH NIETZSCHE, ON THE GENEALOGY OF MORALS

Derrida specifically identifies the feeling of debt anxiety as the shadow side of the gift economy. "If giving is spontaneously evaluated as *good* [...], it remains the case that this 'good' can easily be reversed. We know that as good, it can also be bad, poisonous [...], and this from the moment the gift puts the other in debt, with the result that giving comes down to hurting, to doing harm" (128–29). There is a disquieting threat concealed in the act of benevolence because all exchange is in some way reciprocal exchange. When property changes hands there is an expectation, indeed a demand, for return, for reciprocation. This is the nagging feeling of *owing* something; it is the sense of being indebted to, and under the power of, one's benefactor, one's creditor. Emerson, too, in his essay "Gifts," alludes to this anxiety. "It is not the office of a man to receive gifts. How dare you give them? We wish to be self-sustained. We do not quite forgive a giver [...]. It is a very onerous business, this of being served, and the debtor naturally wishes to give you a slap" (26–27).

In the planter culture of the slaveholding South, this anxiety about reciprocal obligation exists in a particular affective formation with the master-slave relationship. Planter anxiety, I want to argue, is at some level

152 / ANXIETIES OF OWNERSHIP

an anxiety about the terrifying possibility of being indebted to slaves. On the surface, slaveholder culture is obsessed with issues of financial debt, both in terms of slave property and in terms of real estate. These concerns permeate the genre of the plantation romance. But the plantation romance also reveals an underlying anxiety, an unease about the possibility of a looming debt owed to the very slaves whom the masters claim as their own. William Gilmore Simms's novel *Woodcraft* is particularly attuned to the dynamics of this fear. By tracking Simms's account, that is, by unearthing his phenomenology of debt, I aim to show that a darker *debt affect* haunts the sentimental economy of master and slave. In convoluted fashion, Simms's novel effectively displaces a displacement: proslavery ideology (in which the novel is steeped) transforms the property relation of master and slave into a matter of sentimental affect; *Woodcraft* then reroutes the darker aspects of that affective relationship back into an economic register, that is, into fears of financial debt.

Published in 1854, *Woodcraft, or Hawks about the Dovecote* is the fifth of seven Revolutionary War romances written by Simms in the decades leading up to the Civil War.[27] The novel focuses on the exploits of Captain Porgy, a South Carolinian planter and war veteran already familiar to Simms's readers from his cameo appearances in a number of the other war romances. *Woodcraft* takes place in the immediate aftermath of the war as Porgy makes his way home to a plantation that he has not seen in seven years and that has been devastated by British raids. All of Porgy's slaves have been captured or driven off, and to make matters worse, the plantation is mortgaged to the unscrupulous Scottish parvenu, M'Kewn. Porgy does have the support of a few loyal adherents: he is attended by his garrulous sergeant Millhouse, his level-headed lieutenant Lance Frampton, and his faithful slave-cook Tom. In addition, Porgy is aided by the wealthy widow, Mrs. Eveleigh, mistress of a well-managed plantation bordering Porgy's own. The first third of the book details Porgy's rescue of the widow and her son, Arthur, from a wilderness ambush by the villainous squatter, Bostwick (hired for the job by M'Kewn). With that crisis averted, the remainder of the novel tracks Porgy's efforts, with the help of the more pragmatic Millhouse, to get his plantation affairs back in order. The Captain contemplates marrying Mrs. Eveleigh to square away his finances, but the wise woman declines his proposal. Instead, the novel ends when M'Kewn's Tory treachery is revealed and Porgy's debts are released.

Despite the historical premise of the recently ended war, *Woodcraft* is a plantation romance. As such, the novel is replete with the thematic conventions of the genre and with the proslavery discourse that informs those conventions. In addition to the property-focused plot of dispossession, Captain Porgy exhibits the requisite discerning taste, social acumen, and moral virtue of the Southern Cavalier. In his epicurean tendencies and poor financial skills, there are shades of the "Lazy Southerner" stereotype familiar both to Northern and Southern audiences. Perhaps most crucially, the novel pursues several marriage plots, although Porgy's own possibilities never come to fruition.

More important for our purposes, however, is the novel's embrace of proslavery ideology. As the war approached, Simms himself became a passionate advocate of the Southern cause and, like Fitzhugh, wrote defiantly about the virtues of slavery.[28] *Woodcraft*, like many other plantation romances, adapts this proslavery rhetoric into a sentimental portrait of loving slaves and caring masters. When Porgy first reunites with some of the slaves from his plantation, they respond with shouts and cheers, rushing up and seizing his hand "as if they were hosts [. . .] welcoming a favorite guest": "T'ank de Lord, here's maussa g*i*t to he own home at last!—B*r*ess de Lord, Maussa, you come! We all *b*erry glad *for* see you, maussa—glad *too* much!" For his part, Porgy is nearly overcome with emotion. "The tears stood in the eyes of our captain [. . .] and he shook hands with, and spoke to them each in turn—few words, indeed, but they were uttered tremulously and in low tones" (175). Late in the book, Tom demonstrates his own loyalty and affection by rejecting Porgy's offer of manumission. "I's well off whar' I is, I tell you; and I much rudder b'long to good maussa, wha' I lub, dan be my own maussa and quarrel wid mese'f ebbery day [. . .]. *You* b'longs to *me* Tom, jes' as much as me Tom b'long to *you*; and you nebber guine git *you* free paper from me long as you lib" (509). Here, the property relation of master and slave is so completely transposed into an affective register that Tom can imagine he actually "owns" Porgy.

As implausible as Tom's claim to ownership may seem, it hints at the more threatening aspect of debt relation that plagues slaveholders within the novel. Debt concerns are not relegated to the subtext, however.[29] The central conflict revolves around Porgy's prewar mortgage to M'Kewn, "a d——d shark of a Scotchman" (55). Porgy's profligate ways had led him to borrow money from M'Kewn to shore up his finances. He had initially used his plantation, Glen-Eberley, to secure the loans, but during the war real estate values plunged to such a degree that Porgy's debt has now grown to more than twice the value of his estate.[30] At the same time, M'Kewn himself is repeatedly indebted to the squatter Bostwick, an unprincipled woodsman whom M'Kewn hires to steal slaves and ambush the widow Eveleigh. Bostwick has no compunctions about using his knowledge of M'Kewn's illicit activities to extort as much money as he can from the Scotsman, and M'Kewn is driven nearly mad by this feeling of "desperate bondage." "Was there no escape from the arrogance of this enemy? Was he to be plagued perpetually without any hope of relief?" (468). Ultimately, this debt relation proves to be the undoing of both men.

More explicit financial relations of this sort are matched in the novel by the interpersonal debts common to the close-knit planter society. Upon Porgy's return to Glen-Eberley, he has no money or collateral with which to buy supplies or to outfit the slaves. His fellow planter, Mrs. Eveleigh, offers him a loan of goods and money secured only by his reputation and their friendship. "Implements and utensils for working the crop, I can lend you for present use," she tells him. "I have a wagon to spare you for a season." When he protests that he has nothing with which to pay her, she laughs him off. "Oh! I know you have no money, but you have credit [. . .]. If you make a good crop this season, return me what you borrow, *if you can*; if not, you shall pay me, *when able* at the present rates for these articles" (347–48). Part of the reason for Mrs. Eveleigh's largesse is that she also understands herself to be in Porgy's debt for his dramatic rescue of her and her son from Bostwick's ambush. The rescue, she believes, is "a debt which my whole life could not repay," but Porgy graciously absolves her. "Do not talk of any debt to me, my dear Mrs. Eveleigh," he responds, "you owe me none" (341, 342).[31] Such interpersonal debts do not cause anxiety, of course, because they are comfortably ensconced in the realm of social ties and domestic affect. Porgy eventually asks Mrs. Eveleigh to marry him, an act that underscores his belief that such relations are better understood in sentimental and affective, not strictly financial, terms.

Debt narratives, then, of both the financial and interpersonal sort, figure prominently throughout *Woodcraft*. But the novel is interested in debt as more than simply a plot device or a thematic concern. Simms seems especially interested in the affective experience of debt, the phenomenology of indebtedness as it plagues his property-obsessed characters. Porgy spends much of the first half of the novel wrestling with the melancholia that comes with his mortgage to M'Kewn. As he returns to his plantation, he is "pursued by debt and embarrassments, as unrelaxing as the furies that hunted the steps of Orestes" (101). His troubles open up a "distressing prospect" to his view and he considers himself "very nearly a ruined man" (102, 101). His feelings are minutely described:

> There will be always something humbling and oppressive in the survey of such a situation. The questions of 'what is to be

done?'—'whither am I to turn?'—'of what am I capable?'—'what is my resource?' [. . .] are well calculated to fling a pall over the prospect, and make the heart to shrink at the entrance upon the unknown void of life which yet spreads before it. Porgy was the man to feel, thoroughly, the discouraging and sad, in this survey; for he was a man really of good sense and many sensibilities. (102)

The emotional experience of debt here is one of spatial and temporal encumbrance. Not only are the "prospects" and "surveys" of his life curtailed by the gloomy pall, but his future possibilities collapse into a "void" bound by the excesses of his past. The feeling of indebtedness is a shrinking, a contraction and compression under weight, into the bleak confines of absent opportunities. It is, in short, a feeling of subordination and humiliation.

Of course, Simms employs a sympathetic strategy here: we are meant to understand Porgy's affective experience in such detail so that we can better sympathize with his plight. As a result, it seems as if the phenomenology of debt in *Woodcraft* remains firmly yoked to an explicitly proslavery ideology. Debt is horrible, the novel implies, because its cold market calculus interferes with the warm domestic affections of plantation society. But the novel's obsession with debt anxiety does not end with Porgy's despair. Instead, the experience of debt begins to manifest itself in less familiar ways. In one of the stranger passages of the book, Porgy ruminates on his own prodigious girth, subtly equating his massive stomach with his massive debt. "It was with some feeling of reproach and impatience that our captain fixed his eyes on the unnaturally distended member. By what malice of fate was it that it had so greatly grown at the expense of all the rest!" (199). Porgy's stomach serves as the corporeal sign of his profligacy and overindulgence; it is the physical index of his mortgage to M'Kewn. The money he has spent, and now owes, clings to him in the form of embodied debt. The analogy becomes even more pronounced when he considers Mrs. Eveleigh's offer to help: "She can redeem my acres. She can put me on my legs again, however heavy my incumbrance" (200). The pun here on legal encumbrances suggests the ways in which debt contains a bodily component, a phenomenological sensation of weightiness and oppression. But the analogy also helps to symbolically shift the burden, the responsibility for the debt, onto Porgy. His appetites have led to this encumbrance, so there is a certain reciprocal justice in his condition. Porgy's paunch thus becomes an image of not just past indulgence but also future responsibility. This is debt understood as a quid pro quo exchange, as a reciprocal obligation.³⁷

The strange analogy of debt and digestion begins to shift the novel's account of debt affect away from the context of paternal sympathy and toward something more like reciprocity angst. Viewed from the perspective of Porgy's "distended member," the threat of debt is the threat of your own excesses returning to plague you. This shift, we should note, parallels our earlier distinction between the explicit anxiety of masters becoming debt "slaves," and the more subtle anxiety of owning up to reciprocal obligations. One is the fear of financial subjugation; the other is a fear of reciprocity, of egalitarian exchange. But why, we might ask, is this subtler anxiety necessarily an anxiety about slave entitlement? That is, what do Porgy's debt worries have to do with any claims that slaves might make to redress? After all, Porgy's debt is a property relation between two white masters and does not immediately seem to impinge upon the master-slave dynamic.

The link between this reciprocity angst and the master-slave relation gets worked out, I believe, via the novel's vexed treatment of two pivotal white characters: the deputy sheriff Absalom Crooks and the villainous squatter Bostwick. These two characters effectively reroute the novel's anxiety about black slave entitlement through a narrative of white debt. That is, persistent subconscious anxieties about reciprocal obligations owed to exploited black slaves get transplanted into the more palatable context of fears about owing white men, albeit lower-class white men. A close look at these characters reveals an incriminating racial subtext that complicates the novel's phenomenology of debt. The more powerful, because unacknowledged, debt anxiety in the book is a fear of what a truly reciprocal economic relationship between master and slave would look and feel like. The phenomenology of debt here trades on an underlying fear that slaves may have a claim to redress from white masters.

Once Porgy's mortgage finally comes due, M'Kewn calls upon the local sheriff to execute his duties by liquidating Porgy's real estate and by seizing his slaves in partial payment of the debt. The sheriff travels out to Glen-Eberley with the intention of doing just this, but upon arriving he is essentially taken captive by Porgy and his minions. Porgy pretends not to realize that the sheriff is actually a representative of the law; at the same time, he does his best to intimidate the man into not serving the official documents. He succeeds by graphically describing what he would do to the real sheriff if he were to appear on the plantation. At one point, for example, the men sit down to eat and Porgy has a covered dish brought out to the table. When he uncovers it, "the sheriff beheld [. . .] within reach of Porgy [. . .] a pair of highly-polished pistols" (431). "Don't you see," he calmly explains to the sheriff, "that I am prepared to sacrifice my life with my property, and that law can in no way, exact a higher forfeit?" (434). At one point, the sheriff decides to test the waters a bit and asks Porgy what he would do if "the sheriff was suddenly to appear among you, just as I am here now." Porgy uses the opportunity to further terrify the man. "With the wild but determined look and action of a desperate man, he seized both pistols lying in the dish before him, stood up, reached as far over the table as he could, and covered the figure of the amiable but indiscreet sheriff with both muzzles cocking the weapon as he did so" (435).

Porgy's actions, of course, are an elaborate prank. He realizes that he cannot realistically resist the law for any length of time, nor does he intend to do so. The pistols are not loaded. Yet, there is an animosity, an antipathy toward the law that emerges from Simms's account of the sheriff's visit and that conveys a real sense of anger at a meddling legal system. In a rant that echoes the anti-sheriff, pro-property sentiments of Natty Bumppo in *The Pioneers*, Porgy details the service he has done his country and implies that he is owed better treatment than this. "Will I consent, after fighting the battles of my country for seven years, to be driven from my estates by a d——d civilian [. . .]. No! indeed! I will die in harness and in *possession*!" (430). The notion that legal contract and market debt could trump social standing and social debt is utterly rejected by Porgy and, one suspects, by Simms. The moral outrage in the novel is directed at a legal system that would dare to enforce the claims of market debt.

The peculiar flavor of this outrage becomes clearer during the subsequent visit to Glen-Eberley by the sheriff's deputy, Absalom Crooks. Having himself failed to serve the debt papers, the sheriff sends Crooks, a pugnacious Irishman with "red head, red face, red whiskers, red waistcoat" (442). Crooks is likewise taken prisoner by the men at Glen-Eberley, but he is made of sterner stuff. "I am here for the sheriff," he declares, "sent here to make a levy of all the lands, rights, titles, hereditaments, goods and chattels, niggers and stock [. . .] of this plantation, to take and hold thereof, and make sale thereof, in satisfaction of the judgment in the case of M'Kewn *v*. Porgy. Do you hear?" (446). The deputy's authoritative tone inspires an unexpected cruelty in Porgy and his men. Sergeant Millhouse strikes the man across the mouth with the handle of his saber, then repeatedly jabs him in the back with the blade. Once he has been forced into the house, Crooks is tied to a chair while Tom shaves off his beard. Then when the deputy attempts to read his legal documents out loud, Porgy orders his men to force the papers into his mouth, at which point he must swallow them or choke to death. "You love the law, you live on it, and ought to be able to digest it," Porgy taunts him. "Give him another mouthful, sergeant. It must all be eaten" (451).

The agent of debt is tortured for ten pages and again we can detect a latent animosity toward the law boiling under the surface. Clearly, Porgy's out-of-proportion response signals an insistent anxiety about the power of debt to overturn social hierarchies. But it is the particular character of Porgy's rage that merits our attention here. He emphasizes Crooks's red hair and red beard in such a way as to leave no doubt about the ethnic contours of this attack. "What a monster! What a horrible looking creature!" Porgy exclaims. "What a beard! Coppery-red; a perfect jungle, and full, no doubt of all sorts of diminutive beasts" (447). Crooks's Irishness, of course, would signal lower-class stature to Simms's readers, but it would also communicate an ambiguous "ethnicity" closely linked in antebellum discourse to African American identity.[33] This equation of Irish and black becomes explicit as the men hurl racist taunts at the captive deputy. When Crooks tries to tell them that he is protected by the law, Porgy asks Millhouse if he can understand what the man is trying to say. "Not a word!" Millhouse responds. "I reckon it's a sort of nigger speech from Africa" (448). When Frampton suggests that they burn off the deputy's beard, Porgy restrains him: "No! no! he may be human, and that might hurt him. We'll shave it off, and the see what he really is. I suspect he belongs to the monkey species—he's an orang-outang" (448).

The plantation violence and racist taunts suggest that Crooks functions as a thinly veiled stand-in for the figure of the African American slave. His microdrama of imprisonment and humiliation evokes the all-too-familiar slave narrative of subjugation and punishment on the antebellum plantation. At the same time, Crooks is the embodiment of legal debt; he is the personification of the law's ability to demand payment from debtors in default. As a result, *Woodcraft* conflates the figure of the slave and the threat of debt; anxieties that seem at first to be about patrimony and real estate ultimately disgorge the hazy image of the African American. The operative fear underlying Porgy's rage at the deputy is a fear of reciprocity, a fear that slaves, not simply fellow planters, may have some claim, legal or economic or moral, to be reciprocated for all that they have suffered while in chains.

In effect, *Woodcraft* attempts to manage the slaveholder fear of racial reciprocity by rerouting it through the less threatening figure of white legal authority. But the threat becomes even more pronounced, and less manageable, when it resurfaces in the figure of the poor white, a person even more closely related to the slave in the plantation social hierarchy. The squatter Bostwick recapitulates the white-as-black masquerade of

Crooks, but he does so while further emphasizing the specific threat of slave entitlement. Bostwick's relationship with M'Kewn represents a desentimentalized version of the affective bonds that link Porgy and Tom. As such, Bostwick and M'Kewn enact a barely displaced narrative of the slaveholder's worst fear: a reciprocal, market-based relationship between slave and master.

Initially, Bostwick's relationship to M'Kewn appears to be a relatively straightforward economic arrangement; the squatter performs various illegal or unsavory tasks for money. So, for instance, we learn that during the war Bostwick has been raiding plantations, stealing the slaves, and surreptitiously selling them to M'Kewn who then sells them to Moncrieff, the British commander. All three are using the chaos of the war as cover for their own profiteering. One of the jobs M'Kewn sets for Bostwick is the recovery of the widow Eveleigh's strongbox. M'Kewn suspects (correctly) that the widow has secured possession of an incriminating property deed that details the exchanges of slave property between M'Kewn and the British. So long as she has it, M'Kewn's legitimate titles to plantation property are in jeopardy because these purchases have all been financed through his illicit sale of stolen slaves. It is to recover this crucial property record, then, that Bostwick ambushes the widow and her son as they are returning to their plantation home. He manages to recover the strongbox, but his fellow thieves are killed, and he is driven off by Porgy's retinue before he can harm her or steal her slaves.

The strongbox is crucial to understanding Bostwick's role in the novel because it highlights his relationship to debt and property. He maintains possession of the box for almost the entire novel, hiding it in the hollow of an old cypress tree in the swamp. This box, of course, is a record of property transactions; like the property deed hidden in the portrait of Colonel Pyncheon, it promises to reveal the true history of reciprocal exchanges—who owes what to whom. As a result, Bostwick functions in the novel as the symbolic key to understanding the nature of debt. He possesses the box that reveals both the true titles to ownership and the legal record of reciprocal obligation.

Over the course of the novel, Bostwick uses the strongbox to extort money from M'Kewn, and it is through this process that he begins to articulate some unsettling notions of reciprocation and entitlement. The first time he encounters M'Kewn after the ambush, he makes it clear that he expects more money in return for the death and suffering he has witnessed. "You've got to pay for them papers afore you git 'em.—They're worth a sight of money. They're worth them four fine fellows that got knock'd in the head to git 'em. They're worth my horse, my rifle, my trouble, my danger, and the *or*ful fright and hurry, and run, and confusion I've had. Those papers must pay for all." This is a much fuller accounting than M'Kewn is prepared for. "I've paid you punctually for all your services," he insists. But Bostwick is having none of it. "Paid me? And whar's the pay? What am I the better for it? It comes in driblets and it couldn't last no time. Sich rewardings! 'Twon't do to talk of what you've paid me, M'Kewn; it's now that I'm to show you what you've got to pay" (256). Not only does Bostwick invert the power hierarchy here, demanding redress from his social superior, he asserts the financial value of things conventionally excluded from plantation economics. In addition to the lives of men and horses, affective experiences like trouble, danger, fright, and confusion are all given a value. Within the perverse calculus of plantation economics, of course, this fuller accounting is precluded. The suffering of slaves cannot figure into the equation because if it did, if such experiences literally counted, the economy would collapse.[34]

Bostwick's position as emblem of entitlement is most clearly revealed during a three-chapter sequence in which the squatter is playing a game of cards with two other men who also work for M'Kewn. Bostwick quickly loses all of his money, but M'Kewn himself arrives at an opportune moment. "I'm a-looking to you, M'Kewn," he tells the Scotsman, and then he extends his open palm (242). It is an evocative image, one that Simms repeats again and again over the next two chapters. Bostwick loses the gold that M'Kewn initially gives him but immediately hits him up again. "Luck's ag'in me," he tells the increasingly upset planter, "but every road I ever seed has a turn somewhere. I must hev' the guineas, M'Kewn." Then, without looking around, "he extended his open palm" (244). M'Kewn is torn between his own rage at the squatter's insolence and a lingering sense of his own indebtedness. "He [M'Kewn] rose and again sat down, and, all the while, the hand of the squatter was stretched out before him, the fingers working toward the palm [...]. It was with the most desperate reluctance that M'Kewn conceded the demand, and flung down five pieces of gold" (245). Both men realize that M'Kewn's debt to the squatter exceeds anything that can be paid off with a few gold coins. "He owes me a great deal more," Bostwick later tells the card players, "and I'll make him know it afore I'm done with him" (269).

Bostwick and his open palm become a persistent reminder of unpaid debts and unreciprocated obligations. At the same time, his demands on M'Kewn foreground the frustration and anxiety that debt brings with it. In particular, M'Kewn's feeling of indebtedness, his phenomenology of debt, is described in revealing detail. After relinquishing his first three guineas to Bostwick during the card game, M'Kewn "could not keep from showing, in his face, the feeling of scorn and disgust which he entertained for him" (243). This feeling of contempt quickly mixes with a growing anger and resentment: "M'Kewn looked more and more savage. His face had actually grown livid as he listened to the increasing insolence of the squatter" (247). M'Kewn's affective experience here registers the complex constellation of emotion that makes up the feeling of owing someone something. Disempowerment breeds resentment and scorn, which then lead to outright rage. "What was contempt before, in the feeling which he entertained for the miserable wretch whom his cupidity had employed, was rising absolutely into a sentiment of hatred. Unconsciously, vague purposes of resentment and revenge were beginning to work into his mind" (248).[35]

Simms spends as much time as he does on M'Kewn's affective experience because this violent phenomenology of debt figures prominently, albeit tacitly, in the affective economy of the plantation. Within the relatively harmless context of (white) squatter–(white) planter relations, Simms is free to explore the ramifications of a reciprocal relationship. Here, he can consider the unsettling implications of a debt economy, and he can painstakingly describe the phenomenology of debt. What he cannot do is acknowledge the fact that this phenomenology of debt is more appropriate, and more insistent, in relation to the master-slave dynamic than it is to squatter-planter interactions. To admit, or even to realize, that such a phenomenology is at work in master-slave relations would be to destabilize the social and moral economy of the plantation. It would be to acknowledge the ways in which the supposedly sentimental, extra-market relations of master and slave are in fact deeply influenced by a market-derived dynamic of reciprocal debt. Simms is not up to it.

Instead, as with Crooks, the racial subtext that underlies Bostwick's narrative must emerge obliquely, through overdetermined plot sequences and suggestive details. Once the card game has finally come to a close, M'Kewn takes Bostwick's two opponents aside and convinces them to shanghai the squatter, thereby imprisoning him on a boat and removing him as a threat. The two men are happy to oblige M'Kewn, and it doesn't take them long to get Bostwick drunk and lure him to the side of the brigantine. Once there, three sailors appear, grab Bostwick, drag him aboard, and throw him into the bowels of the ship. The description is telling:

> Suddenly, he was let down into the dark but open hold, and slid down and away, as he thought, into the bottomless depths of the sea [. . .]. He rolled over a pile of rice barrels; and grasped at them with the hold of one in mortal dread of sinking. The stars, for a

single instant, were visible overhead. But a single instant. The opening was then darkened by the figures of his captors. He strove to rise and shrieked to them in question, appeals and curses; but, with rude laughter, they clapped down the hatches and left him in unmitigated darkness [...]. When he awakened, he almost swooned with the sickness he felt. The billows were rocking beneath him. He was already out to sea. When suffered to appear on deck, the land was a mere riband along the verge of the ocean. He was flying, perforce, from his familiar swamps and fastnesses, his woman and her children. (277)

Bostwick's kidnapping looks a great deal like the accounts of slave taking that routinely occurred between European slave traders and African tribes.[36] There is his capture and bodily transport onto the ship; there is his confinement in the dark hold and his concomitant terror of the sea; there is the overwhelming nausea and disorientation aboard the vessel; finally, there is his heartbreaking loss of wife and children. The sequence seems to place Bostwick, more or less implicitly, in the role of captive slave, a slave, moreover, who reenacts a kind of reverse Middle Passage. Taken from America, he is sent off to the West Indies, tracing out in reverse one leg of the Atlantic slave trade.

Bostwick disappears from the novel for two hundred pages, but when he returns, his account of his adventures underscores the racial subtext of his experience. Once at sea, he tells a dismayed M'Kewn, "I got the cat! The cat! You knows, I reckon, what they calls the cat?" The reference is to a cat-o'-nine-tails, a whip used to flog both sailors and slaves. Bostwick goes on to emphasize the degree of scarring that occurs. "That cat which they gin to me has left its claw-marks on every inch of my back and body" (463). Bostwick figures here as a displaced version of the abused slave. Like the fugitive slave asked to display his scars to abolitionist audiences as evidence of the horrors of slavery, Bostwick's body testifies to his own suffering and humiliation at the hands of white captors.[37] In effect, the marks on his body index his transformation into the figure of the slave. Dropped into the dark hold of the Middle Passage, he emerges as a thoroughly racialized figure of entitlement.

Indeed, Bostwick's return in the novel is thematized as a kind of return of the repressed. Having gone missing for two hundred pages, M'Kewn imagines himself to be well rid of the importunate squatter. But just as he settles in to enjoy the unchallenged fruits of his deception, Bostwick rematerializes as an almost ghostly apparition. Dozing in his room under the influence of some warm whiskey punch, M'Kewn feels a heavy hand upon his shoulder. "He unclosed his eyes and stared [. . .]. Was it true—was it a dream? Did he really behold the infernal squatter, Bostwick, once more?—or was it his drowned, thrice damned, and ever haunted and haunting ghost, emerging from the depths of the green sea, and following him on the mission of the furies!" (460). M'Kewn has done his best to rid himself of both Bostwick and the debt he represents, but here the squatter returns to haunt his old master. Debt ignored or denied returns to renew its claims. More significantly, it returns newly inscribed with the markings of race. The real threat of indebtedness and reciprocal obligation, the novel suggests, can be found in the figure of the entitled slave, a ghostly presence that persists despite the planters' best efforts to disavow it.

Bostwick's return underscores the reciprocal nature of debt and thus the reciprocal nature of the master-slave relationship. Neither debt nor the entitlement due to exploited slaves can be disallowed or suppressed. It always returns to haunt the debtor. The first thing that Bostwick does when he reappears before M'Kewn is to extend his open palm. "You was intirely wrong," Bostwick tells him, "in trying to git rid of me. You kaint do without me, no more than I kin do without you. We're born for each other, and we've got to work together a long time to come." (462). This is a relationship of reciprocal obligations, a dialectical dynamic in which both sides have a claim to redress, not just one. This is the threat of the entitled slave. Bostwick transforms the uneven moral economy posited by the slaveholders into a reciprocal exchange of equals. "Thar's an account of life and death to settle atween us, M'Kewn, that may be settled up with money. [. . .] You'll pay it out of your pocket, ef you're sensible; ef you're a fool, it comes out of your heart" (466). Bostwick's challenge is twofold: first, he implies that master-slave debts are not confined to the affective realm—they can be settled with money; second, he hints at the potential for violent retribution that lies concealed in an unequal relationship. Both challenges strike at the heart of planter fears: their attempt to transform property relations into affective bonds is rejected, and they are faced with the possibility of violent reprisal.

Bostwick and Crooks represent the return of the novel's repressed anxieties about indebtedness and reciprocal obligation. These two characters highlight the ways in which explicit anxieties about financial debt could conceal more subtle and more specific fears about the legitimate claims of exploited slaves. The possibility that slaves were entitled, simply by virtue of their bondage, to redress of any sort was flatly denied by slaveholding culture. But Simms's novel suggests that this denial was not as confident or complete as Fitzhugh and other proslavery advocates might maintain. Debt resonated as loudly as it did in planter culture, *Woodcraft* implies, because it was intimately tied to the affective dynamics of the master-slave relation. Far from the sentimental myth of benevolent master and grateful slave, the phenomenology of debt that appears in *Woodcraft* points to a very different affective economy. In place of sentimental gift giving, Simms's novel uncovers a reciprocal debt relation characterized by fear and indebtedness on one side, and a sense of injustice and entitlement on the other.

Slave Narrative and the Senses of Entitlement

In "punishing" the debtor, the creditor participates in a right of the masters: at last he, too, may experience for once the exalted sensation of being allowed to despise and mistreat someone as "beneath him."
—FRIEDRICH NIETZSCHE, ON THE GENEALOGY OF MORALS

The insistent presence of Bostwick's outstretched hand in Simms's novel registers the anxiety that slaveholders felt about the slave's potential moral claims to property and redress. Such concerns were not limited to the domain of the plantation romance. In an oft-quoted passage from his *Notes on the State of Virginia* (1785), Jefferson betrays a similar uneasiness about slave entitlement. While describing at length the innate characteristics of the Negro slave, Jefferson pauses for a moment to address the issue of theft. It was widely believed that blacks were *naturally* inclined to steal things, both from their masters and from each other, but Jefferson wants to suggest another possibility:

> That disposition to theft with which they have been branded, must be ascribed to their situation, and not to any depravity of the moral sense. The man, in whose favour no laws of property exist, probably feels himself less bound to respect those made in favour of others. When arguing for ourselves, we lay it down as a fundamental, that laws, to be just, must give a reciprocation of right: that, without this, they are mere arbitrary rules of conduct, founded in force, and not in conscience: and it is a problem which I give to the master to solve, whether the religious precepts against the violation of property were not framed for him as well as his slave? And whether the slave may not justifiably take a little from one, who has taken all from him, as he may slay one who would slay him? (269)

Jefferson's argument is puzzling because although Jefferson himself is a slave owner, and although his larger claim in this section of *Notes* is that blacks are "inferior to the whites in the endowments both of body and mind," here he seems to offer a defense of stealing by slaves and a condemnation of slaveholder morality (270). He concedes the full humanity of the slave by acknowledging his healthy "moral sense" and by conflating both master and slave into the equalizing term "man." Moreover, the whole force of his argument relies on an analogy between white experience ("When arguing for ourselves") and black experience. How, he asks, can we hold slaves to a different standard than we hold ourselves? This egalitarian formulation implies a reciprocal relation, "a reciprocation of right," between master and slave that seems strikingly at odds with the violent hierarchy of the master-slave dynamic. Indeed, Jefferson goes so far as to suggest that the master himself is the real thief, having "taken all" from the slave. And given the magnitude of this theft, he points out, taking "a little" back from the master is entirely justifiable.

Remarkably, Jefferson concedes here the reciprocal property claims of the slave upon the master. He is giving voice to the same anxiety that subtends Bostwick's grasping palm, namely, the idea that slaves are entitled to a piece of the master's property. Jefferson's strategy, however, contra Simms, is to freely acknowledge the moral legitimacy of these claims but then to minimize their significance. Yes, he admits, the slave has a justifiable claim to property. But this "reciprocation of right" is not a full reciprocity; the slave may justifiably take only "a little" from the master. Of course, Jefferson never makes it clear why the slave is entitled to "a little" rather than an equal share and so he effectively re-obscures the problem he sought to address. The anxious slaveholder, after reading this passage, might still wonder about the threatening magnitude of slave claims upon his property.

Jefferson's argument reinforces the cultural prominence of slaveholder debt anxiety that we first saw in *Woodcraft*. At the same time, his writing calls attention to the significance of theft in the moral and financial economy of the plantation. Theft, it seems, is something of a flashpoint for understanding the contested notions of property and ownership that characterized the master-slave relationship. Perhaps the most striking aspect of Jefferson's passage is the way in which it attempts to address the problem of theft by briefly inhabiting the point of view of the slave. Jefferson asks his readers to imagine what it would be like to lack the rights of property, that is, what it would be like to experience ownership as a slave. That slave, he suggests, "probably feels himself less bound to respect those [laws] made in favour of others." This is a strategy of sympathetic identification in which the reader attempts to "feel," however obliquely, a phenomenology of inhibited ownership.

What I would like to suggest is that Jefferson helps draw our attention to two key aspects of property relations within plantation society:

the slave's own experience of entitlement, and the act of theft that helps define it. *Woodcraft* offers us a phenomenology of debt as imagined from the perspective of a slave owner. But what about the other side of the property dialectic? What about the experience of the slave? Simms, like Jefferson, gestures at this alternative phenomenology by obliquely considering a slave's perspective (or quasi-slave's perspective in Bostwick's case). But a much richer account of slave experience can be found in the genre of the antebellum slave narrative. Theft, in particular, figures prominently in such narratives, and, as a result, it provides a crucial perspective on slave views of property and ownership. A close reading of theft themes in a selection of slave narratives will help us to flesh out the feeling, the *sense* of entitlement, hinted at in Jefferson and Simms. This phenomenology of entitlement, I contend, constitutes the flip side of the master's phenomenology of debt. Whereas slaveholders are plagued by feelings of anxiety, contested ownership, and indebtedness, slaves manifest a feeling of entitlement and justified possession. This property, the slave declares, *feels* like mine because in some very real sense it is mine.[38]

Theft, as Jefferson's comments suggest, was a pervasive means of slave resistance in the social world of the Southern plantation. Slaves regularly stole livestock, vegetables, liquor, tools, clothing, and any other pieces of moveable property that promised to ease the pains of life in bondage. For their part, white property owners frequently bemoaned the exorbitant losses they suffered at the hands of their pilfering slaves. Agricultural reformer Thomas Affleck, for example, complained in 1849 that "many planters raise an ample supply of hogs for their families, black and white. Many more find it a thing impossible, from the destruction of their young stock by the negroes, who have all a particular penchant for roast pig, and especially when stolen."[39] The practice was so common that it contributed to the popular white stereotype of the "thieving Negro."[40] And slave narratives corroborate this notion of ubiquitous theft. In *Slavery in the United States* (1837), for instance, Charles Ball describes stealing a sheep, killing it, and surreptitiously boiling the meat in his cabin (92). Moreover, he notes that most masters had no problem with their slaves stealing from other plantations: "I afterwards learned that this was not always regarded as a very high crime by the owner of a slave, provided he would perpetrate the theft so adroitly as not to be detected in it" (84–85).

Slave owners tended to ascribe this penchant for theft to the degraded moral condition of the slave. As one mistress explained, "The conduct of the negroes in robbing our house, store room, meat house, etc. and refusing to restore anything shows you they *think it right* to steal from us, to spoil us, as the Israelites did the Egyptians" (qtd. in Genovese 602). But slaves, not surprisingly, had a much different conception of this property relation. Ball makes it clear that stealing was entirely justified among the slaves he knew: "I was never acquainted with a slave, who believed that he violated any rule of morality, by appropriating to himself any thing that belonged to his master, if it was necessary to his comfort. The master might call it theft [. . .] but the slave reasoned differently when he took a portion of his master's goods, to satisfy his hunger, keep himself warm, or to gratify his passion for luxurious enjoyment" (257). The operative distinction for slaves was between "stealing" and "taking." Stealing was an immoral act that could occur only when one slave stole from another; "taking" was a justifiable appropriation of the master's property. Frederick Law Olmsted, during his first fact-finding tour of the slave South in 1853, learned of this distinction at firsthand. "Even the religious," he explained, "feel justified in using 'massa's' property for their own temporal benefits. This they term 'taking,' and it is never admitted to be a reproach to a man among them that he is charged with it, though 'stealing,' or taking from another than their master, and particularly from one another, is so."[41] Plantation slaves thus developed an alternative moral framework for understanding their relationship to both the master's property and to the possessions of other slaves.

This alternative morality was justified by a variety of essentially rights-based arguments. Most obviously, like Locke, slaves felt that all men had a right to nourishment. Thus, any theft of food from the master was completely justifiable. "I never deprived any one of all the masters that I have served," Ball assures his readers, "of anything against his consent, unless it was some kind of food; and that of all I ever took, I am confident, I have given away more than half to my fellow slaves, whom I knew to be equally needy with myself" (262). At the same time, many slaves also asserted a right to their master's property based on a Lockean notion of labor appropriation. That is, they maintained that they were entitled to pieces of the master's property because they had expended their own hard labor to procure that property in the first place. "The slave sees his master residing in a spacious mansion," Ball explains, "riding in a fine carriage, and dressed in costly clothes, and attributes the possession of all these enjoyments to his own labor; whilst he who is the cause of so much gratification and pleasure to another, is himself deprived of even the necessary accommodations of human life" (257). A deep-seated belief in some version of natural rights then, whether to food or to the fruits of labor, formed the foundations of an alternative moral economy for plantation slaves.

Crucially, the slaves' alternative view of property relations brought with it an alternative phenomenology of ownership. Whereas *Woodcraft* suggests that the master's experience of property is haunted by a persistent anxiety about looming debt, the slave narratives imply that slave experience was characterized by a strong sense, a palpable *feeling*, of entitlement and right to property. This is the other side of the phenomenological dialectic that conditions the master-slave relationship. The master's repressed sense of debt to the slave is counterbalanced by the slave's very conscious sense of entitlement to what has been taken from him. Together, these paired experiences of debt and entitlement constitute a critical component of the phenomenology of property. The affective tug-of-war over property rights that gets played out between master and slave effectively (and violently) amplifies the phenomenology of contested claims that underlies less agonistic experiences of ownership. Thus, understanding the slave's phenomenology of entitlement is vital to understanding ownership itself.

Descriptions of this sense of entitlement, this feeling of what it is to be owed something, appear again and again in a wide range of slave narratives, but Frederick Douglass and Harriet Jacobs provide two particularly illuminating accounts. After living in the North for several years, Jacobs unexpectedly encounters an old slave acquaintance on the streets of New York City. Once the two reacquaint themselves, she asks Luke if he has enough money to reach Canada. His response hinges on the familiar distinction between stealing and taking. "'Pend upon it, I hab," he says, "I tuk car fur dat. I'd bin workin all my days fur dem cussed whites, an got no pay but kicks and cuffs. So tought dis nigger had a right to money nuff to bring him to de Free States" (149). Luke goes on to disclose how after his master died, he took some of the master's money, surreptitiously placed it in the pocket of his master's old pants, and then, once his master was buried, demurely asked his new owners if he could have the old pants as a gift. "With a low, chuckling laugh, he added, 'You see I didn't *steal* it; dey *gub* it to me'" (150). Here, Luke craftily operates within the constraints of planter ideology, allowing the new owners to maintain their sense of themselves as paternal gift-givers while at the same time concealing a theft within the gift.

The image is striking: money hidden in the pocket of a dead master's pants is transferred to a waiting slave. The scene enacts a macabre version of the reciprocal economy so feared by the slave owners. Like some sort of grim puppeteer, the slave forces the master's clothes to act out the property exchange that the master himself would never have performed. In fact, the implied image of Luke "wearing the pants" suggests that the slave is acting out a dramatically reversed vision of the plantation power dynamic: literally "puttin' on ole massa," Luke can now imagine himself as the patriarch, in some sense, and worthy of the reciprocity he has previously been denied. Again, as with Bostwick's "haunting" of M'Kewn, the redress occurs within a gothic register. Luke's master is effectively reanimated after death, and only as a ghost is he able to acknowledge the property claims of his slave.

Luke's sense of entitlement to his master's property is hinted at in the "low, chuckling laugh" that accompanies his story: he takes an understandable pleasure in knowing that he has retrieved at least a tiny piece of the debt he is owed. But Jacob's own analysis of Luke's story underscores the idea that the slave experience of property is characterized by this strong sense of entitlement. "When a man has his wages stolen from him, year after year," she wonders, "and the laws sanction and enforce the theft, how can he be expected to have more regard to honesty than has the man who robs him?" It is a good question, one that foregrounds the divergent moral economies of owner and owned. More importantly, though, it explains how Jacobs can sympathize with Luke's actions. "I have become somewhat enlightened," she explains, "but I confess that I agree with poor, ignorant, much-abused Luke, in thinking he had a *right* to that money, as a portion of his unpaid wages" (150). Jacobs couches her rationale in the language of "thinking" and "enlightenment," but it is clear that this is also an affective identification with the ex-slave. "Poor," "ignorant," and "much-abused," Luke is worthy of her sympathy and his feeling of entitlement of entirely understandable. Jacobs herself has felt the sting of having her wages stolen year after year, so Luke's gleeful "theft" of his master's money makes perfect sense to her.

Like Jacobs, Douglass turns the notion of the "thieving Negro" back on the slaveholders themselves, arguing that they are, in fact, the ones doing the stealing. Once he learns to read, Douglass gradually pieces together a more complete history of the institution of slavery. As he does so, his contempt for slaveholders grows accordingly. When describing these feelings of contempt, however, he focuses specifically on the slaveholders' status as thieves. "I could regard them in no other light than a band of successful robbers, who had left their homes, and gone to Africa, and stolen us from our homes, and in a strange land reduced us to slavery" (33). Douglass reverses the moral economy espoused by the slaveholders by imaginatively restoring the slaves to their original African hearth and home. From this expanded perspective, slaves are the property owners, both of their homes and of themselves, and slaveholders are the thieves who have stolen away cherished possessions. By reframing the master-slave property relation in this way, Douglass justifies a sense of entitlement, a sense of property lost and debts owed.

Moreover, he begins to link this justification of entitlement to the *feeling* of contempt he has for the slaveholders. "As I read and contemplated the subject, behold! that very discontentment which Master Hugh had predicted would follow my learning to read had already come, to torment and sting my soul to unutterable anguish." He "writhes" under this new feeling; it is an "agony" that "presses" upon him (33). These are the affective contours of the slave's insistent sense of entitlement denied. The "torment" and "sting" of his "discontentment" is part and parcel of his sense that he has lost something that once belonged to him and that he is now owed something in return.

Douglass's phenomenology of entitlement becomes even more pronounced once he begins earning his own wages as a caulker in the shipyard of Walter Price. Hired out by his master, Hugh Auld, Douglass is largely independent, able to find his own employment and make his own contracts. He then delivers his wages to "Master Hugh" at the end of every work week. But handing over the fruits of his own labor, week after week, recalls the discontentment he feels when considering the slave traders' theft of African slaves. Here again he is forced to contend with an unequal exchange and with the stinging sense of entitlement denied. "I was compelled to deliver every cent of that money to Master Hugh. And why? Not because he earned it,—not because he had any hand in earning it,—not because I owed it to him,—nor because he possessed the slightest shadow of a right to it; but solely because he had the power to compel me to give it up" (65). Douglass's indignation and moral outrage is directly linked to the perversion of a reciprocal economy. From his perspective, he owes Auld nothing in this relationship; rather, Auld is in his debt for the wages he has stolen from Douglass.

Occasionally, Auld attempts to encourage Douglass's efforts by giving him six cents (out of the six dollars he has earned) to keep as his own. But this only increases Douglass's anger:

> I regarded it as a sort of admission of my right to the whole. The fact that he gave me any part of my wages was proof, to my mind, that he believed me entitled to the whole of them. I always felt worse for having received any thing; for I feared that the giving me a few cents would ease his conscience, and make him feel himself to be a pretty honorable sort of robber. My discontent grew upon me. (66)

As in Luke's narrative, we can see the slaveholder attempting to inscribe a narrative of paternal benevolence here. Auld will magnanimously bestow a gift of six cents upon Douglass as a reward for his dedicated labor. But Douglass sees this for the mockery of reciprocity that it is and persists in characterizing the slaveholder as a thief. More significantly, Douglass gestures at the phenomenology of debt experienced by his master. He perceptively infers that Auld is troubled by his conscience, by a sense of guilt over the exploitation of his slave. In fact, Douglass senses that at some level Auld believes that his slave is entitled to an entirely equitable recompense, "the whole," for his efforts. This, it would seem, is the very same phenomenology that haunts Porgy and M'Kewn: a nagging feeling that the slave is owed something more, much more, than the skewed sentimental economy of affect is allowing him. Auld is made uneasy by the specter of a truly reciprocal economy linking him with Douglass. The flip side of this debt anxiety is Douglass's "discontent," his own conviction that he is indeed entitled to "the whole" fruits of his labor.

These paired phenomenologies of debt and entitlement represent a more accurate account of the affective economy that binds master and slave. In contrast to Fitzhugh's myth of familial love and domestic care, the feelings of master and slave toward one another are better understood as versions of a distorted property exchange. The position of social dominance and paternal power experienced by the master is troubled by a lingering sense of debt, by an insistent anxiety that he is always, in some moral and economic sense, in arrears. The slave, despite his social and economic subordination, or perhaps in part because of it, experiences a feeling of entitlement, a complex sense of outrage, contempt, and right to property that flies in the face of white ownership. Mutually constitutive, these two affective experiences demonstrate the degree to which property and ownership are a dialectical phenomenology. As we turn back to the genre of the plantation romance, we will see this dialectic manifest itself in the space of the plantation itself.

The Structure of the Debt: *Swallow Barn* and the Space of the Plantation

Although the actual building was never constructed, Thomas Jefferson produced three different designs for an observation tower he wanted placed on top of a mountain overlooking Monticello. "Montalto," as he called it (now Patterson Mountain), was a 1,200–foot peak a little less than a mile to the west of Monticello, and it offered a panoramic view of Jefferson's entire plantation. The tower itself was to have been a five-story, one-hundred-foot structure capped by a small octagonal cupola for viewing. While the pragmatic value of such a tower seems questionable, Jefferson's desire to build it reflects his fascination with the possibilities of supervision and surveillance. Such a vantage point would provide what Foucault called "The Eye of Power," a position of centralized observation that can serve as "the focus of the exercise of power and [. . .] the registration of knowledge" (148). From this elevated perch, Jefferson would have simultaneous visual access to everything from his sawmill on the Rivanna River to the family cemetery at the western border of the plantation. In this way, the proposed tower indexed a quintessentially eighteenth-century yearning to render the world entirely visible, entirely transparent, and thus knowable and controllable. Of course, the prospect of panoptical control would have been particularly attractive to a wealthy American planter interested in maintaining a disciplined and productive workforce. Indeed, although the Montalto tower was never built, when Jefferson began remodeling Monticello in 1796, he added an impressive octagonal dome (with six windows) to the top of the new addition. Whether he actually used the structure for observing his slaves, the dome functioned as a reminder of Jefferson's belief in the coercive power of constant supervision.[42]

More significantly for our purposes, Jefferson's architecture of surveillance reflects a broader conception of spatial practice among antebellum slaveholders. Planters were keen to implement Enlightenment notions of geometric order and mathematical precision when organizing the spaces of their plantations. Historian Rhys Isaac notes that in eighteenth-century Virginia, plantations were being "fashioned as declarations of the owners' status, not only by sheer scale but also by means of elaborately contrived formal relationships. Calculated proportion and rigidly controlled symmetry became mandatory" (35–36). What this meant in practice was that plantation houses and their "dependencies," or outbuildings, were being laid out in precise geometric patterns, often a rectangular arrangement around a central yard. The architecture of the buildings themselves often followed a symmetrical Georgian style with precise, mathematical proportions and three-part designs that symbolically emphasized a social hierarchy of the ruling "head" and subordinate "members" (Isaac 37–39).[43] Rigid organizational schemas of this sort encouraged a rational, regimented approach to slave labor; slaves were meant to order their own lives according to the clearly delineated spaces and schedules established by the owner. The strategies of surveillance represented by Jefferson's dome and by the ubiquitous presence of the "overseer" (whose house was often close enough to the slave cabins to watch them) were the counterpart to this geometrical precision. Slaves had to be constantly watched in order to ensure that they remained in the proper spaces and engaged in the proper productive activities.[44]

At the same time that Monticello represented an idealized space of transparency and visibility, however, it also contained within it a paradoxical impulse to concealment. After one visitor complained, for example, that the slave quarters along Mulberry Row (the main road skirting the southern edge of the house and outbuildings) created "a most unpleasant contrast with the palace that rises so near them" (qtd. in Epperson 70), Jefferson had the cabins torn down and rebuilt much further to the southeast, below the sightline from the house. Inside the house itself, he devised his own architectural innovations to minimize face-to-face contact with his house slaves. In the dining room, for instance, he constructed dumbwaiters that would allow fresh bottles of wine to be lifted from the wine cellar without slaves having to enter the room. Similarly, he had a revolving serving door installed that enabled kitchen slaves to move dishes in and out of the room without disturbing the meal.[45] In effect, Jefferson contrived an architecture of concealment at Monticello wherein the presence of slaves was elided for the casual viewer. The economy of exploitation upon which the plantation was based was carefully moved into the background. By so doing, Jefferson fashioned a peculiar spatial paradox in which the movements of slaves were to be both entirely visible—to the overseer and those responsible for maintaining disciplinary control—and largely invisible—to visitors and family members with a vested interest in forgetting the violence and exploitation upon which their idyllic experience rested.

The spatial paradox at Monticello is valuable, I believe, because it alerts us to the dialectical nature of space on the plantation. Underneath the official geometries of planter control, Monticello suggests, there lies another spatial experience, one that unfolds in the largely unseen margins of planter life. This is *slave space*, or what Isaac calls an "alternative territorial system," and it constitutes the flipside, the substrate of the master's symmetrical plantation (53). Behind the revolving door, unseen in the cellars below, and scattered across the plantation in a network of unsanctioned spaces, slaves enacted their own set of spatial relations in the interstices of the master's hyper-visible order. In the fields and slave quarters of the plantation itself, and in the swamps and woods that surrounded it, the slave deciphered "another set of marks, [. . .] signs of the occupancy of his own people," that were invisible to white eyes (Isaac 52). "Their [the slaves'] landscapes were crisscrossed by the trails that led to scenes of communal activities. [. . .] Beyond the storehouses and granaries, but well marked in the memory, were the places deep in the woods where the slaves might slaughter and barbecue the semi-wild hogs that bore on their ears and rumps the marks of a master's claim to possession"

(Isaac 52–53). Architectural historian John Michael Vlach concurs that "slaves used subtle behavioral means to structure alternative landscapes with different spatial imperatives. They would simply ignore the ritual obeisance of a plantation's carefully marked 'processional landscape' and move across its fields, gardens, and grounds more or less as they pleased" (231). In this way, slaves produced a fluid, non-rectilinear subspace that existed in dialectical relation with the "official" space of the plantation.[46]

Crucially, this dialectical contest between competing spatial practices was also a contest of appropriation. That is, as master and slave both worked to inscribe the space of the plantation with their own meanings, uses, and structural systems, they were in effect attempting to take possession, to assert their own title to various locations and patterns of movement within the larger space of the plantation. Of course, legally speaking, the master owned everything, both the plantation real estate and the slaves themselves. But the lived spatial relations of plantation life produced a very different sense of spatial ownership. As Vlach observes, "The simple act of occupying a space was tantamount to appropriating it," and in this manner slaves asserted a variety of counterclaims to aspects of plantation space (xi). "Slaves who claimed their masters' land as their own similarly found that it virtually *was* theirs. Acts of territorial appropriation [. . .] were carried out, in the main, simply by the slaves occupying the spaces to which they were assigned. Slaves gradually identified these spaces as theirs through a routine of innumerable domestic acts" (235). Nor was such ownership merely a fantasy of control on the part of the slaves. Elizabeth Fox-Genovese recounts a confrontation between mistress and house slave in which the slave asserts her ownership of the kitchen space by expelling the white woman: "*Go* inter de *house*, Miss Carrie! Yer ain't no manner er use heah only ter git yer face red wid de heat. I'll have dinner like yer wants it. Jes' read yer book an' res' easy til I sen's it ter de dining room" (142). Spaces on the plantation are thus produced, claimed, and policed by *both* master and slave. As a result, the spatial fabric of the plantation is best understood as a shifting, ambiguous field of contested spaces in which master and slave interact with one another to mutually create the experiential landscape of the plantation.[47]

To some extent, the plantation romance is a record of this dialectical production of plantation space. Novels like *Woodcraft* and *The Planter's Northern Bride* provide some sense of the diverse, and even competing, spaces that make up the plantation landscape. Not surprisingly, however, the overwhelming emphasis in these novels is on a slaveholder-centered understanding of plantation space. Comparatively little effort is made to detail the spaces and spatial practices of the slaves, while the master's fantasy of orderly, and picturesque space is maintained. But as was the case with its sentimentalized view of the master-slave relationship, there is a sense of unease that haunts the sunny spaces of the plantation romance. At the margins of the master's control, the novels betray hints of the submerged slave space that was so important to the everyday experience of the plantation. What I would like to suggest is that this spatial unease is structured by the same threatening dialectic of debt and entitlement that plagues the master-slave dynamic. Through a reading, in particular, of John Pendleton Kennedy's *Swallow Barn* (1832), I want to argue that the spaces of the plantation romance reflect an anxiety about unstable ownership and insistent counterclaims. Underneath the narrative of contented spatial segregation, there remains a more volatile story of hazy boundary lines and uncertain appropriation. This story of contesting property claims extends our earlier discussion of planter debt anxiety and demonstrates the ways in which plantation space both reflected and contributed to this debt phenomenology.

Initially, it seems as if the representation of space in plantation romances is simply another instantiation of the slaveholder's paternalist fantasy of affection and control. In *The Planter's Northern Bride*, for example, Hentz depicts Moreland's plantation as the epitome of productive power and bucolic bliss. "All around, far as the eye could reach, rich, rolling fields of cotton, bearing the downy wealth of the South, stretched out in a boundless ocean of green, spotted with white, like the foam of the wave" (330). Cotton fields evoke both the heroic expanse of the sea and the promise of agricultural wealth. Eulalia, Moreland's wife and mistress of the plantation, is particularly enamored of the picturesque slave quarters. "The cabins of the negroes, each with their own well-cultivated plot of ground, poultry yard, and melon patch, she loved to visit, for wherever she turned her eye she saw abundant proof of Moreland's considerate kindness and liberality" (340). The quarters are transformed here into a vision of domestic order and contentment, all courtesy of the master's largesse.[48] Indeed, as Eulalia tours the plantation, its spaces begin to sound to the modern ear more like an exhibit at Frontierland or colonial Williamsburg than a working plantation:

> She visited the sawmill and grist-mill, built on the margin of a roaring stream; the blacksmith's shop, that, isolated from the other buildings, looked as if it were cooling its fiery forge in the fresh green expanse that surrounded it, and where the stalwart artisan, begrimed by nature, heeded not the black soot that settled on

his dusky skin; the carpenter's shop, where all the furniture necessary for the negroes was made, even to 'a right sharp bedstead or bureau,' as the workman told her. She went to the weaving and spinning rooms, where cotton and woolen webs were manufactured for negro clothing, and counterpanes of curious devices. Everything necessary for comfort and use was of home-work, and everything was done with a neatness, order, and despatch that surprised the young mistress. (340–41)[49]

The "roaring stream," the "fiery forge," and the "fresh green expanse" all work to place this space in harmony with the natural world and to imbue it with the warm glow of domestic affection. It is a quaint picture of industrious domestic life that might recall for readers the preindustrial workshops and manufactories that were mostly fond memories by the 1850s.[50] Plantation space here reflects the needs and desires of proslavery ideology.

Kennedy, too, sentimentalizes the space of the plantation in *Swallow Barn*. The plantation house is "an aristocratical old edifice" that sits "like a brooding hen, on the southern bank of the James River." "It looks down upon a shady pocket or nook, formed by an indentation of the shore, from a gentle acclivity thinly sprinkled with oaks whose magnificent branches afford habitation to sundry friendly colonies of squirrels and woodpeckers" (27). The "gentle," "shady" spot takes on an even more Irving-esque patina of quaintness as Kennedy describes the main outbuilding. "The most venerable appendage to the establishment," the huge barn possesses "an immense roof hanging almost to the ground, and thatched a foot thick with sunburnt straw, which reaches below the eaves in ragged flakes. It has a singularly drowsy and decrepit aspect." And occasionally, "a clownish, hobble-de-hoy colt, with long fetlocks and disordered mane, and a thousand burrs in his tail" will scamper happily through the tableau (29–30). The warm and comfortable image might have been airlifted from Sleepy Hollow.

Charming set-pieces of this sort constitute the predominant representation of space in the plantation genre. Slave spaces are either erased entirely or cloaked in the comfortable terms of the sentimental and picturesque. But there are a few scattered moments in which the novels hint at something else, at the presence of an alternative, sub-rosa spatial system at odds with planter control. In *Swallow Barn*, the narrator briefly describes a disputed piece of property at the boundary line separating Swallow Barn from its neighbor, The Brakes. At first, it appears to be nothing more than an overgrown tract of marsh land. "It was a perfect wilderness," he writes. "No fences had ever been erected on either side, to guard the contiguous territories from encroachment. [. . .] In fact, it may have been said to have belonged to the colts, pigs, heifers, raccoons, opossums and rabbits of both proprietors." Yet, a closer look reveals a more specific effort at spatial appropriation: "The negroes still consider it the finest place in the whole country to catch vermin [. . .] and I myself frequently, in my ranges through this region, encounter their various gins and snares set in the many by-paths that cross it" (145). Such forest trails are precisely the sort of alternative territorial system associated with slave space. Later in the novel, in a chapter entitled "Woodcraft," the narrator, Mark Littleton, and his cousin Ned Hazard, accompany some plantation slaves on a nighttime possum hunt. Once again, the slaves demonstrate a superior knowledge of the plantation's forest spaces.

In *The Planter's Northern Bride*, subversive slave spaces appear briefly and only in relation to the evil machinations of an abolitionist preacher named Brainard. As he furtively preaches the incendiary ideology of freedom and equality to the slaves, Brainard is simultaneously plotting a violent rebellion. So it is only under his influence that the slaves begin occupying their alternative geography. "He had runners," we learn, "employed in traveling secretly from place to place, giving constant information of all that was passing—shuttles on the loom of abolition, weaving a web which should be the winding-sheet of the South" (456). This secret communication takes place on "wild-wood path[s], dark with the shadows of a moonless night" (449). These are the same spatial networks described in slave narratives, but Hentz undercuts their threatening implications by blaming them on the harmful influence of a Northern agitator. Still, this clever displacement draws on what was a persistent spatial anxiety for slaveholders. The nature of this fear becomes more explicit in another scene of midnight rebellion. The same blacksmith's shop that was earlier described in such picturesque terms is now transformed by the revelation of a hidden purpose. "A dusky form could be seen travailing by the burning forge, in the hush of the midnight hour, with closed shutters, to exclude the ruddy beams from flashing on the darkness of night." Gone is the transparent allure of the "fiery forge" in its "fresh green expanse"; instead, the space is closed off, concealed from view so that the "swarthy artisan" can manufacture "rude swords and murderous weapons." "Then, by and by, the black Vulcan would steal forth, and, removing a pile of dried underbrush and moss, crawl on his hands and feet under the building and deposit the hastily-wrought instruments in a dark cavity, dug out, deep and narrow, beneath the forge" (455). This is the haunting threat of slave spaces on the plantation. Concealed behind a façade of affection and submission, slave space threatened to reappropriate and repurpose the orderly, productive spaces of the master's plantation and turn them into a conduit of repressed rage. "Bedsteads" and "bureaus" become "murderous weapons" that get deposited in secret spaces unseen by the planter or his Northern bride.

Still, such moments of spatial tension are relatively infrequent in the plantation romance. Authors seem largely unwilling, or unable, to directly confront the implications of an alternative spatial network at odds with their fantasy of sentimental order and productivity. As a result, the plantation romances at first seem to downplay the influence of slave topography in the dialectical production of plantation space. Yet, as we learned in their treatment of the master-slave dynamic, one way these novels contain anxiety is to reroute it through safer, more acceptable narrative frames. In particular, we saw anxieties about a reciprocal economy, about a dialectic of slave entitlement and master debt, get rerouted through a supposedly de-racialized narrative of white-on-white financial debt. This shift, then, from a raced to an unraced framework, from white-black debt relations to simply "unmarked" debt relations, is a hint as to how we might track planter fears about slave space. *Swallow Barn*, I want to argue, reflects precisely this sort of transference by literally dis-placing the slaveholder's spatio-racial anxieties onto an elaborate account of a property dispute between two wealthy white planters.

The novel as a whole is an Irving-esque collection of loosely connected sketches that detail the idyllic lives of two Southern families. The narrator, Mark Littleton, travels south from New York to visit his cousin Ned Hazard who lives on the Virginia plantation at Swallow Barn. Although the plantation has been in the Hazard family for generations, at present it is owned by Frank Meriwether, husband of Ned's sister, Lucretia. Ned and Lucretia's deceased father, Walter Hazard, had been subject to "some gentlemanlike incumbrances which had been sleeping for years upon the domain," so when Frank paid these off, he assumed title of the estate (27). Littleton's visit allows him to closely observe the manner of life on this Southern plantation; as a result, much of the novel is devoted to humorous descriptions of local characters and rural customs. The novel's plot is notoriously, and self-consciously, unfocused. Kennedy, in his 1832 preface, must reassure his readers that "There is a rivulet of story wandering through a broad meadow of episode. Or, I might truly say, it is a book of episodes, with an occasional digression into the plot" (xxxvii). The book intermittently follows the courtship narrative of Ned and Bel Tracy. Bel is the beautiful daughter of old Isaac Tracy, a cantankerous planter who owns the neighboring estate of The Brakes. But Kennedy's interest in this love plot seems half-hearted, and eventually it drops away altogether. Other sketches involve a nighttime possum hunt, Ned's fistfight with a local brute, a description of the county court, a hike through the "Goblin Swamp," and an account of Abe, a heroic slave from the plantation.

The significance of Abe's narrative has been the focal point of much of the scholarship on the novel. Recent critics have argued that the complex and largely positive construction of Abe's character helps to undercut Littleton's decidedly proslavery perspective. Abe's story immediately follows a chapter in which Littleton and Meriwether visit the slave quarters and Meriwether spontaneously delivers a lecture defending slavery. By the end of the lecture, Littleton seems convinced. But directly on the heels of this harangue, Kennedy offers a lengthy account of Abe's exploits as a slave sailor, an account in which Abe eventually sacrifices his own life trying to save the crew of a capsized ship. Critics maintain that at the very least this juxtaposition of slave heroism with proslavery discourse renders the novel's politics ambiguous; at best, it constitutes a direct challenge to Meriwether's views. Earlier critics were less sanguine, reading the novel as a romanticization of the South and a straightforward embrace of proslavery rhetoric.[51]

What this focus on Abe has obscured, however, is the crucial significance of the elaborate property narrative that winds its way through the novel. Some time before the Revolutionary War, old Edward Hazard, grandfather of Ned and Lucretia, took it upon himself to construct a gristmill on a little branch of the James River called the "Apple-pie." The Apple-pie forms the boundary line between Swallow Barn and The Brakes, and because Edward would need land on both sides of the stream in order to build the mill, he was required to purchase a piece of his neighbor's property. His neighbor at the time, Gilbert Tracy, was happy to oblige, so the two contracted to transfer title "to so much of the said land as it may be found useful and necessary to occupy in the accomplishment of the said design" (142). Edward has badly misjudged the flow capacity of the Apple-pie, however, and the mill quickly proves to be an embarrassing failure. Over the years, it falls into disrepair and the milldam is swept away. The decay of the millworks then calls into question the ownership of the property: without the mill there to justify Hazard's appropriation, Gilbert Tracy and his son Isaac both think that the land should revert back to its original owners, namely, them.

This property dispute forms the central conflict of the novel, and it goes a long way toward explaining Kennedy's complicated politics.[52] Unfortunately, it also weakens the critical claim that Kennedy has concealed a progressive antislavery message in his novel. Instead, the property dispute suggests that the novel is a more canny defense of slavery than existing criticism has realized. More importantly for our purposes, the dispute makes it clear that the novel's principal ideological function is to contain planter anxieties about slave appropriation of, and slave entitlement to, plantation space.

Initially, the novel's representation of space seems to follow the slaveholder fantasy of geometric order and control. Littleton describes the façade architecture at The Brakes, for example, as "built in exact uniformity" and details a line of offices that "sweeps rectangularly along the brow of the hill" (176, 219). "Over all the grounds," he tells us, "an air of neatness prevails, even to an extent that might be called pedantic" (219). In contrast to this Enlightenment order, however, the disputed property bordering the Apple-pie is chaotic and protean, a wild space resistant to clear demarcation. The stream "traverses a range of low grounds for some miles, occasionally spreading itself out into morasses [. . .] overgrown with thickets of arrow-wood, nine-bark, and various other shrubs" (131). Oozing and aqueous, this riparian marsh-space is constantly shifting and overrunning its natural boundaries.

The spatial history of the mill itself underscores the ambiguous nature of the Apple-pie claims. To build the mill, Edward Hazard has to construct a dam across the stream that will gather the waters of the Apple-pie into a millpond. This stored water can then be gradually released to power the waterwheel. But as the waters slowly accumulate, the familiar contours of the stream disappear and, along with them, the boundary line between the properties. Edward remarks on the changing topography as he watches the rising waters of the pond: "It [is] strange," he tells his young son Walter, "to see what results were produced by human art" (132). Once the pond is full and the mill begins operation, it lasts for only two hours before the water supply is again depleted. Surprised and upset by this unexpected development, Edward investigates the mill-pond and finds nothing but a muddy, waterlogged mess. "There were all the little tussocks of the swamp, showing their small green heads above the surface of the water, which would hardly have covered one's shoe-top; and there were all the native shrubs of the marsh, bending forwards, in scattered groups [. . .] dripping wet, and having their slender stalks tangled with weeds" (134). The shifting swamp space stubbornly resists Edward's attempt to harness it for organized, productive labor. Indeed, as the waters are rising, Edward attempts to carve a water-level mark on a tree in the bed of the pond. But "while stooping to take a level with the breast of the dam, he lost his balance, and was upset into a pool, formed by the encroaching element" (133). Here, the submarine plantation space metaphorically consumes the planter, refusing to yield to the dictates of order and spatial containment.

The focus of the Apple-pie property dispute is upon the shifting nature of the boundary line. When Edward and Gilbert initially exchange title to the property, they do so in order that "the western limit of The Brakes [will be] removed from the channel of the Branch to the water edge of the mill-pond" (142). But because the pond is continually filling and emptying, the boundary is continually shifting. Isaac Tracy's subsequent suit against Frank Meriwether is meant to resolve this ambiguity once and for all. But even at the very outset of the case, we learn that "it was hard to determine which should be plaintiff, and which defendant; since it was not quite clear who was in possession" (150). Kennedy underscores the murky, tangled nature of these contesting claims when the lawyers actually visit the property in question. Philpot Wart, counsel for Meriwether, and Singleton Swansdown, Tracy's representative, both agree to a "trial by view," that is, a walking tour of the ground in dispute. The two men disappear into the quagmire, and one of them becomes hopelessly tangled in the undergrowth. "I have encountered shocking obstacles, Mr. Wart," Swansdown hollers at one point. "I have one leg submersed in water and mud, up to the knee; and have had a score of black-snakes hissing at me, ever since I got into this abominable place" (206). The scene is played for humor, but it also represents in concrete spatial terms the difficulty, indeed, the threat, posed by slippery and confusing property claims.

In broad strokes, then, the Apple-pie dispute narrativizes the problem of contested ownership. The protean swamp property enacts a kind of back and forth, push-me-pull-you model of appropriation and expropriation. It is never entirely certain which of the two planters possesses the space. Of course, at one level, Kennedy offers this elaborate property debate as a symbol of the eventual marriage of Ned and Bel; that is, the divisions that have long separated the two aristocratic families will be healed by the union of their two young heirs. But a broad symbolic reading of this sort hardly accounts for the time, space, and complicated treatment that the novel devotes to the Apple-pie dispute. More to the point, it does not account for the persistent racial overtones that cling to the property narrative. What I want to suggest is that the Apple-pie dispute is best understood in precisely racial terms; that, in short, it functions as a phenomenological stand-in for planter anxieties about slave appropriation of plantation space.

Already, Kennedy links the Apple-pie wilderness specifically to the spatial inscriptions of the plantation slaves. This is the landscape upon which "no fences had ever been erected," but upon which Littleton discovers "various gins and snares" set by the slaves "in the many by-paths that cross it." So, even as the legal title to the Apple-pie terrain remains in dispute, the slaves have quietly asserted a pragmatic right of use and occupancy that marks the property as their own. During the fleeting period in which the mill-pond is full and the mill is working, albeit intermittently, it is slaves who are most closely associated with the space. It is they, not the plantation whites, who bring the grain to be milled. "They came there, all through the summer, in crowds; and nothing was more common than to see a dozen ruminative old horses, with as many little bare-legged negroes astride upon them [. . .] all collect of a morning round the mill door, each waiting for his turn to get his sack filled" (137–38). Indeed, the slave "crowds" jostling at the door seem to almost overwhelm the productive purpose of the mill: "Sometimes they made great confusion about the premises with their wild shouts, and screams, and rough-and-tumble fights" (138). The Apple-pie property is slave space, a sliver of land at the margins of the plantation where the surveillance and control of planters and overseers is at a minimum. It is a time and place in which slave claims can push back, however subtly, against slaveholder authority and dominion.[53]

One scene, in particular, reveals the extent to which the Apple-pie property signifies slave resistance within the symbolic economy of the novel. When, after only two hours, the mill's waterwheel runs out of water and comes to a screeching halt, Edward Hazard is upset and embarrassed because the viability of the mill had been justified by his own engineering calculations. As a result, he first attempts to explain away the problem by blaming it on "those rascals of muskrats," or on the mill-pond's "porous, open, filtrating kind of soil" (135). These possibilities are quickly dismissed, however, at which point one of the slaves dares to offer his own analysis: "'It seems to me, master,' said an arch looking negro, who was gaping over the flood-gate upon the muddy waste, 'that the mill's run out of water'" (135). Edward explodes into a fury, cursing the slave, and ordering him to leave at once. The slave complies, but as he's leaving he delivers one last bon mot: "'It's a two-hour-mill,' added the negro, in a voice scarcely audible, taking the risk of my grand uncle's displeasure, and grinning saucily but good-humoredly, as he spoke" (135). The planter responds with an even greater fury. "It is said that my grand uncle looked at the black with the most awful face he ever put on in his life. It was blood-red with anger." Kennedy's proslavery agenda has no room for corporeal violence, however, and so after "bethinking himself for a moment," Edward remains silent and subdues his temper

(135). After all, he reasons, "how could he beat the poor fellow for speaking the truth!" (136).

The scene is valuable because it underscores the link between the Apple-pie property and slave agency. Here, in this marginal space effectively claimed by the slaves, one slave has the courage to mock his master at a particularly vulnerable moment. The slave's behavior indexes the social distance between this space and the more constrained, controlled spaces of the plantation proper. Here, ownership and power are a bit more ambiguous, a bit closer to a reciprocal relationship. Likewise, Edward's dramatic response signals the presence of a more precarious power dynamic between master and slave. The planter realizes at some level that he has been bested and made to look the fool. Such a thing is unbearable for him, of course; it represents a subversion of the entire social structure upon which plantation life depends. But the magnitude of Edward's anger suggests that the interchange has triggered a deep-seated anxiety in the planter: his sense of patriarchal control and security has been rattled. Indeed, we learn that his anger at the mill remains unabated for the rest of his life. "It fretted him exceedingly; and he was sure to get into a passion whenever it was mentioned" (142). When he can even bear to mention it, he calls it "a hyperbolical, preposterous abortion," and believes that "he must have been under the influence of [. . .] Satan when he brought it forth" (142). More specifically, Littleton believes, he says such things because "he was not very patient under contradiction" (142). In other words, Edward recognizes in the failure of the mill and in the words of the slave a challenge to his sense of ownership. Both types of property, real estate and chattel, are pushing back against him, asserting their own versions of a counterclaim.

Edward's affective response is a spatialized version of the debt anxiety that plagues master-slave relations. His emotional experience with the Apple-pie property is an experience of anger and frustration growing out of his inability to order and regulate space according to his desires. What is more, the affective experiences of the later Hazards and Tracys reflect this same anxiety about contested ownership. Isaac Tracy is first inspired to bring the lawsuit because he is possessed by "a kind of exultation and inward chuckling over the certainty of his rights" (147–48). But this possessive exultation is matched by a "seigniorial pride" that will brook no challenges to his rights. "The invasion of the most insignificant outpost," Littleton tells us, "conveys an insult to the lawful supremacy; it manifests a contemptuous defiance of the feudal dignity" (148). Here, then, Kennedy puts his finger on the anxiety that undergirds the master's sense of ownership and entitlement. The "exultation and inward chuckling" that attends the "certainty" of possession is always haunted by the specter of "invasion" and "contemptuous defiance." This is the fear that plagues slaveholders within plantation society. *Swallow Barn* works hard to displace this specifically racialized anxiety onto a de-racialized narrative of space and real estate. But the space of the plantation reveals the same contested claims, and the same anxieties of black and white ownership, that can be found throughout plantation society.

It is not enough, however, for the novel to simply displace ownership anxiety onto the spatial contours of the Apple-pie property dispute. Kennedy must also reassure his readers that this spatial contest is itself nothing to worry about. To do so, he emphasizes the humorous qualities of the lawsuit and makes sure that its eventual resolution merely reestablishes the same old boundaries that were in place originally. Throughout the novel, Kennedy portrays the lawsuit as a silly, frivolous obsession of the Tracy clan. The piece of land in question is only some thirty acres in size and it is worth, at most, a few pennies per acre (200). Meriwether's lawyer, Philpot Wart, is so amused by the case's overblown importance that while he draws up the settlement papers, "it is as much as he can do to prevent himself from bursting out into a horse-laugh" (238). In fact, by the afternoon of the same day the dispute is resolved, "the boundary line and all its concerns were forgotten" (246). The argument that has lasted forty years and the entire first half of the novel is dismissed as nothing more than an amusing anecdote. The terms of this long-awaited resolution place the boundary precisely where it was to begin with: along the banks of the Apple-pie. "There you are, gentlemen," Philpot Wart concludes, "exactly *in statu quo ante bellum*" (245). In short order, Kennedy sweeps away the ambiguities, anxieties, and surreptitious challenges to planter authority that have oozed out of the muck of the Apple-pie. Everything is okay, he assures his readers. The old order remains unchanged and the spaces of the plantation remain firmly in hand.

In spite of Kennedy's dismissal, the spatial contours of *Swallow Barn* remain unsettled and unsettling. Ultimately, the novel's attempt to construct and maintain a quaint, bucolic space of paternalistic control and racial hierarchy cannot hold. At the edges of the plantation, social control breaks down and a contest of appropriation ensues. Subtly but persistently, slave experience asserts a spatial counterclaim, and the planters are confronted by the nagging possibility that their own unobstructed title to the property may be inadequate. Indeed, the very fact that Kennedy devotes as much time and space as he does to the otherwise incidental Apple-pie dispute suggests that questions of ownership, and more specifically, tricky, tangled questions of spatial control, are central to the plantation experience as he understands it. The fact that these spatial anxieties are routed through a narrative of debt and obligation only underscores the importance of the debt-entitlement phenomenology in slaveholding culture. The ownership of space, like the ownership of any other plantation property, unfolds within a dialectical experience of claim and counterclaim.

* * *

Read in relation to slave narratives, and through a phenomenological lens, the plantation romance helps call our attention to both the social and the economic components of the master-slave dynamic. The *social* dialectic of master and slave, we learn, cannot be separated from the *property-centered* dialectic of debt and entitlement. These two interactions are mutually constitutive; they emerge simultaneously, in part because the initial appropriation of a slave, the buying of another human being, necessitates that the relationship unfold within the context of property exchange. That property dynamic then persistently influences the phenomenology of both master and slave as they interact with one another. Within the context of their exploitative, hierarchical social relationship, their affective experiences are continually conditioned by feelings of debt and entitlement. That is, the power relations that bind master and slave, the social and spatial relationships that exist on the plantation, these are all filtered through a phenomenology of property that conditions the affective texture, the qualitative experience, of life in a slave society.

This account of the master-slave dynamic usefully complicates previous scholarly models that tend to emphasize a mostly economic or a mostly psychological framework. Orlando Patterson, in particular, has downplayed the significance of property relations in understanding the "political psychology" of master and slave. Instead, the plantation romances suggest that sociopsychological experience of slavery cannot be separated from a phenomenology of property. Rich, complex, and contradictory, the literature of the period resists some of the stark theoretical taxonomies proposed by modern scholarship.

In a broader sense, the phenomenology of possession we find in *Swallow Barn*, *Woodcraft*, and the slave narratives continues to develop ideas about ownership that we first encountered in other texts and in other spaces. The dialectical nature of debt and entitlement on the plantation, for example, highlights the dialectical nature of property experience more generally. As in *Edgar Huntly*'s body-to-body negotiations, and as in the public circulation of private property in Hawthorne and Stoddard, ownership requires the presence of an other who can contest it. This is Levinas's point when he asserts that "the other possessors—those whom one cannot possess—contest and therefore can sanction possession itself. Thus the possession of things issues in a discourse" (162). This is also Hegel's claim when he argues that property—the externalization of a person's will—is vital because it allows other people to witness and recognize a person *as a person*. "The *existence* which my willing thereby attains," Hegel explains, "includes its ability to be recognized by others.—That a thing of which I can take possession should be *ownerless* is a self-evident negative condition; or rather, it refers to the anticipated relation to others" (*Philosophy* 81). In short, the agonistic nature of ownership on the plantation is especially valuable for calling attention to the relational, dialectical aspects of property more broadly.

The contest of wills between master and slave also continues the tension between reciprocal and gift economies that first appeared in Chapter 2. In *The Morgesons*, of course, a feminine gift economy represented a potential subversion of masculine reciprocity. But the plantation romances reverse the field by trying to insist on the slaveholder as the source of benevolent gift giving. In both contexts, the possibility of the gift is held out as a salutary alternative to dehumanizing market forces. Rising anxiety about that market—and about the abstract forms of property that enable it—demands some form of resistance, some reassurance that property does not only circulate in circuits of ruthless exchange. The gift seems to offer that sort of reassurance, but it is appropriated to very different political ends: progressive redefinition of gender roles versus retrograde fantasies of racial superiority. We are forcefully reminded, then, that the phenomenology of property conforms to its particular historical moment and cultural space.

Of course, the same dialectical tension that characterizes the affective relations of master and slave also structures the fabric of plantation space as it appears in these narratives. Sentimentalized images of happy, productive, and well-regulated plantations are juxtaposed with anxiety-ridden spaces, alternative geographies of resentment and rebellion. So, as in previous chapters, the phenomenology of possession is revealed to be inseparable from the phenomenology of space. Property experience inevitably unfolds within a specific spatial context and with specific spatial implications. Plantation narratives, however, call our attention specifically to the affective dimensions of this spatial experience. The spaces of ownership emerge here not just in relation to sensory experience—to touch, say, or to taste—but also in relation to affect, in relation to powerful emotional imperatives that condition the contours of plantation space.

This focus on emotional phenomenology and affective dynamics locates the plantation narratives right in the middle of the larger cultural shift from eighteenth-century sensation to nineteenth-century affect. No longer beholden to the empiricist paradigms of Locke and his followers, plantation writers increasingly looked to the language and theory of emotion to understand the phenomenology of possession. By repurposing the emotionalism of Romantics like Coleridge, Carlyle, Madame de Staël, and even Hegel, Southern writers contributed to an expansion in the scope of property investigations. They helped move the phenomenology of property beyond the sensory orientation represented by Brown, Hawthorne, and Stoddard and helped call our attention to the ways in which possession and dispossession are shot through with specifically affective investments.[54]

This nineteenth-century fascination with affect will continue in the next chapter as we turn to the space of the city. Here, via the city-mystery novels of George Lippard, we will explore the peculiar feelings of loss that attend the experience of theft. Unlike the entitled "takings" of the plantation slaves, theft in Lippard's city is out-and-out robbery, the greedy exploitation of the poor by wealthy aristocrats. Labor itself will become a contested term as workers and capitalists battle over the nature and definition of work. This phenomenology of dispossession will emerge, like all the rest, in close relation to its spatial context: the growing urban metropole. In this way, we will continue to expand the radius of potential possessive space, attending to sensory and affective elements as they appear in the wider and wider social circuits of the nineteenth century.

4 / Feeling at a Loss: Theft and Affect in George Lippard

> *But be careful, Monsieur [...] that your vigorous metaphysics does not fall into the hands of some sophist of the streets, who would interpret it to a starving mob. In that case we should have looting as a conclusion and peroration.*
> —AUGUSTE BLANQUI, LETTER TO PIERRE PROUDHON, 1841[1]

Although by 1865 Karl Marx had long since lost his early enthusiasm for the writings of Pierre Proudhon, he continued to admire at least one quality of Proudhon's masterwork, *What Is Property?* (1840). "In this book of Proudhon's," Marx observes, "there still prevails, if I may be allowed the expression, a strong muscular style." The Frenchman writes with a "provocative defiance," with a "withering criticism" and a "bitter irony." His "revolutionary earnestness," Marx recalls, "electrified" his readers and showcased a "deep and genuine feeling of indignation at the infamy of the existing order." In short, Marx believes, the book is a tour de force of the "sensational" style.[2]

Marx's comments here are interesting not so much because they betray a lingering fondness for Proudhon's work, but more specifically because they highlight a productive relationship between sensational aesthetics and critical politics. Marx clearly admires the way in which Proudhon was able to link his revolutionary energy, his ardent desire for political reform, to an appropriately "muscular" literary style. In particular, Marx is impressed with Proudhon's ability to "electrify" his readers, a word that suggests a bodily transfer of sensation from text to reader. This sensationalism, Marx seems to believe, is an especially effective technique for inciting revolutionary sentiment in the reading public. Put another way, the literary mode of sensationalism is particularly well-suited to the production and persuasion of readerly affect and is, as a result, brimming with revolutionary potential.

American literary critics of the mid-nineteenth century tended to agree with Marx about the subversive energy contained in the sensational mode. That is, many of them called attention to the subversive political energy contained within the flood of sensational novels and fiction that inundated American literary markets after 1840. Following the impressive commercial success in 1845 of George Lippard's gothic city-mystery, *The Quaker City; or The Monks of Monk Hall*, American writers began churning out stacks of so-called yellow-jacket literature, lurid urban exposés that trafficked in shocking depictions of sex and violence.[3] Unlike Marx, however, American critics found little to admire in such "muscular" sensationalism. Instead, they viewed its subversive potential as a dangerous threat to the political status quo. According to one commentator, this sort of fiction put "our Republican Institutions" at risk:

> We are doubtless, at this moment, fostering within the bosom of this nation, those constituent elements of revolution, which, if we neglect to elevate the masses, by placing before them a healthful and vigorous literature, based upon principles which will prove incentives to morality, will crush us in the might and magnitude of our fancied security, and hold us up to the exulting derision of a crowned world, a torn, bleeding, mangled demonstration, that the problem has been—fearfully solved! (*Confessions* 66–67).

In a suspiciously sensational register of his own, this critic suggests that "the masses," drunk on the heady wine of sensationalism, will run riot over "our fancied security." Like Marx, then, this writer is attuned to the radical possibilities of a sensational aesthetic, but from his perspective, those possibilities are to be feared and avoided.

Noted Boston critic Edwin Percy Whipple went so far as to locate the source of the sensationalist threat in the inflammatory influence of French literature and philosophy. "The leading idea of French romance is opposition to law and obedience to desire; and its mode of proceeding is to exaggerate the defects of social institutions, in order to obtain plausible arguments for the violation of social duties. Thus it practically sides with every form of criminality, and holds up crime, not to hatred, but sympathy" (*Essays* 83). Affective identification with criminals, rather than moral exemplars, destabilizes the social structure, as do the writers' energetic attacks on social inequality. "From the defects or imperfection of social institutions, such writers argue for their total overthrow." Most disturbingly, for Whipple, "this literary compound of English ruffianism and French ethics has invaded the United States in large force; and it comprises at present a considerable portion of the literature which the people read" (84). French socialism, it seems, is gnawing away at the underpinnings of American culture.

But as Whipple's reference to sympathy implies, American critics also agreed with Marx that sensationalism was powerful precisely because it invokes an affective response in the reader. Sensational texts are dangerous, critics warned, because they stir up unsettling, uncontrollable emotions that may then be turned to radical action. The unnamed author of *Confessions and Experience of a Novel Reader* (1850) describes this perilous process: "I candidly affirm, that I never read a [sensational] novel or romance in my life, that I did not arise from its perusal, either under the immediate influence of some one specific passion particularly called forth, because most excited, or the whole catalogue of legitimate effects" (36). These include, among others, "inflamed passions and irritable temper," "sordid desires," "disgust of the world," "Visionary schemes of the future," and in general, "a fevered and excited state of the body, from an undue tension of the nervous sensibilities, wound up as they were, upon the inquisitorial wheel of a protracted, anxious, long looked for denouement!" (36–39). Whipple underscores the same phenomenological register: "According to the philosophy obtaining among the romancers of reality, the fact that an object creates physical disgust is the reason why we should take it to our arms; the fact that a man excites moral reprobation is his claim upon our sympathy" (*Essays* 76). Sympathy, disgust, excitation: this is the language of affect, and it is here that critics found the catalyst for the disturbing politics of sensational fiction.[4]

Of course, the intersection of emotion and politics that emerges in sensational writing at this time also participates—like plantation literature—in the larger cultural transition from eighteenth-century rationalism and empiricism to nineteenth-century emotionalism. Sensational writers, like plantation writers, attend closely to the production and manipulation of emotion, both in their characters and, more importantly, in their readers. More so than plantation literature, however, sensational writing often yokes its emotional dynamics to an overt (if not always coherent) political program. This is Marx's hope and Whipple's fear. But such self-conscious politics only situate sensational writing more firmly in the nineteenth-century Romantic moment; this is because the Romantic emphasis on emotion represents not only a rejection of cold rationalism and empirical science but also a vociferous critique of market society. It is not just "paltry empiricism" that the likes of Carlyle and Coleridge are attacking but the "Gospel of Mammonism," the greedy, heartless ideology of materialism that they believe infects the nineteenth century.[5] Romantic emotionalism is thus closely allied to a revolutionary impulse not just in epistemology, but in politics and economics. Sensational literature manages to blend both discourses: nineteenth-century emotion and pointed political critique.

Neither is it a coincidence that sensational literature develops in a primarily urban context. It is the emerging space of the city that generates the most volatile mix of inequality, class tension, and revolutionary fervor. The expanded social space of the urban metropole creates problems (crime, disease, poverty, and so forth) on a scale unprecedented in the space of the plantation or of the middle-class home. At the same time, the city makes room for social and political organization on a scale also unlikely in the closer confines of plantation or home. This complexity gives rise to a variegated sensational press, a discursive ecosystem that works to record, anatomize, and critique the new urban space. Urban fiction, in particular, emerges as a crucible for representing and reworking this fertile combination of politics and affect. In this way, urban space—and the urban fiction that it enables—opens up potentially new configurations of ownership and phenomenological possession.

As it turns out, antebellum literary critics like Whipple were sensitive to just such a new configuration, and it constitutes the particular focus of this chapter. In considering the political threat posed by sensationalism, nineteenth-century critics repeatedly turned to the topic of theft. At first, they seem to do so only because many sensational novels are crime narratives with thieves as main characters. In an essay entitled "Romance of Rascality," for example, Whipple fumes about the loss of morally upright protagonists and morally uplifting plotlines. "Thieves and cut-throats have come to be considered the most important and interesting of men [. . .]. There is a certain *piquant* shamelessness, a peculiarly ingenious dishonesty, in some of the forms of literary chicane, which nothing can equal in impudence" (74). Whipple's focus on thieves here thus seems to be another version of the common complaint that sensational fiction upends traditional values by valorizing the disgusting and the shameful.

Gradually, however, this straightforward use of the theft trope transforms into a more complex metaphor for the influence of the sensational authors themselves; they too, it seems, are thieves of a sort. "Rascality is now the rage," Whipple writes. "It has forced the passages leading to the temple of fame, and breaks into literature as it was wont to break into houses" (75). Here, authors and novels enact a home invasion of sorts, stealing into both the literary limelight and into the sympathies of the readers. Sensational literature, he warns, "breaks into [the readers'] natures, so to speak,—passes into the very core of their moral and intellectual being" (*Lectures* 201). The *Confessions* critic employs much the same metaphor, equating sensational writers with both thieves and spiders:

> You see him construct from apparent nothing, and to your astonishment in an incredibly short space of time, a curiously wrought trap or den, radiating from the centre in transverse sections, and possessing a tenacity which holds any victim whose luckless star of destiny shoots athwart its cornered domain [. . .]. Like a Bedouin robber he has withdrawn behind an intervening object, or lies concealed within that mysterious ball in the remotest corner. (*Confessions* 19)

For such critics, sensational literature constitutes a perversion of the sympathetic identification essential to more sentimental genres. Instead of encouraging a salutary social bond with the less fortunate, the sensational novel fools the reader, taking advantage of the sentimental impulse in order to forge a subversive bond with thieves or criminals.

The theft trope is attractive to the critics of sensationalism because it effectively encapsulates both the literature's perceived affective threat ("These writers will steal your sympathy") and its perceived political threat ("These writers want to steal your property"). Sensational authors, it seems, are guilty of both crimes. It is no coincidence that these so-called thefts are closely associated with the system of "French ethics" that Whipple derides. By characterizing the values of the sensational authors as both French and criminal, the American critics are vilifying the reformist, quasi-socialist energies circulating in some of the sensational narratives. Proudhon, after all, was famous for his pronouncement that "Property is theft!" and the other proponents of "French ethics" (Fourier, Blanc, Saint-Simon, and so on) advocated various forms of socialism. In other words, the sensational authors were a particularly dangerous threat to the cherished institution of private property. They do not, according to the American critics, respect the liberal values of a possessive market society or the sanctity of the possessive individual. This is why they are best understood as thieves of one sort or another.

Such critiques of sensationalism are valuable, I would suggest, for two reasons: first, they call our attention to the potential link between readerly affect and class rebellion. In the same way that Marx was attuned to the political possibilities inherent in sensationalism, so too are the American critics. (Of course, from their perspective, those possibilities are terrifying—lower-class bodies are an explosive charge requiring only the spark of sensational excitation to detonate and destroy the foundations of a well-ordered capitalist society.) Second, the critiques underscore the central role of the theft trope in this rich discursive context. Radical reformers understood market capitalism itself to be a form of theft, and they viewed capitalist entrepreneurs as nothing more than well-heeled thieves. Defenders of the status quo like Whipple, by contrast, saw the reformers as thieves, as crafty burglars bent on stealing the sympathy and property of naive American readers. The theft trope thus sits at the center of an ideological tug of war between radicals and conservatives.

Philadelphia novelist George Lippard, I believe, is particularly attuned to the theft trope and to its productive intersection with readerly affect and class politics. The progenitor of the sensational novel in America, Lippard was well versed in the affective techniques of sensationalism. At the same time, he was a prominent reformer and labor organizer steeped in the anticapitalist rhetoric of the urban working class. For him, the theft trope served as an ideal platform from which to criticize capitalist excess and to mobilize the affective machinery of sensationalism. What I would like to argue is that Lippard's urban fictions, his city-mystery novels, actively link a radical thematic assault on capitalist exploitation to the aesthetic possibilities inherent in the sensational genre. Sensitive to what Ann Cvetkovich calls the "politics of affect," Lippard attempts to tie the embodied responses of his readers to the emergence of a radical political sensibility. That is, by repeatedly enacting disturbing scenes of expropriation, Lippard seeks to induce in his readers a phenomenology of theft, an affective identification with, and sympathy for, the continuously exploited working class. His novels, I argue, are calculated to convey the feeling of having something stolen, of having your property taken from you, in order that his readers might be continually reminded of the theft-dynamic that he believes is endemic to a possessive market society. Lippard's aim is to sensationalize, to actively embody and concretize, the frustratingly abstract threat of capitalist exploitation.

To accomplish this linkage of politics and affect, Lippard employs two related aesthetic strategies. The first is to repeatedly subject the reader to sensationalized scenes of theft in which a sympathetic character is ignominiously stripped of his property, his dignity, and sometimes his life. Lippard's object here is to induce a feeling of *distress* in the reader, an affective response that includes both conventional sympathy for the character's distressing plight and something more intense, a sense of shared experience and identification. The second aesthetic strategy involves Lippard's representations of urban space. The Gothic contours of his claustrophobic cities, I contend, provide an affective architecture, an emotional proxemics, whose intended effect on the reader is to dramatically heighten the sense of violation, loss, and distress. In particular, the disturbing permeability of Lippard's sequestered urban enclosures intensifies the feeling that ownership is up for grabs. In Lippard's antebellum America absolutely everything is available for expropriation.

Lippard's radical aesthetics are crucial to this book's larger investigation of embodied ownership because they highlight the close connection between increasing antebellum anxieties and emerging phenomenologies of ownership. That is, as anxieties about abstract property and anonymous market forces continue to grow, antebellum writers ferret out new configurations of bodies and properties, new examples of how ownership is ineluctably bound up with embodied experience. As was the case in Chapter 3, however, Lippard's work focuses more on the dynamics of dispossession than of possession. Whereas Chapters 1 and 2 both concerned themselves with the politics and experience of appropriation, Lippard's urban spaces—like the plantation spaces of Southern writers—engage the darker facets of ownership, those of expropriation and loss. Indeed, one way to gauge antebellum society's increasing anxiety is to observe the literary shift from a focus on possession to a focus on dispossession. At the same time, Lippard's aesthetics mark the elevation of affect and emotion in relation to phenomenologies of (dis)possession. Like other urban sensationalists of the nineteenth century, Lippard focuses on the role of affect rather than sensory experience in trying to understand embodied ownership. His particular interest is the affective experience of the reader and, as a result, his work allows us to see phenomenologies of property extending beyond the text itself. Perhaps more than any other writer considered here, Lippard demonstrates the potential of the fictional text to push back against its historical, political, and spatial context.

Recent critical work by Cvetkovich and others is interested in precisely this relationship between affective response and sociopolitical efficacy. But even Lippard himself was fascinated with the link between readerly affect and revolutionary potential. Indeed, he made no bones about the reformist goals he had for his own sensational literary projects. "Literature merely considered as an ART is a despicable thing," he asserted. "It is only, at least mainly, valuable as a MEANS. These people who talk about art, art, art in literature are terrible twaddlers. [. . .] The great object of literature is the social, mental and spiritual elevation of Man" (*Prophet* 279). Literature should serve a progressive social purpose, he believed, and gripping sensational fiction is ideally suited to this task. Moreover, it was the "twaddlers," the pure aesthetes, for whom he saved his most vitriolic disdain. "Here lies the Poet of Twaddle-dom," he sarcastically intoned, "whose whole life was characterized by a pervading vein of Lollypop-itude" (*Prophet* 250). Lippard imagined himself in stark contrast to this sort of apolitical belletrism; his sensational narratives were an opportunity to cultivate widespread, working-class support for political and economic reform. If he could remind his readers about capitalist exploitation by embodying the feeling of theft, he could perhaps change things for the better.

In order to map out the complicated relationship between Lippard's politics and his sensational aesthetics, this chapter is divided into four sections. The first section locates Lippard's own political sensibilities within the historical and cultural context of midcentury urban America. In particular, this section demonstrates how Lippard's fictional narrativization of theft draws on the rich anticapitalist discourse of urban labor movements. The context of labor reform is crucial for Lippard because it directly informs his thinking about the consequences of market capitalism and the distribution of wealth. Sections two and three focus on the specific affective strategies that Lippard uses to concretize the abstract threat of capitalism: one involves a process of "affective scripting" and a second leverages the "affective architecture" of urban space. Finally, the fourth section examines the trope of body snatching and grave robbing as Lippard employs it throughout his work. This particular form of theft, I argue, functions as Lippard's most pointed critique of capitalism and, more provocatively, serves to highlight some of capitalism's more dehumanizing dynamics. Together, the four sections demonstrate exactly how Lippard is able to link specific readerly affects to a radical political program.

A Culture of Theft

If I had to answer the following question, "What is slavery?" and if I should respond in one word, "It is murder," my meaning would be understood at once [. . .]. So why to this other question, "What is property?" should I not answer in the same way, "It is theft," without fearing to be misunderstood, since the second proposition is only a transformation of the first? —PIERRE PROUDHON, WHAT IS PROPERTY?

The notion that unfettered capitalism is a thinly veiled form of theft was not unique to Lippard, of course. On the contrary, this conceit permeated antebellum labor discourse and reflected wider anxieties about the social and economic contours of a rapidly expanding market society, anxieties that were particularly acute in an urban context. Between 1800 and 1850, the largest American cities experienced a dizzying growth in population, immigration, commercial activity, manufacturing, and architectural density. New York City, for example, exploded from just sixty thousand residents in 1800 to more than half a million by 1850. Transportation and communication technologies transformed not just the topography of individual cities but the temporal and spatial relationships between urban centers throughout the northeast and trans-Appalachian west. The familiar pace and scale of America's eighteenth-century "walking cities" were eclipsed by runaway economic growth and unfamiliar new forms of social organization. As the catalyst for many of these anxiety-inducing transformations, market capitalism was regarded skeptically by more than a few urban commentators.[6]

One of the most disturbing results of this rapid urban growth was the dramatic juxtaposition of extreme wealth and extreme poverty. Impoverished immigrants and established entrepreneurs, for instance, could be located in close proximity to one another. These contrasts quickly drew attention to the ways in which market capitalism seemed to benefit the lucky few, or "upper ten" as they were called, and degrade the "lower million." It didn't take long for a scathing critique of this economic disparity to develop. Muckraking sensationalists like Lippard, George Thompson, Ned Buntline, and George Foster continued the tradition of urban exposé pioneered by Eugène Sue in France and G. W. M. Reynolds in England. In his nonfiction *New York by Gas-Light*, for example, Foster took it upon himself to detail "the real facts of the actual conditions of the wicked and wretched classes—so that Philanthropy and Justice may plant their blows aright" (70). These conditions included both the "abominable orgies" of the wealthy and the squalid haunts of the poor, "teeming with destruction and annihilation" (81, 120). Economic inequality in the new urban environment was as obvious as it was breathtaking. As such, it served as a lightning rod for radical critiques of market capitalism.

The source of such critiques was not to be found, however, in the poverty-ridden ranks of the lowest classes. The attacks came instead from an increasingly skittish working class of artisans and laborers. The growing influence of mercantile and industrial capital in cities like New York, Philadelphia, and Boston was dramatically restructuring older artisan and craftwork economies. Master craftsmen, small masters, journeymen, and laborers were all experiencing radical challenges to their traditional ways of working, socializing, and relating to one another. More and more, long-established trades like shoemaking, tailoring, shipbuilding, carpentry, and countless others were becoming centralized and specialized, a development that was concentrating more capital into fewer hands and relegating many tradesmen to the subordinate position of wage-laborer. In response to this economic and social upheaval, a nascent American labor movement took root: journeymen and laborers began to distinguish themselves from master-owners; activist trade unions organized and addressed the increasingly contentious issues of wage compensation and the ten-hour workday; and a sympathetic labor-oriented press emerged to challenge more business-friendly newspapers.[7]

A crucial component of this new working-class consciousness was a firm belief in the intrinsic value of labor itself. American laborites fastened onto a radical reading of what is known as the "labor theory of value." Essentially, this theory maintains that all property and wealth are created by labor; the value of any given piece of property is equal to the labor needed to create it. This perspective, of course, is central to Lockean notions of property and possessive individualism, but perhaps the best-known statement of the theory itself occurs in Adam Smith's *Wealth of Nations* (1776). Smith asserts that "the real price of every thing, what every thing really costs to the man who wants to acquire it, is the toil and trouble of acquiring it" (26). David Ricardo, the English economist, refines the idea in his *Principles of Political Economy and Taxation* (1817), maintaining that "the value of a commodity [. . .] depends on the relative quantity of labour which is necessary for its production, and not on the greater or less compensation which is paid for that labour" (ch. 1, sec. 1). In this way, Smith and Ricardo argue for labor as the basis of exchange-value and thus of equitable market exchange.[8]

American radicals, like their European counterparts, were quick to define "labor" specifically as the activity of working with your hands. Doing so seemed to immediately raise the stature of working-class producers within the new capitalist paradigm. If labor creates all value, then laborers, not capitalist entrepreneurs or speculators, are the real foundation of the economy.[9] Building on the work of English radicals like John Gray, Thomas Hodgskin, and William Thompson, a number of American labor activists began stressing the idea that labor, including both agriculture and traditional trade-based craftwork, was the only true source of wealth and that tradesmen deserved to be compensated accordingly. In 1822, Cornelius Blatchly, an associate of Robert Owen and early proponent of communitarian societies, asked, "Shall he who cultivates the soil be deprived of an adequate share of the fruits which his industry produces, and pine in want, while the labour of his hands feeds luxurious idleness? Shall the right of property be established for *those* who contribute nothing to the *general* stock, and who consume and waste what the industry of others has provided?" (10). A few years later in 1826, a thirty-seven-year-old printer named Langton Byllesby published *Observations on the Sources and Effects of Unequal Wealth*.

In it, he asserted his version of the labor theory of value, stating, "Every thing which is properly entitled to the character of wealth, is the product of labour, and without labour is not to be had." The problem, according to Byllesby, was that "in most cases under the present form of society, the products of labour belong to almost any other than the producer, who generally obtains from the application of his powers, no more than a bare subsistence" (42). In these and countless other writings, American radicals attempted to use the labor theory to revalue people and skills that they felt were being trampled by the juggernaut of market capitalism.[10]

Significantly, however, as labor activists detailed the excesses of capitalism, they did so by obsessively invoking the language and imagery of theft. In a host of speeches, monographs, essays, and newspapers, laborite discourse cast the capitalist "accumulators" as thieves, swindlers, and robber barons greedily siphoning off wealth and property from its true owners, the working-class producers. Blatchly, for example, observed that "to obtain *exclusive wealth*, and *advantages*, men and women are daily tempted to cheat, counterfeit, swindle, extort, oppress, steal, lie, deceive, rob, and murder. By usury, rents, and interest, they feed like drones on the labours of the industrious" (24). Thomas Skidmore, perhaps the most radical of the antebellum reformers, advocated a dramatic seizure and redistribution of this stolen property: "Inasmuch as great wealth is an instrument which is uniformly used to extort from others, their property in their personal qualities and efforts, [. . .] it ought to be taken away from its possessor, on the same principle, that a sword or a pistol may be wrested away from a robber, who shall undertake to accomplish the same effect, in a different manner" (3).[11]

Radical newspapers opted for a more muscular version of the theft rhetoric. Politicians, according to the pugnacious editor and reformer Mike Walsh, were "cowardly dogs who were realizing fortunes by robbing the people to whom they were preaching democracy" ("Working Men's Convention" 3). Fanny Wright's Owenite paper, *The Free Enquirer*, seethed that "taking them in the lump, all the *professions* so called, are so many bloodsuckers of the producing many" ("On the Causes of Existing Evils" 183). The *New-York Daily Tribune* called for workers to "prevent the growth of an unwholesome aristocracy, whose only aim is to acquire wealth by robbery of the toiling masses" (qtd. in Wilentz 378). Mike Walsh, again, captured the general tone of working-class outrage: "I have always contended, and do now, that the laboring classes—the producers of all the wealth, are robbed, oppressed, and degraded, by the plundering schemes and devices of dishonest, grasping, want-producing capitalists; and that no man can be worth what is commonly termed a fortune without being either a *thief* or *a receiver of stolen goods*" ("The Hireling Press" 1). Everywhere in laborite discourse, the labor theory of value was invoked in order to identify and condemn what reformers believed to be a system of exploitation and theft. Like Proudhon in France, American reformers understood capitalism, in its present form at least, to be a version of legalized theft. Classical liberal arguments for private property seemed to actually justify stealing property, to radical eyes anyway, and reformers aimed to establish a more egalitarian framework.[12]

Lippard himself, of course, was a labor activist of no small account. Having cut his teeth as a writer and reporter for a series of penny newspapers from 1841 to 1843, Lippard was introduced early to the genre of urban exposé and to the lively rhetoric of socialist critique.[13] This critical perspective gradually grew into a more sophisticated, and more energetic, espousal of reformist ideals. In 1848, Lippard gave the valedictory address at the national meeting of the "Industrial Congress," an annual gathering of land reformers, socialists, and labor activists. In his speech, he trumpeted reformist visions of change: "To every Man a home, to every Laborer a just share in the fruits of his labor, to every Son of the Poor a foothold on the earth of God!" (*Prophet* 191). Later that same year, he began publication of his own newspaper, the *Quaker City* weekly. It served as a platform not just for selling his fiction, but for espousing his increasingly radical views on social reform.[14] Then in 1849, Lippard founded the Brotherhood of the Union, a labor organization that, remarkably, would become the largest reform association in the United States (and would remain so until the Knights of Labor was formed in 1867). The Brotherhood was national in scope, establishing so-called Grand Circles in nineteen different states by 1850. Like Lippard himself, the Brotherhood advocated a complicated mélange of land reform, cooperative societies, and vigorous anticapitalism. In effect, it served as the institutional expression of reformist impulses Lippard had harbored since his teenage years.[15]

Given his background in labor radicalism, it should come as no surprise that Lippard enthusiastically employed the same theft rhetoric popular with other activists. "The Evils of our Social system are manifold," he observed. "They may be forced into the Compass of two words—DEGRADED LABOR." How is labor degraded? "You can rob it of its fruits by making laws solely *through* and *for* the Wealthy classes; by giving One Man a charter to rob a hundred of his fellows" (*Prophet* 211). In a more militant vein, Lippard even suggested that this capitalist expropriation might require armed resistance in order to stop it. "When Labor has tried all other means in vain," he warns, "[...] then we would advise Labor to go to War, in any and all forms—War with the Rifle, Sword, and Knife [...] and in the name of that God who has declared his Judgment against the Robbers of Labor" (*Prophet* 219). Here, as in other radical writing, both American and European, the labor theory of value underwrites a critique of capitalist exploitation in which the economic system is understood to be rigged and the capitalists themselves are understood to be no better than thieves.[16]

More significantly for our purposes, Lippard's penchant for theft imagery also infuses his city-mysteries fiction. Theft narratives of every sort appear throughout Lippard's urban novels. Avaricious men and unscrupulous women defraud, deceive, swindle, rob, and burglarize just about anyone or anything they can put their nimble fingers on. Monk Hall, for example, the imposing gothic edifice at the center of Lippard's *Quaker City*, is described as a "rookery" in which clueless naïf's are routinely drugged and robbed while sleeping (60). There, Devil-Bug, the diabolical steward of Monk Hall, drops the hapless Paul Western through a trapdoor to his death in order to retrieve the thirty thousand dollars Western carries (70). Indeed, the very foundations of Monk Hall serve as a haven and breeding ground for thieves of all sorts. "'Ha, ha, ha!'" Devil-Bug exults at one point, "'While the broadcloth gentry of the Quaker City guzzle their champagne two stories above, here, in these cozy cellars of Monk Hall, old Devil-Bug entertains the thieves and cut-throats of the town with scorchin' Jamakey spirits and raw Moneygehaley!'" (220). The terms of Lippard's analogy are clear: under the surface of every respectable gentleman there lurks a rapacious crook. This lesson is driven home throughout the course of the novel as one upper-class character after another is revealed to be a fraud or a cheat. The estimable Colonel Fitz-Cowles turns out to be a con man and forger who travels the country impersonating wealthy aristocrats and forging massive checks. The Reverend F. A. T. Pyne, a sort of proto-televangelist, invents "lively fictions" for his congregation in order to better defraud them of their offerings. Virtually everyone, it seems, is a thief of one kind or another.

In particular, however, Lippard sets his sights on narratives of upper-class thievery and lower-class exploitation. In his unfinished novel, *The Nazarene* (1846), for instance, Lippard presents the reader with an impoverished working-class protagonist, Leon, who seeks revenge upon an unscrupulous bank director, Calvin Wolfe. Wolfe has misappropriated Leon's promised patrimony, and he is none too happy about it. "It was you that robbed the Orphan!" he shrieks at Wolfe. "You that have trampled upon the Will of the dead! You that have condemned me to want and poverty for twenty years!" (31). Leon's rage signals an increasing awareness of systemic economic injustice on Lippard's part. "For years I have endured cold, hunger, neglect, despair," Leon soliloquizes. "I have made my bed upon the hard earth, shivered in my rags in the winter's cold, starved on in my rude garret. [. . .] Beaten as a child, trampled upon as a boy, neglected as a man, and all—not because I was criminal, not because I ever harmed a human thing,—no, no! But on account of those terrible words [. . .] 'I am Poor!'" (18). Leon's target here is not just the bank director, but a larger system of exploitation and abuse, a social hierarchy that vilifies the poor and protects the rich.

The theme of capitalist thieves and working-class victims receives its fullest expression in Lippard's final two urban novels: *The Empire City* and *New York: Its Upper Ten and Lower Million*.[17] These two texts (both of which are sequential installments in one continuous narrative) constitute Lippard's most sophisticated, and most overt, critique of capitalist expropriation.[18] Theft narratives proliferate and capitalist "robber barons" take a variety of forms: sleazy slumlords, corrupt politicians, scheming aristocrats, and duplicitous bankers. One representative scene depicts the exploitation of a young seamstress trying to get reimbursed for the garment piecework she has done. The seamstress, Mary, enters the "Canal Street Shirt Store" and presents the proprietor, a Dickensian brute by the name of Screw Grabb, with five shirts she has finished sewing for him. He immediately begins his swindle: "Do you call them stitches? [. . .] How d'ye expect a man to git a livin' if he's robbed in that way?" (*NY* 50). Mary protests at first, but when it becomes clear that he won't pay her the two shillings for each of the five shirts, she asks for her five-dollar deposit back. He refuses and demands that she hand over the remainder of the shirts. Astounded, Mary hurls the accusation of thief back at him: "You cowardly villain!" she cries. "To insult me because I will not permit you to rob me" (51). By this time, their argument has attracted the attention of people on the street and the proprietor appeals to them. "Gentlemen, this hussy has attempted to rob me of my property! I gave her stuff sufficient to make five shirts, and she's spoilt 'em so I can't sell 'em for old rags, and—and she won't give 'em up" (51). The crowd, however, takes Mary's side, immediately seeing through his scam and threatening to pelt him with rotten eggs. Mary is escorted out of the store as a riot threatens to break out, but she takes neither her shirts nor her money with her.

Lippard's theft plots represent a narrativizing of the ubiquitous laborite theft rhetoric that permeated antebellum urban culture. Prolabor newspapermen, high-minded theorists, and rabble-rousing organizers all had recourse to the language and imagery of capitalist expropriation.

Lippard was no exception and his urban fiction eagerly takes up this theme in order to dramatize it, to flesh out and further sensationalize the distressing notion of greedy capitalists preying upon the poor and working class. In this way, Lippard is both a product and a producer of the fertile anticapitalist culture that surrounds him. What sets his fiction apart from other laborite writing, however, is the remarkable manner in which he is able to transform these ubiquitous theft narratives into a kind of powerful affective machinery. He adapts the conventions of sensationalism in such a way as to concretize, to embody in the reader, the omnipresent threat of capitalist expropriation. Lippard, I believe, is keen to induce in his readers the affect of distress and, in particular, the distress of having something stolen. Doing so, he hopes, will render more concrete the unseen economic forces of possessive market society. This is how his fiction will move beyond mere "Twaddle-dom" and "Lollypop-itude." This is how aesthetics can be put in the service of radical critique.

Distress Signals: Theft, Body, Affect

The role of affect in nineteenth-century sensational literature has received a fair amount of critical attention of late. In particular, a number of scholars have called attention to the genre's productive combination of affect and politics. Shelley Streeby, for instance, charts the complex relationship of sensational fiction and American imperialism during the US-Mexican War. She does so, in part, by exploring what she calls the "body politics" of antebellum sensational culture: "Although sensationalism is the idiom of many mid-nineteenth-century working-class cultures, it is also a racializing, gendering, and sexualizing discourse on the body" (27). Streeby is building on the earlier work of Ann Cvetkovich who, in an important study of British mass culture and the Victorian "sensation novel," argues that "like sexuality and other physical processes, affect is not a pre-discursive entity, a fact that is often obscured by the construction of affects or bodily sensations as natural. To study the politics of affect, then, is more broadly to study the politics of cathexis and to explore how meanings are given to the energy attached to particular events and representations" (23–24). For both critics, sensational literature functions as a crucial site for the discursive negotiation and construction of affect.

Implicit within such arguments, however, are two theoretical axes that can help us better survey the critical landscape surrounding sensationalism, politics, and affect. The first axis concerns the ontological assumptions that critics bring to bear on questions of affect. Simply put, is affect a "natural," "pre-discursive" phenomenon or is it entirely discursive in nature, a thoroughly social construct? Cvetkovich and Streeby both adopt a Foucauldian approach and maintain that affect is in fact "created" through discursive negotiation. Cvetkovich contrasts this perspective with an earlier Marxist cultural criticism that, she thinks, makes the mistake of assuming that "culture merely reroutes affect rather than actively constructing it" (28). Marxists like Frederic Jameson, she believes, romanticize affect as "an intrinsically subversive energy whose natural potential is held in check by the repressive force of cultural constructions" (29). At one end of the ontological axis are the strict social constructionists, at the other, the supposedly pre-discursive essentialists.[19]

The second theoretical axis intersects with the first and focuses on the question of political efficacy: Does sensationalism's affective register constitute a subversive or conservative force? In answering this question, Streeby and Cvetkovich part ways. Whereas Cvetkovich sees the social construction of affect as an essentially conservative "mechanism for the containment and discipline of the self" (31), Streeby finds a bit more room for sensational literature to play with and resist cultural hegemonics. "This literature," Streeby writes, "may also register the contradictions between the liberal ideal of abstraction and the material and embodied histories and knowledges that this ideal excludes but nonetheless presumes and exploits" (301n104). Again, the critics position themselves along a continuum, this time weighing the relative social and political energies of sensational literature.

Most critics of sensationalism, like Streeby, now acknowledge that there are both subversive and conservative elements contained within the complex, often contradictory, discourses of sensational culture. An author's stated goals of progressive social reform, for example, may be undermined by his conservative assumptions about race or gender. Thus, as a critic, positioning oneself along the political axis has now become a matter of deciding which set of characteristics, the subversive or the conservative, outweighs the other.[20] My own argument moves toward the subversive end of the continuum. Lippard's scathing and sophisticated critique of capitalism, I believe, mounts a persuasive challenge to such sacred ideological tenets as possessive individualism and laissez-faire economics. What is more, this critique is linked in complicated ways to a powerful politics of affect that leverages the peculiar aesthetic capacities of sensational fiction. But to argue for the subversive energy of Lippard's writing is not to discount those critics who emphasize sensationalism's conservative aspects; rather, it is to accord a bit more respect to the nineteenth-century critics who themselves saw such fiction as a sociocultural threat, and it is to argue also for the disruptive potential contained within the genre's affective apparatus.[21]

In linking politics and affect, however, I need to further distinguish my approach from that of Streeby and Cvetkovich on the question of ontology. Whereas both critics assume that affect is entirely socially constructed, I want to resist that impulse. I want to stop short of completely erasing the physical body. It seems to me that a phenomenology of affect needs to make room for both the physical body and for a discursive interpellation of that body. This is not necessarily to posit the existence of a pre-discursive body, but it is to suggest that in the mutual imbrication of body and discourse, the body can push back; it can help shape a subject's affective experience. In their helpful introduction to the works of psychologist Silvan Tomkins, Eve Sedgwick and Adam Frank take issue with Cvetkovich's discursive model of affect. They point out that for a theory of embodied emotion, her model is distressingly abstract. "*Affect* is treated as a unitary category, with a unitary history and unitary politics. There is no theoretical room for any difference between being, say, amused, disgusted, ashamed, and enraged" (110). The price that Cvetkovich pays, it seems, for pushing affect all the way into the realm of discourse is a loss of embodied particularity. By making room for that body, by attending to more specific phenomenologies of emotion, I aim to improve our understanding of the potential links between politics and readerly affect.

Not surprisingly, perhaps, Silvan Tomkins figures prominently in this effort, not the least because his pioneering work lays out a helpful taxonomy of affects.[22] Lippard's city-mysteries concentrate on producing and managing the specific affect of *distress*. Tomkins describes "distress-anguish" as an affective response generated by a wide variety of sensory stimulations (physical pain, hearing of the loss of a love object, hunger, and so on). In an infant, it is indicated by the crying response, during which "the corners of the lips are pulled downwards" and "there is an arching of the eyebrows" (*AIC* 2: 3). In an adult, the response is generally toned down into a "mute facial cry" involving frowns and grimaces, or into a "substitute cry" of clenched fingers and toes, or into "rhythmic responses" like finger drumming, toe tapping, or gum chewing (2: 56–61).[23] Crucially, distress can be distinguished from the higher-intensity affect of "fear-terror" by virtue of its "more enduring self-punishing response" (2: 9–10). That is, fear causes a person to respond quickly and dramatically so as to reduce immediate threats. Distress, by contrast, is a lower-level response, one that "permits the individual to mobilize all his resources including those which take time (for example, thinking through a problem) to solve the problems which activate distress" (2: 13).

This "more enduring" characteristic of distress is precisely what makes it an ideal affect for Lippard to evoke in the service of his radical politics. This is because distress afflicts societies as well as individuals and can serve as a spur to social and political action. "The presence of distress," Tompkins writes, "indicates a potential for remedial action either by the individual, or with his support. [...] Any society which is not distressed by its illnesses, its injustices, its discrepancies between abilities and achievements [...] is an underdeveloped society" (2: 54–55). By inducing an embodied feeling of distress in readers, Lippard's novels effectively call attention to social inequality at the same time that they marshal the energy to redress it.

Tomkins also emphasizes the fact that literature is fully capable of evoking these affective responses in its readers. In fact, he suggests that words have the capacity to thoroughly "dominate the affective life." He explains:

> Language is the lens of thought through which affects can be brought to a magnifying, searing, white-heat focus. The worlds which have been constructed out of words have promised the wildest excitements, the deepest enjoyments, the most abysmal distress and the ultimate shame and terror. From God, heaven, and the angels, through the bourgeoisie and the proletariat, to hell and the devil, man has been fascinated, dedicated, alienated, humiliated, terrorized by his own linguistic inventions. [...] There is no affect which cannot be activated and maintained endlessly by the magic of the word. (2: 71)

Language and literature are presented here as a privileged medium for "activating" and "maintaining" affective responses in the reader/listener. And it is, I believe, precisely this sort of "white-heat focus" that Lippard hoped to achieve with his city-mysteries. His two key affective strategies, the repetition of theft scenes and the evocative use of urban space, are calculated to produce and manage the readers' political energies. More specifically, I would suggest that these twin strategies constitute a kind of *affective scripting* whereby the reader is repeatedly asked to perform, to feel, the peculiarly distressing experience of having his or her property stolen. These theft-scripts are the means by which Lippard seeks to evoke his readers' "potential for remedial action." Sensational fiction thus becomes the medium for a potentially powerful politics of affect.

Lippard's repeated attention to scenes of theft in his urban novels constitutes the first, more familiar component of his affective scripting strategy. It is more familiar in the sense that some of Lippard's theft scenes, like Mary's mistreatment in the Canal Street shirt store, rely on a sentimental mode of sympathetic identification between reader and character. Common to nineteenth-century sentimental novels, such scenes depict a character undergoing some sort of physical or emotional ordeal and, in so doing, ask that the reader sympathize. We might think, for example, of the famous scene in *Uncle Tom's Cabin* in which Eliza converts Mrs. Bird to the abolitionist cause by appealing to her maternal sensibilities. "Have you ever lost a child?" she asks. Mrs. Bird responds by bursting into tears and then admitting that she has indeed "lost a little one." Eliza presses home the analogy: "Then you will feel for me. I have lost two, one after another" (149). The sympathetic identification in this scene is meant, of course, to include not just Eliza and Mrs. Bird, but the reader as well. "Every one around her," Stowe reminds us, "was, in some way characteristic of themselves, showing signs of hearty sympathy" (150).

Glenn Hendler—citing this same "classic" exchange between Eliza and Mrs. Bird—argues that sympathy was understood in nineteenth-century sentimental novels to be a combination of two affective forms of identification: feeling *like* and feeling *with*. These are relations of analogy and coincidence, respectively. In the first, the reader, like Mrs. Bird, identifies with the character because they have some sort of analogous experience that allows them to effectively imagine the character's pain. This draws reader and character more closely together, but a distance remains because, finally, this is a relationship of analogy. In the second sort of sympathy, however, the reader is thought to actually submerge his or her identity in that of the character, thereby experiencing what the character experiences. This kind of coincidence ostensibly makes for a stronger identification and stronger sense of sympathy.[24]

Hendler notes that both Freud and recent critical work on sentimentalism deny the possibility of this stronger form of total identification. It is a "fantasy of experiential equivalence" that threatens to trivialize the actual suffering of those in pain (7). (Middle-class white women, for instance, could not really vicariously experience the same suffering as slave women.) Nevertheless, Hendler concedes that this fantasy is "at the root of [sentimentalism's] affective and political power" (7). In other words, while nineteenth-century notions of sympathy may not constitute a thoroughly viable psychological model of identification, they do go a long way toward explaining how and why the discourse of sympathy possessed the affective and political power it did.[25]

Hendler's distinction between "feeling like" and "feeling with," between analogy and coincidence, is a helpful framework for understanding how both nineteenth-century readers and twenty-first-century critics make sense of sympathetic identification. What I would like to suggest, however, is a further elucidation of this model, one that takes into account the various modes of analogous identification, the various versions of "feeling like." Clearly, full experiential equivalence is impossible: when I read of a character slamming his hand in a car door, I do not actually feel the same physical pain. "Feeling with," then, does indeed seem to be an unattainable ideal or fantasy of total identification. Relationships of analogy, however, would seem to include different degrees of identificatory immediacy, or "closeness." At one end of the spectrum is a more thoroughly mediated and contextualized mode of identification; call it *sentimental sympathy*. In the Canal Street shirt store, for instance, readers learn the history and context of Mary's troubles: they determine that she has worked hard on sewing her shirts; they discover her father's pitiful plight; they witness the threadbare clothes she must wear. While the readers themselves may never have experienced precisely these circumstances, the narrative of Mary's history and context constitutes a recognizably distressing experience and it invokes a sympathetic response. This sort of mediated sentimental sympathy, in fact, might be better described as "feeling for," a phrase that conveys a greater sense of "distance" from the object of sympathy.

At the other end of the sympathetic spectrum is what we might call *sensational sympathy*. This mode of identification relies on more immediate, embodied responses to sympathy-inducing narratives. Readers recognize the bodily stress or trauma that a character is undergoing and, in so doing, themselves experience a faint phenomenological echo of that trauma. There are countless antebellum examples of this sort of sensational sympathy, but if I might be permitted a more contemporary illustration, we could recall the infamous dental torture scene in John Schlesinger's film, *Marathon Man*. In it, a graduate student played by Dustin Hoffman is strapped into a chair and tortured by a former Nazi dentist played by Laurence Olivier. Olivier slowly and painfully pulls out one of Hoffman's teeth, without the benefit of any anesthetic. The scene is excruciating to watch and results for the viewer in a fit of wincing, gasping, and cringing. This then is the more immediate, more embodied form of sympathetic identification that relies less on context than it does on direct somatic resonance. While not going so far as to fully "feel with" the character, it does represent a "closer," more physically intimate version of sympathy than the more sentimental mode.[26]

Often in Lippard's work, the two modes, sentimental and sensational, are mixed together to varying degrees in the same scene. The affective script that Lippard presents in the Canal Street scene seems at first to mark it as an example of sentimental sympathy. Working-class readers are meant to compare their own experiences of exploitation with Mary's ostensibly similar predicament and to thereby feel her distress.[27] Like their own struggle to secure the "just fruits" of their labor, Mary is denied even her meager reward for the labor she has put into sewing the shirts. "Never saw *wuss* stitchin' in my life," Screw Grabb sniffs (*NY* 50). This sort of capitalist trickery must have seemed like a clear and present danger to readers scrambling to secure their own livelihoods in a rapidly changing market economy. Nor does Lippard hesitate to break out some of the tried and true clichés of the sentimental novel when cementing Mary's position as an object worthy of sympathy. "She was dressed in a faded calico gown," he tells us, "and a shawl as worn and faded, hung about her shoulders. She wore a straw bonnet, although it was a night in mid-winter; and beneath her poverty-stricken dress, her shoes were visible: old and worn into shreds they scarcely clung to her feet" (50). After Mary flees the shirt store, she returns to a squalid, fourth-floor garret apartment, assailed by "drunken shouts, the cries of children, and a thousand other sounds, which, night and day resounded through that palace of rags and wretchedness" (52). Once there, she tries to minister to her invalid father, a "poor man, prematurely old and reduced to a mere skeleton" (53). Without the money from the shirts, however, it is a lost cause: "Oh, my God, and I have not bread to feed him!" she cries. Mary evokes the reader's sentimental sympathy to the extent that she represents a disturbingly familiar narrative. It was not much of a stretch for working-class readers to imagine their own economic situation sliding into a similar nightmare.

At the same time, Mary's experience in the shirt store is meant to convey a sense of what Mary's physical experience is like. That is, Lippard gestures toward a *sensational sympathy*, a phenomenology of affect through which the reader is invited to experience (albeit in a somewhat diluted form) Mary's own feelings of exploitation and theft. When Screw Grabb refuses to pay her for the shirts, Mary responds, "Consider, Sir, you will distress me very much. I really cannot afford to lose that five dollars" (50). The language of distress hints at Mary's specific affect here, and Lippard reinforces this feeling by shifting attention to the *faces* of the two characters: "[Mary] turned toward him a face which, impressed as it was with a look of extreme distress, was also invested with the light of a clear, calm, almost holy beauty" (50–51). According to Silvan Tomkins, the face is precisely the site at which affect is most clearly registered. It makes sense then that Lippard turns to it when he wants to convey

Mary's distress to the reader.[28] Again, when she defies Grabb, Lippard signals her anger by means of facial affect. "The young woman retreated into a corner behind the counter, her face flushed and her eyes flashing with an almost savage light." She rebukes Grabb, calling him a "despicable coward," and "the look of her eye and curl of her lip" make her disgust evident (51). This facial performance serves to heighten the reader's sympathetic identification with Mary by opening up her embodied experience to scrutiny. That is, the reader can better *feel like* Mary by identifying with her embodied affective responses to the deceitful proprietor. This, Lippard insists, is what theft feels like.

Much the same identificatory logic is at work in an earlier theft scene in *Empire City*. In this case, however, the sentimental relationship between reader and character begins to show signs of a more distinctly sensational form of identification. The ironically named protagonist, Nameless, heir to the Van Huyden fortune, has recently escaped from the Quaker-run madhouse he was placed in by his benefactor, Martin Fulmer. He has spent his last few dollars to secure passage on a train from Philadelphia to New York City. En route, he meets a recently released convict named Ninety-One who, Nameless will later discover, was his guardian while he was an infant. The two men are seated in a passenger car directly behind the crooked bank magnate, Israel Yorke. Yorke, unbeknownst to them, has been planning to stage his own robbery. He's carrying seventy-one thousand dollars in gold and bank notes in a leather valise; his plan is to take the money himself, hide it in his own clothes, throw the valise out the train window when no one is looking, and then blame the theft on somebody else. Nameless and Ninety-One are a decidedly suspicious looking pair, so Yorke points his finger at them.

As the affective script unfolds, the reader is again encouraged to sympathize with the unjust plight of Nameless, a penniless indigent accused by a "great Financier." He stands before the assembled passengers in a "faded coat, buttoned to the throat, without the relief of a shirt collar" (92). His partner, Ninety-One, presents an even less prepossessing figure with his "scarred face, harshly relieved by the coarse felon's garb" and his "eyes almost hidden by the overhanging locks" (93). The speed with which the upper-class passengers turn on these two lower-class men is calculated to appeal to a sense of working-class persecution and injustice. Targeted simply for their lack of money and polish, Nameless and Ninety-One stand in for the sympathetic working-class reader. Ninety-One (himself a former mechanic) voices the working-class frustration with this social bias: "Cause a man aint got his Sunday clothes on, must he be suspicioned o' stealin' a dirty little trifle of seventy-one thousand dollars? Redikulous!" (93). The question is a revealing one, and while Ninety-One finds little compassion among the passengers, it seems clear that the real subject of his address is the reader. "With a smile of commiseration for this lamentable mistake of public opinion, Ninety-One, looked from side to side, as if to find a corresponding sympathy" (93). Again, the larger economic context and the specific history of these two characters figures prominently in the identificatory mechanism.

But as in the shirt store scene, Nameless's shame and humiliation are also coded in terms of embodied affect; his facial and bodily gestures encourage the reader to physically feel the distress, that is, to gain a sense of the affective experience associated with being called a thief. When Yorke first accuses him, Nameless stiffens and his "pale features [are] suddenly flushed with burning crimson" (92). Another passenger asks him if he will submit to a body search, but Nameless remains silent, his body alone communicating his affective state. "Hands clenched, his eyes downcast, [the passengers] could remark the nervous tremor of his nether lip, the slight compression of his brows" (93). The questions increase and his emotional state darkens until the "agitation [. . .] fill[s] his eyes with injected blood" and tears tremble on his eyelids (94). Here, the reader's sympathetic identification, signaled by the presence of tears, proceeds via embodied affective resonance. Nameless's bodily affect is made legible to the reader and thus opened to that reader's vicarious experience.

Yet, as the "injected blood" in the eyes begins to suggest, Nameless's body is "opened" in a more visceral fashion here than it is in the more conventionally sentimental scene in the shirt store. Yorke's frame-up still asks the reader to identify, to sympathize, with the two exploited, lower-class protagonists, but in this case the identification starts to rely more heavily on an immediate sense of corporeal suffering. There is a shift away from the narrative contextualizing necessary for sentimental sympathy (for example, Mary has no money; she is being robbed; her father is dying, and so on) and toward the less mediated, more directly somatic response associated with sensationalism. After Yorke's repeated demand that Nameless and Ninety-One be searched (and after rejecting Nameless's more egalitarian suggestion that everyone in the car be searched), a police officer on Yorke's payroll forces the issue. The entire car beholds "the young man standing motionless, his face covered with a blush of burning shame, as the coat [is] torn aside from his naked breast" (97). Quite literally, then, the body is revealed here, opened to the sympathetic gaze of the reader. But it is also specifically a body marked by violence. "By gimini!" cries the officer, "here's a purty feller for the first class cars! Why, the feller aint got no shirt, and his breast is kivered with scars! Marks o' the pennytensherry, no doubt" (97). In a grim echo of the scars on Ninety-One's face, Nameless's mutilated chest is meant to evoke a more visceral sympathy in the reader, a more immediate bodily sensation of physical distress.

Significantly, this movement from sentimental to sensational sympathy seems to parallel a shift from the face as primary site of affective communication to the body writ large. In moving from Ninety-One's scarred visage to Nameless's chest, a kind of literalized de-facing takes place. Scars that initially mark the face as the point of affective contact between reader and character are now inscribed on the body. It is on, and in, this body that Lippard will center his more sensational version of sympathy. Indeed, Nameless's blood-infused eyes underscore this point. Perhaps the most evocative feature of the face, his eyes have now ruptured and succumbed to an invasion of bodily effluvia; the wounded body is beginning to assert its distinctive form of affective connection. The reader's sympathy is being transformed into something more like the flinching, physical distress of *Marathon Man* and less like sentimental compassion. Shared corporeality is emerging from within sentimentalism to become an important avenue of affective identification in its own right.[29]

The full potential of this sensational sympathy, however, is best illustrated in a theft scene that occurs midway through *Quaker City*. In it, Devil-Bug and his Jewish accomplice, Gabriel von Gelt, break into Widow Smolby's house in order to steal her accumulated fortune in gold doubloons.[30] Once again, the reader is encouraged to identify with an innocent victim and to vicariously experience some form of the theft-distress that the widow suffers. But in this instance, the identification proceeds by way of bodily distress. That is, Lippard relies primarily on visceral, sensationalized sympathy that provokes an immediate, somatic distress in the reader, rather than the more mediated response of sentimentalism. After sneaking into her bedroom while she sleeps, the burglars slide her treasure chest from under the bed, open it up and admire the glittering gold. The widow hears them, however, grabs two pistols and prepares to fight: "Rob a poor lone woman, will ye? Take that!" (240). Unfortunately for her, the pistols misfire, but she doesn't hesitate for a moment. "With a wild yell, gathering all her strength for a desperate effort, the old woman, bounded from the bed, and in an instant, came plunging at the throat of Devil-Bug, her arms outstretched, and her long skinny fingers, clutching him by the face and hair." Lippard warms to the scene: "She hung upon him, like a living Night-mare, her arms gathering convulsively around his neck, while her long nails, dug into his cheeks, like the talons of a vulture" (240).

As the violence unfolds, it quickly moves into a sensationalized register calculated to evoke a visceral response on the part of the reader. Hands wet with the blood streaming from his own face, Devil-Bug lifts the old woman above his head and dashes her to the floor, but "in an instant she was on her feet again [. . .] and gathered her hands round his throat." "From one end of the room to the other [. . .] the combatants passed, the old woman muttering a suppressed shriek all the while, as the hand of the robber was pressed upon her mouth." But it ends badly for the courageous old woman when Devil-Bug spies the fireplace andiron. "As the blacksmith with his muscular arms [. . .] brings the hammer, whirling down upon the anvil, so Devil-Bug, with his hideous face, all a-flame with rage, swung the body of the old woman wildly over his shoulder, and with every impulse of his strength, gathered for the effort, struck her head—her long grey hairs streaming wildly all the time—full against the knob of the brass andiron" (241). The image is flinch-inducing enough on its own, but then Lippard tells us that "the brains of the old woman lay scattered over the hearth" and that the corpse Devil-Bug still grasps is "a headless trunk, with the bleeding fragments of a face and skull, clinging to the quivering neck" (241). Once he throws it to the floor, "silently and slowly the blood of the murdered woman [begins] to flow and spread" over "the cold bricks of the fire-place" (242–43). A few minutes later, her cats are walking around her, "staining their feet in the thick blood" (248).

The gruesome scene powerfully conveys a sense of how Lippard's sensationalism, his willingness to dwell on the gory aspects of suffering and pain, translates into a form of embodied distress for the reader. As we read, we wince and cringe at the violence. Our bodies respond to Lippard's descriptions with a kind of corporeal resonance: we imagine that we can feel something of the pain because we have ourselves experienced bodily trauma. Despite its somatic intensity, however, despite its immediate, visceral nature, this affective response is still a form of sympathetic identification with the suffering widow. Readers wince because they can to some extent imagine themselves in the widow's place. It is not primarily, in this case, a sentimental sympathy that requires substantial knowledge of context and narrative; it is instead a sensational sympathy, one that relies chiefly on the reader's own embodied memory. However, narrative context does not disappear altogether here. A crucial part of the reader's distress response in this scene is tied to the fact that the widow is being robbed. This knowledge is what allows Lippard to link the bodily suffering to a phenomenology of theft. Following this affective script, readers can imagine themselves in a position where their property is being violently taken from them. So although the sensational theft scenes shift the emphasis away from the more mediated aspects of theft-distress (like the class-based exploitation that Mary suffers), they do so in order to highlight the more visceral, physically painful aspects of having something stolen.

But there is a bit of a difficulty here for Lippard: Widow Smolby is wealthy, and, as such, she seems like a poor candidate for radical sympathies. That is, if the scene is meant to link theft anxiety to a radical critique of capitalist expropriation, why is the victim wealthy? Wouldn't it be more effective to make her poor or working class? The paradox for Lippard is that while burglary and violent theft of this sort certainly carry a powerful affective charge, it is ultimately the wealthy capitalist who has the most property to lose. The rich make alluring targets for theft and they provide dramatic examples of property loss, but they make poor victims for radical socialist narratives. Lippard's challenge is thus to preserve the magnitude of theft-distress that comes with the loss of Widow Smolby's wealth, but to channel that distress into a critique of the wealthy.

To do this, Lippard relies on several different strategies both large and small. In the immediate context of the Widow Smolby subplot, Lippard is careful to distinguish the old woman from respectable capitalist aristocracy. In contrast to the more opulent mansions of the avowed capitalists, for instance, the widow's house is "old and desolate" with "Thick masses of rank green moss" on the roof and a garret window "stuffed with an old straw hat and bundles of rags." Other windows are "concealed by rough boards, nailed loosely to the window-frame" (199). Far from a glittering testament to capitalist excess, this house is the image of decay and humble poverty. Moreover, the widow herself is coded as lower-class: she neither wore "blue stockings," we learn, nor "talked dictionary" (200). In short, while the widow may be wealthy—and therefore vulnerable to substantial theft—Lippard works hard to distance her from the capitalist upper-class and to associate her more closely with the trappings of the working class.

On a larger scale, Lippard relies on the novel's insistent anticapitalist rhetoric and imagery to effectively constrain and construe any unruly aspects of theft-distress. That is, by repeatedly trumpeting its working-class sympathies and highlighting capitalist thievery, the novel creates a framework, a larger affective script, as it were, for channeling the anxiety generated by the widow's violent robbery and death. The novel is replete with upper-class scoundrels, working-class heroism, and blistering critiques of the inequality and hypocrisy of Philadelphia society.

One representative sample occurs in a dream of Devil Bug's in which he envisions the apocalyptic destruction of the city in the year 1950. His dream guide—a kind of ghostly Virgil to Devil Bug's Dante—explains why the city is convulsed in riot: "The lordlings of the Quaker City have sold their father's bones for gold, they have robbed the widow and plundered the orphan [...] they have turned the sweat and blood of the poor into bricks and mortar" (373). By the end of the dream, a hellish parade of living and dead victims marches by, including "a long line of penniless Debtors," and "the slaves of the cotton Lord and the factory Prince." "Hurrah, hurrah!" the sardonic marchers cheer. "This is a liberal mob; it encourages manufactures. The monopolist forever [...] his enterprise gives labour to the poor, hurrah, hurrah!" (389). Embedded in this sort of passionate anticapitalist rhetoric, Lippard's carefully cultivated theft-distress has a clear political goal: reminding readers what it feels like to have something stolen by a greedy and indifferent upper-class.

Both sensational and sentimental sympathies are at play, then, in Lippard's work. By shifting back and forth between the two sympathetic modes, that is, by allowing the suffering body to both emerge and subside, Lippard's novels marshal a wide range of affective energies, all of which are designed to highlight the larger capitalist culture of theft. Establishing this link between readerly affect and political critique is the centerpiece of Lippard's aesthetic project. But his strategic use of affect does not end with the deployment of multiple theft scenes. Instead, Lippard looks to another aspect of his narrative fiction in order to reinforce the phenomenology of theft. Specifically, he turns to the representation of urban space.

Kleptophobia and the Architecture of Loss

Generally speaking, the representations of space in city-mystery novels draw heavily on earlier Gothic tropes of enclosure and entrapment. Prison cells, dungeon-like basements, tombs and windowless rooms all dominate the urban cityscape. George Thompson, for example, in his lurid 1849 novel *City Crimes*, adapts the long-standing Gothic motif of live burial to the quintessentially urban corridors of Wall Street.[31] In a theft scene of his own, Thompson describes the final, fateful caper of the unfortunate burglar, Fred Archer. Late one night, Archer uses a counterfeit key to let himself into "a large, massive building in the neighborhood of the Exchange." Once inside, he quickly cracks a huge safe, "six feet in height and four in depth [...] made of massive plates of iron and protected by a door of prodigious strength" (175). With the safe open, Archer climbs in and begins happily filling his pockets with banknotes and gold. A moment later, however, he realizes that his candle is casting an incriminating light on the building's outer windows. So, without thinking, he pulls the door of the safe a bit further closed. Unfortunately, "The immense mass of iron swung heavily upon its hinges, and closed with a sharp *click*" (176). The rest of the scene exploits the reader's sense of claustrophobia by detailing Archer's gruesome death: "Vain, vain were his efforts to burst forth from his iron coffin; as well might he attempt to move the solid rock! He shrieked aloud for assistance—but no sound could penetrate through those iron walls!" Just before he dies, Archer's eyes bulge in their sockets and "blood gush[es] from the pores of skin" (176).[32]

Thompson's focus on confinement and claustrophobic enclosure in this scene is emblematic of urban space as it appears in the city-mystery novel. Gothic conventions get rewritten into contemporary urban forms so that the city is transformed into an updated version of the fog-enshrouded castle or the deserted ruin. The small dark spaces, secret rooms, and subterranean crypts of the Gothic reemerge in the modern city, terrifying readers with the possibility that such diabolical structures still exist.[33] What this means in a larger sense is that the urban topography of the city-mystery novel often eschews panoramic vistas, expansive outdoor spaces, and external street scenes, in favor of tightly enclosed interiors. Certainly, this is the case with Lippard's urban novels. His urban spaces are a pastiche of compartmentalized "chambers"; the city is conceived as a collection of closely packed interiors, one right next to the other. Characters often move from the room of one building to the room of another with minimal, if any, description of the outside space that connects them. In *Quaker City*, for example, the vast majority of the plot unfolds within the carefully described interiors of Monk Hall ("The Rose Chamber," "The Painted Chamber," "The Tower Room," and so forth), Ravoni's mansion, and the Hawkewood estate. Lippard's approach, like many of the city-mystery writers, is to represent the city as one immense labyrinth of constricted space and oppressive contiguity.[34]

As the language of claustrophobia and terror should make clear, there is also a set of affective responses traditionally associated with the contours of Gothic space. Anne Williams, for example, emphasizes "the [Gothic] setting's power to evoke certain responses in characters (and in the reader): claustrophobia, loneliness, a sense of antiquity, recognition that this is a place of secrets." Such settings, she believes, "[activate] the 'Gothic' dynamic between image and affect" (39–40). Eve Sedgwick likewise suggests that the ubiquitous imagery of live burial is itself an accurate phenomenology of the reader's experience; that is, claustrophobic enclosure is an accurate description of "the novels' physical ambience" (*Coherence* 3). Gothic architecture is thus understood to induce a range of negative affects in the reader, specifically those associated with loneliness, isolation, and claustrophobia.

Given this legacy of architectural affect, it would seem that Lippard's use of Gothic interiors should result in a similarly claustrophobic experience for the reader. That is, Lippard's urban spaces, like Thompson's Wall Street safe, should cultivate an unsettling feeling of isolation and entrapment in the reader. And to a limited extent they do. But I would like to suggest that Lippard's distinctive urban architecture ultimately emphasizes a different affective response. While Lippard does indeed construct an urban topography of subterranean rooms and tight, enclosed spaces, these spaces are also consistently perforated, opened up to movement and to proliferating connections with other spaces. The affective result of this interpenetration, interconnection, and intercirculation is an unsettling anxiety about possession. Instead of the conventional Gothic fear of immobilization and entrapment, Lippard's urban architecture continually opens a trapdoor under his reader's feet. There is precisely no space of total isolation in this city because every supposedly private or enclosed interior is surreptitiously linked to another private interior. The reader's anxiety, or more properly, the reader's distress response, derives from the notion that there are no impermeable boundaries at all in the city; all property, including the property of one's own body, is susceptible to expropriation via the hidden thresholds that riddle urban space. As Lippard's readers steal from one supposedly sacrosanct space into another, their experience is not one of immobilized claustrophobia but rather of circulating kleptophobia: absolutely everything is vulnerable.

Lippard's perforated urban architectures are important because they effectively cultivate theft anxieties in the reader. But his treatment of urban space is significant too in the broader sense that it indexes the expanding spatial radius of antebellum ownership anxieties. Worries about the abstract nature of property, about its ephemerality, about its susceptibility to expropriation, these have expanded beyond the scale of the home and the plantation and now weave themselves through the very fabric of the city. Disturbing phenomenologies of possession and dispossession, Lippard suggests, now influence spatial experience on the level of the entire city. It is left to the discerning writer of city-mysteries to both reflect and refract this new scale of anxiety.[35]

Before exploring the blueprints of Lippard's urban architecture, however, it will be helpful to consider exactly how it is that literary representations of space are able to produce affective responses in readers.

Tomkins makes it clear that literature, by virtue of "worlds which have been constructed out of words," can bring affects to a "white-heat focus." But spatial experience itself, prior to any linguistic "constructions," also figures prominently in Tomkins's theories of affect. In the simplest terms, affect is produced via sensory perception: a pistol shot, for example, generates a surprise response; or, the sight of a loved one's face may generate excitement. According to Tomkins, however, these affective stimuli are also mapped onto individual phenomenological spaces. In his words, "sounds, heats, smells, touches, kinesthesias, pains, hungers, thirsts must be 'located' by various mapping and nesting transformations in one overall coordinated space so that we know where a sound might be in visual space, where a smell might be, where a pain or a touch might be" (*AIC* 4: 68). Space thus functions as a crucial component of our overall affect-experience; it locates and conditions the stimuli that generate affect.

Literary spaces, it would seem, extend the affective influence of real-world spatial maps into a fictional landscape, or in this case, cityscape. In the same way that real-world spaces produce a variety of affective responses, so too do literary spaces invoke a variety of affects in the reader. From an affective perspective, the difference between real-world phenomenological space and fictional phenomenological space is one of degree not kind. That is, while real-world spaces may invoke more intense, insistent versions of a given affect, literary spaces can at least produce a moderate form of that same feeling. In positing an affective continuum between literary and real-world spaces, I am expanding on Philippe Hamon's notion of an architectural "shifter." In his illuminating analysis of the homologous relationship between architectural theory and literary representation, Hamon underscores the mutual imbrication of real and fictional space. He argues that within a work of literature, architecture "mediates between the text (a semiotic object) and the real (a nonsemiotic object)." Or, put another way, literary architecture "functions as a primary operator of metaphor that allows the real to be rewritten into text or vice versa, in other words, that allows one to be translated into the other" (37). Architectural space thus becomes a pivot point at which the real slides into the textual. As it makes this move, however, I am suggesting that architecture brings with it the affective potential of real-world spaces. Literary spaces generate affective energy because they are phenomenological extensions of real-world space.[36]

Lippard's city-mysteries take full advantage of this affective potential by subjecting readers to a uniquely unsettling architecture of urban space. Lippard's cityscapes are a conglomeration of claustrophobic interiors, juxtaposing one Gothic enclosure with another. *Empire City*, for example, begins with a scene reminiscent of Poe's "Amontillado." Martin Fulmer, the mysterious trustee of the Van Huyden estate, hires the mechanic John Hoffman (who will later be sent to prison and rechristened "Ninety-One") to perform a few crucial tasks for him. He blindfolds Hoffman, leads him through the city and then releases him in a dark, silent room that "might have been an elegantly furnished chamber, or a grave vault for all that he knew." In front of him, illuminated by the doctor's candle, is a brick wall containing "an aperture [. . .] two feet square and sunken in the thickness of the brick and mortar" (11). Through the opening, Hoffman can see the outlines of an iron door. Fulmer instructs John to brick up the opening, quickly and silently, making sure to bury the key to the iron door in the mortar. The job is soon finished: "The iron door with its cumbrous lock was concealed, the key buried in the mortar; the aperture disappeared." But as the two men turn to leave, Hoffman is "tortured by a thousand vague conjectures" because as he worked, "he had heard a groan echoing from that recess [. . .] a low, deep sound, like the half drowned voice of helpless anguish" (11).

The scene is only one of many in Lippard's work that foregrounds a Gothic architecture of confinement and isolation. Everywhere they turn, characters find themselves entombed in rooms of "dim and dusky light," surrounded by "sombre panelling," and breathing an "atmosphere [. . .] heavy with the breath of years" (*QC* 92; *NY* 263). Moreover, the fact that Hoffman is blindfolded while both entering and leaving the chamber nicely demonstrates Lippard's practice of eliding the external, connecting spaces of the city in favor of concatenated interiors. But while such Gothic spaces would initially seem to invoke the familiar feelings of isolation and claustrophobia, this never quite happens in Lippard. The key is never quite buried and the safe door never quite remains shut because Lippard's spaces inevitably reveal another aperture, another passage into or out of the tomb.

The seemingly Gothic architectures of *The Nazarene* offer a representative example of this peculiarly permeable urban space. In a conventionally Gothic subplot, the villainous bank director, Calvin Wolfe, has imprisoned his beautiful daughter Eleanor in the second story of his "dusky and time-darkened" mansion (65). For reasons not entirely clear (she may be the child of an adulterous affair), Wolfe despises Eleanor and has kept her under lock and key for twenty years with only a deaf-mute attendant to watch over her. Lippard goes to some length to emphasize the forlorn isolation of her prison-chambers. As "still as the grave," the rooms' only windows are "closed and grated, like the casements of a gaol" (78). All three of her rooms are separated from the rest of the house by a long narrow chamber "whose length traversed the entire depth of the mansion" (76). The deaf-mute inhabits this room both as a caretaker of sorts and as a prison guard; she lets no one in or out. Most disturbingly, the walls of this barrier room are "concealed in masses of leather, which placed over each other in numerous layers, [add] some inches to their thickness." The rationale for the leather is clear: "It was evident at a glance, that the sound of the human voice, in its loudest and most piercing tones, could never pass these walls from the rooms beyond" (77).

No sooner has he established the claustrophobic isolation of Eleanor's chambers, however, than Lippard turns our attention to a curious "oaken panel" at the back of her closet. The moment she is left alone, Eleanor rushes to the cabinet, climbs in, and slides the rear wall-panel open, revealing another room behind it. As it turns out, this is an upstairs chamber in the house next door, a building whose walls directly abut the Wolfe mansion. What is more, this room is tenanted by none other than Eleanor's beloved, the radical student Leon. The two of them had previously discovered the locked panel, each from his and her own side, and begun a fevered courtship of promises whispered through the barrier. Eventually, Leon was able to locate the secret spring that opened the panel, and the two fell into each other's arms. Reveling in Eleanor's deliverance, Leon reflects on the metaphysical significance of the secret door: "Here we have your father [. . .] making his own child a prisoner, from the moment of her birth. Never does she converse with a human being [. . .]. *Yet an oaken panel, separating one room from another, frustrates the plans of this tyrant, makes a mock of all his cruelty, and tramples his schemes into dust!*" (84). In a subtle architectural reconfiguration of Gothic enclosure, Lippard here opens up a wormhole in the supposedly claustrophobic confinements of Gothic space. The moment he has established a sense of oppressive envelopment, he alters the ground plan, puncturing the prison wall and revealing an escape route.

The cryptal spaces of Monk Hall follow the same logic of perforation. Trap doors are continually opening under the feet of characters who seem to already be in the deepest depths of the mansion. Indeed, we learn that the original architect of Monk Hall "constructed three stories of spacious chambers below the level of the earth" and that each of these communicates with the floors above and below it via a series of spatially aligned trap doors (46). "From the garret to the first story, all in the same line, like the hatchways in a storehouse, sank this range of trap-doors, all carefully concealed by the manner in which the carpets were fixed [. . .]. Beneath the ground another range of trap-doors were placed in the same manner [. . .]. They plunged the victim—God knows where!" (60–61). The claustrophobic rooms of the mansion can never quite sustain their inviolability, their isolation. Instead, openings inevitably appear that transform the dominant spatial affect into something closer to a fear of permeability.

At one point, Byrnewood Arlington, the erstwhile protagonist of *Quaker City*, finds himself imprisoned in the "Tower Room" of Monk Hall. His nemesis, Lorrimer, vows to keep him there until he (Lorrimer) has had his way with Byrnewood's sister. "Scream, yell, cry out, until your throat cracks!" Lorrimer taunts him. "Who will hear you? [. . .] Do you know the thickness of these walls?" (102). The sense of claustrophobia increases when Devil-Bug enters the room and craftily lights a charcoal fire with the intention of suffocating Byrnewood. Before he knows what is happening, the prisoner is on the verge of unconsciousness, gasping for breath. "He sprung to his feet, with a wild bound and his hands clutched madly at this throat, as though he would free the veins from the grasp of the invisible fingers, which were pressing through the very skin" (118). The cloying weight of space and atmosphere in this scene almost seems to literalize the implicit threat of Gothic architecture. It is the room itself that threatens Byrnewood: "The full horror of his situation rushed upon him. He was dying by the gas escaping from charcoal, in a room, rendered impervious to the air; closed and sealed for the purpose of this horrible death" (119).

Yet even in the midst of this ordeal, Byrnewood notices a bizarre feature of the room's architecture. The walls in one part of the room are painted to look like bookcases, complete with real glass doors set into the wall. As he gasps for breath, he spies Devil-Bug's leering face behind the glass. The murderous doorkeeper is laughing as Byrnewood dies: "The charcoal—the charcoal!" he chortles, "Wonder how *that' ill work!*" (119). Disturbing in its own right, Devil-Bug's viewing window nevertheless undercuts the claustrophobic effect of the room's architecture. Suddenly it becomes clear that the room is not as isolated or impervious as it first seemed. Indeed, Byrnewood himself instantly suspects that "these bookcases, conceal secret passages, leading from this den" (115). So again, just as he achieves his most oppressive sense of Gothic entrapment, Lippard alters the affective equation, opting instead for an architecture of permeability and disorientation. Moments after spotting Devil-Bug, Byrnewood accidentally triggers a trap door in the floor and "half of the Chamber [is] changed into one black and yawning chasm" (121). Stifling enclosure yields to a yawning vacuity and Byrnewood plunges through the opening, screaming as he falls. The real threat in Lippard is not the architecture of enclosure, but the disturbing permeability of all city spaces.

With his ubiquitous hidden panels, trap doors, and secret passages, Lippard's representation of urban space cultivates an affective response in his reader not of Gothic entrapment, not of smothering claustrophobia, but of continuous vulnerability. Private space, even the hyperenclosed space of the Gothic, is never truly private, never finally safe from puncture and penetration. The vertiginous threat of a trap door opening under one's feet speaks to an anxiety not about immobility and entombment, but about the unstable, unreliable contours of a society in flux. Lippard's perforated spaces contribute to, and capitalize on, a larger cultural distress about the precariousness of position, be it social, spatial, or economic. More specifically, such spaces trouble already destabilized nineteenth-century notions about the inviolability of property and propertied selfhood. If possessive individualism relies on the sanctity of private property, on the confident ownership of one's own body and possessions, then repeated demonstrations of instability, permeability, and expropriation throw that ideology into question. Just as body snatching will play to a cultural anxiety about theft and loss of the propertied self, so too do Lippard's permeable spaces erode confidence in a person's ability to protect private spaces and control private bodies.[37]

In this way, Lippard's affective architecture transforms Gothic claustrophobia into a kind of lingering kleptophobia. The sense of distress that is invoked for readers is tied not to entrapment but to a persistent openness, a persistent vulnerability to the depredations of thieves who have no respect for private property. This affect is a key component of the phenomenology of theft that Lippard cultivates throughout his city-mysteries. His permeable urban spaces and his canny sympathetic strategies together compose a powerful affective script calculated to induce theft-distress in his audience: readers are encouraged to fear the ever-present possibility of theft as well as to feel the distress of having property stolen.

But Lippard's aim is also to link this phenomenology of theft to a larger critique of capitalist exploitation. That is, in Lippard's narrative economy, the thieves that readers need to worry about are precisely the capitalist proprietors who benefit most from a possessive market society. As he fumes in *Empire City*:

> If there is a sight in this lower world which can draw tears from angels' eyes, it is to witness, not the march of the higher fiend over this world—the fiend who does his work with thunder stroke and with thunder crash—with something of grandeur in his darkest

deeds—but of that lower, baser, viler devil who slimes his way to power over human hearts that have been robbed and crushed, in order to increase to greater magnitude a pile of gold. (156)

This is, he believes, the injustice of an economic system that does not accord to labor its true value. The anxieties and distress that he seeks to evoke with his sensationalism are meant to vilify the capitalists and thus generate the impetus for change. Such distress constitutes that "more enduring" affect that Tomkins argues is necessary to motivate significant social transformations. The capitalists are thieves, Lippard tells his readers, and this is what it feels like to have them steal what rightfully belongs to you.

Again, however, Lippard runs into a difficulty here. More often than not, it seems, wealthy capitalists and property owners are the victims of home invasion, not the perpetrators. As was the case with the Widow Smolby, then, the rich are the ones who stand to lose the most to theft. So Lippard is faced with the paradox of claiming that those with the most to lose are also the thieves. This difficulty becomes apparent, for example, in the case of Calvin Wolfe and his imprisoned daughter, Eleanor. While Eleanor's liberation is certainly meant to be a triumph for the protagonists, it might also be read as a theft of his "property." As problematic as the notion of daughter-as-property might be from a twenty-first-century perspective, it was by no means uncommon in the nineteenth. Thus, the oaken-panel escape might also be understood, paradoxically, as a betrayal of Wolfe's absolute property rights. Squirreled away in the most private of private spaces, Wolfe's daughter constitutes his most prized (if not loved) possession, one that he has secured behind lock, key, and guard. The loss of his daughter thus constitutes a kind of theft and Wolfe becomes not the perpetrator but the victim of a crime.

Lippard is in the Widow Smolby bind. Home invasions and permeable spaces carry a powerful affective charge. Readers could be expected to respond strongly to the suggestion that all private spaces are vulnerable and that no possessions are safe from the depredations of greedy capitalists. But the capitalists themselves were the ones with the most to lose and so represented the most dramatic examples of homes invaded, of private spaces violated. Lippard's challenge is to keep the affective energy of permeable private spaces in his narratives without letting capitalists off the hook. In the case of Widow Smolby, Lippard had recourse to the larger context of anticapitalist rhetoric to channel the reader's affective response. In the present case, Lippard makes a similar move: he takes great pains to counterbalance the tricky class politics of permeable space (that is, the notion that capitalists are the victims, not the criminals) with an additional, and more obvious, geography of capitalist expropriation. In short, Lippard's urban novels embed his permeable rooms and homes within a larger spatial framework of economic disparity.

The opening prologue of *Empire City* immediately translates the economic inequality of the city into a specifically spatial register. Lippard's narrator describes the resplendent architecture of Trinity Church looming over the city as a kind of moral beacon. "Over its wilderness of roofs, there rose, forevermore, a long and tapering spire, surmounted by a cross, which glittered in the light of the noonday sun." The spire seems to figure as "the monument of some holy deed" and apparently shines "peace into the heart of every dweller into the city" (5). As the narrator continues to lay out the space in and around the church, however, the tension mounts between its seeming holiness and the poverty that surrounds it. "The carriages of the rich were there, in front of the great temple [. . .] and diamonds flashed, in the light of the setting sun, within its richly decorated walls." But beside the temple, "rose the dark haunts, where the honor of women was sold, and afar through the night, came the light of unholy places, where poison is given to the poor, the price thereof being their sweat, their blood, their life" (v). Then, throughout the city, the narrator discovers the same spatial juxtaposition of extreme wealth and extreme want: "He saw lofty mansions and miserable huts stand near each other. While the banquet was spread in the lofty mansion, the poor in their miserable huts, crouched on their straw and died" (vi). The effect of this initial city tour is an emphatic spatializing of social and economic injustice. The upper-class exploitation and expropriation that are Lippard's central concern are here inscribed in the architecture and geography of the city itself. While the church spire shines "only for those that were rich and had soft apparel, and rode luxuriously in chariots," for the poor, there is only "the gibbet frowning darkly over the walls of the jail" (vi).

Nor is Lippard content with a simple spatial juxtaposition of wealth and poverty. Elsewhere in the novels, he uses urban space to suggest a systemic economic link between the exorbitant wealth and the widespread poverty. After opening the oaken panel and rescuing Eleanor, Leon remarks that his own "rude home" and Wolfe's luxurious mansion "were one in the olden time" (85). Not only does this suggest an earlier period of greater economic solidarity and equality, it hints at the ways in which contemporary inequalities are still linked to one another. The secret oaken panel points at the possibility of a hidden connection between urban poverty and capitalist accumulation. Likewise, in *Empire*

City Lippard observes that "the merchant's splendid mansion" is often separated from "the rude hovels of the poor" only by a narrow alley, and "it is plainly to be seen, that a man might with great convenience and secrecy [. . .] pass from the yard in the rear of the merchant's mansion, enter the alley, thread its mazes, and seek the hut of the mechanic [. . .] as he pleased" (36). Again, Lippard's organization of urban space suggests a hidden connection, a convenient but secret thoroughfare, linking wealth and poverty. This surreptitious commerce between working-class huts and capitalist mansions erodes any notion of separate economic spheres. Any upper-class assertion of independence or moral superiority is undermined by the revealing contours of urban space. The economic fates of capitalist and worker are as intertwined, ultimately, as their respective architectures.

This is the larger spatial context in which Lippard mobilizes his permeable spaces. In this way, the ambiguous class politics of home invasion and privacy violation is embedded in a more comfortably radical spatial framework. If there is any doubt about which thieves the reader is supposed to fear, Lippard's topography of injustice makes it clear: it is capitalists and the labor-robbing economic system that they represent. Indeed, Lippard's efforts to map economic concerns onto affective space represent a compelling attempt to concretize the abstract threats of capitalism. Capitalists are the most dangerous thieves, he believes, precisely because they conceal their exploitation of the working class behind a façade of legitimate business transactions and financial maneuvers. Exposing this economic legerdemain by translating it into spatial terms is one way for Lippard to demystify the often invisible dynamics of market capitalism. Along with his sympathetic strategies, this spatialization of theft forms the backbone of Lippard's larger project to call affective attention to capitalist excess. Sensationalism offers Lippard the means of radicalizing his readership: through bodies, spaces, and affects, he writes a script for revolution.

Invasion of the Body Snatchers: The Market in the Grave

In Lippard's pursuit of working-class rebellion, there was perhaps no richer vein of sensational polemic to mine than that which surrounded the midcentury bodysnatching hysteria. During the 1840s and 1850s, the largest American cities, particularly New York and Philadelphia, were plagued by an epidemic of grave robbers and body snatchers. Fueled by a spike in medical school enrollment and the corresponding demand for fresh cadavers, body thieves swarmed into poor and working-class graveyards. The result was widespread anxiety about the desecration of family burial grounds and of the bodies they contained.[38] Lippard shrewdly leverages these fears by filling his city-mysteries with plundered graves, dismembered corpses, ghoulish body snatchers, and perverse anatomists. In *Quaker City*, for instance, one of Devil-Bug's many grisly occupations is to procure dead bodies for the sorcerer-anatomist, Ravoni. "The *doctor* sent for me last night," he soliloquizes at one point:

> The one what wants me to steal dead bodies for him. [. . .] he pays me well; and I likes the business. [. . .] To creep over the wall o' some grave yard in the dead o' the night, and with a spade in yer hand, to turn up the airth of a new made grave! To mash the coffin lid into small pieces with a blow o' the spade, and to drag the stiff corpse out from its restin' place, with the shroud so white and clean, spotted by the damp clay! To kiver the corpse with an old over-coat or a coffee bag, and bear it off to the doctor, with his penknife's and his daggers and his gim'lets! Hoo, hoo! [. . .] sich a jolly business! (368–69)

Devil-Bug's macabre enthusiasm mirrors Lippard's own interest in the phenomenon, but more to the point, the body-snatching subtext helps Lippard extend his previously intratextual distress about capitalist thievery into a real-world context. Grave robbing was a real phenomenon, and its presence in Lippard's novels, I maintain, helped to legitimate his claims about capitalist thieves. It effectively amplified the working-class anxieties Lippard worked so hard to generate in his urban fiction.

More subtly perhaps, body snatching raises questions about the nature and limits of market capitalism: Is nothing protected from market circulation? Is absolutely everything susceptible to commodification? Devil-Bug's "jolly business" is in fact just that, a business. As such, it underscores the monstrous reach of this capitalist greed. The grave and the bodies it contains are just another market, just another source of plunder for the relentless capitalist invasion. Slavery, of course, had already called into question the supposed sanctity of the human body; chattel slaves, after all, put the lie to the notion that human beings were somehow immune to appropriation. But grave robbery brought this implication home in most dramatic fashion to white, working-class readers who might otherwise have been able to distance themselves from the depredations of Southern slavery. White, black, poor, even middle-class bodies, all were vulnerable to expropriation in this grim new economy. As a result, grave robbery had the effect of magnifying antebellum misgivings about the ever-expanding reach of the market.

On the one hand, then, Lippard's use of body snatching adds to fears of an all-devouring market—fears about the commodification of human beings that were already taking shape in relation to the contradictions of chattel slavery. On the other hand, I would argue, body snatching appeals to Lippard's socialist sensibilities because it helps highlight certain gothic characteristics of capitalism itself. In particular, the ghoulish buying and selling of dead bodies calls attention to the bleak social relations of the worker-as-object. That is, grave robbery reappears as often as it does in his novels in part in order to repeatedly stage the drama of working-class alienation. In doing so, the novels literalize the objectified status of the worker's body vis-à-vis capitalism and re-present it to the reader. The effect is affect: Lippard's theft-distress is tied to the distressing realization that it is not just personal property that is being stolen in a capitalist economy, it is life itself.

Of course, Lippard's literary uses of grave robbing draw on the already sensationalized discourse circulating in antebellum print culture. In the first half of the nineteenth century, medical schools manifested a growing need for suitable cadavers, but because procurement of bodies was generally illegal, they were forced into all manner of questionable arrangements. Lurid reports appeared in the popular press (some of them true) describing gangs of marauding medical students disinterring bodies from graveyards in the middle of the night. Public outrage was aroused, and a number of violent anatomy riots took place in cities around the country.[39] All of this must have been irresistible to Lippard. Here was a topic that promised to amplify working-class distress to the point of violent resistance. Dead bodies, it seems, were just as effective at cultivating an affective response in readers as were living ones. Indeed, the dramatic antebellum reaction to the desecration and dissection of human bodies might be read as another form of the "sensational sympathy" we explored earlier. Although no doubt inflected in this case by religious taboos and familial sentiment, it seems reasonable to assume that outraged readers were motivated, at least in part, by a visceral, somatic sympathy between their own still-inviolate bodies and the recently exhumed corpses.

Not only did the phenomenon of grave robbery come with a built-in affective charge, it was also thoroughly infused with class politics. Bodies were most often procured from potter's fields or prisons, but during periods of increased demand, working-class graveyards were sometimes plundered. Moreover, the dividing line between poor and working-class burial sites was tenuous at best. Injury or job loss could mean the difference between a respectable burial and an anonymous grave. As a result, the fear of dying indigent was an insistent one for the antebellum working class.[40] Even the passage of the controversial "Bone Bill" in New York in 1854 did not assuage working-class fears. The legislation was designed to eradicate the black market in cadavers by legalizing and regulating procurement. The source of these bodies, however, was to be both the prison house and the poorhouse. (Although legislators removed the word "almshouse" from the final version of the bill, it was generally understood that the unclaimed bodies of the urban poor would constitute the greatest source of cadavers.) The class bias here could not be much more overt and the working class took little solace from the fact that it was, for now, only the very poor who were being offered up as medical merchandise.[41]

Significantly, advocates and opponents of the bill both cast their arguments in terms of class politics and market capitalism. Advocates adopted a utilitarian line of reasoning, asserting that this medical research would ultimately improve the lives of society in general and of the urban poor in particular. Moreover, they claimed that criminals and the poor both owed a debt to society and "by offering up their bodies, to the advancement of a humane science, they will make some returns to those whom they have burdened by their wants, or injured by their crimes" (qtd. in Sappol 130). Opponents (often politicians from immigrant and poor districts) immediately attacked the class prejudice inherent in the language of the bill: "Is poverty a sin—misfortune a crime? Is it not enough that the recipient of these drank life's bitter cup while living, without subject his dead body to insult and sacrilege"? (qtd. in Sappol 131).

At the same time, there was a lively debate over the moral character of those who participated in the body snatching economy. The upper-class professionals who supported the bill were keen to distance themselves from the unsavory lower-class thieves who actually procured the cadavers. Legalization, they believed, would destroy the underground market in bodies and replace it with a more respectable class of entrepreneur, a class with whom they could conduct business without fear of taint. Critics of the bill, however, were quick to point out the flimsiness of this distinction: "If they are remorseless vampyrs who steal a dead body for dissection," one opponent asked, "what will those be who take bodies for dissection under the law?" (qtd. in Sappol 131). Legal sanction or no, the critics imply, a thief is a thief is a thief. More subtly, perhaps, by drawing attention to the similarity of "legitimate" upper-class merchants and reviled lower-class thieves, the body-snatching debates inadvertently underscored the expropriative aspects of market capitalism in general. How are we to distinguish, finally, between the entrepreneurial economies of the body snatchers and of the respectable capitalists? Doesn't the market encourage the same self-interested, amoral behavior in both?

Lippard's answer, of course, is yes. For him, the only distinction to be made between body snatchers and greedy capitalists is the type of property they are interested in stealing. The cultural phenomenon of grave robbery is ideally suited to Lippard's purposes because it seems, from a working-class perspective at least, to be such a stark example of class exploitation. But the disturbing class politics are also intimately linked to the reading public's affective experience. The horrific possibility of having one's own grave violated is an affective script likely to induce a visceral feeling of distress in the reader, particularly in a working-class reader for whom a pauper's grave is an all-too-real possibility. In this way, grave robbery provides Lippard with an almost ready-made politics of affect, a timely body-narrative that also speaks to the inexorable reach of the market.

Clearly, one of the most disturbing aspects of this blackest of black markets is the way in which it transforms human bodies from subjects to objects. When Devil-Bug describes the experience of body snatching for Ravoni, he emphasizes both the lifeless materiality, the thing-ness, of the corpse and the mercantile nature of the exchange. After carelessly smashing the coffin to pieces with his shovel, for example, he rudely drags the body out of the grave and wraps it up in an old "coffee bag." In this gruesome parody of an agricultural harvest, the newly commodified human remains become a bale of goods ready for transport and sale on the market. This, in its starkest form, is the looming threat of capitalism: nothing is spared from the omnivorous appetite of market expropriation. Indeed, in *The Nazarene*, Lippard describes a transaction in which the interested parties contract for a still-living woman. The scene unfolds in a filthy bar called "The Devil's Grave," an infamous transaction point for desperate doctors and conniving body thieves. A sinister barkeep by the name of "Graveyard Crow" proffers his wares to a likely looking medical student. "Doctor, would you like to buy a subject?" Crow whispers. "*She* is not dead yet, but I don't expect her to live more than three or four days [. . .] a very bad case of galloping consumption [. . .]. Give me twenty dollars [. . .] and I will secure the body for you" (142). Even living human beings signify as proto-corpses in this economy, waiting to be stolen.[42]

Such scenes recur obsessively throughout Lippard's work. Female bodies, working-class bodies, all are persistently transformed from persons into property, into fungible commodities. Corpses, for example, are frequently equated with money, as when John Hoffman helps Martin Fulmer entomb the coffin of Gulian van Huyden. As Hoffman lowers the casket into the family crypt, he hears "a strange clinking sound." "Dollars in the coffin?" he wonders. "Corpses and dollars, queer cargo for the other world" (*EC* 13). Living bodies, too, are constantly swept into the currents of market circulation. Frances van Huyden—to name but one of many examples—is sold to one Mr. Wareham for the price of a mansion, some furniture, and ten thousand dollars. Wareham gloats over his new prize. "You used the word 'bought' some time ago," Wareham tells her. "You were right. 'Bought' is the word. You are simply my *purchase*" (*NY* 46). Again and again, Lippard stages the transformation of human bodies into chattel and in so doing heightens the reader's anxiety about encroaching capitalism

One crucial anxiety evoked by grave robbing, then, is this fear of being transformed from person into property: If market appropriation knows no bounds, if body thieves can steal both living and dead human bodies, then what is to prevent the market from stealing you or your loved ones? At the same time, however, there is a more philosophical anxiety underlying the threat of grave robbing. If humans are commodities, Lippard's fiction suggests, if they are in fact alienable property, then the rationale of possessive individualism has a problem. We know from previous chapters that the basis of possessive individualism is the Lockean argument that a person's physical body is their one inalienable possession. As Locke has it, "every Man has a *Property* in his own *Person*. This no Body has any Right to but himself" (287). This body is then the foundation that allows a person's labor to be mixed with external objects, transforming them into private property. Without that body, without self-ownership, there is no foundation for appropriation and no justification for property. The entire edifice of possessive individualism rests upon the inalienability of that individual body.[43]

Lippard's repeated emphasis on commodified bodies, however, calls into question this liberal faith in an inalienable human body. Such bodies draw attention to the fact that the basic assumptions of possessive individualism are undercut by the market ethos itself. The same ideology that produces possessive market society also leads to its own destruction. In short, possessive individualism eats itself. The Locke-inspired, liberal appetite for ever-more property and wealth eventually leads, at least in Lippard's midcentury urban society, to a cannibalism of that same Lockean foundation. There is a contradiction at the heart of possessive market society and Lippard's point seems to be that if possessive individualism is allowed to run amok, it results in a betrayal of its own principles.

Abolitionists, of course, had already capitalized on similar anxieties in relation to the institution of chattel slavery. The slave trade itself was ample evidence of how the market could treat human beings as property to be bought and sold. There was no more insistent philosophical contradiction in antebellum American society than the claim that all men are created equal even as Americans routinely owned slaves. If it is true, as Locke argued and as American political discourse asserted, that every man owns his own body and his own labor, then how are we to countenance slavery? Moreover, anxieties arising from these contradictions haunted slaveholders and slaves alike. Owners worried about their own susceptibility to financial debt; they feared that market forces might reduce them to the position of a beholden slave. And slaves themselves were only too aware of their status as property, constantly vulnerable to violence and to the possibility of being sold away.

In this way, Lippard's account of a voracious market and his critique of possessive individualism were effectively prefigured by both pro- and antislavery discourse in the first half of the nineteenth century. What distinguishes Lippard, I would suggest, is the way in which his work extends and magnifies these antebellum anxieties. For white readers, working-class or otherwise, race slavery did not present an imminent threat. Body snatching, however, was an example of expropriation and dehumanization that was occurring around them and to which they were vulnerable. It demonstrated how capitalism could consume not just slave bodies, but free white bodies as well. This is one effect, for instance, of linking black slaves and working-class laborers in Devil-Bug's apocalyptic dream. When he describes "the slaves of the cotton Lord and the factory Prince" marching in unison, it is not simply an image of class solidarity; it also highlights the expanded scope of capitalist greed. Grave robbing as a cultural phenomenon extended the reach of the market across racial, economic, religious, and familial lines. It even crossed the boundary separating the living and the dead. As a result, theft-distress expands to encompass the entire vulnerable space of the city. Marauding bands of body thieves bring the abstract threat of capitalist expropriation home to white readers in a more insistent fashion than even the horrors of slavery.[44]

The grave robbery trope is attractive to Lippard, then, because it effectively thematizes the ever-expanding reach of capitalist expropriation. But this is not all. I believe there is an additional impetus to Lippard's fascination with this trope. Grave robbery serves his socialist politics especially well, I would suggest, because it stages the alienation of the worker in most dramatic fashion. That is, it literalizes the worker's confrontation with his own bleak existence, with his own status as alienated object. The return of dead bodies as commodities reminds the worker/reader of the dehumanizing, alienating social relations that lie just under the glittering surface of the capitalist machine. In this way, grave robbery performs double duty for Lippard: it presents a sophisticated, proto-Marxist critique of capitalist social relations, and it produces the distressing affects to go along with that critique.

Marx composed his *Economic and Philosophical Manuscripts* in the spring and summer of 1844, almost exactly the same period during which Lippard was crafting his serial installments of *Quaker City*. In the *Manuscripts*, Marx famously details the debilitating effects of capitalist social relations on the experience of the proletarian worker. He argues that the worker is estranged from the products of his own labor because while the worker invests his own vital activity into work, he never actually owns the product—that belongs to the capitalist who has purchased the worker's labor. As a result, Marx explains, "Labour does not only produce commodities; it produces itself and the labourer as a commodity" (86). Moreover, this self-commodification leads to an uncanny kind of doubling in which the externalized object faces and confronts the worker: "His labour becomes an object [. . .] a self-sufficient power opposite him, [and] the life that he has lent to the object affronts him, hostile and alien" (87). The consequences for the worker's quality of life are dire: "He denies himself, feels miserable instead of happy [. . .] mortifies his body and ruins his mind" (88).

It is my contention that Lippard was attempting to convey something very similar to this economic and affective "mortification" through his use of the grave robbing trope. Grave robbery, of course, enacts a macabre transformation of human being into commodity—nicely figured by the coffee bag covering Devil Bug's plunder. In so doing, it forces the living to confront the disturbing prospect of themselves as a commodity, to look at their alienated existence through a glass, darkly, as it were.[45] Put another way, grave robbing reproduces the body of the worker as an estranged object which then "affronts him, hostile and alien." (The class politics of antebellum grave robbing encouraged the poor and working class to imagine that it was their bodies, poor and working-class bodies, that were being stolen.) This is a kind of capitalist haunting in which the ghost of the exploited worker returns to confront the working class with a grim vision of their plight. Part of the affective charge of grave robbing, then, is the way in which it highlights for readers the alienating, dehumanizing effects of capitalism.

The confrontational aspects of grave robbing are particularly pronounced in a bizarre scene of body snatching and resurrection that occurs toward the end of *New York*. Lippard recounts the history of young Marion Merlin who, after a series of disastrous romantic relationships, eventually commits suicide in despair. Her corpse, however, is quickly disinterred by a pair of shifty grave robbers who transport it to the dissecting room of an ambitious medical student, Arthur Conroy. After paying off the grave robbers and indulging in a bit of perverse voyeurism—"Dead, and yet very beautiful" he pants—Arthur settles down to his dissecting work.[46] The moment he begins cutting, however, the corpse sits up and addresses him: "Nay, do not be frightened," she tells him, "I have simply been the victim of an attack of catalepsy!" (227). Marion goes on to relate the details of her interment, but the more striking point here is the way in which the stolen, commodified body is actually given a voice. The alienated object, the commodity, has become a "self-sufficient power opposite" Arthur, one who can attest to the dehumanizing nature of capitalist social relations.

This is precisely what Marion does. She describes the condition of catalepsy in terms that bear more than a passing resemblance to the social condition of the alienated worker. "Catalepsy," she explains, "leaves the soul keenly conscious and in possession of all its powers, but without the slightest control over the body, which appears insensible and dead. The agony of that state is beyond all words! To hear the voices which speak [. . .] and yet be unable to frame a word, to breathe even a sigh." It took her, she tells him, a Herculean effort "to arouse from this unutterable *living death*" (227–28). Loss of agency, of course, is the economic and existential threat that stalks the alienated working class. And the move from artisanal craft work to industrial repetition must have seemed to many like a kind of living death.[47] But more to the point, Marion's resurrected body gives a voice and a face to the experience of alienation, confronting the reader with a grim reminder of how capitalism mortifies the flesh and ruins the mind.

The dynamic of alienation seems to have bothered Lippard throughout his career. In 1849, four years before publishing *New York*, Lippard wrote a vitriolic essay for his *Quaker City* weekly in which he loudly denounced the capitalist banking system. Calling banks the "Temple," banking the "Religion," and money the "God of the Nineteenth Century," he blames the banking system for America's widespread political corruption and economic inequality. In the course of his harangue, however, he offers up a remarkable image of commodified bodies and capitalist theft that also figures forth a quasi-Marxist account of alienation. Lippard writes:

> The Banking System is, in its present state, that legalized form of robbery which enables the Speculator, the Broker, and the Capitalist

to get rich upon the labor and misery of the masses. A Bank is the tomb of dead Labor. From this tomb, by a fearful kind of resurrection, arises the ghost of Labor which scares living Labor from its rights, and bows it into abject slavery. (*Prophet* 169)

Initially, the passage reads like a fairly conventional laborite attack on the greedy robber barons who extort more than their fair share of labor-created wealth. But the metaphor of the bank as the "tomb of dead Labor" is particularly effective. It cleverly conflates the notion of commodified labor with the image of a dead laborer. That is, "dead Labor" here connotes both an alienated, objectified form of work and the corpse of the worker who has been exploited to death. Such an image is right in keeping with Lippard's argument that capitalism reduces workers' bodies to lifeless commodities available for exchange.

More interestingly, Lippard also refers to the "ghost of Labor" that rises from this tomb. Such a ghost would seem to be capital itself. That is, if we understand the wealth that accumulates in banks to be the surplus value extracted from exploited labor, then that wealth is in fact the ghost of labor, the remainder of value that is snapped up by capitalists. In effect, then, Lippard's "fearful kind of resurrection" is a compelling version of what Marx describes as alienation. Living labor is confronted by its own product, by its own commodified labor returning in a threatening and unfamiliar form. It is, in short, haunted by its own ghost.

Reanimated corpses, then, in one form or another, serve a crucial purpose in Lippard's work. Whether they are reintroduced into the ceaseless circulation of capital by unscrupulous body thieves or resurrected in the guise of cataleptics and ghosts, dead bodies bring with them a compelling economic critique and an unsettling affective charge. In economic terms, they attest to the growing influence and the expanding reach of omnivorous capital, a reach that—for white working-class readers at least—no longer remains confined to the circuits of chattel slavery. In affective terms, Lippard's dead bodies distress the reader by forcefully concretizing the experience of alienation. They stand as a grim reminder that not only does capitalism produce "its own grave-diggers," as Marx and Engels famously declared, it also produces its own grave robbers, market forces beheld in a mirror.

* * *

Marx's writings may seem like an odd place to conclude our phenomenological account of property. As the father of dialectical materialism and a vocal critic of Hegel's transcendental phenomenology, Marx hardly seems a standard bearer for the experiential account of ownership we have been pursuing. Yet, as his account of alienation makes clear, Marx himself was interested to some degree in the affective contours of property exchange. It was clear to him that evolving paradigms of ownership were intimately intertwined with human emotional life. Like many other writers and thinkers in the Romantic nineteenth century, then, Marx attended closely to affective experience; he acknowledged the vital role of emotion in human species-being. Thus, he represents a fitting final index of the way in which thinking about property shifted from an eighteenth-century framework of empiricist sensation to a nineteenth-century fascination with affect.

What is more, Marx recognized that literary sensationalism was a crucial discursive mode with which to engage and cultivate such affect. His own writing, of course, famously employs a host of gothic devices—vampires, werewolves, ghosts—in order to catalogue the horrors of capitalism. "Capital," he writes at one point, "is dead labour which, vampire-like, lives only by sucking living labour, and lives the more, the more labour it sucks" (*Capital* 342). Like Lippard, Marx saw the political potential in sensational writing and, as a result, his work helps call our attention not just to the theoretical implications of the city-mystery genre but also to the sophisticated politics of affect that infuse the genre. More particularly, it helps reveal the extent to which Lippard saw emotion and affect as a crucial component of antebellum phenomenologies of possession.

Even the distinctively urban spaces of ownership that we located in Lippard find a kind of sympathetic echo in Marx. As he describes the alienated experience of the worker, Marx alludes to the same spatialized inequalities so important to Lippard. "Labour produces works of wonder for the rich," Marx seethes, "[...] It produces palaces, but only hovels for the worker" (*Selected Writings* 88). Lippard maps out this same geography of class exploitation—"lofty mansions" standing next to "miserable huts." For both writers, then, the space of the city reflects the economic exploitation and anxiety that characterizes a growing market society. Just as the ceaseless circulation of abstract property continues to expand, encompassing larger and larger circuits of exchange, so too do the spaces of ownership anxiety increase, mapping out new geographies of possession and dispossession.

Even here in the newly expanded geography of the antebellum city, we discover once again the persistent figure of the hut, a tenacious reminder of older property paradigms. The miserable huts of Marx and Lippard connote more than just an economic raw deal: they carry with them, still, the implication of rightful ownership. That is, the huts—and the life of honest, physical labor that they are meant to represent—suggest at some level that the working class has a right to a bigger slice of the economic pie than they are receiving. In the same way that Old Deb's hut, Natty's hut, and Matthew Maule's hut all represent original, intimate, and embodied claims to property, so too do these working-class huts signify a kind of moral and economic entitlement.

But like the slave cabins of Southern literature, these huts are also distinguished by their powerful emotional charge. Ownership is more closely linked to a specifically affective politics here than it was in the huts of Brown, Cooper, or Hawthorne. Southern writers used the hut to evoke particular emotional responses in relation to property: the plantation romance figured it as a reassuring marker of slave contentment and paternal benevolence; slave narratives saw it as an emblem of exploitation and neglect. Likewise, Lippard's anticapitalist narrative leverages the emotional charge associated with the hut, in this case, cultivating a sense of anger and outrage at working-class exploitation.

This emphasis on emotion, on the politics of affect, serves as another telling example of how literary accounts of embodied ownership continued to evolve over the nineteenth century. No longer relying only on a phenomenology of physical sensation, writers increasingly explored the affective elements of possession and dispossession. This, of course, was Lippard's forte. Distressing his readers, reminding them what it feels like to have something taken away, he continued the antebellum literary work of exhuming the body of property.

Epilogue. Wisconsin, 2004: Racial Violence and the Bodies of Property

Almost exactly two hundred years after Jesse Pierson and Lodowick Post confronted one another on a Long Island beach and argued over the carcass of a dead fox, another hunting dispute unfolded in the wilderness, this time in the woods of northwestern Wisconsin. On November 21, 2004, a thirty-two–year-old deer hunter from St. Paul, Minnesota, named Chai Soua Vang was involved in an armed confrontation with another group of hunters over the right to use a particular tree-stand. The stand (a raised platform designed to give hunters a better vantage point and line of fire) was located on private land not owned by Vang. When he was discovered on the platform by the legal owners of the property, he was told to leave. Words were exchanged (including, apparently, some racial slurs—Vang is a Hmong immigrant from Laos), and shots were fired. In a manner of seconds, Vang had killed five people and wounded three others. One of those would die the following day (Kinzer A16).

As the surrounding communities struggled to make sense of the killings, many of the residents noted that the concept of private property was a critical point of contention between the established (mostly white) hunters and the Hmong immigrants. According to one Hmong resident, "In our home [in Laos], we do not have private land. All the forest in that country is national forest, so anyone can get into the land at any time. Here, it's different" (Oakes and Meryhew 1A). Different because the forests of upstate Wisconsin and Minnesota are a "patchwork of public lands" in which small private plots are mixed in with federal and state properties (Crenson). An ownership pattern of this sort can make it extremely difficult, if not impossible, to be certain that one is hunting on the appropriate property. Despite this ambiguity, however, owners of hunting property (who are often hunters themselves) expect the full range of their property rights to be assiduously observed. As one longtime resident of the area put it: "Your hunting area, if you own the land, is kind of sacred [. . .]. It's such a touchy thing" (Crenson).

The force of this statement was made clear on the day following the killings when a thirty-eight–year-old man in the nearby town of Menomonie walked onto the property of his Hmong neighbors with a can of white paint and blazoned the word "Killer" on the sides of three homes and a pickup truck (Garza 3B). This crime, while in no way equivalent to the forest killings, is notable in that it further highlights the divergent experiences of property that subtend the white-Hmong culture clash. If we read Vang's tree-stand trespass as, among other things, a challenge to long-held beliefs about the sanctity of private property and to the Western tradition of absolute ownership, then the white-paint vandal begins to look like a response in kind, if not in degree. By invading that most intimate of properties, the space of the home, and by then asserting a kind of territorial right through marking, the vandal is in some ways writing a narrative of imagined consequences. That is, the vandalism implies a kind of worst-case property scenario, one man's vision of a society in which private property rights are not fully respected. Or, to put it in more bluntly, one subtext to the word painted on the walls of the Hmong homes might be understood as: "Look what happens when you don't respect private property."

The Wisconsin killings serve as a dramatic reminder of the deeply embedded, and frequently contested, notions of property and possession that continue to infuse American culture two hundred years after *Pierson v. Post*. As we have seen again and again throughout this book, fraught property encounters of this sort often reveal a complicated tangle of ideological tensions bound up with issues of race, class, and gender. But the confrontation in the woods also returns us to more difficult and persistent questions about the nature of property itself, questions that this book has also repeatedly engaged. How is it, for example, that something like a tree-stand, or a secluded patch of Wisconsin woods, becomes the thing we call property? What kind of discursive assumptions attend that transformation from thing to owned object, and what sort of phenomenological experiences intersect with it? What pathways of action and influence can we trace in the movement from property-as-discourse to violent bodily conflict? And how do historically contingent understandings of property dictate and respond to individual experience?

I would suggest that at least two important conclusions might be derived from the tragedy. First of all, the killings underscore again the intimate relationship between property practice and the organization of space. Property conventions go a long way toward determining where people are allowed to be and where they are not. Space is divided up and organized in relation both to explicit demarcation of property lines (for example, this spot is where my property ends and yours begins) and to the flow of *movable* properties through circuits of exchange (for example, highways become the routes along which commodity goods move to market). The fact that the geography of northern Wisconsin can be described as a "patchwork" of plots attests in a very obvious way to the productive power of property in relation to social space. Secondly, such property-derived space has immediate consequences for individual bodies. The killings, along with the subsequent capture and trial of Vang, make it brutally clear that property practices direct the movement of bodies (as well as other properties) through particular spaces and with particular results. Vang's movements were attracted to and determined by a tree-stand that had been built in a particular spot by the owners of that space. The violation of the property regime in place around that tree triggered a series of events that all had horribly real consequences for the bodies moving through that space. At the same time, it was the movement of individual bodies over time that produced the social space of the Wisconsin woods. Hunters moving along established trails and to certain prime spots created a spatial network, a very real space of the woods.

The tragedy in Wisconsin thus highlights the complex interrelationship of spaces, bodies, and private properties that continues to characterize contemporary American society. At the same time, the killings dramatically underscore the need for a better understanding of such relationships and the power they exert in our everyday lives. In particular, the tragedy calls attention to the ways in which existing accounts of property in America have tended to downplay or ignore the crucial role of embodied experience as it forms and deforms the practice of ownership and possession. Recent legal and literary histories have certainly emphasized the importance of property discourse in the development of American social formations, but they have done so while prescribing a "trajectory of abstraction" according to which our evolving understanding of property has gradually sloughed off a clunky, older notion of property as concrete "thing," and replaced it with a sense of property as purely discursive construct, a "bundle of rights." Thus, while property and property rights are increasingly invoked by both the left and the right as a bulwark of contemporary American political economy—as, for example, when former President George W. Bush describes America as an "ownership society"—this popular invocation brings with it a consistently, and frustratingly, abstract conception of property. In this context, the Wisconsin killings can serve as a kind of cautionary tale, both a bracing reminder of the insistently embodied nature of ownership and a dramatic demonstration of the need for a more flexible, full-featured model of property relations.

It has been the argument of this book that antebellum literature offers us precisely this sort of sophisticated account of property as it emerges within various historical configurations of bodies and spaces. Because antebellum literature appears early on in the development of the abstract "bundle of rights" discourse, it remains open to alternative formulations, alternative models of ownership that still attend to the place of the body, and, indeed, to the space of the body. Antebellum writers and texts are obsessed with questions about the ontological nature of property. Haunted by Blackstone's Anxiety, haunted, that is, by worries about how unclaimed objects or spaces in the world can ever be rightfully claimed, American imaginative writers of the eighteenth and nineteenth centuries write frantically and creatively about how it is that things might become property. Taking up the thorny questions that jurists and legal philosophers have preferred to ignore, American litterateurs of this era delve deeply into the experience and practice of ownership, pursuing lines of thought and flights of fancy that tease out the richness and complexity of property practice. Collectively, these antebellum texts provide us with a remarkably fertile conceptual vocabulary, a vocabulary that the intervening two hundred years has done much to attenuate. In short, these texts offer a range of innovative frameworks—from the phenomenology of alimentary possession to the contested spaces of the plantation—with which to examine the ineluctable links that join together the bodies and spaces of property.

As the Wisconsin tragedy makes clear, the value of such frameworks lies not just in their conceptual complexity but also in their ability to turn our attention to previously unnoticed configurations of people and property. Just as Charles Brockden Brown's tactile phenomenology of the frontier alerts us to the erasure of Native American bodies from the space of the Pennsylvania woods, so too does a phenomenology of property highlight the embodied experience and spatial dynamics at play around the Wisconsin tree-stand. Social spaces, these texts insist, are necessarily structured by phenomenologies of appropriation and possession. But antebellum literature also suggests that this direction of influence can be inverted and that texts, literary or otherwise, can also significantly shape the configuration of properties, bodies, and spaces as these things are experienced by readers. Plantation space after Simms and Kennedy, or urban space after Lippard, all look and feel altered by the mediation of these antebellum texts. The reader's experience of property, of space, of embodiment, all these things are transformed by what Henri Lefebvre calls "representational space," that is, social space as it is lived through its associated images and symbols. The spaces in which we live and move, the spaces that are inextricably bound up with our experience of embodied property, these are spaces mediated, too, by the symbolic matrices of art and literature and discourse. Not just the urban spaces of Lippard's antebellum cities, but also the twenty-first-century space of the Wisconsin woods. These are spaces formed and deformed by the phenomenology of property, the body of property, as it is reflected in and refracted through the texts of American culture.

Notes

Introduction. *Pierson v. Post* and the Literary Origins of American Property

1. The lines are from an early version of "Crossing Brooklyn Ferry" that was found in Whitman's unpublished manuscripts. See *Walt Whitman: Selected Poems, 1855–1892: A New Edition*, p. 432.

2. On the history of *Pierson v. Post* see H. P. Hedges's account on the first page of the October 24, 1895, issue of the *Sag-Harbor Express*. See also Bethany R. Berger, "It's Not About the Fox: The Untold History of *Pierson v. Post*."

3. On the specifics of the initial lower-court proceedings (as opposed to the more famous appeal that was decided in the New York Supreme Court), see Angela Fernandez, "The Lost Record of *Pierson v. Post*, the Famous Fox Case."

4. Stuart Banner offers a succinct account of the growing legal stature of *Pierson v. Post* in his "21st Century Fox: *Pierson v. Post*, Then and Now."

5. *Pierson v. Post*, 3 Cai. 175 (N.Y. Sup. Ct. 1805) at 177.

6. Even the reference to European theorists such as Grotius and Pufendorf indicates the distinctive purview of this decision. The use of such rarefied sources was highly unusual for rulings by this court. Fernandez notes that "no other case in the three volumes of the *Caines Reports* (1804–1806), in which *Pierson v. Post* was reported, had anything like its intensive use of non-English European sources, made most palpable by the odd absence of a commercial context that usually made recourse to the law of other systems a sensible choice at this time" (307).

7. See Carol Rose's "Canons of Property Talk, or, Blackstone's Anxiety." Rose does note, however, that *outside* the Anglo-American tradition, some theorists have been more willing to explore questions surrounding the nature of property. She mentions Proudhon and Marx, specifically. She also points out that very recently legal scholars in the field of Critical Legal Studies have begun reexamining these issues. See Rose, pp. 623–30.

8. We see these coping strategies at work even in *Pierson v. Post*, a case that confronts more directly than most the ontological anxieties swirling around property.

Writing in dissent, Justice Brockholst Livingston concedes that the question of original acquisition is "a knotty point" and that he "feel[s] great difficulty in determining, [how] to acquire dominion over a thing, before in common" (180–81). But in providing his own answer, Livingston ducks the ontological quagmire and opts for a utilitarian justification: he terms the fox a "wild and noxious beast" and argues that it would be of greatest "public benefit" to destroy it. Therefore, the law should recognize the hunter's intent as a useful property claim. Otherwise, without the confidence that his hunting efforts will be rewarded, Livingston reasons, no one will put in the effort to pursue and kill these annoying creatures.

9. The novel itself, of course, is a literary form that developed alongside the rise of market culture. At least since Ian Watt's influential argument in *The Rise of the Novel*, the genre has been intimately associated with the emergence of the middle-class bourgeoisie and of "the acquisitive society" more broadly. But questions of property, in particular, have been an abiding concern of the novel from its inception. Wolfram Schmidgen, for example, observes that "eighteenth-century narratives turn almost inescapably on conflicts over property," that is, on questions over "who gets what, when, why, how" (22). Then later, as the nineteenth century begins to unsettle traditional notions of landed property by replacing them with the more fluid instruments of a credit economy, novels engage this transition, sometimes skeptically, sometimes hopefully. In all of its early instantiations—romance, sentimental, sensational, realist—the novel remained fascinated with property and property practices, persistently placing narratives of ownership, inheritance, and accumulation at the center of its thematic and structural universe.

10. Kent was a longtime friend of the Cooper family, first to James's father William and later to James himself. On the relationship between Kent and the Coopers, see the first volume of Wayne Franklin's biography, *James Fenimore Cooper: The Early Years*.

11. See, for example, Brook Thomas's *Cross-Examinations of Law and Literature*, pp. 21–44, and Susan Scheckel's *The Insistence of the Indian*, pp. 15–40.

12. The quote is taken from the "Editor's Preface" in Tucker's definitive 1803 edition of Blackstone's *Commentaries*.

13. The complex assortment of entails and trusts, for example, were gradually discontinued. On the reform of American land law in early nineteenth-century, see chapter 4 of Gregory Alexander's *Commodity and Propriety: Competing Visions of Property in American Legal Thought, 1776–1970*.

14. For a concise description of the streamlining of American inheritance law, see chapter 1 of Stuart Banner's *American Property: A History of How, Why, and What We Own*.

15. On the Married Women's Property Acts, see Norma Basch, *In the Eyes of the Law: Women, Marriage, and Property in Nineteenth-Century New York*, as well as Marylynn Salmon, *Women and the Law of Property in Early America*.

16. The quote is taken from "Walstein's School of History. From the German of Krants and Gotha," *Monthly Magazine and American Review*, August –September 1799, vol. 1, p. 408.

17. Morton Horwitz's *The Transformation of American Law, 1780–1860* is probably the most prominent exponent of this point of view. But see also Alexander's *Commodity and Propriety* and Banner's *American Property*. Banner challenges the scope of Horwitz's claims by pointing out that eighteenth-century jurists were well acquainted with some forms of intangible property. But, this notwithstanding, Banner ultimately allows the broader contours of the abstraction trajectory to stand.

18. J. G. A. Pocock is perhaps the best-known exponent of this argument; see *The Machiavellian Moment: Florentine Political Thought and the Atlantic Republican Tradition*.

19. In a British context, see Mary Poovey's *Genres of the Credit Economy Mediating Value in Eighteenth- and Nineteenth-Century Britain*, and Catherine Gallagher's *The Body Economic: Life, Death, and Sensation in Political Economy and the Victorian Novel*. For a slightly more Americanist bent, see Marc Shell's *The Economy of Literature*, and his *Money, Language, and Thought: Literary and Philosophical Economies from the Medieval to the Modern Era*.

20. See, for example, Patrick Brantlinger's, *Fictions of State: Culture and Credit in Britain, 1694–1994*, and James Thompson's, *Models of Value: Eighteenth-Century Political Economy and the Novel*. See also Sean Moore's helpful synthesis of recent work in this field, "The Culture of Paper Credit: The New Economic Criticism and the Postcolonial Eighteenth Century."

21. David Anthony, Eric Wertheimer, and Karen Weyler, for example, all utilize the abstraction narrative as an effective framework with which to offer incisive analyses of American cultural anxieties that emerge in relation to economic change. See Anthony's *Paper Money Men: Commerce, Manhood, and the Sensational Public Sphere in Antebellum America*; Wertheimer's *Underwriting: The Poetics of Insurance in America, 1722–1872*; and Weyler's *Intricate Relations: Sexual and Economic Desire in American Fiction, 1789–1814*.

22. In addition to Best's *The Fugitive's Properties: Law and the Poetics of Possession*, see Elizabeth Jane Wall Hinds's *Private Property: Charles Brockden Brown's Gendered Economics of Virtue*, and, a bit earlier, Walter Benn Michaels's *The Gold Standard and the Logic of Naturalism: American Literature at the Turn of the Century*.

23. See, for example, Anthony; Weyler; and also David A. Zimmerman's *Panic!: Markets, Crises, and Crowds in American Fiction*. For economic anxiety in the British context, see Brantlinger; Thompson; Catherine Ingrassia, *Authorship, Commerce, and Gender in Early Eighteenth-Century England: A Culture of Paper Credit*; and Colin Nicholson, *Writing and the Rise of Finance: Capital Satires of the Early Eighteenth Century*.

24. Dana Nelson and David Anthony, for instance, both point out the ways in which middle-class masculine selfhood assuaged its own economic anxieties by projecting those anxieties onto the figure of the white woman, the Native American, or the Jew. See Anthony's *Paper Money Men*, and Nelson's *National Manhood: Capitalist Citizenship and the Imagined Fraternity of White Men*.

25. Jeff Nunokawa, in a British context, makes an argument similar to Michaels. He suggests that Victorian novels assuaged anxieties about the expansiveness and invasiveness of commodity capitalism by imagining fiction as a safe space in which men's most valuable property, women, could be secured against the depredations of a market economy. See *The Afterlife of Property: Domestic Security and the Victorian Novel*.

26. In fact, Marx repeatedly voices his frustration with questions of the ontological variety, calling them an "illusion of metaphysics or jurisprudence" (*Poverty of Philosophy* 168). Indeed, the question of original acquisition—so central to antebellum property narratives—is singled out by Marx for particular disdain. "Let us not be like the political economist," he warns us in the *Economic and Philosophical Manuscripts*, "who, when he wishes to explain something, puts himself in an imaginary original state of affairs. Such an original state of affairs explains nothing" (*Selected Writings*

86). In this way, Marx distinguishes himself from his predecessor, Hegel, who vigorously pursued the "self-developmental" aspects of property relations.

27. See Noëlle Batt's, "'L'Entre-deux,' A Bridging Concept for Literature, Philosophy, and Science."

28. For a helpful overview of phenomenology's rich theoretical ecosystem, see Dermot Moran's *Introduction to Phenomenology*.

29. On William James relationship to phenomenology and to Husserl in particular, see James M. Edie, *William James and Phenomenology*.

30. For Ricoeur's phenomenological account of narrative see volume one of *Time and Narrative*, especially chapter 3, "Time and Narrative: Threefold *Mimesis*." Richard Kearney provides a helpful overview of Ricoeur's theories on imagination and language. See "Study 2" in *On Paul Ricoeur: The Owl of Minerva*. See also Rita Felski's elegant account of the "threefold mimesis" in chapter 3 of *Uses of Literature*.

31. For an involved, if not exactly transparent, explanation of the transcendental reduction, see part III of Husserl's *The Crisis of European Sciences and Transcendental Phenomenology*.

32. The Americanist scholarship on affect and emotion is vast, particularly in relation to the discourses of sensibility, sentiment, and sympathy. A representative sampling might include: Elizabeth Barnes, *States of Sympathy: Seduction and Democracy in the American Novel*; Bruce Burgett, *Sentimental Bodies: Sex, Gender, and Citizenship in the Early Republic*; Peter Coviello, *Intimacy in America: Dreams of Affiliation in Antebellum Literature*; Shirley Samuels, ed., *The Culture of Sentiment: Race, Gender, and Sentimentality in 19th-Century America*; Julie Ellison, *Cato's Tears and the Making of Anglo-American Emotion*; Glenn Hendler, *Public Sentiments: Structures of Feeling in Nineteenth-Century American Literature*; Julia Stern, *The Plight of Feeling: Sympathy and Dissent in the Early American Novel*; and Jane Tompkins, *Sensational Designs: The Cultural Work of American Fiction*.

33. Excellent work on affect and emotion is being done in a range of fields. See Sara Ahmed, *The Cultural Politics of Emotion* and *Queer Phenomenology: Orientations, Objects, Others*; Lauren Berlant, *The Female Complaint: The Unfinished Business of Sentimentality in American Culture* and *Cruel Optimism*; Ann Cvetkovich, *Mixed Feelings: Feminism, Mass Culture and Victorian Sensationalism*; Jonathan Elmer, *Reading at the Social Limit: Affect, Mass Culture, and Edgar Allan Poe*; Sianne Ngai, *Ugly Feelings*; Shelley Streeby, *American Sensations: Class, Empire, and the Production of Popular Culture*; and Rei Terada, *Feeling in Theory: Emotion After the Death of the Subject*.

34. On the broad cultural shift from eighteenth-century rationalism to nineteenth-century emotion, see Henry F. May's seminal work, *The Enlightenment in America*, as well as volume one of Hollinger and Capper's *The American Intellectual Tradition*. See also Russell B. Goodman's *American Philosophy and the Romantic Tradition*.

35. Barbara L. Packer's "The Transcendentalists" remains an excellent overview of Transcendentalism in America and provides a particular focus on the Transcendentalists' rejection of Lockean empiricism. Philip Gura's *American Transcendentalism: A History* offers up a comprehensive cultural biography of the movement. On the influence of Scottish Common Sense philosophy in America, see Terence Martin's *The Instructed Vision*; Bernard Goetzmann's *Beyond the Revolution*; and Daniel Walker Howe's *Making the American Self*.

36. Emerson's views on private property represent a more cautious, perhaps even conservative, counterpoint to the radical inclinations of more reform-minded

Transcendentalists. Although, like them, he devotes little if any thought to the ontology or phenomenology of property, he does take time in *English Traits* to celebrate England's steady protection of private property and the social benefits that flow from it. See, in particular, his chapter on "Wealth."

37. Lefebvre introduces the triad in the first chapter of *The Production of Space*. See pp. 33 and 38–39 in particular. Both Edward Soja and Kim Knott provide helpful discussions of Lefebvre's triad in their respective works. See Soja's *Thirdspace: Journeys to Los Angeles and Other Real-and-Imagined Places*, as well as Knott's, *The Location of Religion: A Spatial Analysis*.

38. Lefebvre's neo-Marxist perspective may seem like an odd match for a neo-phenomenological project, but in fact, as a number of commentators have observed, Lefebvre's close attention to the role of the sensate body in the production of space (particularly in his chapter on "Spatial Architectonics") puts him in direct conversation with more explicitly phenomenological approaches. Indeed, Lefebvre addresses a range of phenomenologists in his book, including Heidegger and Gaston Bachelard. On Lefebvre's affinity with phenomenology, see Andrew Merrifield's "Place and Space: A Lefebvrian Reconciliation."

39. Ricoeur makes this clear in his analysis of time when he asks, "How can we measure expectation or memory without taking support from the 'points of reference' marking out the space traversed by a moving body, hence without taking into consideration the physical change that produces the trajectory of the moving body in space?" (21). Not incidentally, cultural geographer J. Nicholas Entrikin has argued that Ricoeur's model of narrative emplotment facilitates a rapprochement of subjective and objective traditions in contemporary geography. Entrikin believes that narrative allows for a synthesis of place-based individual experience and more abstract, theoretical spatial regimes. See his *The Betweenness of Place: Towards a Geography of Modernity*.

40. On eighteenth- and nineteenth-century American game laws, see chapter 3 of Freyfogle and Goble's *Wildlife Law: A Primer*. See also Thomas A. Lund's *American Wildlife Law*.

41. For an excellent early consideration of game laws in *The Pioneers*, see Charles Swann's "Guns Mean Democracy: *The Pioneers* and the Game Laws," in *James Fenimore Cooper: New Critical Essays*.

42. Nelson effectively highlights the novel's attention to local practices and communal economies as potential alternatives to a capitalist focus on institutions of private property. My reading of communal space in the novel builds on her analysis of the role of the commons. See her "Cooper and the Tragedy of the Commons," in Lang and Tichi's *What Democracy Looks Like*.

43. In addition to the presence of Major Effingham, we might note that once Oliver is awarded the disputed deer carcass, he hops in a sleigh and conveys the meat directly to Leatherstocking's abode (92). In so doing, Oliver effectively relocates the contested property to the space of the hut, underscoring again its link to property disputes. In a similar vein, Richard Godden notes the hut's close connection to property discourse, calling it a "veritable anthology of political iconography" (123). Godden highlights the novel's extensive punning on the word "mine," arguing that this reflects "a particular historical debate about [. . .] the right to define the word 'property'" (123). See his essay, "Pioneer Properties, or 'What's in a Hut?'" in *James Fenimore Cooper: New Critical Essays*.

44. The standoff at the hut has frequently been read as a key instance of the tension between Romantic individualism and the strictures of the law. (See, for example, chapter 1 of Brook Thomas's *Cross-Examinations of Law and Literature*, or, more recently, Jeffrey Insko's "The Logic of Left Alone.") My reading runs parallel to this argument but attends more closely to the spatial implications of the confrontation.

45. Of course, it is Natty himself who destroys the hut in order to prevent the Sheriff and his minions from violating its sanctity. On one level, then, the destruction figures as a final act of defiance against capitalist enclosure. But the gesture is ultimately futile; Natty's actions do nothing to prevent the ascent of exclusive property rights. If the hut represents the ambiguous overlap of communal and private property, its final destruction—at Natty's hand or not—signals the triumph of enclosed space.

46. The intermediate status of the hut—located somewhere between the proximate space of the individual body and the extended space of the middle-class home—will figure prominently in the transition between Chapters 1 and 2. As anxieties about the mobility of property increase, not only will huts mark an expanding sense of spatial crisis, but also they will reflect a desire to control that crisis, to lock down and control the circulations of property. In short, the hut will index a desire for increasingly *private* property.

1 / Walking the Property: Ownership, Space, and the Body in Motion in *Edgar Huntly*

1. Qtd. in the "Appendixes" section of the 1984 Kent State edition of *Edgar Huntly*, edited by Sydney J. Krause and S. W. Reid, pp. 492–93.

2. In the preface to the actual novel, Brown opts for a much more general evocation of the frontier. He promises a narrative springing from "the conditions of our country" and refers only to the "western wilderness." This more inclusive language clearly serves his stated purpose of crafting a national, rather than merely regional, literature, but it also obscures the more specific geographic and historical origins of the book.

3. On the Walking Purchase, see Steven Harper's *Promised Land*. See also Francis Jenning's *The Ambiguous Iroquois Empire*, chapter 17.

4. Most prominently, see Sydney Krause's "Historical Essay," in his edition of *Edgar Huntly*, as well as his essay "Penn's Elm" in *American Literature*. See also John Carlos Rowe, *Literary Culture and U.S. Imperialism*, chapter 2; Peter Kafer, *Charles Brockden Brown's Revolution and the Birth of American Gothic*, chapter 6; and Janie Hinds, "Deb's Dogs" in *Early American Literature*.

5. What is more, Brown suggests that the single most influential subject upon which such writers can focus is property: "The relations by which men, unendowed with political authority, stand to each other, are numerous. An extensive source of these relations, is property. No topic can engage the attention of man more momentous than this. Opinions, relative to property, are the immediate source of nearly all the happiness and misery that exist among mankind" (152).

6. In "Walstein's School of History," Brown describes a literary project very much in line with that of his idol, William Godwin. Godwin, of course, imagined his own Gothic novel *Caleb Williams* (1794) as a "valuable lesson" on "things passing in the moral world" ("Preface," *Caleb Williams*). He also saw his novel as a way to translate the "refined and abstract speculation" of his earlier philosophical treatise, *An Enquiry Concerning Political Justice* (1793), into a language that could be understood

by "persons whom books of philosophy and science are never likely to reach" ("Preface"). Pamela Clemit offers a well-researched account of Brown's relationship to Godwin's writings in chapter 4 of *The Godwinian Novel: The Rational Fictions of Godwin, Brockden Brown, Mary Shelley*. On the relationship between *Political Justice* and *Caleb Williams*, see Maurice Hindle's introduction to the Penguin edition.

7. The question of whether Brown was a "conservative" or a "radical," and whether these allegiances shifted over the course of his life, animates a good deal of Brown scholarship. See, for example, Clemit; Rowe; Tompkins; Steven Watts, *The Romance of Real Life*; and Michael Cody, *Charles Brockden Brown and the* Literary Magazine.

8. W. M. Verhoeven, "'This Blissful Period of Intellectual Liberty,'" in *Revising Charles Brockden Brown*.

9. Larzer Ziff, in "A Reading of *Wieland*," argues that Brown's work undercuts the "optimistic [Lockean] psychology of his day" (51). Several later critics, including Donald Ringe, James Russo, and Beverly Voloshin, consider Brown's relationship to sense psychology. Voloshin specifically attends to the Lockean subtext in *Edgar Huntly*.

10. In *Love and Death in the American Novel*, Leslie Fiedler reads *Huntly*'s frontier as a "symbolic landscape," a feverish projection of the "irrational reality of the id" (142–48). Other critics who read *Huntly*'s frontier as primarily a mental geography include Richard Slotkin, *Regeneration Through Violence: The Mythology of the American Frontier, 1600–1860*; Ringe, *Charles Brockden Brown*; Norman Grabo, *The Coincidental Art of Charles Brockden Brown*; Alan Axelrod, *Charles Brockden Brown: An American Tale*; and George Toles, "Charting the Hidden Landscape: Edgar Huntly." Several critics read Brown's frontier as an aesthetic response to European landscape conventions. See Robert Lawson-Peebles's *Landscape and Written Expression in Revolutionary America*, as well as the work of Dennis Berthold, "Charles Brockden Brown, *Edgar Huntly*, and the Origins of the American Picturesque," and Beth Lueck, "Charles Brockden Brown's *Edgar Huntly*: The Picturesque Traveler as Sleepwalker."

11. In a larger sense, the chapter's efforts to more accurately place Brown in the context of Enlightenment philosophy also add to what Bryan Waterman describes as the recent "post-new historicism" in Brown studies. This includes work that situates Brown in relation to eighteenth-century science, feminism, rural class conflicts, and legal discourse, to name only a few examples. Brown's sophisticated relationship to sensational psychology and to property theory comprises another key aspect of this rich cultural matrix. See Waterman's helpful survey of Brown criticism in "Charles Brockden Brown, Revised and Expanded," in *Early American Literature*.

12. On the subject of the vexed relationship between Locke's *Two Treatises of Government* and *An Essay Concerning Human Understanding*, see Peter Laslett's excellent introduction to the Cambridge edition of *Two Treatises*.

13. Biographies of Brown that discuss his participation in the Friendly Club are those by Watts and Warfel. For the definitive cultural history of the Friendly Club itself—including Brown's participation—see Bryan Waterman's *Republic of Intellect*. See also Frederika J. Teute's helpful article, "A 'Republic of Intellect,'" in *Revising Charles Brockden Brown*.

14. Verhoeven, for instance, notes the influence of the French philosophes on Brown, and specifically identifies, among others, "Montesquieu, Helvétius, Holbach, Diderot, D'Alembert, Buffon, Fénelon, Voltaire, La Rochefoucauld, and Condorcet" (18).

15. Ziff and Ringe both consider "Lockean" psychology in *Wieland*. Voloshin addresses the same issue in "Wieland: 'Accounting for Appearances,'" and then again

in "Edgar Huntly and the Coherence of the Self." Russo looks at *Wieland* in "Chimeras of the Brain," and *Ormond* in "The Chameleon of Convenient Vice." For a book-length study of all of Brown's novels in relation to sensational psychology, see Arthur Kimball's *Rational Fictions* (1968).

16. Brown's invocation of the picturesque, of sublime prospects, and of visual pleasure, all make it clear that he was familiar with the conventions of European landscape description. The discourse of the "Beautiful" and the "Sublime" was first introduced by Edmund Burke in 1756 and then popularized by William Gilpin in his late eighteenth-century work, *Picturesque Tours*. On Brown's engagement with landscape discourse, see Lueck; Berthold; and Robert Lawson-Peebles, *Landscape and Written Expression in Revolutionary America*.

17. Denis Cosgrove, in his seminal study of the "landscape idea" from the fifteenth to the twentieth centuries, distinguishes "insider" and "outsider" experiences of the landscape. He argues that when viewing the environment from a landscape perspective, "The experience of the insider, the landscape as subject, and the collective life within it are all implicitly denied. Subjectivity is rendered the property of the artist and the viewer—those who control the landscape—not those who belong to it" (26). Conventional representations of the landscape (painted, written, or otherwise) effectively translate the complex, subjective, and multisensory experience of the insider into an abstracted and entirely visual format, tailor-made for appropriation by the outside viewer.

18. Voloshin points out that Lockean sense-psychology is closely aligned with Enlightenment visualism. She notes that "Locke's major descriptions of perception are visual, including the famous images of the dark chamber of the mind" and that "sight is still the guiding metaphor" as he presents his theory of memory ("Coherence" 277n5). Voloshin's larger claim that *Edgar Huntly* "reverses the privileging of light and sight in empiricist epistemology" (265) dovetails nicely with the argument I am making here.

19. For a helpful discussion of Berkeley's theory in relation to Locke and Hume (in the context of eighteenth-century English visual art), see Amal Asfour's "Splendid Impositions: Gainsborough, Berkeley, Hume."

20. Initially, it may be difficult to distinguish Condillac's concept of "attention" from Locke's notion of "reflection." Both seem to posit what Roger Smith calls "a reasoning faculty of the mind, an intrinsic capacity to arrange ideas" (235). But as Smith points out, Condillac's approach dramatically shifts the relationship between embodied sensation and mental perception: "When [Condillac] referred to this ability to connect ideas [through attention], he denoted an elemental force, a desire, that expresses a need of both body and mind, and not an intrinsic capacity of mind" (235). In short, Condillac has established a greater role for the sensate body in producing knowledge than it ever had in Locke's system.

21. "When I speak of pure or empty Space, it is not to be supposed, that the Word Space stands for an Idea distinct from, or conceivable without Body and Motion" (*A Treatise Concerning the Principles of Human Knowledge*, section 116). See also sections 111 and 112.

22. This conception of space accords well with contemporary phenomenological theories of space. Merleau-Ponty's work in *The Phenomenology of Perception* is central, of course, but see also Edward Casey's *The Fate of Place*; Robert Sack's *Homo Geographicus*; Yi-Fu Tuan's *Space and Place*; and Michel de Certeau's *The Practice of Everyday Life*.

23. Very few critics of Brown have specifically considered his treatment of space. For two notable exceptions, see chapter 6 of Julie Ellison's *Cato's Tears and the Making of Anglo-American Emotion*, as well as Lisa West Norwood's article, "'I May Be a Stranger to the Grounds of Your Belief.'"

24. For a more explicitly phenomenological account of spatial production (and one on which it seems to me Lefebvre draws), see Merleau-Ponty, *The Phenomenology of Perception*. In particular, see chapter 3, "The Spatiality of One's Own Body and Motility."

25. It is also worth noting here that once again, Brown is echoing Condillac's *Treatise*. In the chapter on discovering space, Condillac writes that the statue is "curious to discover what lies above and it finds itself, as by chance, on its feet. It totters, it walks, leaning against everything that can help it stay up" (240–41).

26. Chapter 4 of John W. Yolton's *Thinking Matter: Materialism in Eighteenth-Century Britain* does an excellent job of summarizing the relevant philosophical positions regarding space during this time.

27. Yolton helpfully explicates this debate. See pp. 67–70.

28. Although not as tactually oriented as Condillac, Hume is much more consistently attentive to the importance of touch than Locke. All of his major arguments regarding space are careful to include both a visual and a tactile example.

29. Frasca-Spada, in *Space and the Self in Hume's Treatise*, maintains that much of Hume's writing on space is "answering Locke directly" (191).

30. In fact, Brown published the review essay, "Parallels between Hume, Robertson, and Gibbon," in the May 1799 issue of the *Monthly Magazine*. This means that in all likelihood he was reading and writing on Hume while he was composing *Edgar Huntly*.

31. See chapter 9 of Certeau's *Practice of Everyday Life*.

32. Brown's earlier reference to the "Blue-mountains" in his preface makes it clear that Edgar's adventures are taking place on the northern side of these same mountains. He has sleepwalked through the cave and under the mountains only to reemerge on the north slope. This is significant because the ridgeline of the Blue mountains had long been recognized, by both Indians and whites, as a boundary separating white and Indian territory. Ogashtash, a Seneca chief, noted of the Blue mountains that "our Boundaries are so well known, and so remarkably distinguish'd by a range of high Mountains." See David L. Preston, "Squatters, Indians, Proprietary Government and Land in the Susquehanna Valley," in Pencak's *Friends and Enemies in Penn's Woods*.

33. See, for example, Slotkin; Krause; Rowe; and especially, Jared Gardner, "Alien Nation: Edgar Huntly's Savage Awakening."

34. Again, see Gardner's "Alien Nation." On the cultural conflation of native Americans and the Irish, more generally, see Joanna Brooks, "Held Captive by the Irish: Quaker Captivity Narratives in Frontier Pennsylvania."

35. Stephen Shapiro, "'Man to Man I Needed Not to Dread His Encounter': *Edgar Huntly*'s End of Erotic Pessimism," pp. 216, 218.

36. Elizabeth Dillon, *The Gender of Freedom: Fictions of Liberalism and the Literary Public Sphere*.

37. See Barry Nicolas, *An Introduction to Roman Law*, pp. 112–13, 130–31.

38. Qtd in Wolfram Schmidgen's *Eighteenth-century Fiction and the Law of Property*, p. 43.

39. On Brown's legal career, see Warfel's *Brown*, chapter 4; Watts, pp. 32–33; and Kafer, pp. 48–51.

40. Carroll Smith-Rosenberg and Julie Ellison both investigate the role of property in relation to the construction of early American gender identities: Smith-Rosenberg sees the appropriation of property as a key component to the construction of a female middle-class subject; Ellison argues that Edgar's desire for sympathetic homosocial relationships obscures any clear understanding of the crucial property issues in the novel. Most recently, Elizabeth Jane Wall Hinds reads Edgar as a character caught between two opposed conceptions of property, the old-style, classical republican ideal of landed, "real" property, and the emergent capitalist conception of movable property and credit. Ultimately, Hinds concludes, "In a culture still habituated to an economy based in visible, 'real' property more appropriately inherited than 'made,' Edgar casts his lot with a visible but disappearing 'myth of civilization'" (134). See Ellison; Hinds, *Private Property*; and Smith-Rosenberg's "Subject Female: Authorizing American Identity."

41. See Krause's "Penn's Elm and *Edgar Huntly*." See also chapter 2 of John Carlos Rowe's *Literary Culture and U.S. Imperialism*. Working within the same context of Indian-white relations, Rowe maintains that *Edgar Huntly* in fact never manages an effective critique of colonial practices. Instead, "Brown's fictitious history in *Edgar Huntly* compounds and elaborates, rather than exposes, the colonists' treachery toward the Lenni-Lenape" (42).

42. See Peter Laslett's lucid introduction to the Cambridge edition of Locke's *Two Treatises* for an excellent overview of Locke's relationship to natural law and of his genealogy of the state. See also James Tully's *A Discourse on Property* for an incisive analysis of the natural law underpinnings to Locke's theory of property.

43. See chapter 7 of Arneil's *John Locke and America*.

44. See footnote 72 on page 324 of Hume's *Treatise*.

45. There is a persistent phenomenological subtext haunting even the most sociodiscursive models of property. As early as 1712, German philosopher Samuel von Pufendorf defined private property as a species of mutual obligations among men. His model in fact directly prefigures Hume's social "conventions." But in describing how people can initially take possession of empty land through "first occupancy," Pufendorf repeatedly has recourse to the language of tactile contact: "We are then said to have *occupied* any thing, when we actually take possession of it; and this commenceth at our joining body to body, either immediately, or by a proper Instrument. The regular Cause therefore is, that the Occupancy of Movables be made with the Hands; the Occupancy of Soil with the Feet [. . .] but the bare seeing a thing, or the knowing where it is, is not judg'd a sufficient Title of Possession" (*De Jure Naturae et Gentium*, Book IV, 175). Likewise, Hume himself invokes the sense of touch when he attempts to explain possession: "We are said to be in possession of any thing, not only when we immediately touch it, but also when we are so situated with respect to it, as to have it in our power to use it; and may move, alter, or destroy it, according to our present pleasure or advantage" (324). A few lines later, Hume strengthens this assertion by undercutting the significance of the "power to use": "Here then it appears, that a certain and infallible power of enjoyment, without touch or some other sensible relation, often produces not property" (325). Hegel continues the emphasis on touch in *The Philosophy of Right* (1821): "From the point of view of sensation, to grasp a thing physically is the most complete of these modes." Though there are various other ways

in which our claims may be expanded to a greater scope, initially, "I take into possession no more than what I touch with my body" (84–85).

46. Even the lesser characters of Weymouth and Sarsefield are distinguished by their seemingly perpetual state of motion. Weymouth tells Edgar that he has traveled all over the world, "changing his abode to England, France and Germany, according as [his] interest required" (765). Sarsefield, for his part, enacts a similar narrative of global circulation, first as an employee of the East India Company and then as an itinerant wandering by foot all over India and the Middle East.

47. Perhaps the more appropriate image is that of the surveyor's staff. Both before and after the Proclamation Line of 1763, frontier settlers frequently purchased land directly from small groups of Indians, whether the Indians had the authority to grant that land. The settlers would then quickly hire surveyors to mark out the tract. Stuart Banner describes one incident in which the Conajoharie Indians of New York accidentally discovered a surveyor's staff stuck in the ground; it had been left behind after the surveyor had completed his work at night. This was the only way the Indians found out that their land was being sold. See *How the Indians Lost Their Land*, p. 90.

48. See Tully's *Discourse on Property*, p. 114.

49. Significantly, Hume repeatedly has recourse to the language of movement when describing the natural passions. He refers to "their partial and contradictory motions" and to "their heedless and impetuous movement" (314). The passions "impel" men in "contradictory directions" (315).

50. Again, Krause does an effective job of outlining this history of conflict. He also helpfully analyzes Brown's sometimes confusing geography, making it clear that the novel takes place in the middle of Walking Purchase territory. See his "Historical Essay."

51. For the most recent, and accurate, map of the Walking Purchase, see Harper, *Promised Land*, p. 70.

52. The account of Edward Marshall I provide here is taken from Davis's *History of Buck County*, chapter 30, and from Steven Harper's "After the Walking Purchase," in *Friends and Enemies in Penn's Woods*.

53. On Hannah Freeman, see John F. Watson's *Annals of Philadelphia and Pennsylvania*. See also, Marshall J. Becker, "Hannah Freeman: An Eighteenth-Century Lenape Living and Working Among Colonial Farmers."

54. On Indian property practices, see Banner, *How the Indians Lost Their Land*, pp. 56–62. On Delaware practices in particular, see Anthony F. C. Wallace, "Woman, Land, and Society: Three Aspects of Aboriginal Delaware Life."

55. It was also being marked, of course, by the rise of the myth of the "vanishing Indian" during the eighteenth and nineteenth centuries, yet another cultural index of Native American erasure.

56. Quoted in Harper's *Promised Land*, p. 67.

57. The rhetoric of erasure is echoed in a Philadelphia conference five years after the Walk. The Delaware had not yet vacated the lands of the Purchase to the satisfaction of the Pennsylvania government. The government called upon the powerful Iroquois nation to apply pressure, so the Onondaga representative Canasatego stood up and lambasted the Delaware in a long harangue. After deriding them as "Women" and "Children," he commanded them to leave the Forks of the Delaware: "We charge You to remove instantly. We don't give you the liberty to think about it. You are Women; take the Advice of a Wise Man and remove immediately. [. . .] We, therefore, Assign

you two Places to go—either to Wyoming [on the Susquehanna North Branch] or Shamokin" (qtd. in Jennings 345).

58. By the middle of the eighteenth century, it was common practice to walk property boundaries (that is, survey them) with representatives from both of the contracting parties, whether Indian or white. This ensured a clear agreement as to the metes and bounds of the property lines. On the joint survey of Indian land purchases, see Banner, *How the Indians Lost Their Land*, pp. 25, 64.

59. Davis, *History of Buck County*, chapter 30.

2 / Eating Dwelling Gagging: Hawthorne, Stoddard, and the Phenomenology of Possession

1. Dwelling and domestic space have long been issues of interest in modern phenomenology. Gaston Bachelard, in *The Poetics of Space*, meditates on the affective and embodied associations that crowd our experience of home. For him, the house provides a "topography of our intimate being" (xxxxvi) and as such it is "a privileged entity for a phenomenological study of the intimate values of inside space" (3). Martin Heidegger makes a similar, albeit more metaphysical argument in his essay "Building Dwelling Thinking." In answer to the question "What is it to dwell?", Heidegger maintains that dwelling "is always a staying with things;" it is a "sparing," "preserving," and "safeguarding" of the four "elements" (earth, sky, divinity, and mortals themselves) so that they are each allowed to unfold in their own essence (353, 351). With his famous example of a farmhouse in the Black Forest, Heidegger goes so far as to describe dwelling as "*the basic character* of Being, in keeping with which mortals exist" (362). For both of these thinkers, then, Heidegger and Bachelard, domestic space functions as an experiential foundation upon which the structures of psychological identity and ontological awareness are built.

2. On the ideology of domesticity, see Nancy F. Cott's influential work, *The Bonds of Womanhood*. See also Barbara Welter's "The Cult of True Womanhood." For a more recent "Foucauldian" assessment of domestic ideology, see the first chapter of Lora Romero's *Home Fronts*.

3. First in equity courts and then in a series of Married Women's Property Acts, antebellum law gradually evolved so that women could own property independently of their husbands. For a comprehensive account of this history and its relationship to separate spheres discourse, see Norma Basch's *In the Eyes of the Law*. For a more concise summary, see chapter 6 of Gregory S. Alexander's *Commodity and Propriety*.

4. We might think, for example, of the countless domestic novels that orbit around inheritance plots, or more progressive explorations of women's property rights like Fanny Fern's *Ruth Hall* (1855).

5. There is no doubt that both Hawthorne and Stoddard were intimately familiar with diet reform discourse. In 1843, Hawthorne's friend Bronson Alcott attempted to start a Graham-inspired, transcendentalist vegan community in Harvard, Massachusetts. Then, in 1857, Hawthorne's sister-in-law, Mary Tyler Peabody Mann (wife of Horace Mann), published *Christianity in the Kitchen, a Physiological Cook Book*. In it, she employs much of the same rhetoric as Graham and Nichols, equating good digestion with virtue and dyspepsia with sin. Hawthorne himself, in his unfinished novel, *Septimius Felton*, explores the fanciful possibility that a "moral dietetics" might be the key to eternal life. Stoddard's novel betrays a similar familiarity: the family cook

is named "Temperance"; Veronica Morgeson implements an extreme version of the Grahamite diet by living "entirely on toast" and an occasional glass of milk (51); and several members of the Somers family are involved in "experiments with temperature and diet" (97).

6. For the clearest account of diet reform as a defensive response to market capitalism, see Stephen Nissenbaum's *Sex, Diet, and Debility in Jacksonian America*. Nissenbaum also describes several alternative explanations of nineteenth-century health reform (including not just dietary practices but the temperance movement, antimasturbation advocacy, exercise programs, and populist physiology). These include the possibility that it was meant to instill discipline in an unruly lower-class workforce, and that it was a "tool of social aspiration" employed by people seeking "bourgeois respectability" (xiii). For their part, feminist historians have persuasively demonstrated the ways in which the sexual ideology associated with health reform sought to minimize or discount female sexuality and to effectively "disembody" women. See Smith-Rosenberg, and Cott's "Passionlessness."

7. Nissenbaum thinks that while Graham's efforts were initially designed to resist the encroachments of the market economy, they also "indirectly hastened" the rise of a middle-class, bourgeois culture (137). Joan Burbick takes a different view in *Healing the Republic* where she argues that Graham's elaborate physiology of the digestive system "implicitly attacks the traditional caretakers of the body, that is, women" (85). In Burbick's view, then, diet reform maintained the divisions of the separate spheres at the same time that it further devalued women's status.

8. In addition to Davidson's preface, see in the same issue Kaplan's "Manifest Domesticity," and Lawrence Buell's "Circling the Spheres." Lora Romero's *Home Fronts* provides an excellent example of the particularized, micropolitical approach that Davidson champions and that I aim for here.

9. See, in particular, chapter 3 of Brown's *Domestic Individualism*. On the "spiritualizing" tendencies of domesticity, see also Nancy Armstrong's *Desire and Domestic Fiction*.

10. In an 1844 letter included in *The American Notebooks*, Hawthorne again describes his culinary aesthetic: "People who write about themselves and their feelings, as Byron did, may be said to serve up their own hearts, duly spiced, and with brain-sauce out of their own heads, as a repast for the public" (107). The same imagery surfaces two years later in the preface to *The Old Manse*, although this time Hawthorne makes it clear that he is no Byron: "nor am I, nor have ever been, one of those supremely hospitable people, who serve up their own hearts, delicately fried, with brain-sauce, as a tidbit for their beloved public" (*Nathaniel Hawthorne's Tales* 287).

11. The significance of the so-called spoilage proviso is a hotly contested point among political theorists. Initially, it seems to imply a limit to capitalist accumulation. But Locke later seems to hold that the introduction of durable goods and money effectively renders the spoilage proviso moot, that is, accumulation is fine so long as the goods accumulated don't spoil. On this topic see C. B. Macpherson's *Political Theory of Possessive Individualism*, pp. 197–221, and Alan Ryan's *Property and Political Theory*, pp. 36–39.

12. Nor is Locke the only precedent for linking eating and property. As my epigraph makes clear, Marx was thinking about the "beginnings" of property along these same lines in the middle of the nineteenth century. Marx and Locke were both preceded by ancient Roman law which utilized the category of *fructus naturales* (natural fruits) to

describe the original acquisition of property. According to this doctrine, a tenant has a right to the fruit produced on land that is legally owned by his landlord. Depending on the textual authority, the tenant becomes owner of this fruit either when he gathers it (*perceptio*), or when it is "separated from the parent thing" (*separatio*). Such separation was frequently understood to mean consumption. See Nicholas, *An Introduction to Roman Law*, pp. 138–40.

13. In a compelling article on "Romantic Dietetics," Paul Youngquist notes that late eighteenth-century English physicians were fixated on the digestive component of Lockean theory, effectively "locating the physiological foundation for political liberalism in the labor of the guts" (242). Youngquist maintains that in Locke's account a person comes to possess his own body through the digestive labor of eating. "The agency of eating transforms common matter into personal property, giving all men a property in their own person. The possessive individual of Locke's liberalism eats his way to ownership" (241). Youngquist's account dovetails nicely with the argument I'm making here.

14. Walter Benn Michaels has persuasively argued that Hawthorne's preface and the book as a whole are an attempt to establish a form of property distinct from both Lockean labor and aristocratic tradition. Hawthorne, he believes, is motivated by "the appeal of a title based on neither labor nor wealth and hence free from the risk of appropriation" (189). While I agree that Hawthorne is interested in exploring alternative forms of property, I do not think he simply rejects Lockean labor theory outright. Instead, he adapts Locke to his own ends, specifically in terms of consumption and nourishment. See Michaels's "Romance and Real Estate."

15. Gillian Brown sees the scene as emblematic of Hawthorne's "revulsion" for commerce and of his fear about the "subjugation" of the body to market forces (83). David Anthony refines this argument by considering the racial implications of the fact that Little Ned eats gingerbread representations of Jim Crow. See Anthony's "Class, Culture, and the Trouble with White Skin in Hawthorne's *The House of the Seven Gables*."

16. Brown qualifies her earlier statements about Hawthorne's fear of commerce and the bodily "subjugation" it represents by acknowledging that within the text commerce "is also imaged as a revivifying and productive force" (90). But she maintains that ultimately this approach erases the "labor of accommodating and incorporating change, the process of domestication" (93). I'm arguing that the text in fact focuses on the labor of incorporation.

17. For an enlightening discussion of cannibalism, self-cannibalism, and incorporation in general, see Maggie Kilgour's *From Communion to Cannibalism*, particularly chapter 4. On possessive individualism, see C. B. Macpherson's *The Political Theory of Possessive Individualism: Hobbes to Locke*.

18. Certainly, it is worth noting that Stoddard names not one but two characters, Locke Morgeson: Cassandra's father and great-grandfather share the name.

19. It should be noted that Veronica does not entirely fit the passive, "angel in the house" stereotype. Although she is endowed with the thoroughly conventional characteristics of "spiritual" and "moral" energy, she also manages to invest at least some of that energy into producing works of music and art. She is described at several points in the text as a musical "genius" (59, 242).

20. Flagroot is another name for sweet flag, or calamus, an aromatic root common to New England wetlands. Significantly, perhaps, the phallic calamus plant has long

been associated with masculine virility and love. Certainly, Whitman capitalized on these erotic significations in his *Calamus* poems. It is interesting to note, therefore, that Aunt Merce's favorite chew toy is a symbol of love, particularly a man's love. The implication would seem to be that her own erotic appetites have gone unsatisfied, another sly indication from Stoddard, perhaps, of the ways in which the separate spheres left little room for women's desires.

21. The trope of the body-house has a long pedigree in art and literature. It was a commonplace in medieval writing and in Renaissance texts like Andreas Vesalius's influential account of human anatomy, *De Humani Corporis Fabrica* (1543). In colonial America, the equation of houses and bodies was commonplace, particularly in New England Puritan culture. On this topic, see chapter 2 of Robert Blair St. George's *Conversing by Signs*.

22. For further examples of the "body as house" metaphor as it was used by health and diet reformers, see Chilion B. Allen's *The Man Wonderful in the House Beautiful* (1891), and Catharine Beecher's *Treatise on Domestic Economy*. Beecher deftly conflates the spatial organization of the home with the bodily health of its inhabitants: an efficiently constructed house results in healthy bodies, and vice versa. See her chapter entitled, "On the Construction of Houses."

23. Nor is Hawthorne shy about using the opposite "body as house" analogy favored by diet reformers. For example, when Clifford returns from his thirty-year imprisonment, blasted and vacant, his world-weary frame is imaged as a "dark and ruinous mansion" in which he struggles to "kindle the heart's household fire" (92).

24. Sigmund Freud, "Negation," in *General Psychoanalytical Theory*, ed. Philip Rieff (New York: Macmillan, 1963), pp. 214-15, qtd. in Kilgour, p. 4.

25. Anthropologists have long emphasized the importance of eating in both the symbolic and literal construction of the home. Janet Carsten and Stephen Hugh-Jones, for example, in their recent reexamination of Lévi-Strauss's seminal work on "house societies," assert that "given its living qualities and close association with the body, it comes as no surprise that natural processes normally associated with people, animals or plants may also apply to the house. Houses may be said to be born, to grow, to mature and die, to move and walk, to feed and be fed, and they may even be said to marry and copulate. Because shared consumption often provides the basic ideas about cohabitation and kinship—it is in this sense that both houses and their occupants are fed—the hearth itself may be the central image and focal point of the house" (42-43).

26. From "Language," in *Poetry, Language, Thought* (1971); qtd. in Richard Lang, "The Dwelling Door," p. 206.

27. Maggie Kilgour remarks on the same: "The need for food exposes the vulnerability of individual identity, enacted at a wider social level in the need for exchanges, communion, and commerce with others, through which the individual is absorbed into a larger corporate body. [. . .] The most basic model for all forms of incorporation is the physical act of eating, and food is the most important symbol for other external substances that are absorbed" (6).

28. Of course, as Witold Rybczynski makes clear in *Home: A Short History of an Idea*, the advent of private rooms in domestic architecture closely parallels the emergence of the bourgeois modern subject. In the eighteenth and nineteenth centuries, he points out, "The desire for a room of one's own [. . .] demonstrated the growing awareness of individuality of a growing personal inner life—and the need to express this individuality in physical ways" (110-11).

29. Levinas himself understands domestic space to spring from precisely this sort of paradoxical openness and exchange. For him, dwelling is ultimately defined not by its interiority, but by its encounter with the outside, with the other. "Recollection in a home open to the Other—hospitality—is the concrete and initial fact of human recollection and separation [...]. The chosen home is the very opposite of a root" (172). In contrast to the pronounced interiority and rootedness characteristic of Heidegger's peasant hut or Gaston Bachelard's dream-house, Levinas conceives of the home as the "opposite of a root." It is created and fostered by a continual exchange with the elements and individuals that exist outside of it. More specifically, this relationship of "welcome" or "hospitality" is characterized by gift giving, by the offering up of one's possessions to the external other. We will return to this crucial issue when we consider the nature of property exchange below.

30. Again, see Heidegger's "Building Dwelling Thinking."

31. Levinas's model echoes the Lockean explanation of the evolution of money. Locke maintains that the primordial process of appropriating food naturally led to the exchange of more durable foodstuffs like nuts for perishable goods like plums. This, in turn, led to the exchange of more symbolic, and more durable, objects like metal and paper; see *Two Treatises*, pp. 300–301.

32. In elaborating Locke's theory of ownership, James Tully helpfully points out that the Greek term for "one's own" is *oikeia* (οικεια) which literally means "belonging to the household or family." "Similarly, the term for appropriation or making something one's own is οικειόω, which means 'to make a part of the family'" (134–35).

33. The distinction Levinas describes here between possession and property follows the evolution of money that Locke proposes. Locke details a gradual historical progression from the gathering of perishable foods, to the trading of longer-lasting foods, like nuts. These, in turn, are eventually traded for "a piece of Metal," or "Shells," or "a sparkling Pebble or Diamond." "Thus," he tells us, *"came in the use of Money"* (300).

34. On Hawthorne and market capitalism, for example, see Brown, *Domestic Individualism*; Michaels, *The Gold Standard and the Logic of Naturalism*; and Anthony, *Paper Money Men*. On Stoddard and ownership, see Weinauer, "Alternative Economies: Authorship and Ownership in Elizabeth Stoddard's 'Collected by a Valetudinarian.'"

35. While such accusations seem to be fairly accurate, commercial bakers did not take kindly to Graham's critique. He was attacked by a mob of angry bakers in Boston in the winter of 1837. So it goes with those who speak truth to power. See Nissenbaum, p. 14.

36. Graham is clearly nostalgic for a romanticized version of domestic life, but his emotion also poignantly marks the historical transition from an eighteenth-century economy in which the household was still the center of economic production, to the market economy of industrializing capitalism. On the transition, see Nissenbaum, pp. 5–8.

37. Gillian Brown, for example, highlights this conventional opposition in terms of the formation of the individual subject: "The domestic sphere provided an always identifiable place and refuge for the individual: it signified the private domain of individuality apart from the marketplace. [...] The 19th-century self-definitions this book explores locate the individual in his or her interiority, in his or her removal from the marketplace" (3).

38. Julia Stern interprets this scene as Alice's effort to "sadistically [rework] the relations of desire, agency, and sensual satisfaction from which she was excluded

during the (unconsummated) love affair between her husband and this younger distant cousin" (119). The "fetal" chicken stands in for Cassy's "blasted hopes."

39. Stern offers a persuasive reading of the dinner scene as "an unconsummated black mass of sorts," in which Mrs. Somers reveals a perverse, even cannibalistic, desire to consume her own child (120). Whether we push our interpretation this far, Mrs. Somers destructive maternal tendencies seem clear.

40. Samuel Otter also explores the subversive, potentially emancipatory energy of alimentary economies in his perceptive reading of the dining scenes in Frank J. Webb's *The Garies and Their Friends*. Otter argues that food in that novel functions as "a medium of struggle," a complex mélange of "freedom, consumption, and constraint" that balances the potential for African American advancement with the burdens of America's violent history of exploitation. In this way, Webb's alimentary economies represent a perhaps more cautious account of eating's liberatory possibilities than do Stoddard's.

41. Cassandra's own mother remains somewhat distant from her daughters. When Veronica is afflicted with one of her lingering illnesses, for example, her mother watches over her but "rarely caress[es]" her (13). Cassy notes that her mother simply "stopped" at a certain point with her children; she maintains an emotional remove "because her spiritual insight was confused and perplexing" (24). Stoddard even hints that this inscrutable distance constitutes a failure to provide emotional and physical sustenance. When Cassy discovers her mother's dead body in the parlor, she is slumped in a chair with "an empty cup [. . .] in her lap, bottom up" (206).

42. A less generous interpretation might argue that Stoddard's account of selfless servants loving their employer's children is an exercise in bourgeois blindness, a bit of wishful thinking on the author's part that misreads economic exigency as emotional commitment. While such is possible, it does not change the fact that Stoddard's novel—wishful or not—holds out the possibility of a gift economy as a viable alternative to market exchange.

43. Lewis Hyde makes much the same argument for the socially cohesive power of gift exchange, a power, moreover, that he explicitly contrasts with commodity capitalism. See the introduction to his book, *The Gift: Imagination and the Erotic Life of Property*. See also Marcel Mauss's *The Gift: The Form and Reason for Exchange in Archaic Societies*.

3 / Anxieties of Ownership: Debt, Entitlement, and the Plantation Romance

1. Letter from Fitzhugh to George Frederick Holmes, March 27, 1855. The letter is quoted on page 130 of Eugene D. Genovese's *The World the Slaveholders Made*. The fullest account of Fitzhugh's biography is C. Vann Woodward's introductory essay, "George Fitzhugh, *Sui Generis*," in the 1960 edition of *Cannibals All!* On the cultural and ideological significance of Fitzhugh's work, see part 2 of Genovese's book.

2. Genovese calls Fitzhugh "the most consistent exponent of the slaveholders' world view," a "ruthless and critical theorist who spelled out the logical outcome of the slaveholders' philosophy and laid bare its essence" (*The World the Slaveholders Made* 130, 128).

3. Fitzhugh is not alone in this effort. Proslavery advocates of all sorts—writers, intellectuals, jurists, politicians—insisted on a similarly sentimentalized version of

the master-slave dynamic. For an insightful account of the role of sentiment in Southern slave law, see Mark Tushnet's *The American Law of Slavery, 1810–1860*. On slavery and paternalism, see Genovese's *Roll, Jordan, Roll*, particularly pp. 3–7. See also Howard McGary's "Paternalism and Slavery," in *Subjugation and Bondage*.

4. Indeed, southerners had been reading Romantic denunciations of the market by the likes of Carlyle and Coleridge long before such critiques were publicly embraced by the Transcendentalists. On the place of Romanticism in Southern culture, see Michael O'Brien's *Rethinking the South*.

5. For a fuller discussion of this cultural shift, see "A Phenomenology of Property" in the Introduction to this book.

6. Of course, the slave's experience of freedom is not to be confused with actual physical emancipation. Legally and practically, the slave may still be in bondage. But Hegel's point is that the slave has come to a clearer sense of himself as a free and independent being than has the dependent master. For helpful explications of Hegel's complicated model, see Dudley Knowles's *Hegel and the Philosophy of Right*, pp. 93–98, and Cynthia Willett's "The Master-Slave Dialectic: Hegel vs. Douglass."

7. Patterson maintains that his model is an improvement on Hegel's because he thinks that it more accurately reflects the variety of asymmetrical power relations that can exist between master and slave. Hosts and parasites present a range of interdependencies, he points out, "from minor dependence or exploitation to major 'Hegelian' dependence on the part of the dominator and grave survival risks for the dominated" (336).

8. More specifically, Patterson thinks that there are many types of social and economic relations in which human beings have a property right in one another. He points to marriage contracts, parent-child relations, and the buying and selling of professional athletes, among other examples. Because property relations between people are so widespread, he thinks it is a mistake to try and define slavery on these terms.

9. Philosopher Dudley Knowles offers a helpful synopsis of Hegel's argument here: "The crucial connection between ownership of property and freedom is revealed as the possibility which the location of will in property affords of the agent being able to identify herself in that portion of the physical world which she has appropriated for use in the satisfaction of her desires. Private property enables us to take an external measure of our desiring selves, and because the measure is external, it affords others, too, the opportunity of identifying the workings of our will in the things that we own. Freedom requires [. . .] that the self be able to detach itself from its desires in order to appraise and order them, in order to determine itself. This detachment is explicit for the first time when the self is recognized (by itself and others) in the publicly accessible medium of private property. Now that I (and others) can see what I am, I can either endorse the pattern of desires thus revealed or alter them. I can use the property or alienate it. Whatever transactions I engage in with respect to my property will attest my freedom" (115–16).

10. Marxist legal historian Mark Tushnet has carefully considered the relationship of "sentiment" and slave law in the antebellum South. Tushnet argues that the "total relation" between master and slave necessarily involved extra-market factors. That is, masters were responsible for providing such things as food, housing, recreation, and religion, which were excluded from conventional market, or "partial," relations. In effect, masters had to attend to the "totality" of the slaves' needs. According to Tushnet, these extra-market factors pushed master-slave relations outside the regulatory

arena of the law. Instead, the policing of the relationship was left to the realm of "sentiment." In this way, his work represents one effort to understand the relative roles of affect and property in the master-slave relationship. Both Patricia Williams and Saidiya Hartman, however, have mounted incisive critiques of Tushnet's work. See Tushnet's *American Law of Slavery*, as well as Williams's *The Alchemy of Race and Rights*, and Hartman's *Scenes of Subjection*.

11. On the property focus of the plantation romance, see John M. Grammer's "Plantation Fiction."

12. For similar critiques, see Joseph Ridgely's *Nineteenth-Century Southern Literature*; Michael Kreyling's *Figures of the Hero in Southern Narrative*; and Wyatt-Brown's "The Evolution of Heroes' Honor in the Southern Literary Tradition."

13. The phrase "new Southern studies" was coined by Houston Baker Jr. and Dana Nelson in their preface to a special issue on the South in *American Literature*. For recent efforts to expand the Southern canon, see the anthology, *Haunted Bodies: Gender and Southern Texts*, as well as Paul Jones's *Unwelcome Voices*.

14. See Derrida's "The Time of the King," in Alan D. Schrift's *The Logic of the Gift*.

15. Fitzhugh is fond enough of the fountain metaphor to return to it in *Cannibals All!* He notes that rich men in the North have no outlet for their paternal benevolence because they have no slaves. So instead, they must give to public charities: "Man is social and philanthropic, and his affections, dammed out in one direction, find vent and gush out in another" (188).

16. Kenneth S. Greenberg details the complex relationship of gift-giving culture and Southern politics in his *Honor and Slavery*. See, in particular, chapter 3, "Gifts, Strangers, Duels, and Humanitarianism." On patronage and the republican political structure in the South, see also Gordon S. Wood's *Radicalism of the American Revolution*, pp. 70–71, 88–89.

17. The common planter practice of ostentatiously bestowing Christmas gifts on slaves represents an obvious example of this self-interested gift giving. Frederick Douglass, for one, recognized the power dynamics concealed behind the façade of benevolence. In his *Narrative*, he observes that "the holidays are part and parcel of the gross fraud, wrong, and inhumanity of slavery. They are professedly a custom established by the benevolence of the slaveholders; but I undertake to say, it is the result of selfishness, and one of the greatest frauds committed upon the downtrodden slave. They do not give the slaves this time because they would not like to have their work during its continuance, but because they know it would be unsafe to deprive them of it" (52).

18. Greenberg, for example, provides a fascinating account of the gift-giving practices utilized by Secretary of State Henry Clay and Senator John Randolph during their pistol duel in 1826. See *Honor and Slavery*, pp. 53–62.

19. This is the altruistic model of one-way generosity described by Stoddard in *The Morgesons* and championed by Cixous as a distinctively *feminine* economy. On the feminine economy of the gift, see the discussion in Chapter 2, above.

20. See Mauss's *The Gift*.

21. Derrida, as I alluded earlier, doubts that a "true gift," a disinterested gift, is even possible, but in attempting to describe it, he helpfully illuminates the distinction between ideal and practice. "For there to be a [true] gift," he writes, "there must be no reciprocity, return, exchange, counter-gift, or debt. If the other *gives me back* or *owes me* or has to give me back what I give him or her, there will not have been a gift, whether this restitution is immediate or whether it is programmed by a complex

calculation of a long-term deferral or difference" (128). In effect, the true gift would have to exist outside any system of exchange at all. Anything less, he believes, is tainted by an expectation of return and "the logic of the debt" (129).

22. In a compelling reading of "debtor masculinity" in George Lippard's *Quaker City*, David Anthony argues that Lippard's fiction reflects a widespread antebellum anxiety about white male masculinity in the face of increasing debt. He suggests that Lippard helped create a new middle-class masculinity based on conventionally sentimental characteristics; this new masculine model would preserve a realm of male achievement outside the dangers of debt and financial ruin. On the transformation of the American economy, see, for starters, Sellers's *The Market Revolution: Jacksonian America, 1815–1846*. For an incisive analysis of the role of debt in early and antebellum America, see Mann's *Republic of Debtors*.

23. Mann uses the examples of the Revolution and the Seven Years' War to demonstrate that Virginia planters were at the mercy of British creditors. See pp. 134–36.

24. Randolph and Jefferson are quoted in Mann, pp. 135–36.

25. See Mann, pp. 125–26.

26. Interestingly, Mann notes that explicit analogies between debt and slavery diminished dramatically in the South after the revolution. He suggests that uncomfortable planters "retreated from the full implications of the argument they had used so freely before the Revolution" (139). My argument, of course, is that their anxieties returned in the guise of the plantation novel.

27. *Woodcraft* was first published in 1852 in semi-monthly serial installments in the *Southern Literary Gazette*. At the end of that year, it appeared as a complete novel with the title, *The Sword and the Distaff: or, "Fair, Fat and Forty," A Story of the South, at the Close of the Revolution*. Two years later, it was published in New York with an entirely new title, *Woodcraft, or, Hawks about the Dovecote*. On the novel's publishing history, see Patricia Okker's "Serial Politics in William Gilmore Simms's *Woodcraft*."

28. He contributed, for example, an essay to *The Pro-Slavery Argument*, an influential defense of slave society published in Charleston in 1852. Likewise, in a letter to John Pendleton Kennedy, Simms asserted, "Negro Slavery is one of the greatest of moral goods & blessings, and [. . .] slavery in all ages has been found the greatest and most admirable agent of Civilization" (*The Letters of William Gilmore Simms*, III, 174).

29. In an early essay on the importance of legal discourse in *Woodcraft*, L. Lynn Hogue calls attention to Simms's knowledge of property law and to the prominence of debt concerns in the novel. See Hogue's "The Presentation of Post Revolutionary Law in *Woodcraft*: Another Perspective on the 'Truth' of Simms's Fiction" in the *Mississippi Quarterly*.

30. Simms uses this unfortunate situation to raise the related issue of the nation's debt, financial and civil, to the veterans of the war who fought for years with little or no compensation. When pressed by M'Kewn, Porgy suggests that perhaps he should be shown a little leniency because of his service. M'Kewn flatly refuses to give him any leeway.

31. Sergeant Millhouse is similarly indebted to Porgy for his life. During the war, Millhouse's right arm was "torn into strips by a brace of bullets"; to stop the bleeding, Porgy cuts off the remains of the arm and thrusts the stump into "hot, seething tar." "But for this proceeding he must have perished" (50). Millhouse then commits himself to Porgy's service for the rest of his life.

32. It is worth noting that as Glen-Eberley's earning potential is restored, via slave labor, and Porgy's wealth again increases, his stomach begins to shrink. When his crops

come in, Porgy tightens "several more inches in his belt and, not infrequently, the sergeant drew his attention, with great concern, to his diminishing dimensions" (401).

33. In antebellum America, Irish immigrants were frequently referred to as "niggers turned inside out," and African Americas were called "smoked Irish." On the ambivalent racial identification of Irish and African Americans, see chapter 2 of Noel Ignatiev's *How the Irish Became White*. See also David Roediger's *The Wages of Whiteness: Race and the Making of the American Working Class*.

34. Saidiya Hartman argues that in behavioral manuals published for freed slaves after the war, emancipation was represented as a debt owed to white people (Northern and Southern) who had sacrificed so much for the slaves' freedom. In this way, she points out, freedom was imaged not as a gift but as a form of indebtedness. But such a claim, she notes, also required that black labor and black suffering be excluded from any calculation of debt. A similarly perverse calculation, I am suggesting, undergirds the antebellum plantation economy. See Hartman's *Scenes of Subjection*.

35. Bostwick plays upon the racially coded power dynamics concealed within his claims to entitlement. He goads M'Kewn by suggesting that being in debt to someone is a condition synonymous with slavery. As the card game wears on, Bostwick's luck changes, and he begins to win hand after hand. His two opponents perceive that M'Kewn wants the game to end, so they declare that they're out of money. Bostwick, however, sees through their ruse and uses the opportunity to prod M'Kewn. "Well, I'm about as poor a dog as ever gnaw'd a bone; but, by Jiminy! I'm not so poor a dog as to let any man say whether I sh*i*ll bark or not [. . .]. In some things, I knows I'm worse than a nigger, but bad as I am, I reckon I'll never let any man put his collar around my neck" (248). A few lines later he tells them that their behavior is "more like being a dog and a slave" (249). The insult is explicitly aimed at his opponents, but its real target is M'Kewn. Bostwick wants to underscore the fact that M'Kewn's dependent position has reduced him to a slave in Bostwick's eyes.

36. See, as just one of many examples, chapter 2 of Olaudah Equiano's *Interesting Narrative*.

37. On the practice of using slave scars as evidence, see, for example, appendix B of *The History of Mary Prince: A West Indian Slave Narrative*. On the politics of embodiment in the abolitionist movement, see Karen Sánchez-Eppler's, *Touching Liberty: Abolition, Feminism, and the Politics of the Body*.

38. The problem of agency and voice in slave narratives is a long-standing issue in both literary and historical scholarship. Due to the fact that many slave narratives were composed by white abolitionist amanuenses, there is considerable disagreement as to how "authentically" these accounts reflect the views and experiences of their slave authors. Mindful of these concerns, my analysis presumes that slave narratives represent a valuable, albeit ideologically smudged, window onto slave experience. That experience itself unfolds, of course, in and through particular cultural, ideological, and spatial matrices. My chapter, in fact, is an attempt to explore one particular aspect of such slave "experience" as it plays out in the spaces and ideologies of the antebellum plantation. On the problem of "experience" in historical analysis, see Joan Scott's essay "The Evidence of Experience." For a helpful overview of the debate about slave narratives as historical documents, see the introduction to Walter Johnson's *Soul By Soul: Life Inside the Antebellum Slave Market*. See also chapters 4 and 5 in William Andrews's *To Tell a Free Story. The First Century of Afro-American Autobiography, 1760–1865*.

39. Quoted from Genovese's *Roll, Jordan, Roll*, p. 600. Genovese provides a useful overview of the widespread practice of theft among slaves. See, in particular, pp. 599–609.

40. On the continuing influence of this stereotype, and on the efforts of black writers to resist it, see Lovalerie King's "Counter-Discourses on the Racialization of Theft and Ethics in Douglass's *Narrative* and Jacobs's *Incidents*."

41. From Olmsted's *The Cotton Kingdom*, p. 83. *The Cotton Kingdom* is a condensed version of three earlier travelogues that Olmsted wrote: *Seaboard Slave States* (1856); *A Journey Through Texas* (1857); and *A Journey in the Backcountry* (1860).

42. Architectural historian Dell Upton suggests that this addition was "a kind of eye on the landscape, a surrogate of its owner. It transformed Jefferson into an all-seeing I" (37). On the architectural history of Monticello, see chapter 1 of Upton's *Architecture in the United States*. See also Terrence Epperson's "Panoptic Plantations," in *Lines that Divide: Historical Archaeologies of Race, Class, and Gender*.

43. John Michael Vlach underscores the planters' rage for order: "Guiding these planters in setting up their estates was a highly rational formalism. The world was, in their view, suitably improved only after it was transformed from its chaotic natural condition into a scene marked by strict, hierarchical order. The planters' landscapes were laid out with straight lines, right-angle corners, and axes of symmetry, their mathematical precision being considered as proof of individual superiority" (5).

44. David Brion Davis proposes that Jeremy Bentham's concept of the Panopticon prison is actually modeled on the fantasy of a perfected plantation space; he calls the Panopticon a "virtual caricature of the planter's ideal" (456). See Davis's *The Problem of Slavery in the Age of Revolution, 1770–1823*.

45. On Jefferson's architecture of concealment, see Upton, p. 30. See also, Jane Webb Smith's review of the 1993 "Worlds of Thomas Jefferson at Monticello" exhibit in *The Journal of American History*.

46. Slave narratives are replete with references to this alternative slave space. Charles Ball, for example, repeatedly attests to his intimate knowledge of the game trails and footpaths that laced the woods around his plantation: "I had by this time, become well acquainted with the woods and swamps, for several miles round our plantation" (277). So much so that in preparing for his escape, he gathers supplies in "a small conical cabin that [he has] built in the woods" (336). Historian Stephanie Camp quotes one ex-slave on the usefulness of alternative geographies: "Dar wus a number of little paths what run though de woods dat nobody ain't watched ca[u]se dey ain't knowed dat de paths wus dar" (550). On the strategic use of the swamp by slave revolutionaries, see M. Allewaert's "Swamp Sublime: Ecologies of Resistance in the American Plantation Zone."

47. In considering the relationship of space and property on the plantation, Saidiya Hartman calls particular attention to the slave practice of "stealing away." This was the phrase used by slaves to describe any sort of illicit trip off the plantation grounds: a prayer meeting in the woods, a surreptitious dance with neighborhood slaves, a nighttime trip to visit nearby lovers or family. Stealing away constituted a crucial form of resistance for slaves precisely because it denied the master's full ownership of the slave's body and asserted a form of agency, via "theft," that posited an alternative view of property relations. At the same time, stealing away represented a challenge to the spatial regime of the plantation. Hartman writes, "Stealing away involved not only an appropriation of the self but also a disruption of the spatial organization of dominance

that confined slaves to the policed location of the quarter [. . .]. Ultimately, the struggle waged in everyday practices [. . .] was about the creation of a social space in which the assertion of needs, desires, and counterclaims could be collectively aired, thereby granting property a social life" (69). The practice of stealing away thus helpfully reveals the continually contested nature of space and spatial appropriation on the plantation.

48. Hentz's picturesque slave quarters stand in stark contrast, of course, to the miserable and inadequate dwellings described in many slave narratives. Indeed, a fair amount of slave suffering seemed to result directly from the cramped confines and scanty shelter afforded by the often dilapidated huts of the quarter. In these contradictory accounts, we can see how the figure of the hut continued to be a flashpoint for issues of ownership and affect. Proslavery texts could employ the hut as a measure of the slaveholder's largesse, adding to the nostalgic image of a contented family under benevolent paternal control. Antislavery texts, by contrast, could leverage the hut to emphasize the exploitation of slaves; here, they could suggest, is a perversion of contented dwelling and rightful ownership.

49. The comparison to Frontierland and colonial Williamsburg is not as far-fetched as it might seem. In her book, *Wounds of Returning: Race, Memory, and Property on the Postslavery Plantation*, Jessica Adams details the ways in which modern-day plantation tours carefully elide slave spaces and slave experience in order to promote an idyllic image of pastoral contentment.

50. Indeed, in this passage and in much of the book, Hentz foreshadows the plantation nostalgia that would come to dominate the genre after the Civil War and on into the twentieth century.

51. For critical work that reads the novel as politically ambiguous, see Jones, *Unwelcome Voices*; MacKethan, "Domesticity in Dixie: The Plantation Novel and Uncle Tom's Cabin"; Ridgely, *Nineteenth-Century Southern Literature*; and Egan, *The Riven Home: Narrative Rivalry in the American Renaissance*. For a more skeptical view, see Cassuto, *The Inhuman Race: The Racial Grotesque in American Literature and Culture*; and Edward H. Foster, *The Civilized Wilderness: Backgrounds to American Romantic Literature, 1817–1860*. Francis P. Gaines, *The Southern Plantation; a Study in the Development and the Accuracy of a Tradition*; Rollin G. Osterweis, *Romanticism and Nationalism in the Old South*; and Charles H. Bohner, *John Pendleton Kennedy, Gentleman from Baltimore*, all emphasize Kennedy's efforts to romanticize plantation culture.

52. It is worth noting that the name of the narrator, Mark Littleton, echoes that of the famous fifteenth-century jurist, Thomas de Littleton. A seminal authority on land tenure and real estate law, Littleton was made famous to early American lawyers through Edward Coke's ubiquitous law text, *A Commentary Upon Littleton*. By naming the narrator after this jurist (and by repeatedly referring directly to Coke's *Littleton*), Kennedy seems to be calling attention to the significance of the property subplot in the novel. On Coke's prominence in American legal education, see Friedman's *A History of American Law*, p. 238.

53. Kennedy links the Apple-pie property with the slaves in more subtle ways as well. At one point, he describes the stream as an "inefficient and trifling imp," language that directly echoes the terms in which he describes slaves throughout the novel (141). Elsewhere, he compares resting slave children to "a set of terrapins luxuriating [. . .] on the logs of a mill-pond" (451). Again and again, plantation slaves are described in relation to the Apple-pie.

54. While acknowledging that the genre of the plantation romance was part and parcel of the broader shift from empiricist sensation to romantic affect, it is important not to forget that such texts were also baldly racist. It is more than a little ironic that this more expansive conception of ownership experience occurred in the context of chattel slavery, an institution dedicated to transforming human beings into property.

4 / Feeling at a Loss: Theft and Affect in George Lippard

1. Proudhon quotes this letter in the preface to his *What Is Property?* (10).

2. Marx's praise of Proudhon's sensationalism appears in an 1865 letter to Johann Baptist von Schweitzer, editor of *Der Social-Demokrat*. See Marx and Engels, *Selected Correspondence: 1846–1895*, 169–77.

3. According to David Reynolds, *Quaker City* sold more than sixty thousand copies in its first year and ten thousand a year after that. It was the highest-selling novel in America before *Uncle Tom's Cabin* (*Quaker City*, vii). On the popularity of sensational fiction, see chapter 6, "The Sensational Press and the Rise of Subversive Literature," in David Reynolds's *Beneath the American Renaissance*.

4. Although the heyday of British sensationalism occurred a decade or two after it did in America, critics there were concerned with precisely the same issues of readerly affect. For a helpful compendium of nineteenth-century British literary criticism on sensational novels, see Andrew Maunder's *Varieties of Women's Sensation Fiction: 1855–1890*. On the dangers of overexcited "nerves," see in particular pp. 32–56 and 69–75.

5. Marx himself was schooled early in Romantic writers like Carlyle and his later work bears traces of that influence, including his critical stance toward market capitalism and his revolutionary commitments. On Marx's relationship to Romanticism, see Michael Löwy and Robert Sayre's *Romanticism Against the Tide of Modernity*.

6. On the startling growth of antebellum cities in America, see Thomas Bender's *Toward an Urban Vision*. See also Howard Chudacoff's *The Evolution of American Urban Society*.

7. On the emergence of the labor movement in America see, for example, Wilentz, *Chants Democratic*, and Laurie, *Working People of Philadelphia*. For the classic work on the British radical movements, of course, see E. P. Thompson's, *The Making of the English Working Class*.

8. For an exacting history of the theory's role in the Revolutionary period, see James L. Huston's *Securing the Fruits of Labor*.

9. Proponents of capitalist entrepreneurship, however, argued that "labor" included work done by lawyers, bankers, merchants, and others outside the traditional working classes. Indeed, the ambiguity of the term "labor" was crucial to the widespread acceptance of the labor theory of value. Both sides could effectively appropriate the theory without conceding their position. On the flexibility of this term, see Glickstein, pp. 122–23, and Wilentz, pp. 157–58.

10. On the place of Blatchly and Byllesby in the antebellum labor movement, see Wilentz, pp. 158–68.

11. French and British radicals employed much the same theft rhetoric. Several years after Blatchly and Skidmore, in fact, Proudhon published *What Is Property?*, a scathing indictment of contemporary political economy and private property theory. While he famously declared that "Property is theft!", Proudhon also rejected the labor theory of value and its assumption that labor creates wealth and property.

12. It should be stressed here that with the possible exception of Thomas Skidmore and a few other "extreme" radicals, most American labor activists never challenged the legitimacy of private property itself. They were interested in correcting the distribution of property under capitalism, but never in abolishing absolute private ownership. Indeed, "free soil" land reformers like George Henry Evans (and Lippard) were advocating a homestead for every worker precisely so they could enact a virtuous, Jeffersonian-style, agrarian existence based on the Lockean precepts of labor and private property.

13. In a serial piece for John DuSolle's *Spirit of the Times*, for example, he created a character named Flib who would spy on and expose the hypocritical transgressions of the upper class. See Reynolds's *George Lippard*, p. 5.

14. David Reynolds's helpful anthology of Lippard's writings includes a wide sampling of his reformist and laborite essays; see *George Lippard, Prophet of Protest*.

15. Surprisingly, The Brotherhood of the Union, subsequently rechristened the Brotherhood of America, lasted well into the twentieth century. Before the nineteenth century was over, it had become an insurance company providing health-care and death benefits for its members. It finally folded in 1994. The best biography on Lippard remains David Reynolds's 1982 work, *George Lippard*. On the Brotherhood of the Union, see Roger Butterfield, "George Lippard and His Secret Brotherhood."

16. Lippard was familiar with the writings of the French socialists as well as the Anglo-Americans. In the *Quaker City* weekly, for example, he published paeans to Charles Fourier and Louis Blanc. He may have read Proudhon (Reynolds sees a "parallel" between their work), but there is no concrete evidence for this (*Prophet* 41). Nor is there any evidence that he read Marx, although bits and pieces of Marx's writings did appear in America (often in German) before Lippard's death in 1854.

17. The title page of *Empire City* actually bears an inscription which promises the reader that in this book George Lippard dedicates his "great talents" "to the side of Labor when opposed by Capital."

18. It seems clear that Lippard was forced to end *Empire City* earlier than he intended, perhaps because of publication pressures. Two hundred pages in, the narrative abruptly ends and Lippard tacks on five brief "tableaus" meant to summarize the remainder of the plot. Happily, *New York* picks up right where *Empire City* left off, ignoring the awkward tableaus and continuing the original storyline. For the purposes of my argument, I will be referring to the two novels as a single narrative. Citations will use *EC* and *NY* to identify the specific novel.

19. Cvetkovich's assessment of Jameson seems a bit reductive to me, but it does clarify the ontological stakes.

20. The question of "subversiveness" has been important to Lippard criticism, in one way or another, for quite some time. Early psychoanalytic critics like Fiedler and Ehrlich emphasized the subversive nature of Lippard's dark eroticism and, in particular, his representations of voracious female sexuality. Michael Denning and David Reynolds both argue for the progressive, reformist impulse in Lippard with Denning highlighting Lippard's efforts to delineate a working-class consciousness. More recently, David Anthony ("Banking on Emotion") and Dana Nelson have reversed the field (following the lead of Cvetkovich and D. A. Miller on British sensationalism), maintaining that Lippard's radicalism is overbalanced by his novels' efforts to police the boundaries of white, middle-class masculinity.

21. That said, there are a number of critics who make persuasive arguments for the regressive aspects of Lippard's writing. David Anthony, for instance, argues that

the male characters in *Quaker City* trade a self-possessive model of Jacksonian masculinity for a more emotional, sentimental "debtor masculinity." He sees this transformation as a regressive process, a "rebound ideology" in which middle-class values are more powerfully reinscribed ("Banking" 721). Likewise, Dana Nelson asserts that *Quaker City* "aggressively advocates, mostly by negative contrast, the regime of the male-purity movement"—female bodies in the novel serve as diseased objects that male protagonists can manage and control, thus restoring a fantasy of masculine power (145). And Christopher Looby thinks that George Thompson's sensational city-mysteries are "more slavishly affirmative of the values of sentimental domestic culture in its most politically regressive form than many of the well-known sentimental novels of the day" (655).

22. Tomkins's central work is the four-volume series, *Affect Imagery Consciousness*. Sedgwick and Frank offer a helpful selection culled from these four volumes in *Shame and Its Sisters: A Silvan Tomkins Reader*.

23. Tomkins is careful to distinguish distress from Freudian "anxiety." Indeed, Tomkins takes Freud to task for what he sees as the sloppy capaciousness of the term "anxiety." "Anxiety has become a weasel word, meaning all things to all men. The common denominator of these meanings is some kind of 'stress,' which all animals will signal by some kind of 'avoidance'" (*Shame* 236). In contrast, Tomkins argues that there is a finite set of more specific negative affects: distress, shame, guilt, disgust, dissmell, surprise, and contempt.

24. See the introduction to Hendler's *Public Sentiments: Structures of Feeling in Nineteenth-Century American Literature*.

25. Hendler, following Raymond Williams, argues that sentimentalism is best understood as a "structure of feeling," a socially-mediated affective experience akin to but distinct from ideology. See Hendler, pp. 10–11.

26. The "sympathetic spectrum" I am proposing here helps synthesize several other critical models of identificatory affect. Marianne Noble, for instance, argues that sentimental writers like Stowe often use scenes of bodily anguish in order to create what Noble calls a "sentimental wound," "an experience of intersubjective connectedness at the level of the body" that links reader and character (296). According to Noble, however, the sentimental writer stops short of fully explicit descriptions of physical suffering, leaving the details to be construed by the reader. Thomas Laqueur, on the other hand, maintains that sensationalist writers do rely on this kind of explicit detail—minute descriptions of suffering bodies—in order to create "sympathetic passions" that connect readers and characters. As he explains, "through this discourse of the body a common ground of feeling is established and the cognitive pathways for intervention laid in place" (190). Read next to one another, then, Noble and Laqueur help outline a sympathetic spectrum stretching across a range of identificatory strategies, bodily proximities, and political possibilities. See Noble's "The Ecstasies of Sentimental Wounding in Uncle Tom's Cabin," and Laqueur's "Bodies, Details, and the Humanitarian Narrative."

27. In *Mechanic Accents*, Michael Denning convincingly argues that "the bulk of the audience of dime novels were workers—craftworkers, factory operatives, domestic servants, and domestic workers—and the bulk of workers' reading was sensational fiction" (27).

28. Tomkins spends a good deal of time describing the specific facial instantiations of various affective states; see chapter 7, "The Primary Site of the Affects: The Face," in *Affect Imagery Consciousness*, vol. 1.

29. Jonathan Elmer's work on affect and mass culture has been instrumental to my thinking about the relationship of sensationalism and sentimentalism. In *Reading at the Social Limit*, Elmer argues that sentimentalism and sensationalism are similar "structures of relation," each of which negotiates the paradoxical "social limit" that both separates and links individual subject to social collectivity. Both structures rely on a form of sympathy, on, that is, "the dynamics of identificatory affect," but each responds in different ways to tears in the social fabric: sentimentalism encourages social cohesion and looks for ways to mend the tear; sensationalism, on the other hand, "lingers at the place of the wound, tarries in the breach of the social limit, explores the affective intensities elicited there, but then rather than allowing for a healing closure, it causes something to rise up in the opening, some horrifying and impossible embodiment" (96). It is a version of this emergent corporeality, I maintain, that Lippard is manipulating in his theft scenes.

30. Despite Lippard's avowedly egalitarian politics, his novels are not without their problematic racial and religious stereotypes. Von Gelt is described in decidedly anti-Semitic terms and Devil-Bug has two African-American servants who are little more than animated stereotypes. A virulent strain of anti-Catholicism figures prominently in the New York novels.

31. *City Crimes* appears in an anthology of George Thompson's work entitled *Venus in Boston, and Other Tales of Nineteenth-century City Life*. The anthology is edited by David Reynolds and Kimberly Gladman.

32. It is interesting to note that Thompson's theft scene effectively reverses Lippard's more radical critique of capitalist expropriation. Here, the Wall Street financiers are the victims and the villainous thief gets his just reward: "How he cursed the money, to obtain which he had entered that safe, wherein he was now imprisoned as securely as if buried far down in the bowels of the earth. [. . .] The remembrance of the many crimes he had committed arose before him" (176).

33. Robert Mighall makes a similar point in discussing G. W. M. Reynolds's sensational novel, *The Mysteries of London*. Mighall argues that this kind of "Urban Gothic" enacts a "transportation" of traditional Gothic scenes into "the contemporary urban context" (30).

34. In his introduction to *Venus in Boston*, David Reynolds observes that for Thompson, "the process of coming to understand the city is represented [. . .] not as gaining an overview or panoramic picture of the whole, but as learning the secret routes and hidden entrances in a particular part of it. [. . .] [The novel] abounds in visions of small or enclosed spaces" (li). Of course, none of this is to say that Lippard and his fellow city-mystery writers absolutely never describe a street scene or an outdoor setting; they do, as Samuel Otter has pointed out in a compelling reading of the urban geography of *Quaker City*. But such scenes are the exception rather than the rule. The overwhelming spatial emphasis is on Gothic interiority. For Otter's argument, see chapter 3 of his *Philadelphia Stories*.

35. Edgar Allan Poe himself briefly attests to this expanded urban anxiety in his 1842 short story, "The Mystery of Marie Rogêt." Like Lippard, Poe's detective narrator, C. Auguste Dupin, is sensitive to the unsettling permeability of urban spaces. "Those who know any thing of the vicinity of Paris," Dupin observes, "know the extreme difficulty of finding seclusion. [. . .] Such a thing as an unexplored, or even infrequently visited recess [. . .] is not for a moment to be imagined." Anyone who thinks he has found a sequestered, protected space will be swiftly disappointed "by the voice and

personal intrusion of some ruffian or party of carousing blackguards. He will seek privacy amid the densest foliage, all in vain. Here are the very nooks where the unwashed most abound—here are the temples most desecrate" (541). Urban space brings with it a fear of permeability, of exposure, of loss of privacy.

36. It is worth noting, á la Hamon, that this affective "shifting" moves in both directions. Thus, literary representations of space also influence our experience of real-world spaces. We might think of the way in which reading a Stephen King novel can transform our own dark or empty house into a site of fear or distress.

37. In fact, one of the more peculiar threats lurking in the real-world spaces of the antebellum city was the so-called panel thief. George Foster, in his nonfiction exposé, *New York by Gas-Light* (1850), describes this curious species of criminal: "The panel thief hid behind a false, moveable panel in the wall of the prostitute's room, emerging at an appropriate moment to rob her customer" (96n6). As Lippard suggests, urban enclosures are never quite as private as they seem and, as a result, property faces the constant threat of penetration and theft.

38. For an engaging cultural history of anatomy in America, in general, and more specifically of the underground cadaver economy, see Michael Sappol's *A Traffic of Dead Bodies*.

39. On the anatomy disputes, see Sappol, chapter 4.

40. On the invasion of working class graveyards, see Sappol, p. 87. On the economics of burial, see pp. 34–39.

41. On the "Bone Bill," see Sappol, pp. 126–32.

42. The notorious Burke and Hare scandal of 1828 in Edinburgh, Scotland, received wide coverage on both sides of the Atlantic. In it, two Irish laborers, William Burke and William Hare, began the lucrative practice of killing indigents they located in the city and then selling their bodies to prominent physicians, including the head of the Edinburgh Medical School, Robert Knox. The two were eventually caught, and Burke hanged, but not before popular culture had coined the term "burking" to designate the grisly technique of suffocation that the two practiced. See Sappol, p. 118.

43. For an enlightening discussion of possessive individualism and ownership of the body (in the context of organ theft), see Stephan Palmié's "Thinking with *Ngangas*."

44. Historian Michael Sappol, in an insightful reading of Quaker City, takes a somewhat different view of bodies and body snatching in Lippard's fiction. Sappol suggests that the novel's fascination with dead and decaying bodies actually signals an antebellum "desire to surrender the boundaries that define bourgeois personhood, a willful annihilation of the propertied self" (234). While the corpse may initially retain some value as the raw material for anatomy experiments, it is ultimately a perishable commodity that will decompose into useless and polluted matter. "Death," according to Sappol, "is what bourgeois morality and aesthetics cannot contain" (235). It seems to me, however, that the market quickly reasserts its all-encompassing grasp by assimilating and revaluing the bones, the nonperishable matter that remains after decomposition. The 1854 legislation was known as the "Bone Bill," after all, and anatomical skulls and skeletons were hot properties in the medical economy. An early satirical poem by Francis Hopkinson emphasizes precisely this point:

Alas! too truly did the wise man say
That flesh is grass, and subject to decay—
Not so the bones—of substance firm and hard
Long they remain th' Anatomist's reward.

> Wise nature, in her providential care,
> Did, kindly, bones from vile corruption spare,
> That sons their fathers' skeletons might have
> And heav'n-born science triumph o'er the grave. ("An Oration" 150)

Hardly the "opposite of value," bones represent the hard currency of the anatomical market. As such, they served not as a subversive challenge to the capitalist system, but as a gruesome reminder of its inescapable reach. Death fascinates in Lippard not because it disrupts the bourgeois economy, but precisely because it fails to disrupt it. Everything, even the last remaining pieces of the laboring body, becomes an opportunity for capitalist gain.

45. Derrida underscores the mirror-like role of the commodity in the experience of alienation. Writing in *Specters of Marx*, he observes that "there is a mirror, and the commodity form is also this mirror, but since all of a sudden it no longer plays its role, since it does not reflect back the expected image, those who are looking for themselves can no longer find themselves in it. Men no longer recognize in it the *social* character of their *own* labor. It is as if they were becoming ghosts in their turn" (155).

46. Many commentators on the genre of the city-mystery have noted its pornographic tendencies and the prevalence of the masculine gaze. See, for an early example, J. V. Ridgely's "George Lippard's *The Quaker City*: The World of the American Porno-Gothic." Dana Nelson argues convincingly that such male-oriented scopic pleasures are closely linked to the wider cultural construction of white masculinity in antebellum America. See chapter 4 of her *National Manhood*.

47. Certainly this was the image that Melville used to such powerful effect in "Bartleby, the Scrivener" as well as his 1855 short story, "The Tartarus of Maids." In *Labor's Text: The Worker in American Fiction*, Laura Hapke points out that metaphor of the worker as "walking dead" became widespread in twentieth-century labor fiction (27).

Works Cited

Adams, Jessica. *Wounds of Returning: Race, Memory, and Property on the Postslavery Plantation.* New Directions in Southern Studies. Chapel Hill: University of North Carolina Press, 2007.
Ahmed, Sara. *The Cultural Politics of Emotion.* New York: Routledge, 2004.
———. *Queer Phenomenology: Orientations, Objects, Others.* Durham, NC: Duke University Press, 2006.
Alcott, William A. *The House I Live in; or, Popular Illustrations of the Structure and Functions of the Human Body: For the Use of Families and Schools.* 1834. 7th ed. London: J. W. Parker and Son, 1852.
Alexander, Gregory S. *Commodity and Propriety: Competing Visions of Property in American Legal Thought, 1776–1970.* Chicago: University of Chicago Press, 1997.
Allen, Chilion B. *The Man Wonderful in the House Beautiful. An Allegory Teaching the Principles of Physiology and Hygiene, and the Effects of Stimulants and Narcotics* New York: Fowler & Wells Co., 1883.
Allewaert, M. "Swamp Sublime: Ecologies of Resistance in the American Plantation Zone." *PMLA* 123, no. 2 (2008): 340–57.
Andrews, William L. *To Tell a Free Story: The First Century of Afro-American Autobiography, 1760–1865.* Urbana: University of Illinois Press, 1988.
Anthony, David. "Banking on Emotion: Financial Panic and the Logic of Male Submission in the Jacksonian Gothic." *American Literature* 76.4 (2004): 719–47.
———. "Class, Culture, and the Trouble with White Skin in Hawthorne's *the House of the Seven Gables.*" *The Yale Journal of Criticism* 12, no. 2 (1999): 249–68.

———. *Paper Money Men: Commerce, Manhood, and the Sensational Public Sphere in Antebellum America*. Columbus: Ohio State University Press, 2009.

Armstrong, Nancy. *Desire and Domestic Fiction: A Political History of the Novel*. New York: Oxford University Press, 1987.

Arneil, Barbara. *John Locke and America: The Defence of English Colonialism*. Oxford and New York: Clarendon Press, 1996.

Asfour, Amal. "Splendid Impositions: Gainsborough, Berkeley, Hume." *Eighteenth-Century Studies* 31, no. 4 (1998): 403–32.

Axelrod, Alan. *Charles Brockden Brown: An American Tale*. Austin: University of Texas Press, 1983.

Bachelard, Gaston. *The Poetics of Space*. Trans. Maria Jolas. Boston: Beacon Press, 1994.

Baker, Houston A., Jr., and Dana D. Nelson. "Preface: Violence, the Body and The 'South.'" *American Literature* 73, no. 2 (2001): 231–44.

Ball, Charles. *Slavery in the United States; a Narrative of the Life and Adventures of Charles Ball, a Black Man, Who Lived Forty Years in Maryland, South Carolina and Georgia, as a Slave*. 3d ed. Pittsburgh, PA: John T. Shyrock, 1854.

Banner, Stuart. *American Property: A History of How, Why, and What We Own*. Cambridge, MA: Harvard University Press, 2011.

———. *How the Indians Lost Their Land: Law and Power on the Frontier*. Cambridge: Belknap Press, 2005.

———. "21st Century Fox: Pierson v. Post, Then and Now." *Law and History Review* 27, no. 1 (2009): 185–88.

Barnes, Elizabeth. *States of Sympathy: Seduction and Democracy in the American Novel*. New York: Columbia University Press, 1997.

Basch, Norma. *In the Eyes of the Law: Women, Marriage, and Property in Nineteenth-Century New York*. Ithaca, NY: Cornell University Press, 1982.

Batt, Noëlle. "'L'Entre-deux,' A Bridging Concept for Literature, Philosophy, and Science." *SubStance* 23, no. 2 (1994): 38–48.

Baym, Nina. *Woman's Fiction: A Guide to Novels by and About Women in America, 1820–70*. 1978. 2d ed. Urbana: University of Illinois Press, 1993.

Becker, Marshall J. "Hannah Freeman: An Eighteenth-Century Lenape Living and Working Among Colonial Farmers." *Pennsylvania Magazine of History and Biography* 114, no. 2 (1990): 249–69.

Beecher, Catharine. *A Treatise on Domestic Economy*. Boston: n.p., 1841.

Bender, Thomas. *Toward an Urban Vision: Ideas and Institutions in Nineteenth Century America*. Baltimore, MD: Johns Hopkins University Press, 1982.

Berger, Bethany R. "It's Not About the Fox: The Untold History of Pierson v. Post." *Duke Law Journal* 55, no. 6 (2006): 1089–143.

Berkeley, George, and Jonathan Dancy. *A Treatise Concerning the Principles of Human Knowledge*. Oxford Philosophical Texts. Oxford and New York: Oxford University Press, 1998.

Berkeley, George, and T. E. Jessop. *Philosophical Writings*. New York: Greenwood Press, 1969.

Berlant, Lauren. *Compassion: The Culture and Politics of an Emotion*. Essays from the English Institute. New York: Routledge, 2004.
———. *Cruel Optimism*. Durham, NC: Duke University Press, 2011.
———. *The Female Complaint: The Unfinished Business of Sentimentality in American Culture*. Durham, NC: Duke University Press, 2008.
Berthold, Dennis. "Charles Brockden Brown, 'Edgar Huntly,' And the Origins of the American Picturesque." *The William and Mary Quarterly* 41, no. 1 (1984): 62–84.
Best, Stephen M. *The Fugitive's Properties: Law and the Poetics of Possession*. Chicago: University of Chicago Press, 2004.
Bierce, Ambrose. *The Unabridged Devil's Dictionary*. Athens: University of Georgia Press, 2000.
Blackstone, William. *Blackstone's Commentaries: With Notes of Reference, to the Constitution and Laws, of the Federal Government of the United States, and of the Commonwealth of Virginia*. 5 vols. Ed. St. George Tucker. Philadelphia, PA: Published by William Young Birch, and Abraham Small, 1803.
———. *Commentaries on the Laws of England*. 1765. 4 vols. Chicago: University of Chicago Press, 1979.
Blatchly, Cornelius C. *An Essay on Common Wealths*. New York: n.p., 1822.
Bohner, Charles H. *John Pendleton Kennedy, Gentleman from Baltimore*. Baltimore, MD: Johns Hopkins Press, 1961.
Brantlinger, Patrick. *Fictions of State: Culture and Credit in Britain, 1694–1994*. Ithaca, NY: Cornell University Press, 1996.
Brillat, Savarin, and M. F. K. Fisher. *The Physiology of Taste: Or, Meditations on Transcendental Gastronomy*. New York: Heritage Press, 1949.
Brooks, Joanna. "Held Captive by the Irish: Quaker Captivity Narratives in Frontier Pennsylvania." *New Hibernia Review* 8, no. 3 (2004): 31–46.
Brown, Charles Brockden. "The Man at Home." In *The Rhapsodist and Other Uncollected Writings by Charles Brockden Brown*, ed. Harry R. Warfel, 25–98. New York: Scholars' Facsimiles & Reprints, 1943.
———. *Three Gothic Novels*. The Library of America. New York: Penguin Putnam, 1998.
———. "Walstein's School of History." In *The Rhapsodist and Other Uncollected Writings by Charles Brockden Brown*, ed. Harry R. Warfel, 143–56. New York: Scholars' Facsimiles & Reprints, 1943.
Brown, Charles Brockden, and Mary Megan Chapman. *Ormond, or, the Secret Witness*. Broadview Literary Texts. Peterborough, Ontario: Broadview Press, 1999.
Brown, Charles Brockden, and Sydney Krause. *Edgar Huntly, or, Memoirs of a Sleep-Walker*. Bicentennial ed. Kent, OH: Kent State University Press, 1984.
Brown, Charles Brockden, and Alfred Weber. *Somnambulism and Other Stories*. Studien Und Texte Zur Amerikanistik. Texte, Bd. 4. Frankfurt and New York: P. Lang, 1987.
Brown, Gillian. *Domestic Individualism: Imagining Self in Nineteenth-Century*

America. The New Historicism 14. Berkeley: University of California Press, 1990.

Buell, Lawrence. "Circling the Spheres: A Dialogue." *American Literature* 70, no. 3 (1998): 465–90.

Burbick, Joan. *Healing the Republic: The Language of Health and the Culture of Nationalism in Nineteenth-Century America*. Cambridge: Cambridge University Press, 1994.

Burgett, Bruce. *Sentimental Bodies: Sex, Gender, and Citizenship in the Early Republic*. Princeton, NJ: Princeton University Press, 1998.

Butterfield, Roger. "George Lippard and His Secret Brotherhood." *Pennsylvania Magazine of History and Biography* 79, no. 3 (1955): 285–309.

Byllesby, Langton. *Observations on the Sources and Effects of Unequal Wealth*. New York: Russell and Russell, 1826.

Camp, Stephanie M. H. "The Pleasures of Resistance: Enslaved Women and Body Politics in the Plantation South, 1830–1861." *The Journal of Southern History* 68, no. 3 (2002): 533–72.

Carsten, Janet, and Stephen Hugh-Jones, eds. *About the House: Levi-Strauss and Beyond*. Cambridge: Cambridge University Press, 1995.

Casey, Edward S. *The Fate of Place: A Philosophical History*. Berkeley: University of California Press, 1997.

Cassuto, Leonard. *The Inhuman Race: The Racial Grotesque in American Literature and Culture*. New York: Columbia University Press, 1997.

Certeau, Michel de. *The Practice of Everyday Life*. Berkeley: University of California Press, 1988.

Chudacoff, Howard P. *The Evolution of American Urban Society*. 2d ed. Englewood Cliffs, NJ: Prentice-Hall, 1981.

Cixous, Hélène, and Catherine Clément. *The Newly Born Woman*. Minneapolis: University of Minnesota Press, 1986.

Clemit, Pamela. *The Godwinian Novel: The Rational Fictions of Godwin, Brockden Brown, Mary Shelley*. Oxford English Monographs. Oxford: Clarendon Press, 1993.

Cody, Michael. "Sleepwalking into the Nineteenth Century: Charles Brockden Brown's 'Somnambulism.'" *Journal of the Short Story in English* 39 (2002): 41–55.

Condillac, Etienne Bonnot de. *Philosophical Writings of Etienne Bonnot, Abbé De Condillac*. 1754. Trans. Franklin Phillip. Hillsdale, NJ: L. Erlbaum Associates, 1982.

Confessions and Experience of a Novel Reader. Chicago: William Stacy, 1855.

Cooper, James Fenimore. *The Pioneers*. Penguin Classics. New York: Penguin Books, 1988.

Cosgrove, Denis E. *Social Formation and Symbolic Landscape*. London: Croom Helm, 1984; reprint, Madison: University of Wisconsin Press, 1998.

Cott, Nancy F. *The Bonds of Womanhood: "Woman's Sphere" In New England, 1780–1835*. 2d ed. New Haven, CT: Yale University Press, 1997.

———. "Passionlessness: An Interpretation of Victorian Sexual Ideology, 1790–1850." *Feminist Studies* 3, nos. 1–2 (1975): 15–29.

Coviello, Peter. *Intimacy in America: Dreams of Affiliation in Antebellum Literature*. Minneapolis: University of Minnesota Press, 2005.

Crenson, Matt. "Whose Woods Are These? Shooting in North Woods Highlights Contrast Between Hmong, Local Hunters." *Associated Press Worldstream* November 30, 2004. Academic. LEXIS-NEXIS. Accessed on June 11, 2008. http://bert.lib.indiana.edu:2093/ us/lnacademic/home/home.do

Cvetkovich, Ann. *Mixed Feelings: Feminism, Mass Culture, and Victorian Sensationalism*. New Brunswick, NJ: Rutgers University Press, 1992.

Davidson, Cathy N. "Preface: No More Separate Spheres!" *American Literature* 70, no. 3 (1998): 443–68.

Davis, David Brion. *The Problem of Slavery in the Age of Revolution, 1770–1823*. Ithaca, NY: Cornell University Press, 1975.

Davis, Thadious M. *Games of Property: Law, Race, Gender, and Faulkner's Go Down, Moses*. Durham, NC: Duke University Press, 2003.

Davis, W. W. H. *The History of Bucks County, Pennsylvania: From the Discovery of the Delaware to the Present Time*. Doylestown, PA: Democrat Book and Job Office Print, 1876.

Denning, Michael. *Mechanic Accents: Dime Novels and Working-Class Culture in America*. 1987. Rev. ed. London: Verso, 1998.

Derrida, Jacques. "Economimesis." *Diacritics* 11, no. 2 (1981): 3–25.

———. "The Time of the King." In *The Logic of the Gift*, ed. Alan D. Schrift, 121–47. New York: Routledge, 1997.

Dillon, Elizabeth Maddock. *The Gender of Freedom: Fictions of Liberalism and the Literary Public Sphere*. Stanford: Stanford University Press, 2004.

Douglas, Ann. *The Feminization of American Culture*. New York: Noonday Press/Farrar, Straus and Giroux, 1998.

Douglass, Frederick, William L. Andrews, and William S. McFeely. *Narrative of the Life of Frederick Douglass, an American Slave, Written by Himself: Authoritative Text, Contexts, Criticism*. 1st ed. New York: W. W. Norton & Co., 1997.

Edie, James M. *William James and Phenomenology*. Studies in Phenomenology and Existential Philosophy. Bloomington: Indiana University Press, 1987.

Egan, Ken. *The Riven Home: Narrative Rivalry in the American Renaissance*. Selinsgrove, PA: Susquehanna University Press, 1997.

Ellison, Julie K. *Cato's Tears and the Making of Anglo-American Emotion*. Chicago: University of Chicago Press, 1999.

Elmer, Jonathan. *Reading at the Social Limit: Affect, Mass Culture and Edgar Allan Poe*. Stanford: Stanford University Press, 1995.

Emerson, Ralph Waldo, and Edward Waldo Emerson. *The Complete Works of Ralph Waldo Emerson*. 1st AMS ed. New York: AMS Press, 1968.

Emerson, Ralph Waldo, Joel Porte, and Saundra Morris. *Emerson's Prose and Poetry: Authoritative Texts, Contexts, Criticism*. Norton Critical Edition. 1st ed. New York: W. W. Norton, 2001.

Entrikin, J. Nicholas. *The Betweenness of Place: Towards a Geography of Modernity.* Baltimore, MD: Johns Hopkins University Press, 1991.

Epperson, Terrence W. "Panoptic Plantations: The Garden Sights of Thomas Jefferson and George Mason." In *Lines That Divide: Historical Archeologies of Race, Class, and Gender,* ed. James A. Delle, Stephen A. Mrozowski, and Robert Paynter, 58–77. Knoxville: University of Tennessee Press, 2000.

Equiano, Olaudah, and Vincent Carretta. *The Interesting Narrative and Other Writings.* Penguin Classics. Rev. ed. New York: Penguin Books, 2003.

Felski, Rita. *Uses of Literature.* Blackwell Manifestos. Oxford: Blackwell, 2008.

Fernandez, Angela. "The Lost Record of Pierson v. Post, the Famous Fox Case." *Law and History Review* 27, no. 1 (2009): 149–78.

Fiedler, Leslie A. *Love and Death in the American Novel.* New York: Criterion Books, 1960.

Fitzhugh, George. *Cannibals All! Or, Slaves Without Masters.* Cambridge, MA: Belknap Press of Harvard University Press, 1960.

———. *Slavery Justified.* Fredericksburg, VA: Recorder Print Office, 1850.

———. *Sociology for the South; or, the Failure of Free Society.* New York: B. Franklin, 1965.

Foster, Edward Halsey. *The Civilized Wilderness: Backgrounds to American Romantic Literature, 1817–1860.* New York: Free Press, 1975.

Foster, George G., and Stuart M. Blumin. *New York by Gas-Light and Other Urban Sketches.* Berkeley: University of California Press, 1990.

Foucault, Michel, Colin Gordon, and Cid Corman. *Power/Knowledge: Selected Interviews and Other Writings, 1972–1977.* 1st American ed. New York: Pantheon Books, 1980.

Fox-Genovese, Elizabeth. *Within the Plantation Household: Black and White Women of the Old South.* Chapel Hill: University of North Carolina Press, 1988.

Fox-Genovese, Elizabeth, and Eugene D. Genovese. *Fruits of Merchant Capital: Slavery and Bourgeois Property in the Rise and Expansion of Capitalism.* Oxford and New York: Oxford University Press, 1983.

Franklin, Wayne. *James Fenimore Cooper: The Early Years.* New Haven, CT: Yale University Press, 2007.

Frasca-Spada, Marina. *Space and the Self in Hume's Treatise.* Cambridge: Cambridge University Press, 1998.

Freyfogle, Eric T., and Dale Goble. *Wildlife Law: A Primer.* Washington, DC: Island Press, 2009.

Friedman, Lawrence Meir. *A History of American Law.* 3d ed. New York: Simon & Schuster, 2005.

Gaines, Francis Pendleton. *The Southern Plantation; a Study in the Development and the Accuracy of a Tradition.* New York: Columbia University Press, 1925.

Gallagher, Catherine. *The Body Economic: Life, Death, and Sensation in Political Economy and the Victorian Novel.* Princeton, NJ: Princeton University Press, 2006.

Gardner, Jared. "Alien Nation: Edgar Huntly's Savage Awakening." *American Literature* 66, no. 3 (1994): 429–61.
Garza, Jesse. "Man Accused of Damaging Neighbors' Property." *Journal Sentinel* [Milwaukee], December 4, 2004, 3B.
Genovese, Eugene D. *Roll, Jordan, Roll: The World the Slaves Made.* New York: Vintage Books, 1976.
———. *The World the Slaveholders Made: Two Essays in Interpretation.* Middletown, CT: Wesleyan University Press, 1988.
Gilpin, William. *Observations on Several Parts of the Counties of Cambridge, Norfolk, Suffolk, and Essex: Also on Several Parts of North Wales; Relative Chiefly to Picturesque Beauty, in Two Tours, the Former Made in the Year 1769, the Latter in the Year 1773.* London: Printed for T. Cadell and W. Davies, 1809.
Glickstein, Jonathan A. *American Exceptionalism, American Anxiety: Wages, Competition, and Degraded Labor in the Antebellum United States.* Charlottesville: University of Virginia Press, 2002.
Godden, Richard. "Pioneer Properties, or 'What's in a Hut?'" In *James Fenimore Cooper: New Critical Essays,* ed. Robert Clark, 121–42. London: Vision; Barnes & Noble, 1985.
Godwin, William. *Enquiry Concerning Political Justice.* 1798. Ed. F. E. L. Priestley. 3d ed. Vol. 2. 2 vols. Toronto: University of Toronto Press, 1946.
Godwin, William, and Maurice Hindle. *Things as They Are, or, the Adventures of Caleb Williams.* Penguin Classics. London and New York: Penguin Books, 1988.
Goetzmann, William H. *Beyond the Revolution: A History of American Thought from Paine to Pragmatism.* New York: Basic Books, 2009.
Goodman, Russell B. *American Philosophy and the Romantic Tradition.* Cambridge: Cambridge University Press, 1990.
Grabo, Norman S. *The Coincidental Art of Charles Brockden Brown.* Chapel Hill: University of North Carolina Press, 1981.
Graham, Sylvester. *A Treatise on Bread, and Bread-Making.* Boston: Light & Stearns, 1837.
Grammer, John M. "Plantation Fiction." In *A Companion to the Literature and Culture of the American South,* ed. Richard Gray and Owen Robinson. Oxford: Blackwell Publishing, 2004.
Greenberg, Kenneth S. *Honor and Slavery.* Princeton, NJ: Princeton University Press, 1996.
Gura, Philip F. *American Transcendentalism: A History.* New York: Hill and Wang, 2007.
Hamon, Philippe. *Expositions: Literature and Architecture in Nineteenth-Century France.* Trans. Katia Sainson-Frank and Lisa Maguire. Berkeley: University of California Press, 1992.
Hapke, Laura. *Labor's Text: The Worker in American Fiction.* New Brunswick, NJ: Rutgers University Press, 2001.

Harper, Steven Craig. *Promised Land: Penn's Holy Experiment, the Walking Purchase, and the Dispossession of Delawares, 1600–1763.* Bethlehem, PA: Lehigh University Press, 2006.

Hartman, Saidiya V. *Scenes of Subjection: Terror, Slavery, and Self-Making in Nineteenth-Century America.* New York: Oxford University Press, 1997.

Hawthorne, Nathaniel. *The House of the Seven Gables.* 1851. Modern Library ed. New York: Random House, 2001.

———. *Septimium Felton: Or, the Elixir of Life.* 1872. Charleston, SC: BiblioBazaar, 2006.

Hawthorne, Nathaniel, and James McIntosh. *Nathaniel Hawthorne's Tales: Authoritative Texts Backgrounds Criticism.* New York: W. W. Norton, 1987.

Hawthorne, Nathaniel, and Randall Stewart. *The American Notebooks by Nathaniel Hawthorne.* New Haven, CT: Yale University Press, 1932.

Hedges, H. P. "Pierson v. Post." *Sag-Harbor Express,* October 24, 1895, 1.

Hegel, G. W. F. *Elements of the Philosophy of Right.* 1821. Trans. H. B. Nisbet. Ed. Allen W. Wood. Cambridge: Cambridge University Press, 1991.

———. *Phenomenology of Spirit.* Trans. A. V. Miller. Oxford: Oxford University Press, 1977.

Heidegger, Martin. *Basic Writings.* Ed. David Farrell Krell. San Francisco: Harper Collins, 1993.

Hendler, Glenn. *Public Sentiments: Structures of Feeling in Nineteenth-Century American Literature* Chapel Hill: University of North Carolina Press, 2001.

Hentz, Caroline Lee. *The Planter's Northern Bride.* Chapel Hill: University of North Carolina Press, 1970.

Hinds, Elizabeth Jane Wall. "Deb's Dogs: Animals, Indians, and Postcolonial Desire in Charles Brockden Brown's *Edgar Huntly.*" *Early American Literature* 39, no. 2 (2004): 323–54.

———. *Private Property: Charles Brockden Brown's Gendered Economics of Virtue.* Newark: University of Delaware Press, 1997.

Hogue, L. Lynn. "The Presentation of Post Revolutionary Law in *Woodcraft*: Another Perspective on the 'Truth' of Simms's Fiction." *Mississippi Quarterly* 31, no. 2 (1978): 201–10.

Hollinger, David A., and Charles Capper, eds. *The American Intellectual Tradition: A Sourcebook.* 3d ed. New York: Oxford University Press, 1997.

Hopkinson, Francis. "An Oration." *American Poems, Selected and Original.* Litchfield, CO: Collier and Buel, 1793.

Horwitz, Morton J. *The Transformation of American Law, 1780–1860.* New York: Oxford University Press, 1992.

Howe, Daniel Walker. *Making the American Self: Jonathan Edwards to Abraham Lincoln.* Oxford: Oxford University Press, 2009.

Hume, David. *A Treatise of Human Nature.* 1739–1740. Ed. David Fate Norton and Mary J. Norton. Oxford: Oxford University Press, 2000.

Husserl, Edmund. *The Crisis of European Sciences and Transcendental*

Phenomenology; an Introduction to Phenomenological Philosophy. Northwestern University Studies in Phenomenology & Existential Philosophy. Evanston, IL: Northwestern University Press, 1970.

Huston, James L. *Securing the Fruits of Labor: The American Concept of Wealth Distribution, 1765–1900.* Baton Rouge: Louisiana State University Press, 1998.

Hyde, Lewis. *The Gift: Imagination and the Erotic Life of Property.* 1979. New York: Vintage Books, 1983.

Ignatiev, Noel. *How the Irish Became White.* New York: Routledge, 1995.

Ingrassia, Catherine. *Authorship, Commerce, and Gender in Early Eighteenth-Century England: A Culture of Paper Credit.* New York: Cambridge University Press, 1998.

Insko, Jeffrey. "The Logic of Left Alone: *The Pioneers* and the Conditions of U.S. Privacy." *American Literature* 81, no. 4 (2009): 659–85.

Isaac, Rhys. *The Transformation of Virginia, 1740–1790.* Chapel Hill: University of North Carolina Press, 1982.

Jacobs, Harriet A., Nellie Y. McKay, and Frances Smith Foster. *Incidents in the Life of a Slave Girl : Contexts, Criticisms.* New York: W. W. Norton, 2001.

Jefferson, Thomas, and Merrill D. Peterson. *Writings.* New York: Literary Classics of the U.S. Distributed to the trade in the United States and Canada by the Viking Press, 1984.

Jennings, Francis. *The Ambiguous Iroquois Empire: The Covenant Chain Confederation of Indian Tribes with English Colonies from Its Beginnings to the Lancaster Treaty of 1744.* 1st ed. New York: W. W. Norton, 1984.

Johnson, Walter. *Soul by Soul: Life Inside the Antebellum Slave Market.* Cambridge, MA: Harvard University Press, 1999.

Jones, Anne Goodwyn, and Susan Van D'Elden Donaldson. *Haunted Bodies: Gender and Southern Texts.* The American South Series. Charlottesville: University Press of Virginia, 1997.

Jones, Paul Christian. *Unwelcome Voices: Subversive Fiction in the Antebellum South.* Knoxville: University of Tennessee Press, 2005.

Kafer, Peter. *Charles Brockden Brown's Revolution and the Birth of American Gothic.* Philadelphia: University of Pennsylvania Press, 2004.

Kaplan, Amy. "Manifest Domesticity." *American Literature* 70, no. 3 (1998): 581–606.

Kearney, Richard. *On Paul Ricoeur: The Owl of Minerva.* Transcending Boundaries in Philosophy and Theology. Burlington, VT: Ashgate, 2004.

Kennedy, John Pendleton, and Lucinda Hardwick MacKethan. *Swallow Barn, or, a Sojourn in the Old Dominion.* Baton Rouge: Louisiana State University Press, 1986.

Kilgour, Maggie. *From Communion to Cannibalism: An Anatomy of Metaphors of Incorporation.* Princeton, NJ: Princeton University Press, 1990.

Kimball, Arthur G. *Rational Fictions: A Study of Charles Brockden Brown.* McMinnville, OR: Linfield Research Institute, 1968.

King, Lovalerie. "Counter-Discourses on the Racialization of Theft and Ethics in Douglass's *Narrative* and Jacob's *Incidents*." *MELUS* 28 no. 4 (2003): 55–82.

———. *Race, Theft, and Ethics: Property Matters in African American Literature*. Southern Literary Studies. Baton Rouge: Louisiana State University Press, 2007.

Kinzer, Stephen. "Motive in Hunting Deaths Is a Riddle." *New York Times*, November 23, 2004, late ed., A16.

Knott, Kim. *The Location of Religion: A Spatial Analysis*. London: Equinox, 2005.

Knowles, Dudley. *Hegel and the Philosophy of Right*. New York: Routledge, 2002.

Krause, Sydney. "Historical Essay." In *Edgar Huntly, or Memoirs of a Sleep-Walker*, ed. Sydney Krause and S. W. Reid, 295–400. Kent, OH: Kent State University Press, 1984.

Krause, Sydney J. "Penn's Elm and *Edgar Huntly*: Dark 'Instruction to the Heart.'" *American Literature* 66, no. 3 (1994): 463–84.

Kreyling, Michael. *Figures of the Hero in Southern Narrative*. Baton Rouge: Louisiana State University Press, 1987.

Lacqueur, Thomas W. "Bodies, Details, and the Humanitarian Narrative." In *The New Cultural History*, ed. Lynn Hunt, 176–204. Berkeley: University of California Press, 1989.

Lakoff, George, and Mark Johnson. *Metaphors We Live By*. Chicago: University of Chicago Press, 1980.

Lang, Amy Schrager, and Cecelia Tichi. *What Democracy Looks Like: A New Critical Realism for a Post-Seattle World*. New Brunswick, NJ: Rutgers University Press, 2006.

Lang, Richard. "The Dwelling-Door: Towards a Phenomenology of Transition." In *Dwelling, Place, and Environment: Towards a Phenomenology of Person and World*, ed. David Seamon and Robert Mugerauer, 201–13. New York: Columbia University Press, 1989.

Lawson-Peebles, Robert. *Landscape and Written Expression in Revolutionary America: The World Turned Upside Down*. Cambridge and New York: Cambridge University Press, 1988.

Lefebvre, Henri. *The Production of Space*. 1974. Trans. Donald Nicholson-Smith. Oxford: Blackwell, 1991.

Levinas, Emmanuel. *Totality and Infinity: An Essay on Exteriority*. 1961. Trans. Alphonso Lingis. Pittsburgh, PA: Duquesne University Press, 1969.

Lippard, George. *The Empire City*. Freeport, NY: Books for Libraries Press, 1969.

———. *The Nazarene, or, the Last of the Washingtons, a Revelation of Philadelphia, New York, and Washington in the Year 1844*. Philadelphia, PA: G. Lippard, 1846.

———. *New York: Its Upper Ten and Lower Million*. Cincinnati, OH: H. M. Rulison, 1853.

———. *The Quaker City; or, the Monks of Monk Hall*. 1845. Amherst: University of Massachusetts Press, 1995.

Lippard, George, and David S. Reynolds. *George Lippard, Prophet of Protest: Writings of an American Radical, 1822–1854*. New York: P. Lang, 1986.

Locke, John. *An Essay Concerning Human Understanding*. 1690. Ed. Roger Woolhouse. London: Penguin Books, 1997.

———. *Two Treatises of Government*. 1690. Cambridge Texts in the History of Political Thought. Ed. Peter Laslett. Cambridge: Cambridge University Press, 1988.

Looby, Christopher. "George Thompson's 'Romance of the Real': Transgression and Taboo in American Sensation Fiction." *American Literature* 65, no. 4 (1993): 651–72.

Lueck, Beth L. "Charles Brockden Brown's *Edgar Huntly*: The Picturesque Traveler as Sleepwalker." *Studies in American Fiction* 15 (1987): 25–42.

Lund, Thomas Alan. *American Wildlife Law*. Berkeley: University of California Press, 1980.

MacKethan, Lucinda. "Domesticity in Dixie: The Plantation Novel and *Uncle Tom's Cabin*." In *Haunted Bodies: Gender and Southern Texts*, ed. Anne Goodwyn Jones and Susan V. Donaldson, 223–42. Charlottesville: University Press of Virginia, 1997.

Macpherson, C. B. *The Political Theory of Possessive Individualism: Hobbes to Locke*. Oxford: Oxford University Press, 1964.

Mann, Bruce H. *Republic of Debtors: Bankruptcy in the Age of American Independence*. Cambridge, MA: Harvard University Press, 2003.

Mann, Mary Tyler Peabody. *Christianity in the Kitchen, a Physiological Cook Book*. Boston: Ticknor and Fields, 1857.

Martin, Terence. *The Instructed Vision: Scottish Common Sense Philosophy and the Origins of American Fiction*. Bloomington: Indiana University Press, 1961.

Marx, Karl. *Capital: Volume 1: A Critique of Political Economy*. 1867. Trans. Ben Fowkes. London: Penguin Books, 1990.

———. *Grundrisse: Foundations of the Critique of Political Economy*. Trans. Martin Nicolaus. London: Penguin Books, 1993.

———. *Karl Marx, Selected Writings*. Ed. David McLellan. Oxford: Oxford University Press, 2000.

———. *The Poverty of Philosophy*. 1847. Trans. H. Quelch. Chicago: Charles H. Kerr & Co., 1920.

Marx, Karl, and Friedrich Engels. *Selected Correspondence, 1846–1895*. New York: International Publishers, 1942.

Maunder, Andrew, and Sally Mitchell. *Varieties of Women's Sensation Fiction, 1855–1890*. London: Pickering & Chatto, 2004.

Mauss, Marcel, and W. D. Halls. *The Gift: The Form and Reason for Exchange in Archaic Societies*. New York: W. W. Norton, 1990.

May, Henry F. *The Enlightenment in America*. New York: Oxford University Press, 1976.

McGary, Howard. "Paternalism and Slavery." In *Subjugation and Bondage*,

Critical Essays on Slavery and Social Philosophy, ed. Tommy L. Lott, 187–208. Lanham, MD: Rowman & Littlefield, 1998.

McKeon, Michael. *The Origins of the English Novel, 1600–1740*. Baltimore, MD: Johns Hopkins University Press, 1987.

Merleau-Ponty, Maurice. *Phenomenology of Perception*. 1945. Trans. Colin Smith. London: Routledge, 2002.

Merrifield, Andrew. "Place and Space: A Lefebvrian Reconciliation." *Transactions of the Institute of British Geographers* 18, no. 4 (1993): 516–31.

Michaels, Walter Benn. *The Gold Standard and the Logic of Naturalism: American Literature at the Turn of the Century*. The New Historicism: Studies in Cultural Poetics. Berkeley: University of California Press, 1987.

———. "Romance and Real Estate." In *The New Historicism Reader*, ed. H. Aram Veeser, 186–205. New York: Routledge, 1994.

Mighall, Robert. *A Geography of Victorian Gothic Fiction: Mapping History's Nightmares*. Oxford: Oxford University Press, 1999.

Miller, D. A. *The Novel and the Police*. Berkeley: University of California Press, 1988.

Moore, Sean. "The Culture of Paper Credit: the New Economic Criticism and the Postcolonial Eighteenth Century." *The Eighteenth Century: Theory and Interpretation* 45, no. 2 (2004): 87–108.

Moran, Dermot. *Introduction to Phenomenology*. New York: Routledge, 2000.

Morgan, Michael J. *Molyneux's Question: Vision, Touch, and the Philosophy of Perception*. Cambridge and New York: Cambridge University Press, 1977.

Nelson, Dana D. *National Manhood: Capitalist Citizenship and the Imagined Fraternity of White Men*. Durham, NC: Duke University Press, 1998.

Ngai, Sianne. *Ugly Feelings*. Cambridge, MA: Harvard University Press, 2005.

Nicholas, Barry. *An Introduction to Roman Law*. Oxford: Oxford University Press, 1962.

Nicholson, Colin. *Writing and the Rise of Finance: Capital Satires of the Early Eighteenth Century*. Cambridge Studies in Eighteenth-Century English Literature and Thought. Cambridge: Cambridge University Press, 1994.

Nietzsche, Friedrich. *On the Genealogy of Morals*. Trans. Walter Kaufmann. New York: Vintage Books, 1989.

Nissenbaum, Stephen. *Sex, Diet, and Debility in Jacksonian America: Sylvester Graham and Health Reform*. Westport, CT: Greenwood Press, 1980.

Noble, Marianne. "The Ecstasies of Sentimental Wounding in Uncle Tom's Cabin." *The Yale Journal of Criticism* 10, no. 2 (1997): 295–320.

Norwood, Lisa West. "'I May Be a Stranger to the Grounds of Your Belief': Constructing Sense of Place in Wieland." *Early American Literature* 38, no. 1 (2003): 89–122.

Numbers, Ronald L., and William J. Orr, Jr. "William Beaumont's Reception at Home and Abroad." *Isis* 72, no. 4 (1981): 590–612.

Nunokawa, Jeff. *The Afterlife of Property: Domestic Security and the Victorian Novel*. Princeton, NJ: Princeton University Press, 1994.

Oakes, Larry, and Richard Meryhew. "A Growing Friction in the Woods." *Star Tribune* [Minneapolis], November 23, 2004, 1A.
O'Brien, Michael. *Rethinking the South: Essays in Intellectual History*. Baltimore, MD: Johns Hopkins University Press, 1988.
Okker, Patricia. "Serial Politics in William Gilmore Simms's *Woodcraft*." In *Periodical Literature in Nineteenth-Century America*, ed. Susan Belasco Smith, 150–65. Charlottesville: University Press of Virginia, 1995.
Olmsted, Frederick Law. *The Cotton Kingdom; a Traveller's Observations on Cotton and Slavery in the American Slave States. Based Upon Three Former Volumes of Journeys and Investigations by the Same Author*. 1861. New York: Alfred A. Knopf, 1953.
"On the Causes of Existing Evils." *Free Enquirer* [New York], April 1, 1829, 183.
Osterweis, Rollin G. *Romanticism and Nationalism in the Old South*. Baton Rouge: Louisiana State University Press, 1971.
Otter, Samuel. *Philadelphia Stories: America's Literature of Race and Freedom*. New York: Oxford University Press, 2010.
Packer, Barbara L. "The Transcendentalists." In *The Cambridge History of American Literature*, ed. Sacvan Bercovitch and Cyrus R. K. Patell, vol. 2, 329–604. New York: Cambridge University Press, 1995.
Palmie, Stephan. "Thinking with Ngangas: Reflections on Embodiment and the Limits of 'Objectively Necessary Appearances.'" *Comparative Studies in Society and History* 48, no. 4 (2006): 852–86.
Patterson, Orlando. *Slavery and Social Death: A Comparative Study*. Cambridge, MA: Harvard University Press, 1982.
Pencak, William A., and Daniel K. Richter, eds. *Friends and Enemies in Penn's Woods: Indians, Colonists, and the Racial Construction of Pennsylvania*. University Park: Pennsylvania State University Press, 2004.
Pennsylvania, et al. *The Statutes at Large of Pennsylvania from 1682 to 1801*. 18 vols. Harrisburg: Clarence M. Busch, State Printer of Pennsylvania, 1896.
Pierson v. Post, 3 Cai. 175 (N.Y. Sup. Ct. 1805).
Pocock, J. G. A. *The Machiavellian Moment: Florentine Political Thought and the Atlantic Republican Tradition*. 2d ed. Princeton, NJ: Princeton University Press, 2003.
Poe, Edgar Allan. *Poetry and Tales*. Ed. Patrick F. Quinn. The Library of America. New York: Viking Press, 1984.
Poovey, Mary. *Genres of the Credit Economy: Mediating Value in Eighteenth- and Nineteenth-Century Britain*. Chicago: University of Chicago Press, 2008.
Prince, Mary. *The History of Mary Prince: A West Indian Slave Narrative*. 1831. Mineola, NY: Dover Publications, 2004.
The Pro-Slavery Argument, as Maintained by the Most Distinguished Writers of the Southern States. Charleston, SC: Walker, Richards & Co., 1852.
Proudhon, P. J. *What Is Property?* 1840. Cambridge Texts in the History of Political Thought. Eds. Donald R. Kelley and Bonnie G. Smith. Cambridge: Cambridge University Press, 1994.

Pufendorf, Samuel. *Of the Law of Nature and Nations. Eight Books. Written in Latin by the Baron Puffendorf, . . . Done into English by Basil Kennet, . . . The Third Edition: Carefully Corrected, with Two Tables. To Which Are Now Added All the Large Notes of Mr. Barbeyrac, Translated from His Last Edition; Printed at Amsterdam, in 1712*. London: printed for R. Sare R. Bonwicke T. Goodwyn J. Walthoe M. Wotton S. Manship R. Wilkin B. Tooke R. Smith T. Ward and W. Churchill, 1717.

Reynolds, David S. *Beneath the American Renaissance: The Subversive Imagination in the Age of Emerson and Melville*. 1st ed. New York: Alfred A. Knopf, distributed by Random House, 1988.

———. *George Lippard*. Boston: Twayne Publishers, 1982.

Ricardo, David, and R. M. Hartwell. *On the Principles of Political Economy, and Taxation*. Harmondsworth, UK: Penguin, 1971.

Ricœur, Paul. *Time and Narrative*. Vol. 1. Chicago: University of Chicago Press, 1984.

Ridgely, Joseph V. "George Lippard's *the Quaker City*: The World of the American Porno-Gothic." *Studies in the Literary Imagination* 7, no. 1 (1974): 77–94.

———. *Nineteenth-Century Southern Literature*. Lexington: University Press of Kentucky, 1980.

———. "Woodcraft: Simms's First Answer to Uncle Tom's Cabin." *American Literature* 31, no. 4 (1960): 421–33.

Ringe, Donald A. *Charles Brockden Brown*. Twayne's United States Authors Series, Tusas 98. Rev. ed. Boston: Twayne Publishers, 1991.

Roediger, David R. *The Wages of Whiteness: Race and the Making of the American Working Class*. Rev. ed. London: Verso, 2007.

Romero, Lora. *Home Fronts: Domesticity and Its Critics in the Antebellum United States*. New Americanists. Durham NC: Duke University Press, 1997.

Rose, Carol M. "Canons of Property Talk, or, Blackstone's Anxiety." *The Yale Law Journal* 108, no. 3 (2006): 601–32.

Rowe, John Carlos. *Literary Culture and U.S. Imperialism: From the Revolution to World War II*. New York: Oxford University Press, 2000.

Russo, James R. "The Chameleon of Convenient Vice: A Study of the Narrative of *Arthur Mervyn*." *Studies in the Novel* 11 (1979): 381–405.

———. "'The Chimeras of the Brain': Clara's Narrative in *Wieland*." *Early American Literature* 16 (1981): 60–88.

Ryan, Alan. *Property and Political Theory*. Oxford: Basil Blackwell, 1984.

Rybczynski, Witold. *Home: A Short History of an Idea*. New York: Penguin Books, 1986.

Sack, Robert David. *Homo Geographicus: A Framework for Action, Awareness, and Moral Concern*. Baltimore, MD: Johns Hopkins University Press, 1997.

Salmon, Marylynn. *Women and the Law of Property in Early America*. Studies in Legal History. Chapel Hill: University of North Carolina Press, 1986.

Samuels, Shirley. *The Culture of Sentiment: Race, Gender, and Sentimentality in Nineteenth-Century America*. New York: Oxford University Press, 1992.

Sánchez-Eppler, Karen. *Touching Liberty: Abolition, Feminism, and the Politics of the Body.* Berkeley: University of California Press, 1993.
Sappol, Michael. *A Traffic of Dead Bodies: Anatomy and Embodied Social Identity in Nineteenth-Century America.* Princeton, NJ: Princeton University Press, 2002.
Scheckel, Susan. *The Insistence of the Indian: Race and Nationalism in Nineteenth-Century American Culture.* Princeton, NJ: Princeton University Press, 1998.
Schmidgen, Wolfram. *Eighteenth-Century Fiction and the Law of Property.* Cambridge; New York: Cambridge University Press, 2002.
Schrift, Alan D. *The Logic of the Gift: Towards an Ethics of Generosity.* New York: Routledge, 1997.
Scott, Joan W. "The Evidence of Experience." *Critical Inquiry* 17, no. 4 (1991): 773–97.
Sedgwick, Eve Kosofsky. *The Coherence of Gothic Conventions.* New York: Arno Press, 1980.
Sedgwick, Eve Kosofsky, and Adam Frank. *Touching Feeling: Affect, Pedagogy, Performativity.* Series Q. Durham, NC: Duke University Press, 2003.
Sedgwick, Eve Kosofsky, Adam Frank, and Irving E. Alexander. *Shame and Its Sisters: A Silvan Tomkins Reader.* Durham, NC: Duke University Press, 1995.
Sellers, Charles Grier. *The Market Revolution: Jacksonian America, 1815–1846.* New York: Oxford University Press, 1991.
Shapiro, Stephen. "'Man to Man I Needed Not to Dread His Encounter': *Edgar Huntly*'s End of Erotic Pessimism." In *Revising Charles Brockden Brown: Culture, Politics, and Sexuality in the Early Republic,* ed. Phillip Barnard, Mark L. Kamrath, and Stephen Shapiro, 216–51. Knoxville: University of Tennessee Press, 2004.
Shell, Marc. *The Economy of Literature.* Baltimore, MD: Johns Hopkins University Press, 1978.
——. *Money, Language, and Thought: Literary and Philosophical Economies from the Medieval to the Modern Era.* Berkeley: University of California Press, 1982.
Simms, William Gilmore. *Woodcraft; or, Hawks About the Dovecote; a Story of the South at the Close of the Revolution.* Americans in Fiction. Ridgewood, NJ: Gregg Press, 1968.
Simms, William Gilmore, et al. *The Letters of William Gilmore Simms.* 6 vols. Columbia: University of South Carolina Press, 1952.
Skidmore, Thomas. *The Rights of Man to Property!* New York: n.p., 1829.
Slotkin, Richard. *Regeneration Through Violence: The Mythology of the American Frontier, 1600–1860.* 1973. New York: HarperPerennial, 1996.
Smith, Adam. *Wealth of Nations.* 1776. New York: Oxford University Press, 1998.
Smith, Jane Webb. "Review: The Worlds of Thomas Jefferson at Monticello." *The Journal of American History* 81, no. 3 (1994): 1222–30.

Smith, Roger. *The Norton History of the Human Sciences*. Norton History of Science. 1st American ed. New York: W. W. Norton, 1997.
Smith-Rosenberg, Carroll. "Subject Female: Authorizing American Identity." *American Literary History* 5, no. 3 (1993): 481–511.
Soja, Edward W. *Thirdspace: Journeys to Los Angeles and Other Real-and-Imagined Places*. Cambridge: Blackwell, 1996.
Stern, Julia A. "'I Am Cruel Hungry': Dramas of Twisted Appetite and Rejected Identification in Elizabeth Stoddard's *The Morgesons*." In *American Culture, Canons, and the Case of Elizabeth Stoddard*, ed. Robert McClure Smith and Ellen Weinauer, 107–27. Tuscaloosa: University of Alabama Press, 2003.
———. *The Plight of Feeling: Sympathy and Dissent in the Early American Novel*. Chicago: University of Chicago Press, 1997.
St. George, Robert Blair. *Conversing by Signs: Poetics of Implication in Colonial New England Culture*. Chapel Hill: University of North Carolina Press, 1998.
Stoddard, Elizabeth, Lawrence Buell, and Sandra A. Zagarell. *The Morgesons*. 1862. New York: Penguin Books, 1984.
Stowe, Harriet Beecher, and Ann Douglas. *Uncle Tom's Cabin, or, Life Among the Lowly*. New York: Penguin Books, 1986.
Streeby, Shelley. *American Sensations: Class, Empire, and the Production of Popular Culture*. Berkeley: University of California Press, 2002.
Sundquist, Eric J. *To Wake the Nations: Race in the Making of American Literature*. Cambridge, MA: Belknap Press of Harvard University Press, 1993.
Swann, Charles. "Guns Mean Democracy: *The Pioneers* and the Game Laws." In *James Fenimore Cooper: New Critical Essays*, ed. Robert Clark, 96–120. London: Vision; Barnes & Noble, 1985.
Tawney, R. H. *The Acquisitive Society*. New York: Harcourt, Brace and Howe, 1920.
Terada, Rei. *Feeling in Theory: Emotion After the "Death of the Subject."* Cambridge, MA: Harvard University Press, 2001.
Teute, Frederika J. "A 'Republic of Intellect': Conversation and Criticism among the Sexes in 1790s New York." In *Revising Charles Brockden Brown: Culture, Politics, and Sexuality in the Early Republic*, ed. Phillip Barnard, Mark L. Kamrath, and Stephen Shapiro, 149–81. Knoxville: University of Tennessee, 2004.
Thomas, Brook. *Cross-Examinations of Law and Literature: Cooper, Hawthorne, Stowe, and Melville*. Cambridge Studies in American Literature and Culture. Cambridge: Cambridge University Press, 1987.
Thompson, E. P. *The Making of the English Working Class*. 1st Vintage ed. New York: Vintage Books, 1966.
Thompson, George, David S. Reynolds, and Kimberly R. Gladman. *Venus in Boston: And Other Tales of Nineteenth-Century City Life*. Amherst: University of Massachusetts Press, 2002.
Thompson, James. *Models of Value: Eighteenth-Century Political Economy and the Novel*. Durham, NC: Duke University Press, 1996.

Thoreau, Henry David. *Walden and Other Writings*. New York: Barnes & Noble Books, 1992.
Thrailkill, Jane F. *Affecting Fictions: Mind, Body, and Emotion in American Literary Realism*. Cambridge, MA: Harvard University Press, 2007.
Toles, George. "Charting the Hidden Landscape: Edgar Huntly." *Early American Literature* 16, no. 2 (1981): 133–53.
Tomkins, Silvan. *Affect Imagery Consciousness*. Vol. 2. 4 vols. New York: Springer Pub. Co., 1962.
———. *Affect Imagery Consciousness*. Vol. 4. 4 vols. New York: Springer Pub. Co., 1992.
Tompkins, Jane P. *Sensational Designs: The Cultural Work of American Fiction, 1790–1860*. New York: Oxford University Press, 1986.
Tracy, Susan Jean. *In the Master's Eye: Representations of Women, Blacks, and Poor Whites in Antebellum Southern Literature*. Amherst: University of Massachusetts Press, 1995.
Tuan, Yi-fu. *Space and Place: The Perspective of Experience*. Minneapolis: University of Minnesota Press, 1977.
Tully, James. *A Discourse on Property: John Locke and His Adversaries*. Cambridge: Cambridge University Press, 1980.
Tushnet, Mark V. *Slave Law in the American South: State V. Mann in History and Literature*. Landmark Law Cases and American Society. Ed. Peter Charles Hoffer. Lawrence: University Press of Kansas, 2003.
Upton, Dell. *Architecture in the United States*. Oxford: Oxford University Press, 1998.
Verhoeven, W. M. "'This Blissful Period of Intellectual Liberty': Transatlantic Radicalism and Enlightened Conservatism in Brown's Early Writings." In *Revising Charles Brockden Brown: Culture, Politics, and Sexuality in the Early Republic*, ed. Phillip Barnard, Mark L. Kamrath, and Stephen Shapiro, 7–40. Knoxville: University of Tennessee, 2004.
Vlach, John Michael. *Back of the Big House: The Architecture of Plantation Slavery*. Chapel Hill: University of North Carolina Press, 1993.
Voloshin, Beverly R. "*Edgar Huntly* and the Coherence of the Self." *Early American Literature* 23 (1988): 262–80.
———. "*Wieland*: 'Accounting for Appearances.'" *New England Quarterly* 59 (1986): 341–57.
Wallace, Anthony F. C. "Woman, Land, and Society: Three Aspects of Aboriginal Delaware Life." *Pennsylvania Archaeologist* 17, no. 1 (1947): 1–35.
Walsh, Mike. "The Hireling Press." *Subterranean, United with the Workingman's Advocate* [New York], December 21, 1844, 1.
———. "Working Men's Convention at Faneuil Hall, Boston." *Subterranean, United with the Workingman's Advocate* [New York], November 22, 1844, 3.
Warfel, Harry R. *Charles Brockden Brown, American Gothic Novelist*. Gainesville: University of Florida Press, 1949.

Waterman, Bryan. "Charles Brockden Brown, Revised and Expanded." *Early American Literature* 40, no. 1 (2003): 173–91.
———. *Republic of Intellect: The Friendly Club of New York City and the Making of American Literature*. New Studies in American Intellectual and Cultural History. Baltimore, MD: Johns Hopkins University Press, 2007.
Watson, John F. *Annals of Philadelphia and Pennsylvania*. 1830. Philadelphia: Leary, Stuart, 1927.
Watts, Steven. *The Romance of Real Life: Charles Brockden Brown and the Origins of American Culture*. Baltimore, MD: Johns Hopkins University Press, 1994.
Weinauer, Ellen. "Alternative Economies: Authorship and Ownership In Elizabeth Stoddard's 'Collected by a Valetudinarian.'" *Studies in American Fiction* 25, no. 2 (1997): 167–82.
Welter, Barbara. "The Cult of True Womanhood: 1820–1860." *American Quarterly* 18, no. 2 (1966): 151–74.
Wertheimer, Eric. *Underwriting: The Poetics of Insurance in America, 1722–1872*. Stanford: Stanford University Press, 2006.
Weyler, Karen Ann. *Intricate Relations: Sexual and Economic Desire in American Fiction, 1789–1814*. Iowa City: University of Iowa Press, 2004.
Whipple, Edwin Percy. *Essays and Reviews*. Vol. 2. 2 vols. Boston: Houghton, Mifflin and Company, 1850.
———. *Lectures on Subjects Connected with Literature and Life*. Boston: Ticknor, Reed, and Fields, 1850.
Whitman, Walt, and Gary Schmidgall. *Walt Whitman: Selected Poems, 1855–1892: A New Edition*. 1st ed. New York: St. Martin's Press, 1999.
Wilentz, Sean. *Chants Democratic : New York City & the Rise of the American Working Class, 1788–1850*. New York: Oxford University Press, 1986.
Willett, Cynthia. "The Master-Slave Dialectic: Hegel Vs. Douglass." In *Subjugation and Bondage: Critical Essays on Slavery and Social Philosophy*, ed. Tommy L. Lott, 151–69. Lanham, MD: Rowman & Littlefield, 1998.
Williams, Anne. *Art of Darkness: A Poetics of Gothic*. Chicago: University of Chicago Press, 1995.
Williams, Patricia J. *The Alchemy of Race and Rights*. Cambridge, MA: Harvard University Press, 1991.
Williams, Raymond. *Marxism and Literature*. Marxist Introductions. Oxford: Oxford University Press, 1977.
Wood, Gordon S. *The Radicalism of the American Revolution*. New York: Vintage Books, 1991.
Woodward, C. Vann. "George Fitzhugh, *Sui Generis*." In *Cannibals All! Or, Slaves Without Masters*, vii–xxxix. Cambridge, MA: Belknap Press of Harvard University, 1960.
Wyatt Brown, Bertram. "The Evolution of Heroes' Honor in the Southern Literary Tradition." In *The Evolution of Southern Culture*, ed. Numan V. Bartley, 108–30. Athens: University of Georgia Press, 1988.

———. *Southern Honor: Ethics and Behavior in the Old South*. 25th anniversary ed. New York: Oxford University Press, 2007.

Yolton, John W. *Thinking Matter: Materialism in Eighteenth-Century Britain*. Minneapolis: University of Minnesota Press, 1983.

Youngquist, Paul. "Romantic Dietetics! Or, Eating Your Way to a New You." In *Cultures of Taste/Theories of Appetite: Eating Romanticism*, ed. Timothy Morton, 237–55. New York: Palgrave MacMillan, 2004.

Ziff, Larzer. "A Reading of *Wieland*." *Publications of the Modern Language Association of America* 77 (1962): 51–57.

Zimmerman, David A. *Panic!: Markets, Crises, & Crowds in American Fiction*. Cultural Studies of the United States. Chapel Hill: University of North Carolina Press, 2006.

Index

affect (emotion): affective scripting, 195, 205–8; the body in, 204, 210; and class rebellion, 192, 194; the face expresses, 208–9; in Gothic literature, 215–16; Lippard focuses on, 194, 202; in master-slave relationship, 138–40, 145; ontology of, 202–3; phenomenology of, 204, 208; in plantation romances, 190; and politics, 190, 191, 193, 202, 203, 204, 235; Romantic celebration of, 22, 187, 190–91; in sensational literature, 190–91, 202; sensation in, 217; shift from sensation to, 18–21, 33, 137, 139, 187, 190, 234; space in, 217; sympathy, 206–8, 210–14, 267n29
Affleck, Thomas, 166
Alcott, Bronson, 21, 107, 252n5
Alcott, William, 87, 107–8
alienation, 14, 74, 125, 226, 229–33, 234, 269n45
alimentation. *See* eating (alimentation)
Americanist scholarship, 11, 18, 244n32
Anthony, David, 12, 13, 243n21, 243n24, 254n15, 260n22, 265n20, 265n21

Ball, Charles, 33, 144, 166–67, 262n46
Berkeley, George, 19, 40, 43–44, 48, 50
Blackstone, William, 4–5, 9, 11, 63, 239
body, the: in affect, 204, 210; appropriation and embodiment, 13, 16, 65, 98; body-as-house metaphor, 107–21, 255n21; body snatching and grave robbing, 224–33; in Brown's *Edgar Huntly*, 38–39, 41, 46, 49–62, 69, 76, 78, 80; commodification of, 226, 228–29, 231, 232; in Cooper's *The Pioneers*, 8–9, 26, 31; disembodiment of property, 14; embodied debt, 155; embodied interpretation, 17; embodied ownership, 6, 12, 13, 15, 16, 18, 19, 21–26, 31, 87, 137, 194, 235, 238; embodied space, 52, 53; in Hawthorne's *House of the Seven Gables*, 89; Locke on, 51–52, 92–93, 97–98, 254n13; mobile bodies, 45, 49, 62, 64, 69–70, 72, 73, 80, 238; the mouth, 101–2, 103, 111–12, 115; phenomenological, 48, 49, 70; sanctity of, 225; sensate bodies, 6, 18, 49, 55–56, 62, 73, 94, 136, 245n38, 248n20; shift from sensation to affect, 18–21; slave bodies, 146, 230; thematics of disembodiment, 89, 103, 136. *See also* eating (alimentation)
body snatching, 224–33
Bone Bill (1854), 227, 268n44
Brotherhood of the Union, 199, 265n15
Brown, Charles Brockden: engagement with empiricist philosophers, 22, 37, 39; and European landscape conventions, 43, 248n16; in Friendly Club, 40, 53, 63, 247n13; legal studies of, 63; national "vertigo" in works of, 12–13;

on opinions about property, 10; on philosophically self-aware literature, 37–38, 246n5; "Walstein's School of History," 37–38. *See also Edgar Huntly*
Brown, Gillian, 89, 103, 254n15, 254n16, 256n37

capitalism. *See* market economy
Certeau, Michel de, 55–56, 57, 60, 70, 73
City Crimes (Thompson), 214–15, 216, 267n31, 267n32
city-mystery novels, 6, 22, 26, 33, 187, 189, 193, 214, 215, 217, 234–35, 267n34
Cixous, Hélène, 132–33, 134, 135
Common Sense philosophy, 20
Condillac, Etienne Bonnot, abbé de: on attention, 41, 44, 248n20; Brown's engagement with, 22, 32, 38, 40, 45–47, 50, 57, 249n25; on a statue acquiring senses, 45–47, 48, 69, 249n25; on touch and sight, 32, 44–45, 47; on touch and space, 48–49
Cooper, James Fenimore, 6–9, 26–32, 71, 86, 157, 235
crime: in sensational literature, 189, 191, 192. *See also* theft
Cvetkovich, Ann, 193, 194–95, 202, 203, 204, 265n20

debt: feeling of, 142, 154–55; gifts incur, 148–49, 150; in market economy, 146, 149; in master-slave relation, 33, 144, 185; phenomenology of, 33, 142, 144, 146, 152, 154–55, 160–61, 164, 166, 168, 171; in plantation romances, 143, 144, 152; reciprocal, 148, 150, 151, 156–57, 159, 161, 163, 164; in Simms's *Woodcraft*, 144, 151–64; in slaveholding South, 145–51, 154; slavery compared with, 149–50, 261n35; slaves seized for payment of, 156, 157; social, 148, 150, 157; social hierarchies overturned by, 158
debt anxiety: in antebellum South, 149, 151–52; Douglass's discontent contrasted with, 171; as feeling, 18; interpersonal debt and, 154; of Jefferson, 165; in Kennedy's *Swallow Barn*, 175, 183–84; Lippard on, 23; in Simms's *Woodcraft*, 155, 156, 158, 160, 163, 168
Derrida, Jacques, 17, 101–2, 103, 145, 151, 259n21, 269n45

diet reform, 87–88; and body-as-house metaphor, 107, 117; in Hawthorne's *House of Seven Gables*, 33, 87, 88, 124, 135–36; in Stoddard's *The Morgesons*, 33, 87, 88, 103–4, 124, 135–36, 252n5; as subject of this study, 18; Thoreau on, 21, 107
distress, 204–5, 208–14, 222, 226, 230
domesticity, 88–89; diet reform and, 87; market economy and emergence of ideology of, 85; in Stoddard's *The Morgesons*, 105–6, 128; thematics of disembodiment in, 89, 103, 136
domestic space: body-as-house metaphor, 107–21, 255n21; in Hawthorne's *House of the Seven Gables*, 84, 113, 115, 117, 118–21; mediates relationship between eating and mobile property, 123; midcentury literary treatments of, 81–82; phenomenology's concern with, 252n1; in Stoddard's *The Morgesons*, 84, 88, 115–19, 134. *See also* home, the
Douglass, Frederick, 169–71, 259n17

eating (alimentation): in construction of the home, 255n25; as exchange, 123, 133; in Hawthorne's *House of the Seven Gables*, 22, 23, 33, 87, 89–90, 95–103, 108, 111–15, 117–18, 123; inside-outside distinction established by, 110, 112, 117, 121; Levinas on, 93–94, 103, 118; Locke on, 91–93, 103, 117; in nineteenth-century domestic fiction, 89–90; phenomenology of, 33, 117, 121, 123; in process of appropriation, 18, 33; in Stoddard's *The Morgesons*, 22, 33, 87, 89–90, 103–6, 108, 116–18, 123, 131–32. *See also* diet reform
Edgar Huntly (Brown), 35–82; amorous contacts for establishment of boundaries in, 58–62; cave sequence in, 32, 42–43, 45–47, 50–51, 56, 73; dispossession and displacement in, 63–64, 75–76, 78, 81; elm tree in, 41, 59, 64, 71, 73; and Hume's theory of property, 66–69; hunger in, 47, 51; hut in, 32, 57, 59, 60, 61, 71–72, 73, 85–86, 235; Indian-settler boundary dispute in, 32, 38–39, 49, 55–58; on mobility and property, 62–82, 251n46; moral dimension of, 80–81; musket thrust into the road, 58, 71, 73; preview of, 34–36, 76–77; on property as social

convention, 66–67; sensation as theme of, 40–41; somnambulism trope in, 41, 59, 67, 73–75, 76; on space, 38, 39–40, 48, 49, 50–55; tactile contact in, 60–62, 71, 86, 115, 239; trajectory of abstraction in, 136; vision and touch contrasted in, 42–43, 45–47; walking in, 70–71, 73; "Walking Purchase" treaty re-imagined in, 32, 36–37, 38, 39, 64–65, 76–81
Ellison, Julie, 250n40
Emerson, Ralph Waldo, 20, 21, 107, 121, 145, 151, 244n36
emotion. *See* affect
Empire City, The (Lippard), 201, 209–11, 218, 221–24, 229, 265n17, 265n18
empiricism, 16, 19, 20, 21, 44, 54, 55, 190, 234
enclosure, 26, 27, 29, 30
Enlightenment rationalism, 19–20, 22, 37, 38, 139
entitlement: in master-slave relation, 33, 144, 185; phenomenology of, 33, 142, 144, 168, 170, 171; in plantation romances, 144; slaves' sense of, 144, 156, 159, 163–71, 180

Fitzhugh, George, 138–40, 141, 145, 153, 171, 259n15
Friendly Club, 40, 53, 247n13

gestures, 50
gifts: commodities versus, 88, 123, 133, 134, 186; debt incurred by, 148–49, 150; in master-slave economy, 145; slaves receive from masters, 146–47, 259n17; Stoddard's *The Morgesons* on, 123, 131, 132–35, 186; between white male planters, 147–48; women associated with, 123, 129, 133, 134
Gothic literature: capitalism's Gothic characteristics, 226; Lippard's novels as, 33, 189, 193, 200, 218; Marx employs Gothic devices, 234; space in, 215–16, 218, 219, 221; tropes of enclosure and entrapment in, 33, 214, 215
Graham, Sylvester, 87, 88, 98, 124–29, 132, 135, 252n5, 253n7, 256n35, 256n36
grave robbing, 224–33
Grotius, Hugo, 2, 62–63

Hawthorne, Nathaniel: *The American Notebooks*, 253n10; on desire for stable property, 12; and diet reform, 33, 252n5; Lockean view of property as influence on, 92; *The Old Manse*, 253n10; property anxiety as catalyst for, 85; *Septimius Felton*, 252n5; and shift from sensation to affect, 23. *See also House of the Seven Gables*
Hegel, Georg Wilhelm Friedrich, 6, 140–42, 144, 186, 233–34, 244n26, 250n45, 258n6
Heidegger, Martin, 17, 111, 114, 118, 245n38, 252n1
heirlooms, 120–21
Hentz, Caroline, 146, 174, 175–76, 177, 263n48
home, the: antebellum writers on property and, 85; body-as-house metaphor, 107–21, 255n21; Graham on, 124, 127; in Hawthorne's *House of the Seven Gables*, 123, 135; Levinas on, 83–84, 118, 121, 134, 256n29; the market versus, 124, 125, 127, 129; midcentury cultural reevaluation of, 87; phenomenology's concern with, 252n1; in Stoddard's *The Morgesons*, 123, 135; women associated with, 124, 125, 127, 129. *See also* huts
House of the Seven Gables (Hawthorne): on alimentary possession, 22, 33, 94–95, 96, 97–99, 117; body-as-house metaphor in, 108–15, 117; choking and failed ingestion in, 99–103, 109, 113–14; on diet reform, 33, 87, 88, 124, 135–36; on domestic space, 84, 113, 115, 117, 118–19, 119–21; on eating, 90, 95–103, 108, 111–15, 117–18, 123; heirlooms in, 120–21; on the home, 123, 135; hut in, 32, 86, 87, 96, 235; on market capitalism, 88, 89, 96, 115, 122–23, 126, 127–29, 135; Preface of, 90, 95, 254n14; Stoddard's *The Morgesons* compared with, 106–7; thematics of disembodiment in, 89; thresholds in, 111–15; trajectory of abstraction in, 136; on women, 89, 128–29
Hume, David: Brown's engagement with, 22, 37, 38, 50, 53–54, 65, 66, 249n30; legal writers influenced by, 63; on passions, 75, 251n49; phenomenological view of space of, 40, 52–53, 67; in "plenum versus vacuum" debate, 22, 32, 48, 52–54; on property, 66–69, 74–75, 80–81, 83, 250n45; skepticism of, 19; on touch and space, 249n8
huts: in Brown's *Edgar Huntly*, 32, 57, 59, 60,

61, 71–72, 73, 85–86, 235; in Cooper's *The Pioneers*, 28–31, 71, 86; in Hawthorne's *House of the Seven Gables*, 32, 86, 87, 96, 235; in Lippard's works, 32, 224, 234–35; as literary trope, 85–87; in Marx, 234–35; as reminders of older property paradigms, 234–35; slave cabins, 32, 173, 235

inheritance law, 10, 26

Jacobs, Harriet, 6, 33, 144, 168–69
Jefferson, Thomas, 149, 164–66, 171–73
justice, property and, 67, 68, 69

Kennedy, John Pendleton. *See Swallow Barn*
Kent, James, 7, 11, 242n10
Krause, Sidney, 39, 64, 251n50

labor movement, 196–98
labor theory of value, 197–98, 199, 264n9
Lefebvre, Henri, 24–26, 49–50, 51, 116, 240, 245n38
Levinas, Emmanuel: on the home, 117, 121, 134, 256n29; on possession without acquisition, 93, 94, 108, 118; on postponement, 118, 120; on property, 83–84, 93–94, 103, 122, 144, 186; on self-possession, 93–94, 103; this study builds on ideas of, 16
Lippard, George, 188–235; aesthetic strategies of, 193–94, 195, 205; affective scripting in work of, 195, 205–8; alienation as concern of, 232; body snatching and grave robbing as theme of, 224–33; claustrophobic space of "city-mysteries" of, 26, 216–21; conservative and subversive aspects, 203–4, 265n20, 265n21; cultural context of, 195–99; distress in works of, 204; emotion as focus of, 194, 202; *The Empire City*, 201, 209–11, 218, 221–24, 229, 265n17, 265n18; and French socialism, 265n16; as labor reformer, 193, 195, 199, 265n12; on literature and reform, 194–95; market society criticized by, 33–34, 193, 195, 199, 203, 222, 232–33; *The Nazarene*, 200–201, 218–19, 228; *New York*, 201, 218, 232, 265n18; sensational literature of, 33, 193–95, 207, 212, 222, 224, 234; sentimental and sensational mixed in, 207–8; and shift from sensation to affect, 23; stereotypes in works of, 267n30; theft in works of, 187, 193, 199–202, 205–6, 208, 209–14; urban architecture in works of, 216–21; working-class huts in works of, 32, 224, 234–35. *See also* Quaker City; or, The Monks of Monk Hall
Locke, John: Brown's engagement with, 22, 37, 38, 39, 65; on eating and acquisition, 91–93; empiricism of, 19, 20, 21, 44; legal writers influenced by, 63; on money, 256n31, 256n33; in "plenum versus vacuum" debate, 32, 48, 51–55, 248n21; on property, 3–6, 65–66, 67, 69, 74, 80–81, 83, 91–93, 103, 197; on reflection, 44, 248n20; on right to nourishment, 167; scientific and political works as connected, 39; on self-possession, 92–94, 97–98, 229, 230, 254n13; visual bias of, 40, 43, 45, 48, 248n18

market economy (capitalism): abstraction of property in, 31, 81, 84–85; body snatching and grave robbing as challenge to, 225–33; debt in, 146, 149; diet reform and, 87–88; economic inequality in, 196, 223–24, 234–35; Fitzhugh's proslavery criticism of, 138, 139; gifts versus commodities, 88, 123, 133, 134, 186; gothic characteristics of, 226; Graham on, 124, 125, 126, 127; Hawthorne's *House of the Seven Gables* on, 88, 89, 96, 115, 122–23, 126, 127–29, 135; the home versus, 124, 125, 127, 129; Lippard's opposition to, 33–34, 193, 195, 199, 203, 213, 222, 232–33; men associated with, 123, 125, 131, 133, 135; Romantic denunciations of, 258n4; search for stable economy insulated from, 13; sensational literature critiques, 190; slavery and challenge to, 10, 230; Stoddard's *The Morgesons* on, 122–23, 126–27, 129–35; as theft, 34, 192, 195–96, 198, 199–202, 213, 221–24; thefts from capitalists, 222; transition from agrarian economy to, 11, 12
Married Women's Property Acts, 10, 252n3
Marx, Karl, 14–15, 21, 91, 141, 188–90, 192, 203, 231, 233, 243n26, 253n12, 264n5, 265n16
Michaels, Walter Benn, 12, 13, 243n25, 254n14

INDEX / 295

Morgesons, The (Stoddard): on alimentary possession, 22, 33, 94–95, 103–4, 106, 117; body-as-house metaphor in, 108, 115–18; on collection of goods, 119; on diet reform, 33, 87, 88, 103–4, 124, 135–36, 252n5; on domesticity, 105–6, 128; on domestic space, 84, 88, 115–19, 134; on eating, 22, 33, 87, 89–90, 103–6, 108, 116–18, 123, 131–32; on gift economy, 123, 131, 132–35, 186; Hawthorne's *House of the Seven Gables* compared with, 106–7; on the home, 123, 135; on market capitalism, 122–23, 126–27, 129–35; trajectory of abstraction in, 136; on women, 89, 103–6, 115, 129–35
mouth, the, 101–2, 103, 111–12, 115

Nazarene, The (Lippard), 200–201, 218–19, 228
Nelson, Dana, 28, 143, 243n24, 245n42, 265n20, 266n21, 269n46
New York: Its Upper Ten and Lower Million (Lippard), 201, 218, 232, 265n18
Nissenbaum, Stephen, 88, 125, 126, 253n6, 253n7

ownership. *See* property

Patterson, Orlando, 141–42, 185, 258n7, 258n8
Penn, John and Thomas, 36, 77, 79
phenomenology: of affect, 204, 208; of appropriation, 121, 136; in Brown's *Edgar Huntly*, 38, 39; of debt, 33, 142, 144, 146, 152, 154–55, 160–61, 164, 166, 168, 171; of dispossession, 187, 194, 235; on domestic ideology, 136; domestic space as concern of, 252n1; of eating, 33, 117, 121, 123; of entitlement, 33, 142, 144, 168, 170, 171; Hegel's, 233–34; Lefebvre and, 245n38; as middle way between empiricism and idealism, 16, 19, 21; neo-phenomenology, 18, 19; of ownership, 13–14, 25, 139, 144, 165, 167; phenomenological body, 48, 49, 70; of possession, 9, 12, 17, 19, 21, 23, 24, 31, 32, 39, 76, 81, 85, 86, 89, 101, 122, 137, 139, 185–86, 194, 234, 235, 239; of property, 12, 14, 15–23, 142, 168, 171, 186, 233–34, 239; sensation and affect in, 9, 19; and shift from sensation to affect, 18–21; of slavery, 142, 168; of space, 39, 40, 49, 51, 52–53, 55–56, 62, 89, 186, 217; of spatial boundaries, 64; subject-object interrelationship in, 16, 21; tactile, 239; of theft, 33, 193, 212, 214, 221

Pierson v. Post (1805), 1–4; Blackstone's view of property compared with, 5; Cooper's *The Pioneers* compared with, 7, 8, 26–27; and legal coping strategies, 241n8; and Vang shooting incident of 2004, 236, 237
Pioneers, The (Cooper), 6–9, 26–32, 71, 86, 157, 235
plantation romances, 142–44; debt in, 143, 144, 152; emotion in, 190; huts in, 235; Kennedy's *Swallow Barn* as, 175; on plantation space, 174–75, 186–87; as proslavery, 143, 264n54; and shift from sensation to affect, 187; Simms's *Woodcraft* as, 152–53; slave narratives compared with, 143, 144, 185
Planter's Northern Bride, The (Hentz), 146, 174–77, 263n48
possessive individualism, 93, 98, 131, 135, 197, 203, 221, 229, 254n13
private/public divide, 85, 89, 96, 129
property: alimentary possession, 22, 33, 94–95, 96, 103–4, 106, 117, 118; American literature and problem of, 4–9; America seen as ownership society, 239; in antebellum culture, 9–15; anxieties regarding, 11–15, 31, 33, 81, 85, 122, 136, 239; beginning of, 91–107; in Brown's *Edgar Huntly*, 35–82; as bundle of rights, 10–11, 84–85, 238, 239; common, 3, 27–28, 30–31; contractual models of, 38; in Cooper's *The Pioneers*, 6–9, 26–32; dialectical nature of, 25, 144, 185, 186; discursive models of, 9, 13, 31, 69, 72, 74, 122, 144, 186, 250n45; domestication of, 85, 136; as dwelling, 82; eating and exchange of, 123, 133; embodied ownership, 6, 12, 13, 15, 16, 18, 19, 21–26, 31, 87, 137, 194, 235, 238; feeling of, 137; and the feminine economy of the gift, 121–35; French socialists on, 192, 264n11; in Hawthorne's *House of the Seven Gables*, 95–103; Hume on, 66–69, 74–75, 80–81, 83, 250n45; justice and, 67, 68, 69; in Kennedy's *Swallow Barn*, 179–85, 263n52; legal justifications of, 5; Levinas on, 83–84, 93–94, 103, 122,

144, 186; literary shift from possession to dispossession, 194; Locke on, 3–4, 5, 6, 65–66, 67, 69, 74, 80–81, 83, 91–93, 94, 97–98, 103, 197; in master-slave relation, 141–42, 144; mobility and, 62–82, 238; ontological nature of, 4–6, 15, 241n8, 243n26; original acquisition in, 2, 3–5, 10, 66, 241n8, 250n4; phenomenology of, 12, 14, 15–23, 142, 168, 171, 186, 233–34, 239; phenomenology of appropriation, 121, 136; phenomenology of dispossession, 187, 194; phenomenology of ownership, 13–14, 25, 139, 144, 165, 167; phenomenology of possession, 9, 12, 17, 19, 21, 23, 24, 31, 32, 39, 76, 81, 85–87, 89, 101, 122, 137, 185–86, 194, 234, 235, 239; *Pierson v. Post* on, 1–4, 236, 237; in plantation romances, 143; possession without acquisition, 91–107, 108, 117, 118, 120–21; relational models of, 67, 69; sanctity of, 221, 237; self-possession, 92–95, 98, 103–6, 108, 113, 115–16, 119, 122, 229, 230, 266n21; shift from landed to portable, 13; as social convention, 66–69, 75; social relations model of, 15; space of, 23–40, 238; spaces of ownership, 26, 85, 186, 234; stable, 12, 13, 86; trajectory of abstraction of, 10–14, 31, 81, 84–85, 122, 136, 238–39; and Vang shooting incident of 2004, 236–40; violence and legitimacy of, 80, 81; virtualization of, 11, 12, 32, 34, 67, 69, 81, 84, 136; walking boundaries of, 252n58
proslavery texts: of Fitzhugh, 138–40, 141, 145, 171; Kennedy's *Swallow Barn* as, 179, 180, 182; plantation romances as, 143, 264n54; Simms's *Woodcraft* as, 33, 152, 153, 166; slave cabins in, 32
Proudhon, Pierre, 34, 188, 192, 195, 199, 264n11, 265n16
Pufendorf, Samuel von, 2, 63, 250n45

Quaker City; or, The Monks of Monk Hall (Lippard): as anticapitalist, 213; architecture of, 215, 218, 219–21; body snatching and grave robbing in, 225, 228, 231, 268n44; debtor masculinity in, 260n22, 266n21; the face in, 208–9; sales of, 264n3; as sensational, 189; slaves and working-class laborers associated in, 230; sympathy in, 207, 208, 210, 211–14; theft narrative in, 200, 208, 211–14

Ricoeur, Paul, 17, 25, 245n39
Romanticism, 20, 22, 139, 187, 190–91, 234, 258n4, 264n5

Sedgwick, Eve, 204, 215–16
sensation: in affect, 217; Lippard focuses on affect rather than, 194; sensational sympathy, 207, 208–9, 212; shift to affect from, 18–21, 33, 137, 139, 187, 190, 207–8, 234. *See also* touch
sensational literature, 33, 188–95, 202–4, 207–8, 210, 211, 212, 222, 224, 234, 264n4, 267n29
sensational psychology, 22, 38–43, 58, 247n9, 247n11, 248n18
sentimental literature, 206, 207–8, 211, 266n25, 266n26, 267n29
"separate spheres" ideology, 85, 88–89, 125, 127
Simms, William Gilmore: knowledge of property law of, 260n29; as proslavery, 33, 153, 260n28. *See also Woodcraft, or, Hawks about the Dovecote*
Skidmore, Thomas, 34, 198, 265n12
slave narratives, 164–71; agency and voice in, 261n38; anxiety-inducing questions about property in, 6; huts in, 235; master-slave relationship in, 33; plantation romances compared with, 143, 144, 185; slave space in, 262n46; slaves' sense of entitlement in, 144; theft as theme in, 166
slavery, 138–87; and abstract forms of commodified personhood, 12; as challenge to established property paradigms, 10, 230; debt compared with, 149–50, 261n35; debt in slaveholding South, 145–51; gifts from masters to slaves, 146–47; Hegel's master-slave dialectic, 140–42; Jacobs on hypocrisies of, 6, 168–69; in Kennedy's *Swallow Barn*, 33, 175–85; phenomenology of, 142, 168; in plantation romances, 143; reciprocity in master-slave relationship, 146, 148, 150, 151–52, 156, 158–59, 161, 163–65, 168–71, 183; sanctity of the body and, 225; sentiment and slave law, 258n10; slave bodies, 146, 230; slave cabins, 32, 173, 235; slaveholders as thieves, 165,

169–71; slaves' evolving relationship with ownership, 14; slave space, 174–78, 181–83, 262n46, 263n49; slaves seized for payment of debt, 156, 157; slaves' sense of entitlement, 144, 156, 159, 163–64, 165–71, 180; space of the plantation, 31, 171–85; "stealing away," 262n47; taking of slaves, 162, 169, 170, 185; theft by slaves, 166–69, 173. *See also* proslavery texts; slave narratives
Slavery in the United States (Ball), 166–67
Smith, Adam, 3, 197
space, 23–40; in affect, 217; antebellum texts operate in two directions with respect to, 25; in Brown's *Edgar Huntly*, 38, 39–40, 48, 49, 50–55, 80; in city-mystery novels, 214; Condillac on, 48–49; in Cooper's *The Pioneers*, 26–32; dialectical nature of, 24, 49, 173–74, 178; as discourse, 69–70; embodied, 52, 53; empty, 48, 52, 54; Gothic, 215–16, 218, 219, 221; Hume on, 40, 52–53, 67; increasing scale of ownership anxiety, 86; lived, 24, 25, 37, 49, 55; Newtonian, 48, 51–52; permeable private, 33, 222–23; phenomenology of, 39, 40, 49, 51, 52–53, 55–56, 62, 89, 186, 217; of the plantation, 171–85; "plenum versus vacuum" debate, 32, 48, 51–55, 248n21; of property, 23–40, 238; representational, 25, 240; slave, 174–78, 181–83, 262n46, 263n49; social, 23, 24–26, 28, 31–34, 49–50, 56, 72, 191, 238, 239, 240; as socially constructed, 24, 39–40, 116; spaces of ownership, 26, 85, 186, 234; spatial appropriation, 32, 72–73, 75, 76, 80, 177; spatial boundaries, 27, 28, 38, 40, 55–58, 60, 62, 64, 70, 71, 72, 80, 112; urban, 26, 33, 191, 193–96, 205, 214–18, 221, 223, 224, 234, 240, 267n35. *See also* domestic space
spoilage proviso, 92, 253n11
Stoddard, Elizabeth: and diet reform, 33, 252n5; Lockean view of property as influence on, 92; property anxiety as catalyst for, 85. *See also Morgesons, The*
Stowe, Harriet Beecher, 84, 136, 206, 266n26
Streeby, Shelley, 202, 203, 204
Swallow Barn (Kennedy), 175, 85; debt and entitlement in, 144; debt anxiety in, 175, 183–84; gift-giving in, 146–47; as

plantation romance, 175; plot of, 178; property narrative in, 179–85, 263n52; as proslavery, 179, 180, 182; slaves' bodily appropriation of counter-spaces in, 33, 175, 176–78, 181–83
sympathy, 206–8, 210–14, 267n29

theft: body snatching and grave robbing, 224–33; capitalist-as-thief imagery, 34, 192, 195–96, 198, 199–202, 213, 221–24; from capitalists, 222; in Jacobs's narrative, 168–69; in Lippard's novels, 187, 193, 199–202, 205–6, 208, 209–14; phenomenology of, 33, 193, 212, 214, 221; in sensational literature, 191, 192; slaveholders as thieves, 165, 169–71; in slave narratives, 166; by slaves, 166–69, 173; slave "stealing away" as, 262n47; "stealing" versus "taking," 167, 168; taking of slaves as, 162, 169, 170, 185
theft-distress, 18, 33, 211, 213, 214, 221, 226, 230
Thompson, George, 214–15, 216, 267n31, 267n32
Thoreau, Henry David, 21, 107
Tomkins, Silvan, 33, 204–5, 208–9, 217, 266n23
touch: Condillac on, 32, 44–45, 47, 48–49; tactile encounters in Brown's *Edgar Huntly*, 60–62, 71, 86, 115; tactile encounters in delineation of spatial boundaries, 80; tactile phenomenology of the frontier, 239; in theories of property, 250n45; and vision contrasted in Brown's *Edgar Huntly*, 42–43, 45–47; walking and, 70
Transcendentalism, 20–21

vandalism, 237
Vang, Chai Soua, 236–40
vomit, 102

walking, 70–71, 73
"Walking Purchase" treaty, 32, 36–39, 64–65, 76–81
"Walstein's School of History" (Brown), 37–38
Whipple, Edwin Percy, 189–90, 191–92, 193
women: commodification of, 228; diet reform and, 88; evolving relationship with ownership, 14; gifts associated with, 123, 129, 133, 134; Graham on

bread and, 124–26; in Hawthorne's *House of the Seven Gables*, 89, 128–29; the home associated with, 124, 125, 127, 129; inheritance law changes regarding, 10; Married Women's Property Acts, 10, 252n3; property and the feminine economy of the gift, 121–35; "separate spheres" ideology, 85, 88–89, 125, 127; in Stoddard's *The Morgesons*, 89, 103–6, 115, 129–35

Woodcraft, or, Hawks about the Dovecote (Simms), 151–64; debt anxiety in, 144, 155, 156, 158, 160, 163, 168; gift-giving in, 147; as plantation romance, 152–53; on plantation space, 174; proslavery ideology in, 33, 152, 153, 166; publication of, 152, 260n27; return of the repressed in, 162–63; slave narratives compared with, 167–68

yellow-jacket literature, 189

www.ingramcontent.com/pod-product-compliance
Lightning Source LLC
Chambersburg PA
CBHW030435300426
44112CB00009B/1008